*From Old Standards
to the Latest Favorites,
DRINKS FROM A–Z:*

Aperitifs • Bob Danby • Cupid • Daiquiri • El Diablo • Fallen Angel • Gin • Highball • Irish Coffee • Jo'burg • Kangaroo • Liqueurs • Mai-tai • New Orleans Fizz • Old-fashioned • Pansy • Quaker • Russian • Screwdriver • Thunder • Union Jack • Vodka • Wassail • Xeres • Yodel • Zombie

The Drink Guide brings the knowledge of the experts into your own home—and makes it easy to choose and prepare the most exotic drinks, even if you've never mixed a drink in your life.

House & Garden's
DRINK GUIDE

Edited by
Collette Richardson

PUBLISHED BY POCKET BOOKS NEW YORK

POCKET BOOKS, a Simon & Schuster division of
GULF & WESTERN CORPORATION
1230 Avenue of the Americas, New York, N.Y. 10020

Contents

II. Spirits and Wines—What They Are and How to Use Them 39

III. What Drinks to Serve When—And How to Make Them 87

Foreword

Mixed drinks run the gamut from a gin and tonic that is simplicity itself to concoct, to a strong punch that involves umpteen ingredients and considerable concentration. No one—not even the most experienced professional bartender—has all the good drink recipes tucked away in his memory bank, and no host in his own house will ever want to try all of them. But it's a reassuring, satisfying feeling to know that you can look up any particular drink recipe you want, or get new ideas if that is what you're hankering for, right in one place and without trouble or fuss. Hence this book.

Here is a treasury of useful information that will make it easy for you to cope on any occasion when liquid libations are indicated. You will find more than 850 individual recipes in this guide, plus innumerable variations that require only slight changes from the basic recipes. In addition to these specific instructions, there is a fund of sound general advice about choosing, mixing and serving drinks of every type, including wine and delicious non-alcoholic thirst quenchers.

All the expertise in this book derives from columns in HOUSE & GARDEN—columns originally written by renowned gourmets and connoisseurs. They are responsible for the fascinating facts, helpful ideas and excellent, easy-to-follow recipes collected in these pages, and for this the editors thank them all: Sam Aaron, James A. Beard, Alexis Bespaloff, Philip Brown, Robert Farrar Capon, William Clifford, Nika Standen Hazelton, Hugh Johnson, C. G. Martinez, Henry McNulty, Robert Neville, William Olcott, and José Wilson.

HOW TO USE THIS BOOK

You can locate every recipe in this book three different ways, for the simple reason that when you want to look up a drink recipe, it is almost invariably for one of three reasons:

REASON I. You wish to serve a drink that is just right for a specific occasion. It may be an important party or an informal get-together, a picnic on a hot day or a thaw-out after a football game, a short hour before lunch with that dear old couple from across the street or a long, lazy afternoon with a few cronies. How do you find the ideal drink for the particular situation?

Chapter III, "What Drinks to Serve When," tells you just that. It contains all the recipes, grouped in sections to suit various occasions. Turn to the section that best meets your requirements. Read its introduction—for fun, for suggestions, for dependable information. And then choose the recipe you like best. Simple.

REASON II. You want to serve a drink based on a particular liquor, liqueur or wine. Perhaps you've been given a bottle of tequila, or you have invited guests for cocktails who have a passion for rum. Or your wife wants you to make a delicious after-dinner drink with a coffee-liqueur base which she can serve in place of dessert. You're nonplussed, or you want to find a recipe that is a little less prosaic than those you already know. What do you do?

Chapter II, "Spirits and Wines," will solve your problem. Turn to the spirit or wine that interests you. Read about it. Then look over the list of drinks that are based on, or include a goodly proportion of, that liquor or wine. Simple.

REASON III. You want to make a drink that you've heard about, but the only thing you're sure of is its name—which tells you nothing. It might be a Negus, a Grasshopper, a Queen's Peg. And you want to try it, but how do you find it?

The Index lists every single drink by name, alphabetically, and gives the page number for the recipe. Simple.

I

What Every Drink Maker Should Know

Mixing good drinks deftly and easily is a skill that not only affords a host a fine sense of accomplishment but gives guests a great deal of pleasure. It is a skill worth having, one that enhances hospitality and can make jovial a gathering of any size. But there is more to mixing a drink than following a recipe. You need to know certain facts about measures and quantities, ice and mixers, garnishes and flavorings, glasses and decanters. You need to have the right equipment and know when and how to use it. In addition to the basics, there are flourishes that may come in handy—how to make pink ice, for example; when to use canned or bottled cocktails; how to give a wine-tasting party or make an appropriate toast. Virtually all the necessary background information and many intriguing extras are included in this short chapter. If you pay close attention to the former and take what you want from the latter, you will be well prepared to browse among the recipes in Chapter III.

The Measures That Matter

A successful mixed drink depends as much on accurate measuring as on a happy combination of ingredients, so every amount used in recipes—from a quart to a teaspoon —is translated here into ounces. Even a "dash" is defined. Wine measures are listed in a second group and this will take the guesswork out of such words as "wineglass" and "Methuselah."

1 quart	32 ounces
1 fifth (4/5 quart)	25.6 ounces
1 pint (½ quart)	16 ounces
1 cup	8 ounces
1 split	6.6 ounces, approx.
1 jigger	1½ ounces
1 pony	1 ounce
1 tablespoon (3 teaspoons)	½ ounce
1 teaspoon	1/6 ounce
1 dash	3 drops
1 wineglass (as a measure)	4 ounces
Average bottle of wine	26 ounces
Standard bottle of champagne	27 ounces
Magnum (2 bottles)	52 ounces
Jeroboam (4 bottles)	104 ounces
Rehoboam (6 bottles)	156 ounces
Methuselah (8 bottles)	208 ounces
Demijohn	1- to 10-gallon jug

It should be noted that the word "bottle," when referring to a measure of liquor, usually means a fifth. As a rule, "quart" is reserved for the actual quart measure. Although the sizes of wine bottles may vary a little, you can figure that one holds approximately a fifth. With the exception of a magnum, oversize bottles of champagne are seldom practical, for they are awkward to handle. Demijohns of still wines, however, are often good buys, but the wine should be decanted.

One final point about measures: Although a tablespoon,

pony and jigger can be used to give you ½ ounce, 1 ounce and 1½ ounces, respectively, you will find that some of the recipes in this book call for ¾ ounce of one or more ingredients. This is half a jigger, so it is recommended that you keep both a pony and a jigger handy, unless you have a measuring cup that is marked off for various amounts.

The Right Glass to Use

Although large glasses are popular today, there is nothing stingy about pouring 4 ounces of wine into a 10-ounce or larger wineglass or 1 ounce of brandy into a 12-ounce snifter. In fact, this is the proper thing to do because the large glass allows a person to enjoy the aroma as well as the taste. On the other hand, a strong, short drink on the rocks looks more inviting in a standard 7- or 8-ounce Old-fashioned glass than lost in the bottom of a huge double one. With cocktails, a too large glass gives the drink more time to lose its chill and initial zest, and a half-filled glass looks unexciting, so an average size cocktail glass of 4½ ounces is the most satisfactory. Long drinks that call for ice and a mixer such as soda require glasses big enough to hold three or more ice cubes plus the drink itself. Shaved ice, so essential to frappéed concoctions, is a great space-taker, filling up perhaps two-thirds of a glass, so figure accordingly.

An ebullient and generous sense of hospitality tends to make many of us feel that we are being ungenerous and even stingy if we do not fill a glass to the brim when pouring a drink. This is not true; too full a glass always requires careful handling to avoid spilling. Allow adequate space at the top—anything from ¼ to ¾ inch, depending on the size of the glass—if you wish to set your guests at ease and protect your rugs and furniture from damage. And remember that it is infinitely better to fill a glass two-thirds full, or even less, than to add more liquor than the required measure. More ice—yes, if necessary—but a double quantity of spirits—no.

TULIP
CHAMPAGNE
(9 oz.)

SAUCER
CHAMPAGNE
(6 oz.)

BRANDY
SNIFTER
OR
INHALER
(12 oz.)

LIQUEUR
OR
CORDIAL
(2 oz.)

MUG
(9 oz.)

PUNCH CUP
(6 oz.)

COCKTAIL
(4 oz.)

WHISKEY
SOUR
OR
DELMONICO
(5 oz.)

SHOT
(1½ oz.)

These are the most usual sizes and shapes of glasses in use today. You don't, by any means, need all of them. For example, if you serve punch once a year, you can rent the punch cups. One size of wine glass will serve all purposes, although a larger glass is preferred by connoisseurs for very fine red wines. Furthermore, there are all sorts of possible substitutions that work out very satisfactorily: a 16-ounce

Many Ways

OLD-FASHIONED (9 oz.) OLD-FASHIONED (16 oz.) HIGHBALL (20 oz.) HIGHBALL (12 oz.)

SHERRY (6 oz.) WINE (15 oz.) WINE (9½ oz.) WINE (7 oz.)

Old-fashioned glass can be used for a highball or any other "tall drink"; a cocktail glass or a sherry glass can be used for a whiskey sour; sherry can be served on-the-rocks in an Old-fashioned glass; and you could serve a Martini on-the-rocks in a brandy snifter. In short, you don't have to be too rigid about what's right and what's wrong.

Glasses for various purposes are illustrated and described on pages 6–7, but standard capacities of the most basic glasses are explained here, with the various other measures that are important to drink mixers and hosts.

Wineglasses range from quite small—approximately 4 ounces—to very large. In general, the smallest are best suited to aperitifs, cocktails (if you don't have special cocktail glasses) and white wine served at the table when it will be followed by a red with the main course. All-purpose wineglasses, however, of any size from 8 ounces up to 12 or even more, are excellent for most wines and many other drinks.

Water goblets are among today's pet choices for all kinds of mixed potables and often wine or beer as well. Their customary size: 8 to 10 ounces.

Old-fashioned glasses average anywhere from a 6- to 10-ounce capacity. Double Old-fashioneds are exactly that and really belong in the tumbler class.

Tumblers for drinks of various length range from about 8 (small) to 21 ounces (very large). One rule of thumb about them that you might follow is this: The milder the drink and the hotter the day, the bigger the glass should be, because lots of ice and plenty of soda or other mixer require a generous container.

Liqueur glasses usually have a capacity of about 1 to 2 ounces.

Brandy snifters that make the most sense range from 6 to 12 ounces or a little larger. Steer clear of too small ones that turn sniffing into a chore, and don't invest in those enormous inhalers: they're a waste of money and space that could be better used for the brandy itself.

As you see, you have considerable latitude. Also, as you know, there are many special-purpose glasses not listed above; the better-known glasses are shown on pages 6–7 because there is no point in confusing the issue here with too many measures.

How to Buy Spirits

Periodically, the efficient host checks over his liquor cabinet and wine cellar and makes plans to replenish his stocks. The *wise* host studies the catalogs of his local dealers and orders with an eye to future entertaining of all kinds, from small dinners to large buffets and open-house parties. He selects a varied list of wines and liquors, knowing that a best buy is essentially what best suits the occasion.

Building your drinking stock: Even if you don't foresee a run of big galas, it is always a good idea to buy liquor by the case, provided you have the storage facilities. This practice almost invariably means a saving. Also, in some states you can buy popular liquors such as bourbon, rye, gin and vodka in half-gallon, full-gallon and even 5-gallon jugs—and the advantage in price is considerable.

How do you serve liquor from such large containers? You don't. You use decanters. Many people consider this by far the most attractive way to serve spirits, in any event. If you object to decanters because you feel that your guests expect to see the labels on the bottles, remember that the quality of a liquor is in its taste and no one should need a label to proclaim it. Those who do are unable to appreciate the product. It is a good idea to hang identifying metal, pottery or porcelain tags around the necks of the decanters to avoid mistakes. (Collecting decanters can be an interesting and rewarding hobby, and for more about it, see pages 32–33.)

It is also sensible to buy your favorite wines by the case —not just for the saving but also because good wines are usually in limited supply and sell out quickly. You can't always depend upon being able to get the same wine you liked last month. When buying by the case, sample a single bottle before ordering. This applies particularly to unfamiliar wines, toward which many people are gravitating, as the increasing demand for great wines of outstanding vintages has sent prices sky-high. For everyday drinking, it would be sheer folly to buy superb wines. If you are willing to expend a little time and effort, there are various ways to get good wine at a reasonable price, but in the end, your best guide to wise buying will always be a reputable, knowledgeable dealer. Select your liquor and wine merchant with care and talk over your needs with him. It is his business to give you sound advice.

Stock up for cooking: Consider cooking as well as drinking when you stock up for the season. Sherry, port and Madeira are a boon in the kitchen. Each contributes a great deal to various dishes, and each adds a fillip to sauces. These fortified wines vary greatly in price and quality; try some of the domestic sherries and ports for kitchen use. They cost less than their imported counterparts.

Liqueurs, too, are a great asset in cooking. The less expensive varieties are fine for that purpose, but for sipping straight, have a selection of the "greats."

A well-stocked bar: What constitutes a well-stocked bar varies from region to region and group to group. For example, in some areas bourbon is the popular whiskey and Scotch is seldom called for, while in other circles, Scotch is the choice. In some regions vodka is in much greater demand than in others, and the same is true of rum. But the thoughtful host, no matter what he and his friends prefer, keeps on hand at least one good bottle of each of the standard liquors, which will cover most contingencies.

Here is a list for a thoroughly well-stocked bar. All you have to do is tailor quantities to your needs.

WHISKEYS

2 Scotch—one light, one heavier
2 bourbon—one light, one heavier
1 blended whiskey in decanter for mixed drinks
1 Canadian whiskey
1 Irish whiskey, primarily for Irish coffee

GINS

1 American gin
1 English gin for those who
prefer it

VODKAS

1 American vodka for mixed
drinks, cocktails
1 Zubrowka (Polish) vodka

for drinking straight (keep
Zubrowka chilled in the
refrigerator)

RUMS

1 light rum

1 dark rum

BRANDIES

1 fine old cognac
1 or 2 lesser brandies
(for example: 1 armagnac

and 1 lesser brandy **or** 1
white alcohol fruit brandy
and 1 lesser brandy)

LIQUEURS

2 famous-name liqueurs
3 fruit liqueurs for flavoring

1 cassis for Vermouth Cassis
and Kir

VERMOUTHS

1 dry vermouth

1 sweet vermouth

BITTERS

1 Italian bitters: Campari or
Punt e Mes (serve as an
aperitif)

1 Angostura bitters for
cocktails

FORTIFIED WINES

1 excellent dry sherry
1 good medium-dry sherry
1 good American dry sherry
1 fine vintage port
1 good port for cooking and flavoring

1 fine vintage Madeira
1 lesser Madeira for sauces and flavoring

TABLE WINES

Imported wines of your choice
Varietal domestic wines of your choice
2 gallons of domestic white wine (to decant)

2 gallons of domestic red wine (to decant)
1 gallon of domestic rosé (to decant)

Buying for a Party

Buying for a well-stocked bar is quite a different matter from buying liquor for a specific occasion. For the latter you should first decide what drinks you are going to serve. Then, on the basis of how many guests you expect, you should figure out quantities. These depend, to some extent, on the drinking habits of your friends, which you can ascertain only by experience. But a knowing host always buys too much rather than too little. Telephoning or rushing out to get additional supplies during a party can be very discomforting to both host and guests and indeed may hasten the end of a party. Liquor that is not drunk or wine that remains unopened will keep until another day.

There are certain broad calculations that you can make about the quantities you will need, and they are as follows:

Cocktails and highballs: On the average, figure that each person will drink two or three, and allow for 2 ounces per drink, even if you usually use 1½. On this basis you will need 2 fifths for six to eight guests, 3 fifths for ten to twelve, 5 fifths for twenty, and 8 fifths for thirty people. If you buy the same number of bottles but quarts rather than fifths, you will have a still wider margin of safety.

Brandy and liqueurs: A straight serving of either should be about 1 ounce. Most people like no more than one or two of these drinks after dinner, so you can figure that 1 fifth will take care of a party of twelve. You'll need 2 fifths for twenty and 3 fifths for thirty.

This is a very general estimate. But because of their high alcoholic content, brandy and liqueurs keep well, so overstock rather than understock your liquor closet with them.

Wines: Champagne or any other sparkling wine should be drunk promptly once it has been opened, because the effervescence does not last long. Many domestic reds, whites and rosés—particularly the generic types such as Burgundy and Chablis—can be kept for a while after opening. This is especially important to know if you buy large jugs. As far as more perishable wines go, you can always keep an opened bottle for a couple of days without risking a significant change in the character of the wine.

Again, in figuring quantities the margin must be broad. Some people like 1 glass of wine with a meal; others drink as many as 3 or 4. Using two servings per person as an average and allowing for about six servings per standard bottle, you will need 1 bottle for three people, 2 for six, 4 for twelve. But what about a dinner for four? One bottle may not be enough and 2 may be too much, but err on the generous side and console yourself with the cheery thought that you can always drink whatever is left with dinner the next night!

Depending on both the sizes of the glasses and the amounts poured, you can count on about 8 glasses per standard-size bottle of champagne. People tend to drink more of this wine at a prolonged festivity such as a dance or wedding than before or with a meal, but 3 glasses apiece is a fair average; those who drink 2 will compensate for others who drink 4! (Also see pages 55–56.)

Indispensables for the Drink-Dispensing Host

Efficient equipment does not guarantee an efficient performance when mixing drinks, but it certainly contributes a great deal. The most important implements and accessories a home bartender needs are relatively few in number, easy to come by and not too space-consuming or highly priced. There are additional items that are helpful although not essential. These are listed separately on pages 16–17.

A double-ended measuring cup, or a graduated measuring glass, for pouring a jigger (1½ ounces) and a pony (1 ounce) without guesswork. Although you may learn through practice to measure with your eye, it is always a wise idea to have a measuring cup handy, because the eye tends to become careless as hospitality and joviality increase! Do *not* get an automatic pourer that fits over the top of a bottle and measures one jigger at a time; such a gadget belongs in a second-rate public bar.

A lever-action corkscrew. As the screw is twisted into the cork the levers rise; lowering them does the work of actually pulling the cork.

A bar shaker and wire strainer: The shaker consists of two containers—one glass for the ingredients, one metal for the ice. They fit together for shaking the drinks. The strainer has a coil rim. This equipment is professional, efficient and a far cry from the obsolete cocktail shaker of former days.

A mixing pitcher or glass and a long-handled **stirring spoon,** also called a bar spoon, for making drinks that should be stirred rather than shaken.

A pitcher to hold plain water.

A bottle opener which is, above all, sturdy.

An ice bucket that holds at least two trays of ice cubes. A much larger insulated bucket or chest that can stand on the floor is useful for reserve ice supplies at a large party.

A small wooden cutting board and sharp knife for slicing fruit.

A lemon stripper for cutting citrus fruit peel.

A lime squeezer that you can hold over a glass and operate with one hand. Used also for lemons.

A bar muddler, strong, good-sized and heavy—for muddling sugar, crushing mint or cracking ice cubes.

A generous tray to hold the various mixings and protect the table. It should be made of liquor-proof metal or plastic.

Less mandatory but very welcome on occasion are an electric blender, fruit juice squeezer and ice crusher. The operations performed by these machines can also be performed by hand; it simply takes longer and uses more energy. Lacking an automatic ice crusher, you can use a manual one or wrap cubes in a thick towel or canvas bag and crush them with a mallet.

Garnishes and Flavorings

Most of those listed here are used quite frequently when mixing drinks. A few may never be in demand among your friends, and others, not mentioned, may be essential for one or more of their favorite drinks, but the checklist on pages 18–19 is a good starter.

Olives, green and pitted but not stuffed, for Martinis. (Let drain before adding to drink.)

Cocktail onions, for Gibsons. (Again, let drain or wash off.)

Fresh citrus fruit: Fresh fruit is best but when absolutely necessary you can fall back on canned, frozen or bottled juices. Lemons should be first on your list, followed by limes and oranges, depending on your drink-mixing plans. To get the most juice out of any of them, roll the uncut fruit back and forth several times on a counter or cutting board, pushing down hard with the palm of your hand. This softens the pulp inside, which, in turn, releases the juices.

Slices of citrus fruit should be cut less than a quarter of an inch thick, and orange slices should be halved. When

A double-action corkscrew. The screw is worked into the cork, and then the crosspiece at the top enables you to pull the cork by turning. The circular frame fits over the rim of the bottle.

A two-handed corkscrew. The corkscrew is worked into the cork, which automatically raises the side arms. When the corkscrew is down all the way, depress the side arms, and the cork will slide up and out.

A sommelier's corkscrew. It has a small knife for cutting the foil off the neck of the bottle, a corkscrew, and a prong to give you leverage against the rim of the bottle. The prong doubles as a bottle opener for mixers.

a wedge of lime or lemon is required, quarter the fruit lengthwise; if a quarter seems too big, halve it. When you need fruit peel, use a lemon stripper and cut off only the colored surface of the peel. If you need the peel of an entire lemon in one piece, it should be removed carefully in a continuous spiral; start at one end and circle the fruit until you reach the other. Do this as nearly before serving as you can, to better preserve the oils.

Sugar: Use the finest granulated sugar—called "superfine"—in mixing drinks, except for those few recipes that require lump sugar. Confectioner's (powdered) sugar is not the most satisfactory for sweetening drinks. However, sugar syrup—or simple syrup, as it is often called—is easy to make, requires no dissolving or stirring and can save you a great deal of time when preparing a drink that needs sugar. Its only disadvantage: most recipes give you the precise amount of finely granulated sugar to use, but if you prefer sugar syrup, you usually must judge the right quantity for yourself.

Recipe for sugar syrup: Put 3 cups of sugar in a saucepan with 1 cup of cold water, heat and allow to boil vigorously for a few minutes, then cool and bottle. Sugar syrup will keep almost indefinitely.

Bitters: The most often used are Angostura bitters (pages 23–24). Small bottles retain their character and particular flavor longer than large ones, after opening.

Maraschino cherries: Although these are not necessary, many people like them in certain drinks, and they are very decorative. Buy those with long stems attached, and keep the lid tightly screwed on the jar when not in use.

Recipe for coconut milk, or coconut cream: For the most part, these two terms are interchangeable in the Hawaiian Islands. (Milk is actually a misnomer for the liquid inside a coconut.)

Coconut milk is easily made: Grate fresh coconut until you have 4 cups, pour 2 cups of boiling water (part of which may be the liquid from the nut) over it and let stand ½ hour. Strain through a strong white cloth, squeezing and pressing to extract all liquid. Put in a jar and store in the refrigerator.

Although many Hawaiians do not distinguish coconut cream from coconut milk, to some the cream is the thick, creamy part that rises to the top of coconut milk when it is thoroughly chilled. This can be whipped. Some recipes from the Islands distinguish between the two by designating "thin" or "thick" coconut milk. Coconut milk can also be bought frozen in fancy food stores on the mainland, but this type is often sweetened, which rules out its use in many recipes.

Clever Ways with Ice

Iced drinks are very dear to American hearts and palates, so be sure that you have plenty of ice on hand at all times, and that it is both fresh and clear. Cubes that have been in trays in the refrigerator too long tend to take on a slight unwelcome odor, particularly if they have been near certain foods. If possible, remove cubes from a tray without running water over them, which is apt to make them stick together after you put them in an ice bucket. (To remove cubes easily, let the trays sit a few minutes at room temperature.)

An obvious but often overlooked fact about cold drinks is that they require less ice and it melts more slowly if all the other ingredients and the glasses have been pre-chilled. The easiest way to chill a glass is to put it in the refrigerator for half an hour or in the freezing compartment for a few minutes—slightly longer if you want to frost it. Another method is to fill the glass with shaved ice before you start mixing a drink, then to empty out the glass when you're ready to use it. If you want a heavily frosted glass, dip it in tepid water and put it in the freezer for a couple of hours. To sugar-frost a glass, chill it, then moisten the rim with a wedge of lemon or lime, a bit of citrus peel or a liqueur; dip the rim into superfine sugar, lift the glass out and gently tap off the excess sugar. Proceed in the same way but use lime peel and dip the glass in salt if you are preparing a Margarita. When making a Mint Julep the trick is to stir the shaved ice, bourbon and crushed mint mixture together so thoroughly that the glass becomes frosted in the process. If the ice reduces substantially in volume during the stirring, add more ice and additional bourbon to taste.

Large pieces of ice melt more slowly than small ones. A big block, such as you would put in a punch bowl, is the slowest to dissolve; cubes melt less quickly than crushed or shaved ice. When serving drinks on the rocks, crack the ice cubes with a heavy muddler or other tool before you put them in the glasses, because cracked ice chills quicker and better than cubes. It also dissolves faster, however, so be sure to empty out any water before pouring the liquor over the ice.

The iciest of all drinks are the frozen or frappéed type. If you make them in a blender, take the following precautions or they may turn to water rather than the desired sherbetlike consistency. Be certain the liquor is at room temperature—from 65° to 70°F. Use finely shaved ice, about 1 cup per drink. Pour all ingredients into the blender, then the ice, turn on the blender and keep close watch. If the mixture begins to get watery, switch off and add more crushed ice. If it forms a solid mass, switch off and break it up with a spatula.

To freeze a bottle in a block of ice—an especially good treatment for vodka, gin, aquavit, the white fruit brandies or even a bottle of made-up Martinis—you will need a mold or container deep enough to hold the bottle up to its neck. A large tin such as an empty two-pound coffee can, a half-gallon milk container of plastic or waxed cardboard, a plastic bucket or even a large saucepan or the bottom of a double boiler is suitable. Put the bottle in the center of the container and fill the container with water (tinted, if you like, with blue or green food coloring). Leave them in the freezer until the water is solidly frozen, then unmold the block. The "iceberg" will hold for several hours, and it makes a great conversation gambit. To pour, wrap a folded linen napkin around the ice block to hold it securely and protect your hands. Tequila and rum are other liquors that take happily to this kind of chilling.

Flavored or garnished ice can be made easily at home. If a punch recipe calls for a fair quantity of tea, for example, you can make a couple of big blocks of tea ice by putting strong tea in large containers and freezing it. Cubes of frozen tea or coffee are preferable to ice for chilling tea and coffee drinks, because there is no dilution of strength or flavor. For any drink requiring a dash of Angostura bitters, you can use cubes tinted and flavored with bitters. Add about 2 drops per cube to the water when you are making ice, so that it turns pink. The aroma of the bitters is trapped until the ice begins to melt in a drink.

If you freeze garnishes in cubes, choose the individual ice containers that sit in a tray; the cubes are larger and easier to extricate. Among your frozen assets might be twists of lemon or orange zest (see pages 104–05), tiny sections of lime and lemon, cubes of pineapple, strawberries, cherries, mint or borage leaves. If you can find the really minuscule currant tomatoes, they make an appropriate frozen garnish for a Bloody Mary or a non-alcoholic tomato juice cocktail.

Consider, too, the artful ice you can create with food coloring, but approach the job thoughtfully. Green cubes would add nothing to the appeal of an Old-fashioned, for example, whereas one ice cube surrounding a maraschino cherry, plus plain cracked ice, would look delightful. And blue or green cubes would be smashing in a pale, nearly colorless drink such as a Tom Collins, a gin and tonic or a simple glass of Perrier water (see page 29).

One last word about ice. Remember that the longer it remains in a drink, the more watery that drink becomes. Therefore, make cocktails in small batches (they can be pre-mixed except for the ice), and do not pour a second iced drink of any kind into an undrained glass unless a person asks for it that way.

Bitters—The Tangy Mixers

Bitters are the antidote to too much sweetness. In a drink —especially in a summer drink—sweetness can be cloying. It needs to be balanced, set off, with a tang. We drink dry wines, coolers with the sharpness of limes and lemons and now more than ever the, as it were, cryptically herbal, alchemical concoctions made with Campari, Angostura, Fernet Branca and the whole gamut of patent bitters.

Bitters are mixers. Few people like them straight. Italy does produce wonderful half-bitters, so to speak, with the sweet additive already in them, and another variety of bitters, complete with soda, in a one-shot bottle—a galloping success. Out-and-out bitters, however, are too pungent and positive for most palates. Their role is in partnership, and at this they excel.

More than anything else bitters are the mixers of leisure and lazy days. They were born in the nineteenth century in Turin, known as the city of pensioners, so fond were the citizens of sitting in cafés, watching the paving stones go by. Turin was a cynical city, a city that had grown up, been around, seen the world. It liked nothing better than to stretch its legs out, have its talk, and sip and sniff at a sophisticated glassful.

Turin café proprietors were masters of their trade. They studied (for they had time) every sip their customers took. The coffee was good. The cakes were good. The cigars were of the finest Havana leaf. But these were mere background for the cordials, the *specialità della casa*. Under the arcades—the cafés still exist today along the streets with big-bellied balconies sailing overhead and with much of the same unhurried atmosphere—all was calm. The last big meal was merely a prelude to the next. A little business might be concluded meanwhile, much as one might play at cribbage or admire the waitress—dispassionately but carefully, making no mistake.

Such an atmosphere accounts for the slightly bizarre development of bitters. They have their ultimate roots in alchemy—in the studies of the restless dreamers who passionately believed that somewhere in the mixing of this and that lay the elixir of life, the philosophers' stone, the heart's desire. It is impossible to tell how much, if at all, bitters have changed from the old prescriptions. In essence they remain the same—the infusion of herbs, roots and spices in alcohol.

Secrecy remains the attitude of the great aperitif and bitters houses today. In vain the researcher, with the best will in the world, knocks at their doors for a clue to—the merest hint of—the ingredients they use. "A family secret," they all say. One member alone of the staff or family knows the whole recipe. He is under oath to tell no one. Only on his deathbed, it is said, is his chosen successor ushered into his chamber. Then the doors are locked, the blinds are drawn and in the faintest, hoarsest whisper the secret passes for a second through the air and is locked in another heart.

It is almost equally difficult to describe the taste of the great bitters. No associations come to mind to help us. Perhaps if we knew what was in them we would be able to ascribe to them qualities of scent and flavor. There are Alpine herbs in this one or that, we are sure. Certainly orange peel accounts for something in the aroma of another. But the only associations they hold for us are the corner cafés, the beach terraces, the mountain resorts where we have drunk them.

Angostura bitters are the bitters of the New World. Dr. Siegert, the latter-day alchemist who developed them, had served in a Prussian cavalry regiment against Napoleon Bonaparte. The war over, he took up arms again to become surgeon general under the heroic, disillusioned Simón Bolívar. It was in Bolívar's service in Venezuela that Siegert compounded his medicinal bitters, christening them Angostura, the name of his post. Effective as they were against the inevitable stomach disorders of military life in South America, their taste was the attribute that secured Angostura's fame. In a few years the doctor was shipping them via Trinidad to England, where they were used for every purpose except the medicinal—especially, for a long time, as an additive to sherry.

The doctor's family (who runs the company to this day) eventually found that Venezuela, despite Bolívar's efforts, was a treacherous and unstable headquarters for a growing firm. There was an understandable unwillingness to invest capital in such a restless state. So the Siegerts left (secretly, for the government would never have let such a prosperous business out of the country) and settled in Port of Spain, Trinidad. They are still there.

Angostura bitters crop up in more mixed drinks than we could name, and soft drinks too; their special sphere of influence is designated by the word "pink."

Pink Gin, or Gin and Bitters, is dry gin and Angostura. Some people like it with an equal quantity of water.

The newest and most ingenious way of exerting the subtle influence of Angostura on a drink is by using pink ice (page 21). Put pink ice in almost any summer drink, from lemonade to a collins. It goes well in an Old-fashioned or a glass of Russian tea. Whatever the rare plants are that lurk in the dark confines of Dr. Siegert's concoction, they freshen and enrich everything they come in contact with.

Peychaud's bitters, although difficult to find outside the state of Louisiana, have been enjoyed for generations in many of the traditional drinks of New Orleans, such as the Sazerac. They are similar to Angostura in color and flavor, although slightly more pungent.

Amer Picon (*amer* is French for "bitter"), black as it looks, is not as strong in either flavor or alcohol as Angostura. Angostura is only dripped into drinks; Picon and the rest of the bitters family are drunk.

Picon comes as near as any bitters to giving the game away about its ingredients. It is based, it admits, on orange, quinine and gentian roots—three ingredients probably present to some degree in all bitters. The technique of making bitters is much the same for all, too: the flavorings are steeped in pure alcohol and distilled water for a certain length of time, sometimes in glass tanks, sometimes in casks of Slavonian oak. Then the flavored spirit is filtered away and mixed with an appropriate amount of sugar syrup, colored, matured awhile, bottled and finally consumed.

In France, Picon is most often drunk simply diluted with water and sweetened with a dash of grenadine syrup. Grenadine is, in fact, frequently used in conjunction with bitters —more to the advantage of the grenadine than of the bitters. Picon's best partner is the orange, which is, after all, one of its ingredients.

Campari must be the biggest-selling bitters of all. It is as smart to drink Campari in Scotland as it is to drink Scotch in Milan. Unlike Angostura, and to some extent Picon, Campari is not a subtle flavoring agent for other drinks but a drink in its own delicious right.

Gaspare Campari learned his trade in Turin, although the Campari café became famous at its present site on the corner of the Galleria Vittorio Emanuele in the center of Milan. The Galleria is actually a huge shopping arcade, the favorite promenade of the gentry of the city. There they stroll and, sitting down for a rest, order a Campari soda. The waiter takes them to mean the little single-measure bottle, in which the soda is already mixed with the Campari. Sticklers sometimes call for the big red bottle and a siphon for the pleasure of doing it themselves. The redness of Campari is one of its most attractive attributes; it is clear, pale garnet.

Campari, although bitter, is distinctly less so than most of the other tangy mixers. Its taste, like that of any bitters, comes as a bit of a surprise at first. But generally one acquires a liking for it very quickly—quicker still through the intermediary stages of drinks such as the Americano and the Negroni.

Fernet Branca was the prescription of the Swedish Dr. Fernet at the time of a cholera epidemic. This does not sound like a promising start for a drink, but its gastronomic qualities outlived its original purpose, as Angostura's survived the Bolívar campaign, to establish it as a digestion-promoting aperitif. Fernet Branca also has the reputation of being a last-resort head clearer for the morning after a party. There are even those who recommend it half-and-half with brandy for this purpose; others put it in their coffee. Its distinguishing ingredient is rhubarb.

Orange and peach bitters are less aromatic, simpler and more distinctly fruity than their more sophisticated counterpart, Angostura. Where their particular tastes are desired, in drinks or in cooking, they are effective flavoring essences.

Punt e Mes means "point and a half" in Italian. The story goes that the drink was the favorite in a café frequented by stockbrokers, and the proprietor borrowed a term he often heard in their conversation. The sign-language gesture that accompanied it—one straight finger and one crooked one—still constitutes an order for a Punt e Mes in some very well-traveled bars.

The drink is not, strictly speaking, a bitters. We are moving away into the world of what should properly be called aperitifs. Punt e Mes lies somewhere between an Italian vermouth and Campari. Its base, unlike that of a real bitters, is wine rather than spirits; the bitterness is due to quinine.

Punt e Mes is perhaps the finest "bitter vermouth." It is very sweet and at the same time extremely bitter—a crossing of tastes that makes it extraordinarily appetizing. It is best drunk on the rocks or with a splash of soda.

Mineral Waters and Carbonated Mixers

If you have changed your brand of whiskey time and again, trying to find one without a slightly medicinal taste, it's probably not the Scotch or bourbon that is at fault but the water you mix it with. Because of the pollution of most of our water these days, it is treated with chlorine and other chemicals to make it safe to drink. Safe it may be, but often not very tasty, which accounts in part for the re-awakened popularity of bottled spring or mineral waters.

Spring water is called "mineral water" because in passing

through the earth it picks up a certain mineral content. Varying amounts of bicarbonates, sulfates, chlorides, calcium, magnesium and iron are absorbed, depending upon the region. The water may be still or sparkling, pungent or tasteless. Waters with a very strong mineral flavor are usually not bottled but are consumed at the particular spas where they flow. Very flat-tasting waters usually have a small amount of salts added when bottled. (Even our bottled club sodas and/or charged waters have minerals added to compensate for the dull taste of the distilled water from which they are made. Some spring waters bubble naturally, the gas having been acquired on their way to the surface, but many of them are artificially carbonated—that is, carbonic acid gas is introduced when they are bottled.)

Since the earliest times, mineral waters have been highly valued for their healthful qualities, whether justifiably or not. Ancient Roman and Greek temples to Aesculapius were frequently built in the vicinity of mineral springs, to make things easier for the god of medicine. Down through the centuries, "taking the waters" has been believed to be a cure for almost every ailment known to man, and generally speaking, the worse the taste of the water, the more efficacious the remedy was presumed to be. Along in the eighteenth century, it became fashionable to spend a week or two at a spa, and great hotels sprang up around many of them. (The fact that the health of the patrons improved at such places was probably due to the substitution of water, however obnoxious, for excesses of wines and spirits, plus a controlled regimen of exercise and rest.) As bottling procedures and shipping facilities improved, the waters were sent far and wide, and the need for protracted "cures" at the source diminished. However, the French (who have always been concerned with the state of their digestions and livers) and to a lesser extent the Italians still patronize curative spas, and they are the world's greatest consumers of mineral waters, bottled and otherwise.

Another reason why bottled water appears on many tables in Paris, the world's capital of gastronomy, is that the knowing Frenchman may rely on the alkalinity of the water to offset the acidity of the wine he drinks. Elsewhere, especially in out-of-the-way places, European diners will ask for bottled water rather than risk the perhaps dubious local water. In this country, imported bottled waters are bought mainly by people who have had them in Europe and have developed a liking for their peculiar mineral flavor. Some are drunk solely because of their taste, some on the basis of their reputation for health-giving properties, some for their purity. Nearly all mineral waters, by the way, are best when chilled, for chilling minimizes their earthy flavor.

In addition to imported waters, there are a number of well-established brands of American mineral spring water, and the demand for them is increasing. Every state in the union contains mineral springs, and the water from many of them is bottled for regional use. . . . However, the most famous American water—Poland Water, originally from Poland Springs in Maine, now springing in Wayside, New Jersey, is sold all over the country. It is a natural still water, neutral in flavor with a refreshing tang, ideal for table use. Another popular domestic water, also nationally distributed, is Mountain Valley Mineral Water from Hot Springs, Arkansas. It too is non-sparkling, with a bracing smoothness and a faint taste of minerals, although it is very low in salt content.

There are two other American waters which are now widely distributed and gaining in popularity. Deer Park, with its distinct bite, is a natural still water from springs at the Maryland resort of Deer Park. It became celebrated as "the great water" served on the B&O railroad trains. The second, Saratoga Geyser, is the only naturally carbonated water in the United States. It has a hearty flavor and is from one of the springs at the famous spa in New York State.

Literally scores of mineral waters are bottled in all parts of the world, but here are the major waters imported to this country:

Apollinaris: This naturally carbonated water from Germany's Rhineland is one of the oldest bottled waters to be shipped. It has a lively flavor and is refreshing at any time of day, by itself or as a mixer.

Vichy-Célestins: There are several springs at Vichy in France, of which Célestins is the only palatable table water. Far and away the best seller among bottled waters, it has a distinct mineral flavor, even when chilled. Other waters from Vichy are so strong as to be medicines and are taken in limited doses. The Vichy springs are owned and operated by the French government; over 80 million bottles of Vichy-Célestins are shipped annually.

Perrier: Another French water, this one is highly effervescent but not strong in flavor. It is ideal for highballs and is widely used in France in place of club soda. It is equally refreshing to drink upon rising in the morning and before retiring at night.

San Pellegrino: An Italian sparkling water, pleasantly brisk, with a marked mineral taste.

Vittel: This non-sparkling, slightly alkaline water from France is used principally as a table water. It should be well chilled.

Evian: A sweet, pure, still water from the Cachat Spring in France, its taste can best be described as innocent.

Garci-Crespo: This is one of several waters bottled at Mexico's largest spa and by far the most popular. It is slightly effervescent, and although it contains traces of a dozen or more minerals, it has no strong flavor and is an excellent mixer.

Although many sparkling mineral waters mix well with spirits, club soda is of course still the most widely used. Next in popularity as mixers are ginger ale and quinine water. Ginger ale originally was made by a brewing process, like beer, and the bubbles were the result of natural fermentation. Now a ginger-flavored syrup is combined with carbonated water to produce this tangy drink.

Quinine water, or "tonic," was first used by colonials in the hot countries as a sort of specific against the ever present threat of malaria. Although not very effective for that purpose, it made a good excuse for having a drink. Now tonic is mixed with everything—gin, vodka, rum, even whiskey—and consumed in every season. Its curious bitter-sweet flavor seems to have an almost universal appeal, even though it pretty well conceals the flavor of whatever spirit is mixed with it. Some people drink it straight and consider it most refreshing, especially on a hot midsummer afternoon. Often a twist of lemon is added, or a quartered lime, to impart a little piquancy. Today, quinine water is even bottled pre-flavored with lemon and orange.

Everyone is familiar with Coca-Cola and the other colas, of course. Besides being immensely popular on its own, Coke is often mixed with various liquors, rum being the most usual.

Carbonated water (club soda, effervescent mineral water or other beverages containing carbonic acid gas), besides adding sparkle and zest to mixed drinks, is believed by some to have the peculiar property of carrying the alcohol into the blood stream faster than plain water. When in a hurry for alcoholic exhilaration, they use a sparkling mixer.

Just about everyone knows how to make highballs, col-linses and rickeys, but the average home bartender is apt to get into a rut, serving the same drinks time after time. If you would welcome a change of pace, here are a few suggestions. Fizzes are rather like cocktails with club soda added. Puffs are pretty to look at, beneficial and delicious to drink, and are mixed with club soda. There are count-less other drinks that are made with charged water, ginger ale or other carbonated beverage. They range from mild to strong, from moderate to long, from drinks served in large wineglasses to those served in pitchers and punch bowls. All have one thing in common: if they are allowed to stand too long after mixing, they lose most of their bubbles.

Packaged Drinks and Drink Mixes

Today, some of the best-known cocktails can be bought canned or bottled in many liquor stores. Bottled and frozen mixes that require only the addition of the alcoholic ingredients, and even powdered mixes that—in the case of long drinks—also require the addition of water, soda or other dilutant, are available in certain supermarkets. All have their uses, but their flavor is usually not as good as that of a drink made from carefully measured and mixed fresh ingredients turned out by an experienced host-bartender. Of course, this is no more surprising with drinks than it is with food, although it is less universally known.

There are times, however, when the best packaged cocktails and mixes can be very handy to have. An inexperienced host, for example, may find better success with these than when left to his own devices. Again, if time is an important factor, selected packaged products can come to the rescue with considerable aplomb and make bartending an instant success. And they dramatically simplify life on a boat, in an automobile, on a camping trip or picnic—in fact, at almost any outing. Probably here is where they shine at their brightest and best.

During the Christmas holidays some grocery stores sell cartons of eggnog base which you will find in their refrigerator cases; all you have to do is add liquor. And some liquor stores sell bottled eggnog complete with liquor (which prevents the non-alcoholic ingredients from spoiling). You simply chill the brew and serve. This shortcut is particularly convenient if you want to offer drop-in guests individual glasses of eggnog on the spur of the moment.

Be forewarned that packaged drinks are more expensive than the homemade varieties. This is most conspicuously true when canned and bottled products include liquor. Mixes to which the liquor must be added will make less of a dent in your budget per drink, even after allowing for the price of the gin, whiskey or whatever.

Remember that you can always perk up the appearance, and often the flavor, of partly or fully packaged drinks with appropriate garnishes—citrus peel, mint, nutmeg and so on. If you want to serve anything out of the ordinary, you will have to fall back on your own resources and skills, plus a dependable recipe.

For the most part, you really don't have to rely on pre-made drinks or fixings in your own home, provided your friends will settle for simple concoctions. Such drinks as gin and tonic or bitters, Scotch, bourbon or brandy on the rocks with a little soda or water, or in a tall glass with ice and more soda or water, can be whipped up quickly and correctly with a minimum of fuss. They are excellent standbys in almost any community. They'll come to the rescue when you're out of lemons, low on sugar or pressed for time. They can be made with no past experience, no tools but a measuring cup and a long-handled stirring spoon, no concern about suitability. But even a sophisticated host woud do well to investigate the various packaged drinks and mixes on the market. He should sample those that interest him before he stocks up. He may find that he likes all the products of a particular firm, or that he prefers one firm's Martinis and another's Manhattans, one brand of Tom Collins mix and another brand of Daiquiri mix. If you don't consider yourself a good judge, ask a friend or two whose opinion you respect to help you make a decision. And in the making, have a good time.

Decanters Old and New

A handsome decanter is always a decorative addition to the dining or serving table. It is also a very practical serving accessory for the host who buys his liquor and wines in large jugs or outsize bottles, and for the connoisseur who serves vintage wines, which are bound to have some sediment and therefore benefit from being decanted. And fine decanters are satisfying possessions for the esthetically minded person who prefers to pour his liquor, wine and liqueurs from them rather than from commercial bottles. For any or all of these reasons, decanters make excellent gifts, particularly when accompanied by a bottle of wine or cognac, in which case the decanter should be of clear glass. Green or amber decanters are better used for whiskey—

and gin or other colorless liquors. You can give the decanter already filled if you like, but if you fill it with good wine, be sure you attach the cork from the bottle to identify the wine.

If you are buying a new decanter for someone who might like to add others to make a set, choose a design that can be easily matched or that will go well with a variety of types. But if you have a friend who collects antique drinking accessories, give a beautiful old decanter complete with a silver chain and label. A true antique collector will not be concerned about whether his decanters match; he may even deliberately seek a wide range of styles.

The earliest decanters probably evolved from the green bottles used for shipping wines and for drawing wines and brandies from casks in English inns and pubs. These bottles were usually square, so they could be easily packed for shipping, and they came in a soft bottle-green. They were blown of flint glass; the cooling process often left the surfaces concave and the bottle slightly irregular in shape. The necks were very short and the corks or stoppers very small.

Later, the bottles were made from gunmetal molds which gave the surface of the glass a dappled texture. Such bottles were used not only for wines and brandies but also for other precious liquids such as scents and medicines.

You can still find some of these square green bottles in antique shops here and in England. Sometimes they're available at bargain prices because people think they are merely old medicine bottles and do not realize their true age and charm. They make a fine addition to a collection of decanters, and although transparency is preferable for wines or cognacs, the green bottles are attractive containers for whiskies, gin or vodka.

Occasionally you may come across crude but interesting examples of early American decanters. They are irregular in shape and frequently rather dirty. But when cleaned up and polished, they can be appealing as decorative accessories.

In the eighteenth century, decanters became quite elegant and were important additions to every well-appointed dining room in the colonies as well as in England. They were filled from wine or brandy casks in the cellar, then brought to the dining room and placed in large wine chests or coolers, which might hold as many as six or seven decanters. You will find some decanters of colonial design among the Colonial Williamsburg reproductions.

In the southern colonies, slaves were generally entrusted with replenishing the decanters, and since many of them could not read, the bottle stoppers were made in different designs to indicate what the bottle should hold—a diamond design for sherries, perhaps, a heart design for port, etc. Also used were crowns, spades, circles, flowers and many other designs. Occasionally such decanters turn up in antique shops in the tidewater regions of Maryland and Virginia. If you see one, buy it. Today it is a rarity.

Toward the end of the eighteenth century, it became the fashion to have sets of square decanters fitted into a case of fine wood equipped with lock and key. This was known, appropriately enough, as a "tantalus," because the case was designed so that the bottles could be seen but not removed unless the case was unlocked. In addition to serving the obvious function of making it impossible for anyone to deplete the owner's supply of liquor without his knowledge, some of these tantalus sets were extremely handsome. The polished wood was embellished with rich silver ornamentation, and the bottles were elaborately cut in sunburst or diamond patterns. The decanters had chased or cut labels, or chains hung around their necks with engraved silver labels attached to indicate the contents. A good antique tantalus set, with all its bottles and stoppers intact, adds great distinction to a sideboard or buffet.

Modern decanters come in an amazing array of designs, from the simple, severe bottles of Scandinavia to the elegant Baccarat of France and the famed classical Waterford designs of Ireland. A truly elegant gift for someone who is a connoisseur of fine old beverages might be a Baccarat or

Waterford decanter with a bottle of vintage port or excellent cognac decanted into it. Another would be a modern three-decanter tantalus containing port, a good sherry and an outstanding Madeira.

Liqueur decanters are smaller than those designed for wine or liquor, and come in a variety of shapes, the most common having a graceful long neck. Some of these, both old and new, are accompanied by matching liqueur glasses. Clear glass is the most effective, because it permits the subtle or vivid color of the liqueur to be seen and enjoyed. True, certain cordials are colorless; if these are decanted, cut, colored or gold-enriched glass makes them look more interesting.

Carafes are somewhat different from decanters. Designed to hold simple, pleasant wines that are drunk freely during informal meals, carafes are never elaborate. They have sturdy necks that can be grasped easily, and they are often used without stoppers.

(Speaking of corks, it is sometimes possible to buy an old decanter that is most attractive but lacks a stopper and is therefore quite reasonably priced. It is also possible to find a crystal or silver stopper that suits the design and proportions of a particular decanter. Proprietors of antique, secondhand and near-junk shops frequently have a box of old stoppers tucked away on a shelf. Occasionally, one that harmonizes with a decanter may fit it, too, but if a stopper is too large, it can usually be ground to the right size.)

From a practical point of view, and often an esthetic one as well, separate identifying labels on chains are more satisfactory than those that are applied permanently to decanters by cutting, etching or some other process. Removable labels can always be switched, and many of them are well designed, but permanent lettering is inflexible and—particularly on contemporary decanters—apt to be in bad taste. Metal bottle labels make charming and relatively inexpensive presents, but they should be chosen to harmonize in mood and design with the decanters on which they will be used. The most adaptable labels are simply shaped, made of silver or undecorated white enamel and marked with classic block letters.

Some Tips for Drink Makers

Every host collects his own little bag of tricks that add to his efficiency or prowess as a bartender. Some of these he discovers by accident or experiment; others he copies from friends or professional bartenders who know their business. Here, however, are a few simple suggestions:

To stir or to shake? For years the controversy raged, but in this sophisticated era, it is recognized that some drinks take more kindly to stirring, others to shaking. The old wives' tale about bruising gin if you shake it is particularly asinine, if only because gin is sturdy stuff indeed! The reason to stir it is that it's a clear liquid. So are vermouth, whiskey, vodka and a number of other liquors. If all the ingredients in a drink are clear, or if any are effervescent (such as champagne), you stir them together with the ice for the best results. (Especially, drinks made with soda or any other carbonated mixer should be stirred quickly and very briefly so that they will keep their sparkle.) There are few exceptions to this, the Stinger being one of them. But if the ingredients include items that are difficult to blend— eggs, cream, fruit juice, heavy liqueurs, etc.—they should be shaken well so that the drink becomes creamy. Tall drinks like a Brandy Milk Punch or an eggnog should be shaken.

Straining a cocktail of any type is a good procedure because, if nothing else, it prevents little pieces of ice from getting into the glass.

Pouring mixed drinks into glasses sounds easy, but there is a trick to doing it so that all the drinks will have the same consistency. Set the glasses in a row, fill each halfway, then return to the head of the row and fill each to about a half-inch from the top. This distributes the ingredients evenly.

Separating an egg looks simple but takes a little practice. If you need egg whites for drinks you plan to serve, get them ready ahead of time. Take each egg and crack the shell in half by rapping it sharply across the middle with a knife or against a counter edge. Holding the two half shells side by side, pass the yolk back and forth between them while allowing the white to drop down into a bowl underneath. The most important part of this procedure is to keep the yolk intact and unbroken so that none of it mixes with the white. Should some of the white persist in clinging to the yolk, gently separate it with the edge of the empty half shell, but don't cut into the yolk.

The right order when mixing an individual drink in a glass may vary, but there are some basic principles that are often followed. For one thing, if an iced drink calls for sugar, put it in the glass first, add a few drops of water or soda and muddle until the sugar has dissolved. (It will not dissolve quickly in liquor.) Mint that must be crushed should be muddled along with the sugar. As a rule, any fruit juices come next, then the ice, the alcoholic ingredients and any mixer, in that order. There are two reasons for adding the ice before the liquor. First, the liquor cools faster when poured over ice. Second, the longer you postpone pouring the liquor, the more chances you have to correct any mistakes or to start again without wasting your precious whiskey, brandy or whatever.

You should change the above order, however, if you are measuring by eye rather than with a measuring glass. Nobody can pour liquor over ice freehand, as it were, and be certain when to stop. Ice can arrange itself in a glass so that it is closely or loosely packed; it can take up more or less space; it can create all kinds of optical illusions. Even the simplest mixed drink—bourbon or Scotch on the rocks with a little water—is difficult to make properly without a measuring cup if the "rocks" are already in the glass. Of course, all this is one more proof that you should have that measurer right at hand.

Floating brandy, liqueurs or cream on the top of a drink is another skill that the drink-mixing host should acquire. Hold the bowl of a teaspoon face down just above the drink and pour the "float" gently over the back of the spoon. It will slide onto the top of the drink and stay there, provided of course it is less dense. (Also see "Floats," page 327.)

II

Spirits and Wines—
What They Are and
How to Use Them

You are missing a lot if you don't know something more about spirits and wines than which brands you prefer and what they cost. A little knowledge of the various qualities for which they are famous and their backgrounds—where they originated, how and from what they are made—gives alcoholic beverages a more interesting, more personal and certainly more individual appeal. Certain bits of information are particularly intriguing, for example: why gin was once the most demoralizing influence in England; what the letters "D.O.M." on a bottle of Benedictine stand for; how you can flavor vodka in the bottle before you use it; the meaning of a *trou Normand*. Once you acquire such facts, you will find that other people enjoy hearing them as much as you enjoy knowing them.

At the end of this chapter is a section on wines of all kinds: natural and still; champagne; the great fortified wines; and vermouth, the famous aromatized wine. A capsule guide to the wines of various European countries and the United States, plus suggestions about how to treat and handle all types, makes it easy for you to choose and use wine with assurance.

APERITIFS

The dictionary defines an aperitif as "a short alcoholic drink taken before a meal as an appetizer," but as the word is used today, it almost invariably also means a mild drink. Dry sherry, sweet and dry vermouth and dry white wines are often drunk as aperitifs, and there is a sizable group of bottled potables known as patent aperitifs. Some of these are aromatized wines; besides being fortified, they are flavored with various herbs, quinine or other ingredients that change the natural taste of the red or white wine into one that is highly individual—and rarely entirely definable. Spirit-based aperitifs fall into two categories —bitter and sweet—and each of them is made according to a special, sometimes secret formula. A French patent aperitif of the nineteenth century was named *Quoique Ce Soit* ("Whatever This May Be") which might still apply to the entire group and their secret formulas. All, however, are constant from bottle to bottle. If you like one, you can continue to buy it without fear that its characteristics will change.

Because vermouth is best known in this country as an ingredient of mixed drinks, particularly cocktails, it is discussed separately on pages 66–67. The patent aperitifs are reviewed briefly here. Most are French or Italian. Americans developed a taste for them as a result of wide travel in Europe after World War II (and lately, because of increased interest in healthful and low-calorie diets). People found it very pleasant to follow the continental custom of lingering in a sidewalk café before lunch or dinner, sipping a light aperitif and watching the world go by. Today many men and women prefer these pleasant little drinks to cocktails before meals. It is possible to buy a wide range of them, and several make good bases for various mixed drinks as well as being delicious on their own.

Among the best-known French aperitifs is Dubonnet, either red or white (it is also now made in the United States). The red is the sweeter, but a slice of lime or lemon gives it a touch of tartness. Other French favorites are white or red Lillet, white or red Raphäel, and Byrrh, which is red. The outstanding Italian aperitif—actually a drinking bitters—is Campari, which combines well with soda and is sold already bottled that way all over Italy. Others are Punt e Mes (a contradiction of sweetness and bitterness that needs icing) and Cynar, made from artichokes. Both of these aperitifs contain quinine.

The sweet, spirit-based aperitifs are all aniseed drinks —Pernod and Ricard from France, and ouzo from Greece (see pages 47–48). Unlike those mentioned above, they are not mild, being stronger than brandy, and must be drunk diluted with water, which turns their yellow-tinged clearness cloudy.

As you can see from these short descriptions, there is such great variety in aperitifs that you must find your preferred way of drinking each. Most, however, are served chilled in small wineglasses, or on the rocks, or diluted with soda or water in Old-fashioned glasses. You can dress them up with orange, lemon or lime slices or peel.

APPLE SPIRITS AND CIDER

What brandy is to wine, applejack is to cider—the distillation of the alcohol to a concentrated essence of the fruit. Like all country liquors, cider has in its history a strong element of the old moonshining tradition. In the United States, applejack, or "Jersey Lightning," has been produced commercially for about three hundred years; the oldest operating distillery in the country, Laird's of New Jersey, has been producing it since the seventeenth century. The French equivalent of applejack, calvados, comes from Normandy (and is named for one of its departments). The difference between the two is that pure cider is used for applejack, whereas all but the very best calvados is distilled from the pressings after the cider has been made. Calvados, therefore, tends to have a slight underlying rankness that needs covering up with caramel. Either the American or French version of apple brandy makes a marvelous change from cognac as an after-dinner straight drink. In Normandy there is a tradition known as the *trou Normand*—drinking a glass of calvados between courses in the middle of a meal. The theory is that the fiery spirit burns out a *trou,* or hole, for the food that will follow.

Cider is fermented apple juice. The unfermented juice, however delicious, can no more lay claim to the name "cider" than grape juice can be called "wine." Real cider has about the same alcoholic strength as normal beer—sometimes less, often much more. It is made by pressing fresh ripe apples, adding yeast and letting the natural sugar in the juice ferment. In its natural state, cider—like table wine—is completely dry and free of sugar, and it is almost unobtainable today.

The great British cider houses produce ranges of cider from a slightly sweetened, almost still table drink to a "champagne" version in which, in order to make it sparkle, the cider is caused to ferment a second time after bottling. This drink is available here.

Cider is a great thirst-quencher either on its own or made into Cider Cup. Its fresh tang is also incomparably good with coarse, simple country foods, salads and cold dishes, and on picnics, served thoroughly cooled in tall tumblers. Only at dinner does it seem too bulky and too plain at the same time. It lacks the appetizing quality of wine.

AQUAVIT, TEQUILA AND SOME OTHER WHITE SPIRITS

The principle is the same for making all grain or fruit alcohols. No matter what you start with, the *original* end product is always a clear, waterlike liquid. The kind of raw material used and the flavoring that may be added make an almost limitless number of liquors possible. Some of the best known—gin (pages 55–57), vodka (pages 67–68), rum (pages 62–63) and brandies (pages 48–51), which are distilled dry spirits—are briefly discussed on the pages given. Some of the less familiar ones are explained here.

Aquavit

In Denmark, Norway and Sweden, the native white spirit is aquavit (Danish *akvavit*), a ginlike liquor made from grain or potatoes and flavored with caraway seed rather than juniper berries. Aquavit means "water of life," which, in some form or other, is a phrase used by various countries when referring to one or more of their distilled spirits. Aquavit is a pungent, strong drink (90 proof) that is not a good mixer. It is best taken straight, icy cold, in small stemmed glasses. The usual drink is 1 ounce, and the Scandinavians do not sip it but take it in one swallow, most often with a beer chaser. It should be accompanied by fish such as herring and smoked eel, or substantial appetizers, canapés or sandwiches. Aquavit is a very satisfactory drink to serve with the first course of a meal, whether at the dining table or in the living room, but it is not the best choice at a cocktail party when little emphasis is put on food. For the best results, and the most spectacular, freeze the bottle in a jacket of ice (see instructions, page 20). It is traditional, when drinking aquavit, to raise your glass to your companion, look into his eyes, say "Skoal," down the spirit in a gulp, lower the glass and again meet the person's eyes.

Tequila

Mexico's own contribution to the world of white spirits (touched with a gleam of gold) is tequila. Described as the cactus whiskey, it is made from the sap of the century plant, a very superior kind of cactus. Although enormously popular among Mexicans, its distinctive flavor is definitely an acquired taste for Americans. Nevertheless, tequila has loyal advocates in the United States, many of whom probably became familiar with it when traveling in Mexico and vacationing in that country's popular resorts.

This fiery drink may be taken straight by those who like it that way, but there is a traditional technique for doing so that helps to offset the red-hot shock. You tilt back your head, squeeze the juice of half a lime into your mouth, follow it with a pinch of salt and then down a shot glass of tequila in one gulp. Another method is to place a little salt on the back of your hand, put a pinch in your mouth, drink the tequila and follow up with a bite into a slice of lime. Whatever the sequence, the accompaniments remain the same, although you can substitute lemon for lime if necessary.

Pernod, Ouzo and Arak

All are Mediterranean spirits; all are almost colorless, licorice-flavored, highly potent and cloud up when mixed with water. The usual way to drink any of them is to pour about 2 ounces over a few ice cubes in an 8-ounce goblet or tumbler and then fill the glass with water. This procedure is almost always followed by the knowing French in drinking what, on the face of it, is the whitest spirit of all—Pernod—known as pastis on the Riviera, and the favored drink of southern France.

Pernod is today's successor to the notorious absinthe, the inspiration of poets and painters that presumably drove them to madness and death. Indeed, absinthe, green in color, was such a favorite in France at the end of the nineteenth century that the aperitif hour before dinner became known as *l'heure verte.* Today this legendary potion is illegal in Switzerland (where it originated), France, the United States and some other countries. However, the approximate flavor, the pretty appearance and some of the effect are produced with all the original ingredients (consisting of aromatic plants and high-proof spirits) except *Artemisia absinthium,* more familiarly known as wormwood, which was erroneously held responsible for the evils of absinthe. The coloring is chlorophyll, derived from spinach, stinging nettles, lettuce or other innocent leaves which water precipitates as an opalescent cloud. The flavor is overwhelmingly that of aniseed. The most satisfactory ways to enjoy Pernod are to dilute it with a great deal of water and ice, as explained above, or to use it as an added ingredient or flavoring in cocktails.

Ouzo, a product of Greece with a grape spirit base, aniseed flavoring and chlorophyll additive, is similar to Pernod. It is said that certain of the cheaper kinds use a sort of gum instead of chlorophyll, but since all Greek ouzo is remarkably inexpensive and many men have drunk it freely and lived to tell the tale, this cannot be very important.

Arak is made from grapes in Lebanon and Syria, from dates in Iraq and Egypt. In Turkey and the Balkans it is called "raki," and is made from such things as wine, grain, potatoes, molasses and plums. Natives of the Middle East feel that it is important to nibble something while sipping arak; they favor small savories of cheese, hard-boiled eggs and radishes.

Okolehao

This liquor is used in a few drinks that originated in Hawaii and can be bought there and in some other areas of the United States. Often referred to as "oke" in the Islands, it is made from sugar-cane molasses and other ingredients native to that part of the world. (One of these, taro, is also the base for poi, Hawaii's famous food.) One type of okolehao is dark in color, with a smoky smell and flavor. Another almost colorless type, also called arnack, can be drunk straight or used in mixed drinks.

BRANDY, THE BELOVED

There are two types of brandy—that distilled from wine and that distilled from a fermented mash of fruit. True, wine is the product of grapes, which are themselves a fruit, but the process of making the grape juice into a wine before distilling is not involved when producing fruit brandies.

Of the wine-based brandies, the finest is cognac.

Wine-based Brandies

Cognac: The reputation of cognac as the best brandy in the world is unchallenged. And its excellence is not, as some people think, simply a matter of age. To make good brandy, you need thin, indifferent wine; ideally, a wine with the character found in the Charente region around the town of Cognac in the west of France. Only the vineyards located here are allowed by French law to call their distilled wine "cognac." The wine itself from this area is so acid that it is practically undrinkable, but it distills superbly. This step is handled most often by the farmers who make the wine, and the spirit is then sent to the

QUALITIES OF BRANDY

FIRM	I	II	III
Bisquit Dubouché	St. Martial	V.S.O.P.	Extra
Courvoisier	V.S.	V.S.O.P.	Napoleon
Delmain	R.D.		Pale and Dry
Denis Mounie	Gold Leaf		
Hennessy*	Bras Armé	V.S.O.P.	Extra
Hine	★★★★★	V.S.O.P.	Triomphe
Martell	★★★	V.S.O.P. Medallion	Cordon Bleu
Monnet	★★★		Anniversaire
Otard	★★★	V.S.O.P.	
Polignac	★★★	V.S.O.P.	
Remy Martin		V.S.O.P.	Louis XIII
Robin	★★★		

* Hennessy has two cognacs, Bras d'Or and X.O., which are rated between V.S.O.P. and Extra.

big shipping houses around Cognac—Courvoisier, Martell, etc.—for blending and aging. It takes 10 barrels of wine to make 1 barrel of brandy.

Age is vital. When brandy is first distilled, it is hot as fire and undrinkable. At three years it is bearable, and at eight or nine years an ordinary brandy is as good as it will ever be. No amount of aging will make an indifferent brandy good; but the better a good one is, the longer it will continue to improve. The maturing of spirits can take place only in wooden casks; once bottled, brandy ceases to age, so don't be lured by a cobwebby bottle into thinking that the contents are automatically old. Those stars and letters on the labels do not necessarily indicate age, either. "V" stands for "very," "S" for "superior," and "O" for "old" and "P" for "pale," but the nomenclature of brandy has become very complicated. The simplified chart above will help you understand it.

Armagnac: The only other brandy that is recognized as equal to any but the very finest old cognacs—and even on a par with them in a different way. Armagnac comes from the Basque area in the northwest foothills of the Pyrenees and is often described as "earthier" than cognac.

Serving Brandy: Brandies fall into two categories— those you drink neat as a special after-dinner pleasure and those that make admirable bases for long and short drinks. All the Star brandies are really mixers. They have neither the delicacy nor the age to stand up to truly critical examination on their own, although there is absolutely nothing wrong with them and they are among the finer brandies. Three Star brandies are perfect on the rocks, with soda, or with dry ginger ale and ice. They are also fine to use in cooking, for flavor and flaming. Liqueur cognacs (and everything from V.S.O.P. upward can bear that name) should never be mixed or diluted. The traditional way of serving them is to pour a small measure into a large glass after a good dinner or lunch. Do not interpret "large glass" to mean the great goldfish-bowl type that is sometimes used. There is no need to be able to get your head into the glass. Any generous-looking glass with a decidedly narrower top than middle, so that the scent is directed toward the drinker's nose, is good. It should be thin, to permit the temperature of the hand to penetrate the glass and warm its contents quickly.

Fruit Brandies

Known in France as *alcools blancs*, these are the brandies made from fruits, and not to be confused with liqueurs. (For an explanation of the basic difference between fruit brandies and liqueurs, see page 57.)

With the exception of calvados and sometimes slivovitz, fruit brandies are colorless because they are not aged in wood, which would affect the flavor of the fruit, but in earthenware, glass or wax-lined casks.

One of the best known of the fruit brandies is kirsch or kirschwasser, made from black cherries—originally a wild variety found in central western Europe but today usually cultivated. Other notable fruit brandies are calvados made from apples grown in Normandy orchards, and brandies produced from plums: slivovitz from Yugoslavia, Quetsch or Mirabelle from France. The stones are mashed along with the flesh of cherries and plums, which is responsible for the slightly bitter almond flavor of these brandies. Poire Williams or Williamine is a Swiss pear brandy distilled from Williams pears. Framboise is the product of wild raspberries from the Vosges, and increasingly rare (and expensive) because of the cost of labor involved in picking the berries. These and all other fruit brandies are sold at very high strength to preserve their freshness, which is their great quality. The fruit is crushed and fermented the moment it is picked. Distillation follows quickly, and then the spirit matures for a few months only. Drinking it is uncannily like biting on fresh-picked fruit.

Although fruit brandies are often served before or during a meal in various countries abroad, they are customarily drunk only after lunch or dinner here. Serve them at room temperature. Half-fill small, balloon-shaped glasses that have been iced so they are frosted; this chilling emphasizes and points up the aroma of the brandy.

Some of the recipes in this book call for small or sometimes large amounts of cherry brandy, peach brandy and others of that type. They are not true fruit brandies *distilled* from the fruit, but brandy *flavored* with the fruit, and are actually liqueurs.

CHAMPAGNE

No drink in history has such a mystique or gives rise to such a sense of self-indulgence and luxury as champagne. This many-faceted wine tastes delicious at any hour—brunch or supper, cocktail time or four o'clock in the morning. It complements most foods. It is the felicitous choice for a large party—easier to cope with than a battery of mixed drinks, not much more expensive if you buy magnums instead of quarts and probably the most elegant of all potables. It is the classic wine for drinking toasts (see Chapter V), for weddings and christenings. It is also a first-rate mixer.

To be precise, true champagne comes from one place only, the French region of Champagne around Rheims and Epernay northeast of Paris. Some of the champagnes from other countries are made in the careful, complex French manner, and others by a simplified procedure. Many are highly satisfactory—and the most sensible choice for mixed drinks such as punches and Black Velvets or for serving on those occasions when guests are more appreciative of quantity than quality.

Classic French champagne is made from a combination of black and white grapes; quick pressing prevents the skins from coloring the juice. Two other types of champagne are pink, or *rosé,* and *blanc de blancs.* The color of pink champagne comes from the black grape skins, which are left in the wine just long enough to tinge it, or from the addition of a little of the local still wine made from the same black grapes. *Blanc de blancs* is made from only white grapes.

Most champagne is blended and carries no date on the label. Only when the shippers feel they have a truly great year do they declare a vintage. But the primary aim of each firm is to produce, through skilled blending, a champagne with definite characteristics that distinguish it from its competitors and to keep these characteristics constant year after year. Non-vintage does not imply inferior quality.

Care and handling: Unlike many still wines, champagne is not temperamental and does not need babying. All it requires is that it be stored on its side in a relatively cool place and chilled to a temperature of 44° to 48° F. before serving. (If it is any colder, you can neither smell nor taste the wine.) Usually three-quarters of an hour in the refrigerator is sufficient. Unless the bottle is cool to start with, an ice bucket will take longer. Don't put champagne in the freezer for any length of time; if it actually freezes, it will never be the same again. But if you are in a great hurry, a brief fifteen minutes in the freezer will help. So will chilling the glasses. Don't put ice cubes in straight champagne unless you want a considerably diluted drink.

Aside from improving its taste, chilling champagne has a practical advantage: you will find it easier to control the wine as it comes out of the bottle. When cold, it flows out smoothly; warm champagne shoots out wastefully and messily.

Should you not finish a bottle at one sitting, there are special stoppers that will prevent champagne from going flat; also, it should be kept in a cool place. If you have left a fine champagne open and it has gone flat, it will still be good enough to drink the next day, though not bubbly. Or you can use it for cooking.

How to open and serve champagne: The type of glass to use for champagne has a stem and a base, and its shape is much more a matter of choice than it used to be. The shallow-bowled saucer has one drawback—its large surface allows the wine to go flat more quickly. A hollow-stemmed glass is difficult to clean, and the wine warms in the stem when the glass is held. The tall tulip shape and, less traditionally, a deep-bowled all-purpose wineglass are both excellent for champagne (see pages 6–7).

To open a bottle of champagne, unwind the twisted end of the wire cap that holds the cork firmly in place. Loosen the wire cap and foil covering over the cork and remove them from the bottle. Tilt the bottle at a slight angle away from you. Protecting your hand with a napkin, twist the cork toward you while turning the bottle clockwise with your other hand. Continue to twist gently. As the cork nears the top of the bottle, gas inside will force it up and out. For the least waste, the cork should make only a discreet pop. The simplest way to pour is to grasp the bottle around the center, with your index finger on the neck for control. There is usually a fair amount of bubbles at first, so begin by pouring only a little, pause until some of the foam subsides, and then continue pouring until the glass is slightly more than half full. As you stop, turn the bottle slightly to the right to prevent wine drips.

How to Open Champagne

Unwind the twisted end of the wire cap between foil and cork that holds the cork firmly in place. Loosen wire and foil covering and remove from the bottle.

Tilt bottle at a slight angle. Protect hand with napkin and twist cork toward you while turning bottle clockwise with other hand. As cork nears top of bottle, gas inside will force it up and out.

(If the cork fits so tightly that you can't move it, try pressing it upward with your thumbs firmly but steadily, going all around the cork; then try to turn the bottle again. If the cork breaks off at the top before you get it out, stick a skewer or thick needle through it to release the immediate pressure behind it, after which you can use an ordinary corkscrew to get the cork out in the usual way.)

How to buy champagne: The three types most often sold in this country are *brut,* which is the driest; *extra sec,* or extra-dry, which is, confusingly enough, sweeter than *brut;* and *sec,* or dry, which is quite sweet, most suitable with dessert and not sold in any great quantity. Of the three, *brut* is the best choice for serving alone and in many mixed drinks.

One standard bottle holds about 8 glasses; a half-bottle, 4; a magnum, or double bottle holds 16, and a jeroboam, the equivalent of 4 bottles, 32 glasses. There is also a split, which holds only a scant 2 glasses and is usually a waste of money. Estimate the amount you will need and buy accordingly. Standard-size bottles are the easiest to handle, but the larger magnums and jeroboams are festive and their size means that less air comes in contact with the wine.

THE GENIALITY OF GIN

Gin is a colorless liquor made from grain, and one of the oldest of spirit drinkers' favorites. Actually, it is simply a pure grade of alcohol with flavoring added. The Dutch really started the fad for *genever,* which was their word for juniper—the herb they used to flavor their pure grain alcohol—and which the English shortened to "gin."

When William of Orange came to the British throne he brought a love of gin with him and pushed it for all he was worth in his newly adopted country, because he didn't like the French and wanted to eliminate imports of French wines. (Heavy taxation put these wines beyond the reach of most people.) William, and later Queen Anne, succeeded better than they expected and almost ruined England because gin became too cheap, too popular and too easy to get. Whole sections of the population were in a constant state of euphoria—sloshed, to put it bluntly. The price of gin was so low that one inn sign of the times lured customers with this succinct message:

> Drunk for a penny,
> Dead drunk for two pence,
> Clean straw for nothing!

The rowdiness of taverns in the eighteenth century and the effects of gin drinking were popular subjects with many artists of the period such as Hogarth. It took stiff taxation—the tried and true means of control—to reduce gin consumption to a sensible level, and many generations to upgrade it to its present "respectable" and palatable level as cocktail ingredient number one around the world.

Age is no virtue where gin is concerned. It is as good as it will ever be straight from the still. Its flavor comes from various herbs, and these differ somewhat depending on the country where the liquor is made. The gin distiller's business is to redistill the spirit with the addition of flavoring matter so that what emerges tastes as though juniper (and cardamom, orris, angelica, orange peel and a dozen others) were in its blood.

Although there are as many different kinds of gin as there are distillers, the liquor falls into two broad categories. One of these, dry or London gin, is universally popular and the most useful, because the spirit has just enough flavor to stamp its character on a cocktail or other mixed drink without being overwhelming. It has no rival as a mixer, but is not often drunk straight, although on the rocks with lemon and a splash of water it is a very refreshing hot-weather drink. Pink gin drinkers usually make their favorite drink with London plus 2 or 3 drops of Angostura bitters. This drink has long been popular with the British, and is also known as gin and bitters. English gin is made primarily of corn, plus some malt and a small percentage of other grains. Juniper berry is the most important flavoring, although very limited amounts of other ingredients are used.

Holland or Dutch gin is too pungent and sweet for mixing, but is most enjoyable when drunk neat, on the rocks. The basis of Holland gin is barley malt, flavored with juniper berries. Holland is the one country where you can still see shops that sell gin and nothing else. Like pretty little apothecaries, they have painted blue-glass jars on shelves behind the counter, a low bar and no seats or stools. Delicate, bell-shaped glasses on stems, like eighteenth-century rummers, are filled until surface tension causes a little flat dome of gin. It is impossible to pick up the glass for a first sip without spilling, so the custom is to stoop and drink the top without touching the glass. The gin is available in any strength from 40 to 120 proof and the measures are by no means small. Holland gin, very well chilled or on the rocks with a sliver of lemon, makes an excellent alternative to a dry Martini. You probably should not serve it at a party without offering an alternative, however, as the taste takes a little acquiring.

American gins have a slightly different character from London gins; the water and spirits used are different. But both products are first-rate mixers.

Sloe gin, flavored with sloe berries from the blackthorn bush, is really a liqueur (page 57).

LIQUEURS

There is considerable confusion in many people's minds about the difference between liqueurs and fruit brandies, so it might be a good idea to define and clarify. Most liqueurs—or cordials—are produced by macerating fruit or herbs, or both, in spirits and then adding sugar. Fruit brandies are distilled dry spirits made from the fermented mash of fruits. In other words, a number of liqueurs are *flavored* with the essence of a fruit, whereas all fruit brandies *are* the essence of fruit. It is easy to be misled, however, by the labeling that permits certain European liqueurs to be called cherry or apricot (or other fruit) brandy; some of them may be good, but they are not fruit brandies. The fact that brandies and liqueurs are drunk most often after dinner can be another source of confusion. (For fruit brandies, see pages 50–51.)

After the Arabs learned to distill, the art rapidly went West, where chemists used it in their search for the secret of eternity. Distilling became the monopoly of the chemists. But because of the healing qualities of spirits and because medicine was mainly in the hands of religious orders, the stills tended to shift from the scientists to the theologians, and monks got into the liquor business. Roots, bark, leaves, rind, flowers, nuts, herbs, fruits, juices, gold dust, coffee—you name it—almost everything was tried, not only for taste but for medicinal effect. Thus there were created hundreds of liqueurs.

Our forefathers all thought of liqueurs as agreeable but potent and effective medicines. They warded off fevers and also gave sufferers the benefit of medicinal herbs like caraway seeds (still used in some lands to soothe infant stomachache). The French called liqueurs *digestifs* because of the soothing herbs in so many of them. And the synonym "cordial" comes from the Latin for heart, *cor,* because the drink was originally a heart stimulant.

A liqueur is made by combining a spirit (usually brandy) with various flavorings, and adding sugar. Many of the liqueurs we drink today have fascinating histories.

One of the early practitioners of the distilling art, Arnaud de Villeneuve, a Spanish-born chemist of the late thirteenth century, managed to fend off the terrors of the Inquisition by giving the pope an elixir made with spirits and herbs, flecked with gold, which saved the Holy Father's life. As a result, Arnaud was absolved from Torquemada's third degree. Even today, Goldwasser which, despite its name, is water-clear is well thought of in Europe because the caraway in it is supposed to be good for digestion, the anise for taste and the tiny gold flakes for protection against various unnamed diseases.

D.O.M. Benedictine is still made where it was first brewed in 1510. A monk, Dom Bernardo Vincelli, dreamed up his new elixir in the Benedictine abbey at Fécamp in France, where he found that it made other monks feel better if they were tired or sick. D.O.M., never omitted from the label, stands for the Latin *Deo optimo maximo,* "To God, most good, most great." Nowadays this liqueur is made by a family-owned firm founded in Fécamp almost a hundred years ago, but the formula is so closely guarded that only three people know it. Every effort, and there have been hundreds, to copy Benedictine has failed. It is made of several different plants, herbs, peels, etc., on a fine cognac base. A while back, the firm discovered that many people were mixing Benedictine and brandy (or B and B) to create a drier liqueur, so the company now produces its own B and B liqueur, D.O.M.

Chartreuse has an equally famous history. It continues to be made according to a secret formula which was a gift from the Maréchal d'Estrées to the Carthusian fathers of the convent of the Grand Chartreuse near Grenoble, France, in 1607. A century and a half later, one of the monks slightly altered the formula to make the drink even more superb. Chartreuse has a brandy base, but the names and proportions used of other ingredients remain unknown to all people but its makers. Yellow chartreuse is 86 proof and green is 110.

Many other liqueurs are of ancient origin and have intriguing backgrounds, but their stories are more interesting than necessary to their enjoyment. Because almost all liqueurs are sweet, strong and good aids to the digestion, they are most often served straight in small liqueur glasses, and usually at room temperature, after dinner. But these colorful, flavorful drinks can be more than a cordial postscript to dinner. Several adapt with ease to everything from cocktails to cooking. Now that virtually every liqueur is sold in half pints and miniatures as well as full-size bottles, it is no extravagance to keep a supply on hand.

You'll find that some liqueurs are excellent in mixed drinks, while others enhance iced tea and coffee. All of them combine well with brandy and vodka; Scotch has a special affinity for chartreuse. Sleight of hand with liqueurs can lift a simple dessert into the gourmet class. During Prohibition, liqueurs were frequently used in cocktails because their dominant flavor effectively disguised the raw taste of bootleg liquor. Some of these pre-Repeal cocktails still survive and other, more recently created recipes involve a dash of liqueur in a cocktail to give it special character. Most liqueurs mix well with very black, very hot after-dinner coffee and others are excellent frappéed.

Here is a list of the leading liqueurs, the nationality of each (although many are also made in the U.S.) and its flavor.

A Guide to Liqueurs

LIQUEUR	NATIONALITY	FLAVOR
Apry	French	Apricot
Apricot liqueur	French, Amer., Dutch	
Cheri-Suisse	Swiss	Cherry and chocolate
Cherry Heering	Danish	Cherry
Galliano	Italian	Herbs and flowers
Grand Marnier	French	Orange
Aurum	Italian	
Cointreau	American	
Curaçao	Dutch	
Triple Sec	American	
Mandarine	French	Tangerine
Peach liqueur	French, Amer., Dutch	Peach
Framberry	French	Raspberry
Crème de violette	French, Dutch	Violet
Kümmel	French, Amer., Dutch	Caraway

LIQUEUR	NATIONALITY	FLAVOR
Tea liqueur	French	Tea
Pimento dram	Jamaican	Rum and allspice
Liqueur d'or	French	Aromatic herbs
Danziger Goldwasser	German	(Contains bits of gold leaf)
Strega	Italian	Herbs, citrus
Chartreuse	French	Herbs
Benedictine	French	Aromatic herbs
B & B or Benedictine and brandy	French	Aromatic herbs
Crème de cassis	French	Black currant
Crème de cacao	French, Dutch, Amer.	Cocoa
Tia Maria	Jamaican	Coffee
Kahlúa	Mexican	
Espresso	Italian	
Crème de vanille	French, Amer., Dutch	Vanilla
Crème de Noyaux	French, Dutch	Almond-hazelnut
Crème de menthe	French, Amer., Dutch	Mint
Fior de Alpe	Italian	Aromatic herbs with rock-candy base
Izarra	French	Aromatic herbs
Anisette	French, Amer., Dutch	Anise
Anis	French	
Ouzo	Greek	
Drambuie	Scottish	Scotch and honey
Lochan Ora	Scottish	Scotch, honey, orange
Irish Mist	Irish	Irish whiskey and honey
Sloe gin	English	Blackthorn berries
Vandermint	Dutch	Dutch chocolate and mint

THE RANGE OF RUM

Down where the trade winds blow, in the islands of the West Indies, rum is the staple spirit. Called many things during its long career, from "a hot, hellish and terrible liquor" to "comfortable waters," rum is the distilled spirit of molasses.

Sugar cane was introduced to the West Indies by Columbus on one of his later voyages, and numerous plantations were flourishing by 1520. Some time later, it was discovered that molasses, a by-product of the sugar refining process, could be distilled into high-grade firewater, and the history of rum as we know it began. In the early days of its production in the West Indies during the sixteenth and seventeenth centuries, rum was distilled carelessly and drunk at once, mostly by slaves on the plantations. Their masters sipped French wines and cognacs. Later, as stills improved and the rum was aged in casks, it developed into the smooth, suave drink we know today. Its popularity became so widespread that, for many years, the term "demon rum" stood for all alcoholic beverages from whiskey to champagne.

There are two main types of rum made in the West Indies today: the very light Puerto Rican and Virgin Islands rums and the heavy, dark varieties from Jamaica, Guyana (Demerara rum) and Puerto Rico. In between are medium rums from Barbados, Haiti and other islands. The light rums, being tasteless and odorless, are suitable for simple mixed drinks, light highballs and collinses. The dark aromatic rums are better for drinks containing lots of fruit juice or flavorings, as they have enough character to counteract other assertive tastes. With the in-between varieties, you can go both ways.

Certain rum drinks contain lemon or lime juice and sugar. As sugar is very difficult to dissolve in spirits, it is a good idea to blend it with the fruit juice first. Better yet, have some simple sugar syrup on hand. (For how to make it, see page 18.) Other sweetening ingredients include orgeat and falernum, both of which have a delicate almond flavor that goes well with rum drinks. Orgeat is non-alcoholic; falernum contains from 6 to 10 percent alcohol. Grenadine, a non-alcoholic, sweet syrup made from pomegranates, is also frequently used, especially if a pink- or red-colored drink is desired. Often a rum drink recipe will call for charged water from a soda siphon; if you don't have one, hold your thumb over a bottle of charged water, shake it several times, then squirt into the glass.

SHERRY, PORT AND MADEIRA

These wines are fortified with alcohol, usually grape brandy, which arrests fermentation so that the wines retain some of the natural grape sugar. Due to fortification, they are almost twice as rich in alcohol as natural table wines. The best known of the fortified wines are sherry and port; sherry originated in the south of Spain, port in the north of Portugal. When made in other countries, although lacking the specific characteristics of classic sherries and ports, they often have a great deal to recommend them. A third fortified wine with which some people are familiar is Madeira.

All fortified wines have certain advantages. Because of their high alcoholic content, they keep well once they have been opened. They improve with age. They will generally take extremes of temperature and rough handling much more equably than non-fortified wines. They are marvelously suited to leisurely and civilized sipping. They are useful in cooking.

Sherry

The name is an anglicization of Jerez, an archetypal Andalusian town in the far south of Spain that is the sherry center of the world. The wine made in the country around Jerez and blended and matured in the huge white buildings called *bodegas* begins as an ordinary white wine. By various processes of aging, blending and sweetening, however, this basic wine is transformed into sherries with differing characteristics which divide them into three broad categories with the Spanish names *fino, amontillado* and *oloroso*.

Fino is normally very dry and the least alcoholic of the three. It is the sherry that should be treated most gently and drunk up soonest after the bottle has been opened. It should be chilled in the bottle, not with ice in a glass. Although most often served as an aperitif before a meal, fino is also good with hors d'oeuvre, shellfish, hot or cold soups.

Amontillado is probably the most generally useful. Less dry than fino, it is the typical "medium" sherry that is suitable not only as an aperitif but on those occasions when coffee is not quite appropriate and whiskey seems too potent.

Oloroso, from the Spanish word for fragrant, is the technical classification for all sweet sherries, but the descriptive adjective "cream" or "golden" is more often seen on labels. Olorosos are prepared specifically as dessert wines and usually served with dessert or just before or after coffee, but many people enjoy cream sherry as a morning "reviver" or an afternoon or evening drink. If used as an aperitif, sweet sherry should be very well chilled. At other times, it is best served at room temperature.

When you open a bottle of good sherry, decant it into a container with a ground-glass stopper; it will keep better that way than in the bottle. Avoid the usual V-shaped sherry glass; it holds a poor drink and is easily upset. Instead, use the long, straight-sided Spanish glass or a small, tulip-shaped wineglass (which is very good for port and Madeira, as well).

Port

This fortified wine originated in the north of Portugal, and the classic types come from that area today, although a large number of approximations are available and some are particularly suited to mixed drinks. There are innumerable ways of blending and maturing port, but only one way of making it. When the wine has fermented to the proper point, grape brandy is added to stop the fermentation and leave the wine sweet and rich. Most port ages in wooden barrels and is bottled when it is ready to drink. According to its age and style, wood-aged port is described as ruby or tawny. Ruby is younger, darker, sweeter, and has more kick. Tawny pales and refines itself, over the course of ten to twenty years, to a very smooth, mellow drink that is somewhat drier than ruby. Both are blended.

Vintage port, however, is unblended and not aged in the wood but in the bottle. When the wines of one vintage appear outstanding, they are kept aside from the blending wines. Instead of being allowed to mature quietly in their barrels (called pipes), they are bottled when only two or three years old and still completely undrinkable. In bottle, they very slowly go through the same maturing process that tawny port undergoes more quickly in wood. Eventually —it may easily be twenty or twenty-five years later—the wine has a character and style that is unique. Vintage port must always be decanted, because during its adolescence it has thrown off all manner of things to form a crust which looks unpleasant in your glass.

Madeira

Although little vintage Madeira is still around, it is the longest-lived wine in the world. It resists heat and extreme changes of temperature and can survive two centuries with its flavor, vigor and bouquet intact.

All modern Madeiras, like our own premium wines, are

known by their grape variety and the merchant's brand name. Of the former, *sercial* is the driest of all, *verdelho* less so; *bual* is soft and sweet, *malmsey* really full and fruity. Rainwater Madeira, an American invention, combines lightness with softness, and is somewhere between a scrcial and a verdelho.

The flavor of Madeira is unlike that of any other wine. In its youth it is slightly cooked, and the resulting hint of burnt sugar stays with it. As with sherries, the drier a Madeira, the better suited it is to sipping, chilled, as an aperitif before lunch or dinner. The rich, mellow Madeiras are good with desserts, after dinner, or in midafternoon or evening, served at room temperature and accompanied, if you wish, by nuts, biscuits, cake, etc.

VERMOUTH THE VERSATILE

Vermouth is an aromatized wine, fortified with alcohol and flavored with various spices and herbs, roots, seeds, flowers, peels—you name it! One of them is wormwood— *Wermut* in German—which has given the drink its name.

Vermouth is produced in many countries including, in this hemisphere, the United States and Argentina. France and Italy, however, have long been acknowledged the producers of the world's finest. It is made along either side of the French-Italian border in the foothills of the Alps, with the city of Turin as the center.

Basically, there are two kinds of vermouth—dry and sweet. The dry type is the most popular in America for drinking solo. Its delicate aromatization has an enjoyable subtlety and it is as low in calories (105 per 4-ounce glass) as one could wish. Sweet vermouth is more deeply aromatized and heavier in base, pungent and richly flavored, with a bittersweet aftertaste to round it off. It has a natural affinity for orange just as dry vermouth has for the flavor of lemon. Two of our most popular cocktails, Rob Roys and Manhattans, are made with sweet vermouth.

The dry variety is essential to making a Martini, even when the proportion used is very small.

All vermouths become darker in color as they age, and the variations have nothing to do with quality. There is an enormous difference in the blending and resultant flavor of the top ten brands available here. Some which are touted as being the driest taste best only in the comforting company of gin. Others are more versatile. There are no absolute standards of taste to guide you, and the only way you can be sure of finding the vermouth that best suits your purpose is to test and decide for yourself. Being fortified, all last a long time once they have been opened. And, among their other virtues, vermouths are very useful in cooking.

Vermouth has great éclat, whether served on the rocks, frappéed, or in a long or short mixed drink. It is a simple but ideal aperitif. If you offer it before a meal when there are fine wines to follow, you need not fear that it will spoil your palate. On the contrary, a good dry vermouth frappé, more than almost any other drink except very dry champagne, will tend to prime your appreciation of the more delicate flavors to come. Probably every well-equipped drink-mixing tray or setup in American homes today is stocked, among other potables, with a bottle of dry and another of sweet vermouth.

VODKA—THE COLORLESS, FLAVORLESS SPIRIT

Vodka is the logically ultimate alcoholic drink—alcohol from which all harmful and other foreign bodies have been removed by distillation, rectification and repeated filtration. As a mixer it does nothing but make soft drinks hard, and hard ones harder. Its effect on flavor is minimal, on morale wonderful.

Vodka didn't really catch on in America until the late forties. But in Europe, it ranks as one of the oldest and most versatile of liquors. Vodka is a diminutive of the Russian word for water, and, according to one theory, the liquor originated in that country. According to another, it began life in Poland as a sure preventive for flu. Vodka is produced from grain, not potatoes, as many people think. In Poland it is served ice-cold, neat, in tiny glasses that are repeatedly filled and refilled. The vodka ceremonial starts before a meal and continues throughout. The bottle starts wrapped in a jacket of ice and ends in a pool of water, while conversation flashes onward and upward.

Vodka has no taste of its own, but it easily acquires one, according to what is put into it—or what it is put into. One of the most venerable of Polish vodkas is Starka, which is made from rye grain, aged in wine casks, finally blended with wine and bottled at a potent 100 proof. The color is reminiscent of rye whiskey, but the flavor is distinctive and unusual. Zubrowka, produced in Poland and Czechoslovakia and available here, is flavored by insertion of a blade of buffalo grass, which gives it a subtle taste and perfume. Zubrowka should always be served very, very cold in chilled glasses. Keep the bottle in the freezer or, better yet, freeze it in a block of ice, as you would aquavit.

If you are drinking any of the plain vodkas straight, either alone or with food, you should also have them ice-cold. There is a wide assortment of these unflavored vodkas available, made in Russia, Poland, Czechoslovakia, France, and right here in the U.S. Unless you are a true connoisseur of subtle variations in spirits, it makes little difference which one you drink because all of them are, by definition, unflavored.

Given this neutral spirit to work with, you can invent your own flavorings. Flavored vodkas make interesting bases for long drinks and summer punches. Experiment with lemon, orange or tangerine peel, and caraway seeds. This is the procedure to follow: For lemon vodka, add the rind of 2 large lemons to a fifth of the spirit; for orange vodka, the rind of one large orange; for tangerine vodka, the rind of one tangerine; for caraway vodka, 3 tablespoons (or less for a fainter flavor) of caraway seeds tied in a cheesecloth bag. Cork the bottles and allow them to stand for two weeks, then test by sniffing and sipping, to see if they have infused enough. If they have, transfer the vodka to another bottle and throw away the additives.

THE WONDERFUL WORLD OF WHISKEY

The word "whiskey" comes from Gaelic, the language of the Celts of Ireland and the Scottish Highlands. The old Irish name for this favorite drink was *uisgebeatha,* the Scotch version was *uisgebaugh,* and in both countries it meant "water of life." *Uisge* was pronounced oo-ees-gee, which has been anglicized in the course of time to our familiar word. And right here it should be pointed out that the Irish spell whiskey with an *e,* and so do we; the Scotch and Canadians drop the *e.*

All whiskeys, regardless of their country of origin, are made from grain of one sort or another. Of the six basic types, three are imported—Scotch, Irish and Canadian—and three are made in this country—bourbon, rye and corn. Each, however, is offered in its own shadings of flavor and color—depending on various factors such as the grains and water used, the way the whiskey is distilled, its proof rating, whether it is straight or blended, and its age when bottled.

Proof is a measure of the alcoholic content in any distilled beverage. You can always figure the amount of alcohol simply by dividing the proof stated on the label by 2. Thus a 100-proof whiskey is 50 percent alcohol.

Proof influences a whiskey's character in two ways—its proof at the time of distillation and then the proof at which the liquor is bottled. The proof at distillation time establishes a whiskey's flavor and body, and the proof at bottling time determines its potency. To satisfy the public taste for light-bodied liquors today, most whiskeys are distilled at a relatively high proof—say, around 140 or 150. Then, to lower the alcoholic content, the proof is reduced before bottling by the simple expedient of adding water. You will find most whiskey is bottled at 85 to 100 proof.

Straight whiskey is bottled from the cask in which it is aged, with only water added to reduce the proof.

Blend has two meanings today. It describes the art of combining two or more straight whiskeys of the same general type to achieve a distinctive product; thus you will read on some labels such a phrase as "a blended straight bourbon" (or Scotch). Blend also refers to the largest classification of American whiskey now being made. Somewhat less expensive than bourbon or Scotch, a blended whiskey is a blend of whiskey and neutral spirits. The word "whiskey," when used alone, most often means such a blended product.

Aging varies depending upon the particular product, but distillers agree that no amount of aging will make an inferior whiskey good. Whiskey is a raw, colorless liquid when it goes into a charred oak barrel. Several years later, when it is drawn out, mature whiskey is smooth tasting and amber colored. It is generally believed that a caramel-like layer at the base of the char accounts for the amber tone. The charred oak and air circulation (or "breathing") are thought to remove impurities.

Scotch Whiskey

Real Scotch can only be made in Scotland. "Château Bottled Scotch" and "Scotch Bottled at Buckingham Palace" do not exist, the Japanese imitations to the contrary notwithstanding. Even though there are hundreds of Scotch castles, Scotch whiskey comes from humbler origins and most of the malt distilleries are in small communities hidden in the hills—"hidden" because in the early days a good deal of hanky-panky went on and hefty quantities of illicit whiskey found their way down Scottish gullets.

Scotch was an unappreciated drink, however, until about a hundred years ago. Up to that time, the chic potable was brandy, but in the mid-nineteenth century, the European grape vineyards were all but wiped out by a bug called phylloxera, and supplies of brandy became short. The elite began to turn to Scotch. By the time phylloxera was foiled, it had been discovered that a blended whiskey cut down the strong, peaty taste of the straight malts the Scots love, and the resulting liquor could be sold to delighted foreigners. The Scots never looked back. Today, Scotland exports over 59 million gallons of blended Scotch whiskey per year.

Back in 1905, there was a famous law case in England, known as the "What Is Whiskey?" case. The pure malt whiskey distillers—pure malt being virtually the original Scotch—were upset that their brew was being cut with grain whiskey to make its strong taste more palatable to the unreconstructed British. The blenders won, and the blend is *legally* Scotch, but opinion is still divided in Scotland as to whether it is *really* Scotch. However, without blending, it probably would have been impossible to sell the stuff to non-Scots.

Malt whiskey is one of the four basic types of ingredients the Scots believe must be part of any good blend. Since blending is done by smell rather than taste, a blender is known as a "nose." According to the "noses," every bottle of fine drinking Scotch should have an island malt, a highland malt, a lowland malt and a grain whiskey. Considering the fact that a quality blend has sixty-five different whiskeys in it, you can hardly miss having some of all four essentials in any good brand you are likely to buy. To the real aficionado, however, the only true Scotch is the "single" malt whiskey—one that comes from a single distillery and is made exclusively from malt. Most people would consider this fairly heavy, perhaps because of its pronounced peatiness. From that extreme, through blending with other types of whiskey, especially grain whiskey, the taste of the pure malt is subdued until you get what the American whiskey fancier likes, which has a higher percentage of grain whiskey. (Some Scots complain that a number of these very "light" varieties are not Scotch at all!)

To make Scotch, the barley must first be allowed to begin to sprout. Upon sprouting, it is malt (which is germinated grain). Then the sprouting is stopped by drying the malt on screens over peat fires, which gives it tanginess and a smoky aroma that flavors the spirit distilled from it. "Pure burn water," as they always describe it, is added and the mess, or mash, is fermented with yeast. This makes a kind of weak beer, which is then distilled twice to produce a clear alcohol, the raw whiskey. This is matured in old casks that gradually give it color. After about four years "in the wood," the whiskey is smooth enough to drink.

There are over a hundred distilleries making malt whiskey and more than a dozen grain distilleries, and the number of brands is legion—something like five hundred in Scotland. If you want to taste what Scotch whiskey must have been like in the good old days, you should try one of the great single malts, such as Glenrothes, Tamdhu or Talisker, all available in the U.S.

The Park Avenue of the whiskey-making area in Scotland consists of about nine hundred square miles on the River Spey. Some of the local inhabitants think the healthy quality of the air in the region is due to the 3 million gallons or so of evaporated Scotch suspended in it and thus supposed to be "lost" each year. These evaporated fumes from the kegs where the whiskey is aging are a form of pollution many of us might like more of!

Irish Whiskey

For at least seven hundred years, the Irish have been making and drinking whiskey. In fact, most authorities agree that the art of distilling the malted grain originated in Ireland and the knowledge spread from there to western Scotland. Even some Scotsmen admit this, if reluctantly. Ireland's whiskey is as unlike Scotch whiskey as an Irish accent differs from a Scots one. Although Irish is softer, sweeter and more beguiling and, in a sense, less sophisticated, its character is too outspoken for many people. As with all good flavorful drinks or foods, you need to get used to Irish whiskey to appreciate its quality.

It tends to be old and more mature than Scotch, because it is not bought at anything like the same rate. You might find a twelve-year-old Irish whiskey in an ordinary bottle as easily as a four- or five-year-old Scotch.

The pot still whiskeys of Ireland are produced in much the same way as those of Scotland, except that the malted grain is not smoked over a peat fire, but cooked gently with a smokeless coal fire. Thus, there is no smoky taste. Some Irish whiskeys are made with pure barley mash, some with a mixture of oats and barley and still others with a combination of several grains. The flavors, of course, vary. A number of people find the brew made with pure barley malt the richest and tastiest; others prefer whiskeys based on mixed grains.

In addition, there are blended Irish whiskeys. These are pot still whiskeys blended with pure grain whiskeys from patent stills. The blends are lighter, less strong in flavor, and often preferred by Englishmen and Americans, who are accustomed to more delicate liquors.

Much fine Irish whiskey is exported to the U.S., although the number of brands is small. Among the most important are John Power & Sons, John Jameson's, Tullamore Dew, Old Bushmills and Paddy. Tullamore is a town in the center of the country where a family named Williams has been distilling for over a century. Power's and Jameson's fine whiskeys are produced in the traditional way at Dublin. Both firms make a standard blend as well as the special-quality ones they are known for abroad. Paddy is a strong-tasting countryman's drink, brownish in color and rather sweet in taste. Old Bushmills' flavor is not so pronounced because, like Scotch, it is blended with the lighter product of the patent still. There is also a liqueur based on Irish whiskey—Irish Mist (page 61).

The Irish themselves drink the full-bodied pot still whiskey, and they drink it neat. To them it is a sin to adulterate the precious liquid with ice and soda water. There are many outside Ireland who think the same way and feel that Irish whiskey is not a good mixer. Some like it diluted with a good dose of very cold water, but without ice. Another way to enjoy it is in that wonderful whiskey-laced brew called Irish Coffee, a concoction that may be partly responsible for making Irish whiskey better known in this country.

Canadian Whiskey

A blend of heavy- and light-bodied whiskeys, Canadian is distilled from a mash in which the proportions of corn and rye are much like those in American whiskeys. Some experts believe that this whiskey's distinct taste may be attributed in part to special grain varieties that have been developed to withstand the severe Canadian climate. Other contributing factors: the region's water, plus the fact that the blending takes place immediately after distilling. Canadian whiskeys are considerably lighter than those made in the United States.

American Whiskeys

In colonial days, whiskey was a frontier drink. The more sophisticated people of the eastern seaboard drank rum, brandy, wines, cider and beer; but the settlers in the backwoods made their own liquor with their surplus grain. They were immigrants from Scotland and Ireland, and they brought the knowledge of whiskey-making with them. Most of the farmers had home-constructed pot stills and made their brew from whatever grain was available. In western New York and Pennsylvania it was rye; farther south it was corn.

The whiskeys they made were undoubtedly crude and fiery concoctions, but once the frontier was tamed and the descendants of the pioneers became interested in living well, whiskeys were upgraded, produced with care and properly aged in wooden casks.

The Prohibition era forced most of us to rely on the products of the moonshiner, who produced a firewater similar to the raw liquor of frontier days. To drown its rough taste, we doused it with many other flavors. When Repeal finally came, there were few Americans who could identify or appreciate really good, flavorful American whiskeys.

A truly mellow, rich bourbon or a well-made rye has the distinctive taste of the grain from which it is made, and appreciation of the flavor must be cultivated. So it happened that through the late thirties and World War II, a whole generation that had never tasted fine straight whiskeys plumped for the blends because these were blander and cheaper. But during the past twenty or twenty-five years there has been a change. Americans have become more conscious of the characteristics of the whiskeys they are drinking. Women are now regular customers at the liquor stores. This development has brought with it a demand for lighter whiskeys with less pronounced flavors and a preference for the 86-proof liquors rather than the stronger 100-proof varieties. "Lightness" can be a confusing term. In the U.S. trade, it *does* mean a lower alcoholic content, but many customers think of lightness in terms of color and flavor. (It should be noted that the so-called light Scotches have the same amount of alcohol as other Scotches—this is regulated by the British government—but they are paler and blander.)

The U.S. government has recently authorized a new category of whiskey to be called "light whiskey." It is distilled at a much higher proof—161 to 189—than traditional whiskeys and is aged in matured (i.e., reused) barrels rather than in new charred barrels. The result is a whiskey that is much lighter in flavor than any of its predecessors. "American Light Whiskey" is all light whiskey; "American Blended Light Whiskey" has no more than 20 percent straight whiskey at 100 proof added to light whiskey.

American whiskeys are made by a process very similar to the one used for making grain whiskeys in Scotland, except that the grains are different and the whiskey is distilled out at a lower proof.

Western Pennsylvania, Kentucky, Tennessee and surrounding areas are the center of the American whiskey industry because of the plentiful supply of very pure limestone water that is so important in the making of whiskey.

Sour-mash whiskey is produced from a mash containing yeast from a previous fermentation which is added to the new yeast in a proportion of 1 to 2. A more stable fermentation is achieved in this manner, with less chance of "wild" yeasts entering. This process is used primarily for bourbon, which was first made in 1789 by Elija Craig from corn ground in his mill in Georgetown, Bourbon County. The county, then in Virginia and now part of Kentucky, had been named in honor of the French royal family, a thank-you for their help to the colonists during the Revolution. The liquor was named after the county.

All straight American whiskey sold today is actually straight bourbon, rye or corn. The main ingredient of bourbon is corn. To qualify as straight bourbon or rye, a whiskey must be made from at least 51 percent corn or rye, respectively. Straight corn whiskey must be made from 80 percent corn. Of the three, straight bourbon is the overwhelming favorite. While a quality bourbon is recommended as a drink to be sipped plain or on the rocks with or without a little good, bottled spring water, blended whiskeys have grown in popularity as the base for mixed drinks.

WINES

It is only sensible to save outstanding wines for solo performances because they are best appreciated and enjoyed on their own. When choosing wines for mixed drinks, they should certainly be good and pleasing—but not outstanding. Therefore, because this book is essentially a drink-mixing guide, emphasis here is on wines which are appropriate for that purpose. All of Chapter IV, however, is packed with suggested types of wines to serve with various foods, and it is included for the very good reason that mixed drinks are seldom served at meals, whereas wines are becoming increasingly popular on the dining table. The true purpose of that chapter and this section is to supplement your drink-mixing information with enough wine know-how so that no occasion will find you unprepared.

As you know, we import wines from most European countries and South America, in addition to making a great deal of it ourselves. In fact, we have such a wide range available that choice can become something of a problem. Most people, unless they are true wine connoisseurs, know little about brands, years, labeling and so on. They may be familiar with such words as Burgundy, claret, Chablis and some of the American vintners' names, but that is about all. They are often under the mistaken impression that no wines are really good unless they are imported, that only Spanish sherry or French rosé is drinkable, that wines sold in half- or full-gallon jugs are invariably poor. And too often, they rely on price as the prime criterion. All of which is unfortunate. Character, flavor, smoothness, suitability are the essentials, but these are corked inside the bottles and there are only two ways to find out about them, short of becoming an expert. You can experiment, taste and test on your own, or you can deal with a dependable wine merchant, and ask his advice. But if you do, be sure to tell him exactly what you're looking for—for example, a white wine to use in spritzers, a red for iced sangría or one for a hot mull, a champagne for a party punch. And if you like what he recommends after sampling, go back and buy a case. But if you think there is room for improvement, tell him so and why, and try again.

Following are very brief guidelines to the important wine-growing areas of various foreign countries and the United States, and some of their best-known products. But, as Thomas Jefferson once said, "Taste cannot be controlled by law." In the last analysis, it is up to you to find the wine you like best to use for a particular wine-based drink.

Natural, Still Wines

These fall into three broad categories, based on color: red, white and rosé. All may be served alone, with food, or used as the bases for certain mixed drinks. Champagne, the most important of the sparkling wines and an excellent mixer, is discussed separately (pages 51–56), as are the fortified and aromatized wines (pages 63–67).

With few exceptions (and these are spelled out in the recipes in Chapter III), dry wines are the best choice for mixed drinks. The lighter whites are ideal for summer coolers and most punches that call for a still white wine. The light reds and rosés are good in mild mixed drinks, while the more robust reds make hearty and heartwarming drinks which have greater substance.

France turned winemaking into an art centuries ago, and several regions have become famous for their bottled delights. Climate, soil, grape variety, production methods —all affect wine and give it individuality, and these factors vary from area to area. The region of Bordeaux, where wine has been made for over two thousand years, is roughly half the size of Rhode Island, but produces literally hundreds of wines ranging from dry to sweet, and including red, white and rosé. Bordeaux reds are the original clarets. The dry and medium dry Graves and the sweet Sauternes are the best known of the white Bordeaux wines. The best Bordeaux are "château-bottled," but there are a number of regional blends that are good and not expensive, and make fine mixers.

The red and white Burgundies from the area of the same name run the gamut from very fine to pleasant. The ones most suitable for mixing are the village wines, labeled simply with the name of the village in which the grapes were grown.

Beaujolais is a vast district that produces wine of the same name. Most of it is sold as simple Beaujolais. It is a clear red, light and fresh in flavor, and should be drunk young.

The Côtes du Rhône area is best known for its red wines, those of Châteauneuf-du-Pape being the most famous. But the dry Hermitage whites are good, as are the Tavel rosés. The delightful white wines of Alsace on the French banks of the Rhine are the only ones of that country which are sold under the grape variety name, as Riesling, Gewürtztraminer, Traminer, Sylvaner—although "Alsace" is usually on the label, too. These Alsatian whites should be drunk young. The rosés from the Côtes de Provence in the south are excellent. And the Loire valley produces a wide range, of which the most familiar are dry whites.

Germany is renowned for its white wines—Rhine and Moselle, after the rivers of those same names along whose banks the vineyards flourish. Rhine wine is round, full and ripe, and is sold in brown bottles. Moselle wine is very dry, crisp and fresh, and is sold in green bottles. It has been calculated that there are over 52,000 different wine names in the country. Among those shipped to the United States, there is the richest imaginable choice, with prices ranging from modest to very high, and flavors from flinty to syrupy. Within this vast spectrum are many whites that are dry without being too acid, pleasant to drink and highly satisfactory mixers.

Italy grows wine from top to toe. The great virtue of Italian wine is variety; the great failing is inconsistency as there are few imposed standards or controls. The superior wines come from the north and middle of the country. Soave is one of the better-known whites. Tuscany produces Chianti which, in its straw-covered *fiasco,* has become the archetypal Italian wine. The best of it is made to keep for seven years, the least to be drunk tomorrow morning. Great, classic Chianti is recognized by a black cock seal on its label, and is sold in traditional Bordeaux bottles, but you can find cheerful, young Chiantis that are most enjoyable, reasonably priced and satisfying in mixed drinks. Barolo is a big full red wine, Valpolicella a light, delicate red, and Asti Spumante is the sweet Italian version of champagne.

Spain exports vast quantities of inexpensive, agreeably young table wines (in addition to its famous sherries), a large percentage of which is bought by France for day-to-day drinking. A great deal, however, is available in the United States. Look for the name "Rioja." This northern valley produces pleasing "Chablis" and a "Burgundy" that are worth investigating. A famous wine from the south of Spain is Montilla, made in the mountains near Cordoba. Montilla is not strictly sherry, although it has given its name, Amontillado, to the type of sherry which comes nearest its light, dry, nutty flavor. Try some of the less well-known wines of various Spanish firms and vineyards. This is a fertile field if you are looking for a good mixer at a reasonable price.

Portugal, particularly the northern part, is noted for its wines. The Douro valley is not only the home of port (page 65), but of a white wine that has a dry bite and clean finish. This area produces large quantities of both reds and whites, but the red tends to harshness and is rarely better than dull. A northern Portuguese product is *vinho verde,* meaning "green wine." The "green" refers to its character, which is as fresh as an early morning at vintage time. Actually the wine may be red, white or pink, and—because a good deal of the gas of fermentation is still in it—is in a half-champagne state, lightly prickly on the tongue and slightly tart on the palate, extremely gay and refreshing.

Dão wines, also from the north, are almost always blended and have a real character of their own that is very easy to like. Farther south, Colares wine, both red and white, is the product of vineyards that are literally sand dunes on the Atlantic littoral near Sintra. The Portuguese rosés with their mellow, not-quite-dry flavor have become extremely popular in America.

Other countries: Switzerland has important vineyards

on the north shore of Lake Geneva in the canton of Vaud, and also in the canton of Valais, higher up in the valley of the Rhone. White wine comes from the lakeside, called La Côte, and the best reds from high up the Rhone. Here, as in Germany, cultivation is hard work, with vineyards at improbable angles on near-precipices. The most familiar wines are the red Dole, the white Neuchatel, Fendant (very dry) and Johannisberger (which has no relation to the great German wine of the same name). The Italian-speaking province of Ticino grows much red *vin ordinaire*.

Austria's white wines, made from the German grape varieties but lighter and drier, fall into the immediate-drinking category. The country also produces some passable reds. All Yugoslavian wines are fairly good, and some are very good.

England now exports Stone's ginger wine regularly to this country. It was first produced in the mid-eighteenth century and is made from very ripe currants. After the wine matures, Jamaica ginger is steeped in it. Ginger wine can be drunk neat in a small glass or over ice cubes, and it is delicious on fruit or ice cream.

The United States has two major wine regions—California and the country around the Finger Lakes in New York State. There is considerable difference in climate between the two, in the grapes grown and the wine produced. The grape varieties used for California wines were originally brought over from Europe and planted here. Those in New York State are largely native American varieties that flourish in a cold climate.

California provides more than three-quarters of the wine we drink in this country. The best of it is excellent, and much of the less-than-best is very good and inexpensive. The premium wines sold as varietals—meaning that the name of the grape variety which went into the wine as well as the name of the winery appears on the label—are among the finest. Red varietals include Cabernet Sauvignon, Pinot Noir, Zinfandel and Gamay. All except vintage Cabernet Sauvignon, which improves with age, are very good when drunk young. Among the best of the whites are

Pinot Chardonnay, Pinot Blanc, Chenin Blanc, Sauvignon Blanc, Semillon and Riesling. Although these are among the classic European grape varieties grown in the finest vineyard districts of France and Germany, the soil and climate of California are so different and so influential that it would be fruitless to look for identical characteristics simply because, for example, the same type of grapes makes a California Pinot Noir and a French Pommard.

Although vintages vary in California, most producers do not put the year on their wines, partly because the vintages are usually blended to create a more standardized product, and partly to avoid making people unnecessarily "vintage conscious" about California wines. There are exceptions, of course; certain producers will indicate the vintage year on a wine they consider especially good. But due to the pressures of marketing and demand, most American wine is sold shortly after it is bottled and is given no time to mature. This is unfortunate in the case of some of the red wines, which would improve immeasurably with aging.

Most of the great California wine firms make good rosés that lose nothing by comparison with the French products.

In addition to the premium wines, most California vintners produce great quantities of less expensive types, many of them very good and excellent mixers. They are simply called Chablis, Burgundy, claret, and so on, or even more directly Mountain Red or White. Although they do not resemble their European namesakes very closely, as a rule, you will find many of them highly satisfactory on their own. Oddly enough, California Sauterne is dry (and spelled without an *s* at the end), whereas French Sauternes is sweet.

The name of the wine firm is important, because each tries, with commendable success, to maintain a consistency of quality and character in its products. For example, Almadén's Chablis varies little from bottle to bottle and, indeed, from year to year. If you find a wine you like, do not hesitate to buy it in large bottles. Decant into smaller ones and cork them if you plan to use only a little at a time. The money you will save is worth the trouble.

Probably the most famous of the New York State wines is champagne, although reds, whites and rosés are also made on the slopes around the Finger Lakes. The outstanding grape varietal names—all native—are Delaware, Elvira, Catawba and Concord, all of which seem to flourish in the area. Conditions there are more like those of Germany than of any other country in Europe. Although Lake Ontario and the Finger Lakes help to moderate the climate, the summers are short and very hot, and the long winters are bitterly cold. More and more, however, as time goes on, efforts are being made to cultivate some of the European vines in New York State, and there are signs of progress. The word most often used by connoisseurs to describe the special flavor of the wines from American native vines is "foxy," but this particular taste is less evident in the sparkling wines—primarily champagne—and the New York State sherries.

How to Treat and Serve Wines

All you have to do with a small wine or a young one is to put it on the table, pour and drink. But a good wine needs time to bring it gradually to the right temperature: cool for white, very slightly warm—about 68° F.—for red. If you have to chill wine quickly, submerge the bottle up to the neck in cold water (not cracked ice) with three or four ice cubes floating in it. To bring red wine to room temperature naturally, stand the bottle in the room for several hours. As it has been stored on its side, this also gives any sediment time to settle at the bottom.

The only function of a wine cradle is to keep the bottle as nearly lying down as possible while you pull the cork and decant the contents. For the latter, pour in a continuous movement until you reach the dark and dirty wine at the bottom of the bottle; then stop. If you use a cradle for pouring directly into glasses, you will find that every time

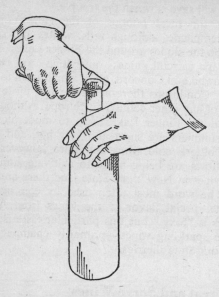

*Take a sharp knife and cut foil
just below rim of neck. Peel
foil from top of bottle,
exposing cork and rim.
With a cloth, carefully wipe
them clean before drawing
cork.*

Table Wine

Grasp corkscrew firmly. Brace thumb on top and press wing at side down toward bottle with index finger. Draw cork upward. As cork rises, pull slowly and evenly so it emerges smoothly without jerking bottle. Carefully wipe inside neck of bottle.

Hold bottle steady with left hand and twist corkscrew into center of cork.

you stop pouring to move on to the next glass, the wine will flop back in the bottle and mix with the sediment. These details do not affect young or inexpensive wines, or white wines, since they have no sediment. Therefore a cradle is unnecessary unless you are decanting a red wine at least six years old. Decanting, on the other hand, is a good idea for any red wine, however young, because this gives it contact with the air before you drink it. There is no reason why white wines should not be decanted too, and certainly any wine that you buy in half- or full-gallon jugs or that has a garish label should be decanted.

A glass that is good for one wine is good for all wines. It should be big, clear and uncolored, with a stem and a round or roundish bowl that curves in slightly at the top to collect and hold the wine's aroma. The important points are that you should be able to pour a reasonable portion (3 to 4 ounces) without filling more than half the glass, to see the wine clearly and to enjoy its bouquet.

How to open table wine: Red wines should be opened an hour or two before serving, and others a few minutes before. With a sharp knife cut the foil below the rim of the neck. Peel the foil to expose cork and rim; wipe both clean. Twist the corkscrew into the center of the cork; as you do this, the side levers will rise automatically. Grip the corkscrew firmly and press the side levers down. As the cork rises, pull slowly so it emerges without a jerk. Wipe the inside of the bottle neck before pouring wine. Fill the glass half full or less, depending on its size, then turn the bottle slightly to prevent drips.

III

What Drinks to Serve When—And How to Make Them

You will find more than 850 recipes for mixed drinks in this chapter, plus an enormous number of variations on them; the variations are known by other names but differ only slightly in ingredients. Of course, not all the recipes will interest you or even suit your particular needs, but with such a wide choice you can find just about any drink you want or have heard about. And no doubt you have sampled or heard about many of them, because the mixed drink—nurtured by Prohibition—is a true tribute to American inventiveness. We have no peers—in fact, no close contenders—in the combining of liquors and liqueurs in mixed drinks. It is safe to say that nine out of ten of the most frequently ordered bar drinks are American in origin. Even such words as "cocktail" and "highball" are Americanisms. There are theories about the origin of the first term (for two of these theories, see page 94), but "highball" presents no problem; it's an early railroading expression signifying "all clear ahead." How "julep" found its way to this country is indeed a mystery, because it is

Arabic in origin for a sweet drink flavored with aromatic herbs.

Many famous drinks, such as the Daiquiri and Margarita, which are associated with other countries, were originally created by or for visiting Americans. (Oddly enough, the Americano was dreamed up by an Italian for Italians, in spite of its name.)

In the days before Prohibition, the consumption of mixed drinks was enjoyed almost exclusively in barrooms; home drinking was limited mainly to neat spirits, beer and wine. The saloons were patronized by men only; the women stayed at home and found solace in one of the numerous "tonics" and "elixirs" then available. When entertaining at home, the men had drinks before dinner, everyone drank wine with the meal, and then the ladies withdrew while the gentlemen lingered over their port, Madeira or brandy. This strongly entrenched procedure was drastically affected by two historic developments—women's suffrage and Prohibition. The first gave women new freedom in their daily life; Prohibition created a demand for the speakeasy, which, in sharp contrast to the old-time saloon, encouraged convivial drinking in public by both sexes. Prohibition also saw the start of another big movement—the mixing of elaborate drinks at home, because much of the available bootleg liquor was unfit for straight drinking and its flavor had to be disguised. During that short period, more new drinks were concocted than at any other time in history. By now, fortunately, the worst of them have been consigned to oblivion.

Such has not been the fate of some of the famous drinks invented in the pre-Prohibition era when bars were presided over by a professional and rare breed of mixologist who not only knew how to make hundreds of mixed drinks but could create new ones at the drop of a request! Many have survived from the good old days, more or less altered to suit today's tastes but still recognizable. Among them are the rickey, named for Colonel Joe Rickey, a bibulous, high-flying lobbyist in turn-of-the-century Washington; the collins family, of which the Tom Collins is the founder; the Planter's Punch; the Manhattan, Old-fashioned and Martini. (For more about the history of these last three, see page 95.)

Once a specially good drink was invented, it was natural enough that numerous versions of it also came into existence. Thus we have such basic potables as bucks, cobblers, daisies, fixes, puffs and rickeys, and there are many more. Each can be made with a choice of liquors, although one particular liquor is usually the most popular. The flexibility of these basic recipes is a great asset to a home bartender because he can ring changes with minimum fuss. Even many of the one-of-a-kind recipes have near relatives. All of which should reassure you that mixing memorable drinks is not a complicated task.

Before you start getting out the liquor and lining up the flavorings, however, you need to decide what drinks to serve, unless you leave the choice to your guests. This is an easy solution if you are entertaining only a few people and have an assortment of standard spirits on hand and some experience in making a range of well-known drinks. But you will often find it more satisfactory (in fact, necessary with a gathering of any size) to offer drinks of your own choosing. You may suggest an alternative or two, if you like, but this is not always important or practical. The prime problem is to come up with a drink that is *suitable* —in terms of the time of day, the temperature, the occasion and, when possible, the people (old or young, experienced drinkers or not, conservative or free-wheeling, etc.).

To make the decision easier for you, the recipes that follow are divided into six groups. Each group (except one) is particularly suited to certain situations which are discussed in the introduction to that group. One group consists of all the cocktails, another the after-dinner drinks, another punches and eggnogs for parties and alternates for single servings, another the whole gamut of non-alcoholic drinks, and another the low-calorie drinks for dieters. The remaining, large group of potables is designed for clock-round hospitality and is very varied in its types and also very flexible. Some of these drinks can hold their own during the cocktail or after-dinner period. All the mixed drinks that can rise successfully to dozens of occasions are rounded up in this chapter, which opens with numerous suggestions and ideas on which of them to offer when, and how to serve them with style.

When you follow a recipe for the first time, follow it exactly. That way, you can find out what glass size is best, whether you want to use more or less ice and/or mixer, and whether the various flavoring agents are too strong or too weak to suit you. No recipe can please everyone, and there is no rule against making slight alterations or exercising your own creative prerogative. But be very discreet in one area—alcoholic strength. No guest really appreciates too-strong drinks.

Convivial Drinks for the Cocktail Hour

Whether you share a cocktail with one person or a few friends, serve drinks as the prelude to a meal or give a bang-up cocktail party, certain basic factors remain constant; others depend upon circumstances.

According to Webster, a cocktail is "a short, iced drink containing a base of rum, whiskey or other spirituous liquor or occasionally wine with the admixture either by stirring or shaking of flavoring or coloring ingredients (as fruit juice, egg, bitters, liquor or sugar) and often garnished (as with a sprig of mint or slice of lemon)." All very fine so far as it goes. But since Repeal, the availability of dependable, palatable whiskeys, rum, gin and the like has made a difference in American cocktail habits. During Prohibition, complicated mixtures and those calling for a goodly measure of fruit juice or some other flavoring agent were in demand because they disguised the raw taste of poor liquors such as the legendary bathtub gin. Today,

Martinis, Manhattans and Rob Roys, which combine a liquor with vermouth and little if anything else, are high on the popularity list. So, too, is that simplest of all drinks —a measure of liquor poured over ice in an Old-fashioned glass, with a little water or soda added and sometimes a garnish such as a twist of lemon peel or a sprig of mint. Old-fashioneds—the drink, not the glass—are also in demand, but they take more time to make, and considerate guests don't ask for them at any but the smallest gatherings.

There is also a large group of mild drinks, some with no alcoholic content at all and others with a low one, that may be served at the cocktail hour. For those who are on the wagon or calorie-conscious or simply light drinkers, these potables are ideal.

The cocktail hour is somewhat flexible, but only within certain established limits. Because cocktails, and some of the other drinks that have joined that category, are short and relatively strong, they are almost invariably served _before_ a meal—brunch or lunch, dinner or supper—the idea being that a substantial meal in the offing will cancel the influence of the alcohol and bring one back to par. Even though that meal may be omitted or extremely sketchy if it is not provided by the host, the service of cocktails should be limited to late morning and late afternoon. "Late" is, of course, a vague word. Some people, for example, feel that once "the sun is over the yardarm" around noon, they may legitimately enjoy a cocktail. Furthermore, the length of the cocktail "hour" is extremely variable. It may start early and be very prolonged, or run its course in forty-five minutes. There are no precise rules, because community custom and individual preferences are the most decisive factors. Of course, a host can always control the timing when he invites guests to a meal and serves cocktails before it. But even so, opinions differ widely on how much time should be allowed for imbibing.

Only one rule is fairly hard and fast: Bona fide cocktails are not served _after_ a meal or late in the evening. Although you may see the phrase "after-dinner cocktails" in many drink-mixing books, it is highly misleading. It is used probably because a large group of after-dinner drinks which are liqueur- or brandy-based and essentially sweet are served in cocktail glasses. Of these only the soothing milk- or cream-based concoctions such as Alexanders might be enjoyed before a meal—usually before brunch. Their alcoholic content is well disguised, and they are a palatable example of the old theory that if one is feeling shaky "a hair of the dog" may steady one's nerves and stomach. But it stands to reason that sweet drinks are a poor prelude to meals; they should either follow or even take the place of dessert.

Cocktail Lore and Legend

Although the cocktail is acknowledged to be an American invention, the origin of the word is a matter of conjecture. One patriotic if probably apocryphal story concerns a Betsy Flanagan, whose tavern was frequented by the French soldiers in Washington's army. One evening she served them a pre-dinner mixed drink or bracer and stirred or decked it with the tail feather of a cock snitched from the roost of her neighbor, a Tory farmer. The gallant Frenchmen greeted this show of spirit with an admiring cry of "Vive le coq's tail" or "Vive le coquetel." (Coq's tail, an unlikely medley of French and English, sounds less probable than *coquetel,* a French word for a mixed drink current in eighteenth-century Bordeaux.) A less romantic story insists that the word "cocktail" came from the stable, being a strong draught given by unscrupulous horse traders to old nags to make them prance and "cock their tails" for potential buyers.

Whether "cocktail" sprang from stable or tavern, by 1806 it was part of the American language. An American periodical of the day described a cocktail as "a stimulating liquor, composed of spirits of any kind, sugar, water and bitters—it is commonly called a bittered sling and is supposed to be an excellent electioneering potion." Cocktails crop up with increasing frequency in nineteenth-century literature, from Hughes's *Tom Brown's School Days* to Hawthorne's *The Blithedale Romance,* which contains a character "famous for nothing but gin cocktails."

In those days, a cocktail was served as a morning bracer or afternoon pick-me-up and was quite de rigueur for fishing and hunting parties. The Gilded Age industrialists Armour and Vanderbilt helped to popularize cocktails, which even today are regarded as the proper solace of the tired businessman.

Although literally hundreds of cocktails have been invented, the old standbys—the Martini, Manhattan, Old-fashioned and Daiquiri—have sustained their popularity. The stories behind them are fun to know.

Whiskey cocktails: The most famous bourbon drink (aside from the Mint Julep, which is not, strictly speaking, a cocktail although it may be served at the cocktail hour) is the Old-fashioned. It is known that a bartender at the old Pendennis Club in Louisville, Kentucky (the state whence bourbon sprang), added soda and Angostura bitters to a whiskey-and-sweetened-water concoction and called it an Old-fashioned, probably because it resembled an old-fashioned toddy. But this drink is believed to have originated in the turn-of-the-century Union Saloon in Honolulu.

The Manhattan is said to have been named for the old Manhattan Club in New York, although the Dry Manhattan, compounded with dry rather than sweet vermouth, came into being during Prohibition in the speakeasies in the environs of East Forty-first Street.

Gin cocktails: The most celebrated gin cocktail is, of course, the Martini. There are two schools of thought about its origin. Some people believe that the name came from the brand of vermouth with which it was made—originally sweet, later dry. But writers of San Francisco history claim that the Martini began there and credit its invention to Jerry Thomas, a famous bartender and author of the *Bon Vivant's Companion, or How to Mix Drinks.*

The life of Thomas was as spectacular as the Martini. At twenty-two, he shipped out of New York aboard the

Annie Smith and docked at San Francisco in the autumn of 1849, where he left the ship and became bartender in the El Dorado, a gambling hall. After an unsuccessful venture into the goldfields, he set out from San Francisco for the metropolitan areas of the South and East, making his living tending bar in the best places. At the famous Planters House in St. Louis he invented the Tom and Jerry (Jerry Thomas).

About 1860 he returned by covered wagon to San Francisco, where he became principal bartender at the Occidental Hotel. One morning, it is said, a customer came into the bar asking for a drink to cure his hangover. Thomas decided to invent one, which he did with considerable care and gave to the customer, who promptly recovered. As the man was leaving the bar, Thomas asked him if he lived in San Francisco. "No, I'm on my way to Martinez" (the county seat of Contra Costa County in the San Francisco Bay area). Thomas wrote down the recipe and named it the Martinez. It is included in his *Bon Vivant's Companion.* If this was indeed the forerunner of today's Martini, not only the name but the ingredients have been considerably modified since 1862.

The Pink Lady, named for a popular show of 1912, enjoyed a brief revival during the Broadway run of *Happy Birthday,* produced in 1947. In the play, the shy and proper young heroine (played by Helen Hayes) danced on the bar after a mixture of drinks, including a Pink Lady.

Rum cocktails: An early American version was the Stonewall or Stone Fence, a heady mixture of rum and cider. Later palates preferred the Daiquiri, originated by American engineers in Cuba after the Spanish-American War. It began as a long drink, then shrank to cocktail size. Rum is the base for innumerable cocktails that have less historic associations.

Vodka cocktails: The fashion for vodka drinks is relatively new; it originated on the West Coast, where the Moscow Mule cocktail was dreamed up by Jack Martin, of Heublein, and Jack Morgan, owner of Hollywood's Cock 'n' Bull restaurant. The Bloody Mary, famous morning-after restorative which is also popular with many cock-tail-partygoers, is claimed by George Jessel and at least two New York bartenders, and the Screwdriver, which tastes like orange juice but is considerably more potent, is believed to have originated with American oil workers in Iran who drank vodka and orange juice, stirring it with the screwdriver they attached to their fatigue pants by loops. The Gimlet, on the other hand, began as a British drink of gin and Rose's lime juice, much favored in Hong Kong and Singapore (Americans substituted vodka). A gimlet is a small boring tool, but its relationship to the Gimlet cocktail is extremely obscure.

Brandy cocktails have never been as popular as those made with gin, whiskey, rum or vodka. The Sidecar, an ingratiating mixture of brandy, Cointreau, and lemon juice, is believed to have been invented in Paris and brought here during Prohibition, to become the rage of the speakeasies. It is supposedly named after the motorcycle sidecar in which an army captain was driven to and from his pet Paris drinking spot, variously claimed as the Dôme, the Ritz Bar, Harry's Bar or the Rotonde. Like many stories about the origin of cocktails, this sounds farfetched, but it may well be true, and at least it's colorful.

The Outsize Cocktail Party

This can be a fearsome thing to contemplate, or it can be a festivity that you look forward to staging. Much depends on your reasons for giving a big cocktail party and on your approach to planning it. If you are simply resignedly pay-ing off innumerable social obligations, you are actually fooling no one as to your motive and you are also letting yourself in for an exhausting production that you may well find isn't worth it. If, however, you really want to bring a large number of your friends and acquaintances together, an outsize, gala cocktail party can be a first-rate catalyst and extremely rewarding. But do not overestimate your own capacities. Unless you can afford and find well-trained professional help to do all or most of the work, trim your dreams and your guest list to a scale that you can handle.

Being Your Own Bartender

It is quite possible to manage a cocktail party of fifteen, twenty or even twenty-five on your own, and do it gracefully. In fact, the atmosphere never seems to be as hospitable as when you are your own bartender. A self-assured and thoughtful host presiding over the bar at his own party gives a feeling of personal warmth that no professional bartender can ever impart to the occasion. The do-it-yourself party means a bit of work, but if you prepare well in advance, you will have no fuss or confusion when the guests arrive.

The bar: First of all, decide which is the best place to set up your bar. Even if you have a built-in bar, it may be inconvenient for parties. At these times, a temporary bar arrangement is usually preferable. To avoid a commercial look, don't rent a portable bar. If you are expecting relatively few guests—perhaps ten people—you can set up drink mixings on a serving tray on a table or handy buffet. For larger groups, place a good-sized table—your dining table may be right for the purpose, or you can always put two card tables together—at one side of the room but away from the wall so that you can stand behind it when bartending. This allows guests plenty of space to move up for refills. The table should be close enough to the conversation centers so that you can pour and mix casually while entering into the general talk. Always remember that you are host as well as bartender. Unless the table's surface is liquor-proof, take the precaution of covering it with a plastic cloth underneath a plain linen or brightly printed one.

Basic drinks: Being your own bartender for a sizable group means that you should limit the types of drink served. This is not only necessary but suitable. It is tasteless to imitate, even partly, the procedures of a professional bar. You should never feel that you must offer everything from a Pink Lady to a Sazerac. (Nor should your guests ever ask for such special drinks or request any liquor by brand name.) Your simplest course is to serve one kind of liquor-based cocktail (a Martini, Manhattan or other generally liked type), one light drink and one non-alcoholic drink. The light drink can be chilled dry sherry or white wine. For a non-alcoholic drink, seasoned tomato juice is a good choice. If you keep a bottle of vodka on hand, offer the tomato drink spiked with vodka for a tasty Bloody Mary. When you are serving Martinis or, in fact, any cocktails that are combinations of two or more liquors without fruit juice or other non-spirituous elements, mix them in advance except for the ice and put them in the refrigerator to chill. Mixing ahead saves time and trouble at the bar. This is true of makings as well as entire drinks: a spiced bouillon concoction (absolutely no consommé; it jellies upon contact with ice) for Bullshots, a spicy tomato juice for Bloody Marys, sour juices, simple sugar syrup, a rum-based mix.

If you are not a good cocktail mixer, try bottled cocktails. Many of them are better than those served by amateurs.

Plenty of people nowadays have learned the wisdom of asking for cocktails on the rocks, because the ice dilutes the drinks and makes them last longer. Various types of straight liquor served on the rocks with a little water or soda are also popular, and easy on a host. So are highballs of all sorts; although not cocktails, or even variations of them, highballs are perennial favorites in some areas of the country and are often in demand during hot weather.

Ice and glasses: Make sure to have plenty of ice on hand. This requires a good-sized, decorative ice bucket on the bar, and two or three utility buckets or an ice chest—well stocked—nearby or in the kitchen, ready for resupplying. Also set out an ample number of glasses. If you happen to own a fine large punch bowl, you might fill it with ice and place it on the bar. In it stand the pitcher of pre-mixed cocktails, the bottle of dry sherry or white wine, the vodka bottle and any other drinks that need chilling. Ice-filled punch bowls are also excellent for chilling glasses.

If you have double Old-fashioned glasses, use them only for highballs. A normal on-the-rocks drink looks like a mere drop when poured into one of these giant containers. For those guests who enjoy their liquor on the rocks, use the smaller Old-fashioned glasses. These are also suitable for sherry and cocktails, although simple all-purpose wine-glasses or stemmed cocktail glasses are more classic. For a serving of sherry or other wine, fill a stemmed glass about two-thirds full.

The importance of measuring: Don't guess. Have a measurer. Professional bartenders can gauge correctly by eye, but if you lack experience, measure each drink accurately. Leading restaurants and bars pour about 1½ ounces of liquor per drink. Some offer 2 ounces, but it takes very few of these generous helpings to finish off the drinker. If you feel that measuring at your party makes you look stingy, practice a bit in advance so that you can pour the right amount.

Cocktail food: If you are giving a party on your own, with no help, eschew fancy hot tidbits that must be rushed from the oven every fifteen minutes. Content yourself with a few simple foods that can be bought or prepared well in advance and placed at strategic points in the living room or arranged attractively on a second table (never on the same one used for a bar). Concentrate on such edibles as a good pâté with crackers or toast, cheese, nuts, olives and a bowl of *crudités*—crisp, raw vegetables—with a smaller bowl of a sharp dip beside it.

Keeping alert: Many host-bartenders make the mistake of adding a little "sweetener" to their own drinks every time they pour one for a guest. This is dangerous. Stay on your feet, bright-eyed and coherent. Remember, you are not only in charge of dispensing liquids but also responsible for catering to your guests' whims and wishes. If you feel you cannot nurse a mild drink for the better part of the party, sip Perrier water with a twist of lemon. You should not start your own cocktail indulgence until the gaiety has begun to taper to a close.

As the party progresses, watch the pattern of drinking. You may notice two types of guest—those too shy to ask for a second and who must be approached, and those who are only too eager to help themselves and also to help *you* at the bar. Beware of the latter.

Should you have, as sometimes happens, an overly gay guest, make his refills progressively less potent. This is particularly essential if he will be driving himself home. Ideally, no guest should depart feeling more than pleasantly warmed and elated. If need be, do not hesitate to slack up on the flow of liquor. People will be grateful; no one likes to wake up the next day with a decided feeling of having overdone a good thing.

When Guests Mix Their Own Drinks

Some hosts at a cocktail party prefer to circulate among their guests rather than stay by the bar making drinks most of the time. And while allowing people to mix their own drinks involves certain hazards and takes total control of the party out of the host's hands, it often works out well. For one thing, no matter what time each person arrives, the host can be on hand at the door to welcome him, tell him where to leave his coat and then, if necessary, make introductions. The bar should be equipped with various types of liquor—gin, Scotch, perhaps bourbon as well, and vodka or rum, depending on the particular tastes of the community. Such mixers as tonic, plain and carbonated water, Angostura bitters and spiced tomato juice should be set out, as well as cocktail olives and onions and twists of lemon peel. If a mixed-ahead cocktail is served, it should stand on the bar in a clearly labeled pitcher. And of course plenty of ice is essential. The host should check frequently to replenish any supplies that are running low.

The "make your own" approach presupposes a sizable party, no help and some confidence that guests know their own capacity and require little or no overseeing. But it does not mean that the host has no drink-making responsibilities at all. After he greets new arrivals and chats with them for a bit, he should offer them a drink, lead them to the bar and make the first one, suggesting that they help themselves to another when they wish to. Even if he cannot make *every* first drink, he should certainly show this courtesy to any women who arrive unescorted by a man, and keep an eye on these guests to be sure they are well looked after.

Two bars are often an easy solution to possible traffic problems. People tend to gather around the source of drink supply and linger there long after they have filled their glasses. This can create a real jam-up if you have one bar, small rooms and lots of guests. Two moderately sized bars, placed in separate rooms and as far from each other as possible, automatically make the most use of the available space and help to eliminate crowding. Food, of the type mentioned above, should be scattered strategically around the rooms where it can be readily seen and reached.

The Small Cocktail Party

Sometimes it isn't even called a party. You invite a number of people to "drop in for a drink" on a specific afternoon around six. Or you might say, "Come for cocktails," giving the day and hour. The usual procedure, in such instances, is to set up a cocktail tray on a table in the living or dining room, or to mix the drinks on the kitchen counter. This last method is the least convenient, because the host must trot back and forth to make the drinks, rather than mix them in the same room as the guests. There are those, however, who prefer to keep the cocktail tray out of sight, and do so on all occasions.

Again, quick but thorough preparations are the best guarantee of easy, smooth service with minimum strain. The necessary bottles of liquors, an aperitif, perhaps a non-alcoholic drink, mixers, garnishes and ice, should all be assembled in an organized way. The smaller the space, the more efficient the arrangements should be. Some bottles—those that may be the least in demand—can be placed on the floor under or beside the table. A second good-sized bucket of ice saves trips to the refrigerator. Plenty of glasses also cut down on extra legwork.

At such a gathering, informality is invariably the keynote. Upon occasion, if guests linger for a long time and imbibe quite a lot, the host may find himself slightly overworked, in which case old friends, particularly men, usually help out by making drinks for themselves and the person they are talking with. When a woman alone entertains in this fashion, she should ask one man she knows well to help her, or simply indicate to all the men that they are to look after themselves and the women who come with them. Or she can be her own bartender and do the work herself, but most women prefer to relinquish the job after the first round or so.

Cocktails Before a Meal

When you invite guests to a meal and offer them cocktails first, you can be as casual or as precise as you wish. You can ask people what they would like to drink, give them a specific choice or decide on one drink that seems to suit the time, situation and menu that will follow. You can have a long or short cocktail hour simply by continuing to serve more drinks or saying gently but firmly that the meal is ready. Custom varies from place to place, but it is usual to offer guests a second round of drinks when they have finished the first one. This is true whether the potables you serve are strong or mild or a mixture of both. The same range of drinks that is suitable for a cocktail party is appropriate as the prelude to a meal. But to spare yourself too much confusion, offer those particular drinks that you believe will be the most popular with your guests. If you know your guests well, however, and want to be adventuresome, you might depart from standard drinks and try something unusual. But have the old reliables available for friends who prefer to play it safe.

When a couple entertain, the man tends bar, freeing his wife to cope with last-minute meal preparations. When one person alone must combine the responsibilities of bartender and cook, he should plan a menu that keeps him away from his guests as little as possible. When he must repair to the kitchen for a short time just before the food is served, he can quite easily ask his friends to make themselves another drink if they want one during his absence.

Any cocktail food served before a meal should be simple and not too filling. Crisp raw vegetables accompanied by coarse salt or a sharp dip are always a good choice, as are olives, nuts, cheese sticks and the like.

Knowing Tips for Cocktail Time

Standard cocktail parties are given all the time, but the most successful hosts are those who delight their guests by touches of originality in the preparation of drinks and food. Here is a compendium of convivial ways and means that help to make a party memorable.

Your own way with a Bloody Mary: Some people who entertain frequently with Sunday pre-brunch cocktails like to serve Bloody Marys. Here's one excellent way of going about it—at any time. Chill the glasses thoroughly, well in advance, dampen the rims and then dip them into coarse salt to give a glaze to the edges. When your guests arrive, pour tomato juice and vodka, in the right proportions and both icy cold, into each glass. Then pass a tray containing a bottle of Tabasco sauce, a pepper grinder and slivers of lemon. Each guest seasons to suit himself.

Beef broth with a bounce: The Bullshot—beef bouillon laced with vodka—is another drink that gains distinction with the addition of a few subtle touches. Be sure both bouillon and vodka are chilled until icy. Mix the drink in proportions to suit each individual taste and serve without ice in chilled glasses, or over ice in large wineglasses. Add bits of lemon zest (see below) and pass a tray with a pepper mill and a bottle of Tabasco sauce.

Lemon, orange or lime zest: Using a lemon stripper, you can do all sorts of things with citrus zests (peels), and do them quickly. Although some of the following drinks are not cocktails, they are, upon occasion and request, served at the cocktail hour. Try a spiral of lemon zest in whiskey highballs, Whiskey Sours and Whiskey Mists to give these drinks more character. Twists of lime zest add interest to many rum drinks. Use a bit of orange zest for color and flavor in a long gin drink, such as a collins.

The kick of vodka: The ever popular Screwdriver —orange juice and vodka—is too often served in a highball glass with too much orange juice and ice. As a result, it becomes weak fruit juice, lightly spiked. Serve it, instead, in a well-chilled regular Old-fashioned glass, with little or no ice, and be sure both vodka and orange juice are extremely cold. Or serve the drink in a wineglass, with a finger of pineapple, chilled and sugared, for garnish.

The coolth that counts: All the drinks made with fruit juices, such as Daiquiris and collins, seem cooler and more appetizing when the glasses are as cold as you can get them, dampened and then frosted with sugar.

The true perfection of the classic Martini depends as much on how cold it is as on the proportions of gin and vermouth. Put the glasses in the deep freeze or freezer compartment of your refrigerator for an hour or two before serving. Chill both the gin and vermouth in the refrigerator or in ice buckets.

Onions, olives and cheese: If you plan to use onions or olives for garnish, open the jars and drain well ahead of time: brine from either does not improve the drink. Although Martini enthusiasts tend to be fussy, with strong preferences for onions, olives or lemon twist, not all of them are opposed to innovation. At your next cocktail party, you might offer a new Martini garnish that has gained some adherents—a small cube of sharp cheese impaled on a toothpick.

The switch to sherry: Many people also offer a good dry sherry at cocktail time for those who prefer a light drink. This is a thoughtful gesture, but the host should bear in mind that dry sherries are best if nicely chilled. Chilling improves the flavor and brings out a brisk quality in the wine. Chill the bottle and serve the sherry preferably in small, clear wineglasses.

Varying glasses: While we are on the subject of glasses, nobody expects you to have a stock of fine crystal in cocktail, highball and Old-fashioned glasses. There are many inexpensive yet nicely designed glasses—of glass or plastic—on the market today. For a change, you and your guests may enjoy drinks in unorthodox glasses— Martinis in iced wineglasses, Bloody Marys in Burgundy glasses, highballs in simple, good-looking goblets. Stemware avoids the need for coasters, which at times can be a nuisance.

Respect for the bons mots: When planning the kind of food to have at a cocktail party, by all means choose a style of serving that doesn't necessitate constant intrusion on your guests' conversations. The host who is forever circling the room with tidbits cannot possibly enjoy the party—and may be a bit of a nuisance to his guests. If you don't have someone to pass the food, it should be displayed in a convenient and inviting place where your guests can help themselves at will.

Kindness to all appetites: Nothing is more confusing and uninteresting than a miscellaneous collection of canapés. There are too many mixed flavors, and too many of the canapés grow soggy. Instead, why not provide the simplest of snacks for those guests who wish to drop by briefly, plus a hearty buffet table with meats and salads for those who linger!

Manufacturing ice: Just as it's wise to have a basic liquor supply always on hand, as well as mixers, lemons, olives, onions and so on, it's smart always to have lots of ice available, made day after day whenever the domestic consumption is low, and stored in the freezer in double plastic bags.

Chilly plastic: Store plastic bar glasses in the freezer to keep them chilled, transferring them before a party to a big plastic foam cooler to use as needed. Nested plastic glasses insulate a drink against warm hands; a double glass per person serves the purpose nicely.

APERITIF- AND WINE-BASED COCKTAILS

Most of these cocktails are made with rather mild aperitifs or wines. (Pernod is an exception, as are those drinks that call for a liquor such as gin or brandy in addition to the central ingredient.) For this reason, some of the potables in this group are longer than standard cocktails and should be served in goblets, Old-fashioned glasses or large wine-glasses.

The largest number of recipes are based on vermouth, sweet or dry or both; sherry-based cocktails are second. Although not many Dubonnet cocktails are listed, this aperitif is becoming more popular all the time; many people like to drink it, in one form or another, before a meal as well as in midmorning or midafternoon. Cocktails made with port, Amer Picon, Byrrh and so on are grouped together under "Miscellaneous" at the end of the section.

ADDINGTON

1½–2 ounces sweet vermouth	2 or 3 ice cubes
	Club soda
1½–2 ounces dry vermouth	Twist lemon peel

Combine the vermouths and ice in a mixing glass and stir well. Strain into a goblet, fill with soda and drop in the lemon peel. Serves 1.

This is also known as **Vermouth Half-and-Half.**

Vermouth Cocktail: Add a dash of orange bitters and a maraschino cherry.

Crystal Bronx: Add 2 tablespoons orange juice and omit lemon peel.

Duplex: Omit club soda and serve in a cocktail glass.

ADONIS

2 ounces dry sherry
1 ounce sweet vermouth

1 dash orange bitters
3 or 4 ice cubes

Combine all ingredients in a mixing glass and stir well. Strain into a cocktail glass. Serves 1.

ALICE MINE

½ ounce dry vermouth
4 dashes sweet vermouth
1 ounce Grand Marnier

½ ounce gin
Dash Angostura bitters
3 or 4 ice cubes

Combine all ingredients in a mixing glass and stir well. Strain into a cocktail glass. Serves 1.

AMERICANO COCKTAIL

3 ounces sweet vermouth
1½ ounces Campari

3 or 4 ice cubes
Twist orange or lemon peel

Combine the vermouth and Campari in a mixing glass with ice cubes and stir well. Strain into a large cocktail glass and garnish with orange or lemon peel. Serves 1.

The proportions may be varied to 2 ounces each sweet vermouth and Campari.

APPETIZER NO. 1

1½ ounces Dubonnet
¼ cup orange juice

3 or 4 ice cubes

Combine all ingredients in a cocktail shaker, shake vigorously and strain into a cocktail glass. Serves 1.

BOB DANBY

2 ounces Dubonnet   3 or 4 ice cubes
1 ounce brandy

Combine all ingredients in a mixing glass and stir well. Strain into a cocktail glass. Serves 1.

BOMB (FOR 6)

9 ounces sherry   2 dashes Pimento Dram
1½ ounces Cointreau   3 cups crushed ice
1½ ounces orange juice   6 olives
1 dash orange bitters

Combine all ingredients except the olives in a cocktail shaker and shake vigorously. Strain into 6 cocktail glasses. Garnish each glass with an olive.

BONSONI

3 ounces sweet vermouth   2 or 3 ice cubes
1 ounce Fernet Branca

Combine all ingredients in a mixing glass and stir well. Strain into a cocktail glass. Serves 1.
   Italian: Add 2 dashes sugar syrup, 1 dash Pernod.

BRAZIL

1½ ounces sherry   1 dash Angostura bitters
1½ ounces dry vermouth   3 or 4 ice cubes
1 dash Pernod   Twist lemon peel

Combine all ingredients except the lemon peel in a mixing glass and stir well. Strain into a cocktail glass, twist the peel over the drink to release oil, and then drop it in. Serves 1.

BROKEN SPUR

3 ounces white port
½ ounce dry gin
½ ounce sweet vermouth

1 egg yolk
1 teaspoon anisette
3 or 4 ice cubes

Combine all ingredients in a cocktail shaker and shake vigorously. Strain into a large cocktail glass. Serves 1.

BRUNELLE

1 ounce Pernod
3 ounces lemon juice

1½ teaspoons superfine
   sugar
3 or 4 ice cubes

Combine all ingredients in a cocktail shaker and shake vigorously. Strain into a cocktail glass. Serves 1.

BUTTONHOOK

½ ounce Pernod
½ ounce apricot brandy
½ ounce brandy

½ ounce white crème de
   menthe
3 or 4 ice cubes

Combine all ingredients in a cocktail shaker and shake vigorously. Strain into a cocktail glass. Serves 1.

BYCULLA

1 ounce sherry
1 ounce port
1 ounce curaçao

1 ounce Stone's ginger wine
3 or 4 ice cubes

Combine all ingredients in a mixing glass and stir to mix well. Strain into a cocktail glass. Serves 1.

BYRRH

1 ounce Byrrh
1 ounce rye whiskey

1 ounce dry vermouth
3 or 4 ice cubes

Combine all ingredients in a mixing glass and stir well. Strain into a chilled cocktail glass. Serves 1.

BYRRH CASSIS

2 ounces Byrrh
1 ounce crème de cassis

2 or 3 ice cubes
Club soda

Pour the Byrrh and crème de cassis into a goblet, add ice cubes and fill with club soda. Serves 1.

BYRRH SPECIAL

1½ ounces Byrrh
1½ ounces gin

3 or 4 ice cubes

Combine all ingredients in a mixing glass and stir well. Strain into a cocktail glass. Serves 1.

CHRYSANTHEMUM

1½ ounces dry vermouth
1½ ounces Benedictine
3 dashes Pernod

2 or 3 ice cubes
Twist orange peel

Combine all ingredients except orange peel in a mixing glass and stir well. Strain into a cocktail glass and drop in the twist of peel. Serves 1.

CINZANO

3 ounces Cinzano vermouth   2 or 3 ice cubes
2 dashes orange bitters   Twist orange peel
2 dashes Angostura bitters

Combine all ingredients except the peel in a mixing glass and stir well. Strain into a cocktail glass. Twist the orange peel over the glass to release the oil and drop peel in. Serves 1.

CORONATION

¾ ounce dry vermouth   ¾ ounce gin
¾ ounce Dubonnet   ½ cup crushed ice

Combine all ingredients in a mixing glass and stir well. Strain into a cocktail glass. Serves 1.

CUPID

3 ounces sherry   Pinch cayenne pepper
1 egg   3 or 4 ice cubes
1 teaspoon superfine sugar

Combine all ingredients in a cocktail shaker and shake vigorously. Strain into a cocktail glass. Serves 1.

DEVIL'S

1½ ounces port   2 dashes lemon juice
1½ ounces dry vermouth   3 or 4 ice cubes

Combine all ingredients in a mixing glass and stir well. Strain into a cocktail glass. Serves 1.

DIPLOMAT

3 ounces dry vermouth
1 ounce sweet vermouth
Dash maraschino

3 or 4 ice cubes
Maraschino cherry
Twist lemon peel

Combine vermouths and maraschino in a mixing glass with ice and stir well. Strain into a cocktail glass. Garnish with cherry; twist the peel and drop it in. Serves 1.

DUBONNET MANHATTAN

1½ ounces Dubonnet
1½ ounces whiskey

3 or 4 ice cubes
Maraschino cherry

Combine all ingredients except the cherry in a mixing glass and stir well. Strain into a cocktail glass; garnish with cherry. Serves 1.

DUBONNET ON THE ROCKS

Twist lemon peel
3 or 4 ice cubes

4 ounces Dubonnet

Put the twist of lemon peel in the bottom of an Old-fashioned glass, add ice cubes and pour in the Dubonnet. Serves 1.

DUCHESS

1 ounce Pernod
1 ounce dry vermouth

1 ounce sweet vermouth
3 or 4 ice cubes

Combine all ingredients in a cocktail shaker and shake vigorously. Strain into a cocktail glass. Serves 1.

DUKE OF MARLBOROUGH

1½ ounces sherry
1½ ounces sweet vermouth
3 dashes raspberry syrup

3 tablespoons lime juice
3 or 4 ice cubes

Combine all ingredients in a cocktail shaker and shake vigorously. Strain into a cocktail glass. Serves 1.

EAST INDIAN

1½ ounces sherry
1½ ounces dry vermouth

Dash orange bitters
3 or 4 ice cubes

Combine all ingredients in a mixing glass and stir well. Strain into a cocktail glass. Serves 1.
Reform: Reduce vermouth to ½ ounce.
Greenbrier: Substitute peach bitters for orange bitters and garnish with mint sprig.
Coronation No. 1: Add a dash maraschino.

FIG LEAF

1½ ounces sweet vermouth
1 ounce light rum
1½ tablespoons lime juice

Dash Angostura bitters
2 or 3 ice cubes

Combine all ingredients in a cocktail shaker and shake vigorously. Strain into a cocktail glass. Serves 1.

GREEN ROOM

1½ ounces dry vermouth
½ ounce brandy

2 dashes curaçao
2 or 3 ice cubes

Combine all ingredients in a mixing glass and stir well. Strain into a cocktail glass. Serves 1.

HARVARD WINE

1 ounce dry vermouth
¾ ounce brandy
Dash orange bitters

1 or 2 ice cubes
Club soda

Combine all ingredients except the soda in a mixing glass and stir well. Strain into a large cocktail glass and fill with soda. Serves 1.

ITALIAN APERITIF

3 ice cubes
3 ounces Punt e Mes
Dash dry vermouth

Dash Campari
Squeeze of lemon
Lemon slice

Put the ice cubes in a goblet, pour the Punt e Mes over them, add vermouth, Campari and a squeeze of lemon. Garnish with lemon slice. Serves 1.

KIR

6 ounces dry white wine
1 tablespoon crème de cassis

2 or 3 ice cubes
Twist lemon peel

In a goblet or large wineglass combine all ingredients except the lemon peel, and stir gently. Twist the peel to release the oil and then drop peel into the glass. Serves 1.

MACARONI

1½ ounces Pernod
½ ounce sweet vermouth

3 or 4 ice cubes

Combine all ingredients in a cocktail shaker and shake vigorously. Strain into a cocktail glass. Serves 1.
Glad Eyes: Substitute white crème de menthe for the vermouth.

MARY GARDEN

1½ ounces Dubonnet   2 or 4 ice cubes
1½ ounces dry vermouth

Combine all ingredients in a mixing glass and stir well. Strain into a chilled cocktail glass. Serves 1.
Spion Kop: Increase Dubonnet and vermouth to 2 ounces each.

MERRY WIDOW NO. 1

1½ ounces sherry   3 or 4 ice cubes
1½ ounces sweet vermouth   Twist lemon peel

Stir the sherry and vermouth with the ice cubes in a mixing glass. Strain into a chilled cocktail glass. Twist lemon peel over the glass and drop it in. Serves 1.
Bamboo: Omit lemon peel; add a dash of Angostura bitters.

NEGRONI

1½ ounces sweet vermouth   2 or 3 ice cubes
1½ ounces Campari   Twist lemon peel
1½ ounces gin

Put all ingredients except lemon peel in an Old-fashioned glass and stir. Garnish with the peel. Serves 1.
Perfect Cocktail: Use dry vermouth in place of Campari. Make the drink in a mixing glass and strain into an Old-fashioned glass. Garnish with the peel.

NINE-PICK

1 ounce Pernod   1 egg yolk
1 ounce curaçao   3 or 4 ice cubes
1 ounce brandy

Combine all ingredients in a cocktail shaker and shake vigorously. Strain into a cocktail glass. Serves 1.

NINETEEN NO. 1

3 ounces dry vermouth
½ ounce gin
½ ounce kirsch

Dash Pernod
3 dashes sugar syrup
3 or 4 ice cubes

Combine all ingredients in a mixing glass and stir well. Strain into a cocktail glass. Serves 1.

NINETEEN-PICK-ME-UP

1½ ounces Pernod
¾ ounce gin
1 dash Angostura bitters
1 dash orange bitters

1 dash sugar syrup
3 or 4 ice cubes
Dash club soda

Combine first six ingredients in a cocktail shaker and shake vigorously. Strain into a cocktail glass and add the club soda. Serves 1.

PANSY

1½ ounces Pernod
6 dashes grenadine

2 dashes Angostura bitters
3 or 4 ice cubes

Combine all ingredients in a cocktail shaker and shake vigorously. Strain into a cocktail glass. Serves 1.

PANTOMIME

1½ ounces dry vermouth
Dash grenadine
Dash orgeat syrup

1 egg white
3 or 4 ice cubes

Put all ingredients in a cocktail shaker and shake vigorously. Strain into a cocktail glass. Serves 1.

PERNOD NO. 1

2 ounces Pernod   1 dash Angostura bitters
½ ounce water   3 or 4 ice cubes
1 dash sugar syrup

Combine all ingredients in a cocktail shaker and shake vigorously. Strain into a cocktail glass. Serves 1.
Pernod No. 2: For this weaker drink, use 1½ ounces each of Pernod and water.

PERPETUAL

1½ ounces sweet vermouth   2 dashes crème de cacao
1½ ounces dry vermouth   3 or 4 ice cubes
4 dashes Crème Yvette

Combine all ingredients in a mixing glass and stir well. Strain into a cocktail glass. Serves 1.

PHILOMEL

2 ounces sherry   1½ ounces orange juice
¾ ounce rum   Pinch pepper
1½ ounces Quinquina   3 or 4 ice cubes

Combine all ingredients in a cocktail shaker and shake vigorously. Strain into an Old-fashioned glass. Serves 1.

PICON

1½ ounces Amer Picon   2 or 3 ice cubes
1½ ounces dry vermouth

Put all ingredients in a mixing glass and stir well. Strain into a cocktail glass. Serves 1.

PICON GRENADINE

1½ ounces Amer Picon　　　2 or 3 ice cubes
¾ ounce grenadine　　　　　Chilled club soda

Place all ingredients in an Old-fashioned glass and fill with club soda. Serves 1.

PICON PICON

1½ ounces Amer Picon　　　1½ ounces chilled fresh
　　　　　　　　　　　　　　　　orange juice
　　　　　　　　　　　　　Dash chilled club soda

Pour all ingredients into a cocktail glass and add club soda. Serves 1.

Although this drink is served without ice in France, it may be made in a mixing glass with 2 or 3 ice cubes, stirred to chill well and then strained into a cocktail glass.

PINEAPPLE COCKTAIL

1 cup crushed pineapple　　　1 tablespoon lemon juice
6 ounces dry white wine　　　9 ounces sherry
3 ounces fresh pineapple　　　6 very small wedges
　juice　　　　　　　　　　　　pineapple

Soak the crushed pineapple in the white wine for two or three hours. Pour into a cocktail shaker and add all other ingredients except the pineapple wedges. Chill mixture thoroughly in the refrigerator. Stir and strain into 6 cocktail glasses. Garnish with pineapple wedges. Serves 6.

PLAIN SHERRY COCKTAIL

3 ounces sherry　　　　　　2 dashes Pernod
2 dashes maraschino　　　　3 or 4 ice cubes

Combine all ingredients in a cocktail shaker and shake vigorously. Strain into a cocktail glass. Serves 1.

PLAIN VERMOUTH

15 ounces dry vermouth	6 ice cubes
1 teaspoon Pernod	6 maraschino cherries
1 teaspoon maraschino	

Combine all ingredients except cherries in a mixing glass and stir thoroughly to chill. Strain into 6 cocktail glasses and garnish each with a cherry. Serves 6.

PORT NO. 1

3 ounces port	3 or 4 ice cubes
1 dash brandy	Twist orange peel

Combine first three ingredients in a mixing glass and stir well. Strain into a cocktail glass, twist orange peel over top to extract oil, then drop peel in. Serves 1.

PORT NO. 2

3 ounces port	1 dash Angostura bitters
2 dashes curaçao	3 or 4 ice cubes
1 dash orange bitters	

Combine all ingredients in a mixing glass and stir well. Strain into a cocktail glass. Serves 1.

QUEEN ELIZABETH WINI

1 ounce dry vermouth	1 tablespoon lime or lemon
1½ ounces Benedictine	juice
	2 or 3 ice cubes

Combine all ingredients in a mixing glass and stir well. Strain into a cocktail glass. Serves 1.

RAYMOND HITCHCOCKTAIL

3 ounces sweet vermouth
¼ cup orange juice
Dash orange bitters

3 or 4 ice cubes
Slice pineapple

Combine all ingredients except the pineapple in a mixing glass and stir well. Strain into an Old-fashioned glass. Garnish with pineapple slice. Serves 1.

ROY HOWARD LILLET

2 ounces Lillet
1 ounce brandy
1 ounce orange juice

2 dashes grenadine
3 or 4 ice cubes

Combine all ingredients in a cocktail shaker and shake vigorously. Strain into a cocktail glass. Serves 1.

ST. RAPHAEL AND VODKA

2 or 3 ice cubes
3 ounces St. Raphae
1½ ounces vodka

Club soda
Twist lemon pee

Put the ice cubes in a wineglass or goblet, add the St. Raphael and vodka and a little club soda. Stir lightly and garnish with lemon peel twist. Serves 1.

SANCTUARY

2 ounces Dubonnet
1 ounce Amer Picon

1 ounce Cointreau
3 or 4 ice cubes

Combine all ingredients in a mixing glass, stir well and strain into a cocktail glass. Serves 1.

SHERRY TWIST NO. 1

9 ounces sherry
3 ounces dry vermouth
3 ounces brandy
2 ounces Cointreau

1½ tablespoons lemon juice
1" piece stick cinnamon
6 ice cubes

Combine all ingredients in a cocktail shaker and shake vigorously. Strain into 6 cocktail glasses. Serves 6.

SHERRY TWIST NO. 2

8 ounces sherry
6 ounces whiskey
1½ ounces Cointreau
½ cup orange juice

1 tablespoon lemon juice
2 cloves
Pinch cayenne pepper
6 ice cubes

Combine all ingredients in a cocktail shaker and shake vigorously. Strain into 6 cocktail glasses. Serves 6.

SHIP

4 ounces sherry
½ ounce whiskey
2 dashes rum

2 dashes prune syrup
2 dashes orange bitters
3 or 4 ice cubes

Combine all ingredients in a cocktail shaker and shake vigorously. Strain into a large cocktail glass or a wineglass. Serves 1.

STIRRED VERMOUTH

2 ounces dry vermouth
2 or 3 ice cubes

Twist lemon peel
Slice lemon

Put all ingredients except the slice of lemon in a mixing glass and stir well. Strain into a cocktail glass and garnish with the lemon slice. Serves 1.

SOUL KISS NO. 1

1½ ounces sweet vermouth
1½ ounces dry vermouth
1 ounce Dubonnet
1 ounce orange juice
3 or 4 ice cubes

Combine all ingredients in a mixing glass and stir well. Strain into an Old-fashioned glass or large wineglass. Serves 1.

STRAIGHT LAW

3 ounces dry sherry
1 ounce dry gin
2 or 3 ice cubes
Twist lemon peel

Combine all ingredients except lemon peel in a mixing glass and stir well. Strain into a cocktail glass; drop in the peel. Serves 1.

SUISSE OR SUISSESSE

1½ ounces Pernod
4 dashes anisette or sugar syrup
1 egg white
3 or 4 ice cubes

Combine all ingredients in a cocktail shaker and shake vigorously. Strain into a cocktail glass. Serves 1.

Sometimes a dash of heavy cream is added.

THIRD RAIL NO. 1

1½–3 ounces dry vermouth
1 or 2 dashes curaçao
1 or 2 dashes crème de menthe
2 or 3 ice cubes
Twist lemon peel

Combine all ingredients except the lemon peel in a mixing glass and stir well. Strain into a cocktail glass and garnish with lemon twist. Serves 1.

TROCADERO

1½–2 ounces sweet vermouth	Dash grenadine
	Dash orange bitters
1½–2 ounces dry vermouth	2 or 3 ice cubes

Combine all ingredients in a mixing glass and stir well. Strain into a cocktail glass. Serves 1.

Cherry Mixture: Use a dash each of maraschino and Angostura bitters in place of the grenadine and orange bitters. Garnish with a maraschino cherry.

TROPICAL

1½ ounces dry vermouth	Dash Angostura bitters
1½ ounces crème de cacao	Dash orange bitters
1½ ounces maraschino	2 or 3 ice cubes

Combine all ingredients in a mixing glass and stir well. Strain into a goblet or wineglass. Serves 1.

TUXEDO

3 ounces sherry	Dash Peychaud's bitters
¾ ounce anisette	3 or 4 ice cubes
2 dashes maraschino	

Combine all ingredients in a mixing glass and stir well. Strain into a cocktail glass. Serves 1.

UPSTAIRS

3 ounces Dubonnet	2 or 3 ice cubes
1 tablespoon lemon juice	Club soda

Pour the Dubonnet and lemon juice into a large cocktail glass, add ice cubes and fill with club soda. Serves 1.

VERMOUTH CASSIS

3 ounces dry vermouth
1 ounce crème de cassis

2 or 3 ice cubes
Club soda

Pour the vermouth and crème de cassis into an Old-fashioned glass, Whiskey Sour glass or 8-ounce wineglass. Add ice cubes and fill with club soda. Serves 1.

VERMOUTH NO. 1

3 ounces dry or sweet
  vermouth

2 dashes Angostura bitters
2 or 3 ice cubes

Combine all ingredients in a mixing glass and stir well. Strain into a cocktail glass. Serves 1.

VERMOUTH NO. 2

2 ounces sweet vermouth
1 teaspoon curaçao
1 teaspoon Amer Picon
½ teaspoon superfine sugar

Dash Angostura bitters
3 or 4 ice cubes
Twist lemon peel
Maraschino cherry

Combine all ingredients except the lemon peel and cherry in a mixing glass and stir well. Strain into a cocktail glass. Add peel and cherry. Serves 1.

VERMOUTH ON THE ROCKS

3 or 4 ice cubes
4 ounces dry or sweet

vermouth, Vermouth Fraise
or Framboise

Put the ice cubes in an Old-fashioned glass and pour in the preferred vermouth. Serves 1.

Lillet, St. Raphael and similar aperitifs may also be served in this way, as may sherry, Madeira and dry port.

VICTOR

1 ounce sweet vermouth   ½ ounce brandy
½ ounce gin   3 or 4 ice cubes

Combine all ingredients in a mixing glass and stir well. Strain into a cocktail glass. Serves 1.

VICTORY

1½ ounces Pernod   3 or 4 ice cubes
1½ ounces grenadine   Club soda

Combine the Pernod, grenadine and ice in a cocktail shaker and shake vigorously. Strain into a cocktail glass and fill with club soda. Serves 1.

WASHINGTON

2 ounces dry vermouth   2 dashes Angostura bitters
1 ounce brandy   2 or 3 ice cubes
2 dashes sugar syrup

Combine all ingredients in a mixing glass and stir well. Strain into a cocktail glass. Serves 1.

WEEP NO MORE

1½ ounces Dubonnet   Dash maraschino
1¼ ounces brandy   3 or 4 ice cubes
1½ ounces lime juice

Combine all ingredients in a mixing glass, stir well and strain into a cocktail glass. Serves 1.

WYOMING SWING

2 ounces sweet vermouth
2 ounces dry vermouth
2 ounces fresh orange juice

1 teaspoon superfine sugar
2 or 3 ice cubes

Combine all ingredients in a mixing glass and stir well. Strain into a goblet or Old-fashioned glass. Serves 1.

XERES

3 ounces sherry
Dash peach bitters

Dash orange bitters
2 or 3 ice cubes

Combine all ingredients in a mixing glass and stir well. Strain into a cocktail glass. Serves 1.

Sherry Cocktail: Substitute 4 dashes dry vermouth for the peach bitters and increase orange bitters to 4 dashes.

YODEL

1 ice cube
2 ounces Fernet Branca

2 ounces orange juice
Club soda

Place the ice cube in a goblet, pour in the Fernet Branca and orange juice and fill with club soda. Serves 1.

YORK SPECIAL

3 ounces dry vermouth
1 ounce maraschino

4 dashes orange bitters
2 to 3 ice cubes

Combine all ingredients in a mixing glass and stir well. Strain into a cocktail glass. Serves 1.

Humpty-Dumpty: Omit the bitters.

ZEUS

2 or 3 ice cubes
2 ounces Campari

1 ounce vodka
Twist lemon peel

Put the ice cubes in an Old-fashioned glass and pour in the Campari and vodka. Stir lightly. Twist the lemon peel over the drink to release the oil and then drop the peel in. Serves 1.

APPLEJACK COCKTAILS

APPLE BRANDY

1½ ounces applejack
1 teaspoon grenadine

1 teaspoon lemon juice
½ cup crushed ice

Combine all ingredients in a cocktail shaker and shake vigorously. Strain into a cocktail glass. Serves 1.

APPLE TREE

1½ ounces applejack
1½ ounces sweet cider or
apple juice

Dash dry vermouth
2 or 3 ice cubes
Twist lemon peel

Combine all ingredients except the peel in an Old-fashioned glass and stir. Drop in the peel. Serves 1.

APPLEJACK COCKTAIL

2 ounces applejack
1 teaspoon superfine sugar
1½ tablespoons lime juice
4 dashes curaçao
½ cup crushed ice

Combine all ingredients in a cocktail shaker and shake vigorously. Strain into a cocktail glass. Serves 1.

APPLEJACK NO. 1

1½ ounces applejack
1 teaspoon sugar syrup
2 dashes orange bitters
Dash Angostura bitters
3 or 4 ice cubes

Combine all ingredients in a mixing glass and stir well. Strain into a cocktail glass. Serves 1.

APPLEJACK NO. 2

1½ ounces calvados or
    applejack
½ ounce sweet vermouth
Dash Angostura bitters
3 or 4 ice cubes

Combine all ingredients in a mixing glass and stir well. Strain into a cocktail glass. Serves 1.
BVD: Omit the bitters and add a twist of lemon peel.

APPLEJACK OLD-FASHIONED

1 cube sugar
Dash Angostura bitters
Dash club soda
1½ ounces applejack
½ cup cracked ice
Twist lemon peel

Muddle the sugar and bitters in an Old-fashioned glass with the soda. Pour in the applejack, add the ice and stir. Garnish with lemon peel. Serves 1.

APPLEJACK SOUR

See "Sours," page 216.

HONEYMOON

1½ ounces applejack
⅔ ounce Benedictine
2 tablespoons lemon juice

3 dashes curaçao
3 or 4 ice cubes

Combine all ingredients in a cocktail shaker and shake vigorously. Strain into a cocktail glass. Serves 1.

JACK-IN-THE-BOX

1½ ounces applejack
¾ ounce pineapple juice
2 tablespoons lemon juice

2 dashes Angostura bitters
3 or 4 ice cubes

Combine all ingredients in a cocktail shaker and shake vigorously. Strain into a cocktail glass. Serves 1.

JACK ROSE

1½ ounces applejack
½ ounce grenadine

1½ tablespoons lime juice
3 or 4 ice cubes

Combine all ingredients in a cocktail shaker and shake vigorously. Strain into a cocktail glass. Serves 1.

JERSEY LIGHTNING

2–3 ounces applejack
Dash Angostura bitters

Sugar syrup to taste
3 or 4 ice cubes

Combine all ingredients in a cocktail shaker and shake vigorously. Strain into a cocktail glass. Serves 1.

LIBERTY

1½ ounces applejack
¾ ounce light rum

Dash sugar syrup
3 or 4 ice cubes

Combine all ingredients in a cocktail shaker and shake vigorously. Strain into a cocktail glass. Serves 1.

OOM PAUL

1 ounce calvados or applejack
1 ounce Dubonnet

Dash Angostura bitters
3 or 4 ice cubes

Combine all ingredients in a mixing glass and stir well. Strain into a cocktail glass. Serves 1.

Bentley: Omit the Angostura.

ROYAL SMILE NO. 1

1 ounce applejack
½ ounce dry gin
½ ounce grenadine

1 tablespoon lemon juice
3 or 4 ice cubes

Combine all ingredients in a cocktail shaker and shake vigorously. Strain into a cocktail glass. Serves 1.

SAUCY SUE NO. 1

2 ounces applejack
½ teaspoon apricot brandy

½ teaspoon Pernod
½ cup cracked ice

Combine all ingredients in a mixing glass and stir well. Strain into a cocktail glass. Serves 1.

SPECIAL ROUGH

1 ounce applejack	Dash Pernod
1 ounce brandy	½ cup crushed ice

Combine all ingredients in a mixing glass and stir well. Strain into a cocktail glass. Serves 1.

STAR NO. 1

1 ounce applejack	Dash orange bitters
1 ounce sweet vermouth	½ cup crushed ice

Combine all ingredients in a mixing glass and stir well. Strain into a cocktail glass. Serves 1.

TINTON

1½ ounces applejack	3 or 4 ice cubes
¾ ounce port	

Combine all ingredients in a mixing glass and stir well. Strain into a cocktail glass. Serves 1.

TULIP

¾ ounce calvados or applejack	½ ounce apricot brandy
	1 tablespoon lemon juice
¾ ounce sweet vermouth	3 or 4 ice cubes

Combine all ingredients in a mixing glass and stir well. Strain into a cocktail glass. Serves 1.

TWELVE MILES OUT

¾ ounce calvados or applejack	¾ ounce Swedish Punch
	3 or 4 ice cubes
¾ ounce light rum	

Combine all ingredients in a mixing glass and stir well. Strain into a cocktail glass. Serves 1.

WHIST

1 ounce calvados or
    applejack
½ ounce light rum

½ ounce sweet vermouth
3 or 4 ice cubes

Combine all ingredients in a mixing glass and stir well. Strain into a cocktail glass. Serves 1.

WIDOW'S KISS

1 ounce calvados or
    applejack
½ ounce yellow chartreuse
½ ounce Benedictine

Dash Angostura bitters
3 or 4 ice cubes
Strawberry (optional)

Combine all ingredients except the strawberry in a cocktail shaker and shake vigorously. Strain into a cocktail glass and drop in the strawberry. Serves 1.

BRANDY COCKTAILS

ALEXANDER OR BRANDY ALEXANDER

¾ ounce brandy
¾ ounce crème de cacao

¾ ounce heavy cream
3 or 4 ice cubes

Combine all ingredients in a cocktail shaker and shake vigorously. Strain into a cocktail glass. Serves 1.

This drink is often called a "Brandy Alexander" to distinguish it from variations.

Alejandra: Use Kahlúa instead of crème de cacao.

AMERICAN BEAUTY

¾ ounce brandy   Dash grenadine
¾ ounce dry vermouth   3 or 4 ice cubes
¾ ounce orange juice   1 ounce port
Dash white crème de menthe

Combine all ingredients except the port in a cocktail shaker and shake vigorously. Strain into a cocktail glass and carefully float the port on top. Serves 1.

BALTIMORE BRACER

1 ounce brandy   1 egg white
1 ounce anisette   3 or 4 ice cubes

Combine all ingredients in a cocktail shaker and shake vigorously. Strain into a cocktail glass. Serves 1.

BOMBAY

1 ounce brandy   2 dashes curaçao
½ ounce sweet vermouth   1 dash Pernod
½ ounce dry vermouth   3 or 4 ice cubes

Combine all ingredients in a mixing glass and stir well. Strain into a cocktail glass. Serves 1.
    Whip: Use 1 teaspoon curaçao and shake rather than stir the drink.

BOOSTER

2–3 ounces brandy   3 or 4 ice cubes
1 teaspoon curaçao   Nutmeg
1 egg white

Combine first four ingredients in a cocktail shaker and shake vigorously. Strain into a cocktail glass and grate a little nutmeg on top. Serves 1.

BRANDY

2 ounces brandy
½ ounce curaçao
Dash Angostura bitters

3 or 4 ice cubes
Twist lemon peel

Combine all ingredients except lemon peel in a mixing glass and stir well. Strain into a cocktail glass and drop in the lemon peel. Serves 1.

BRANDY GUMP

2–3 ounces brandy
2 dashes grenadine

2 tablespoons lemon juice
3 or 4 ice cubes

Combine all ingredients in a cocktail shaker and shake vigorously. Strain into a cocktail glass. Serves 1.

BRANDY OLD-FASHIONED

1 cube sugar
Dash Angostura bitters
Twist lemon peel

2 or 3 ice cubes
2–3 ounces brandy

Put the sugar cube in an Old-fashioned glass and sprinkle with bitters. Add the lemon peel and ice cubes. Pour in the brandy and stir. Serves 1.

BRANDY SOUR

See "Sours," page 216.

BRANDY VERMOUTH

1½ ounces brandy
½ ounce sweet vermouth

Dash Angostura bitters
3 or 4 ice cubes

Combine all ingredients in a mixing glass and stir well. Strain into a cocktail glass. Serves 1.

This drink is sometimes called **Sink or Swim**.

CARROL

1½ ounces brandy
¾ ounce sweet vermouth

3 or 4 ice cubes
Maraschino cherry

Combine all ingredients except the cherry in a mixing glass and stir well. Strain into a cocktail glass and add the cherry. Serves 1.

CHAMPS ELYSEES

1 ounce cognac
½ ounce yellow chartreuse
1 tablespoon lemon juice

½ teaspoon superfine sugar
Dash Angostura bitters
3 or 4 ice cubes

Combine all ingredients in a cocktail shaker and shake vigorously. Strain into a cocktail glass. Serves 1.

CHARLES

1–1½ ounces brandy
1–1½ ounces sweet
    vermouth

Dash Angostura or orange
    bitters
3 or 4 ice cubes

Combine all ingredients in a mixing glass and stir well. Strain into a cocktail glass. Serves 1.

Metropolitan: Add a dash of sugar syrup.

CHERRY BLOSSOM

1 ounce brandy
1 ounce cherry brandy
¼ teaspoon curaçao

¼ teaspoon grenadine
¼ teaspoon lemon juice
½ cup crushed ice

Combine all ingredients in a cocktail shaker and shake vigorously. Strain into a cocktail glass. Serves 1.

CHICAGO

1 lemon, cut in quarters
Superfine sugar
1½ ounces brandy
Dash curaçao

Dash Angostura bitters
3 or 4 ice cubes
Iced champagne

Rub the rim of a chilled cocktail glass with the lemon and dip into sugar to frost. Combine the brandy, curaçao, bitters and ice cubes in a mixing glass and stir well. Pour into the prepared glass and fill with champagne. Serves 1.

CLASSIC

1 lemon, cut in quarters
Superfine sugar
1 ounce brandy
½ ounce curaçao

½ ounce maraschino
1 tablespoon lemon juice
3 or 4 ice cubes
Twist lemon peel

Rub the rim of a chilled cocktail glass with the lemon and dip into sugar to frost. Combine all remaining ingredients except the peel in a mixing glass and stir well. Strain into the prepared glass. Twist the lemon peel over the drink to release the oil and then drop the peel into the glass. Serves 1.

COFFEE NO. 2

This drink does not contain any coffee but derives its name from its coffee color.

1½ ounces brandy
¾ ounce port
2 dashes curaçao
2 dashes sugar syrup

1 egg yolk
3 or 4 ice cubes
Nutmeg

Combine all ingredients except nutmeg in a cocktail shaker and shake vigorously. Strain into a cocktail glass and grate a little nutmeg on top. Serves 1.

COGNAC WITH CASSIS

2 or 3 ice cubes   1 teaspoon crème de cassis
2 ounces cognac

Put ice cubes in an Old-fashioned glass and pour in the cognac. Add crème de cassis and stir lightly. Serves 1.

CORONATION NO. 2

1½ ounces brandy   Dash white crème de menthe
¾ ounce curaçao   3 or 4 ice cubes
Dash peach bitters

Combine all ingredients in a mixing glass and stir well. Strain into a cocktail glass. Serves 1.

CUBAN NO. 1

1½ ounces brandy   2 tablespoons lemon juice
¾ ounce apricot brandy   3 or 4 ice cubes

Combine all ingredients in a mixing glass and stir well. Strain into a cocktail glass. Serves 1.

CRUSTAS

All crustas are made the same way, with applejack, brandy, gin, rum or whiskey as a base. The Brandy Crusta is probably the most popular.

Basic Recipe

Cut lemon   Dash Angostura bitters
Superfine sugar   1 teaspoon maraschino
Rind of a lemon or orange   1 teaspoon lemon juice
   cut in a spiral   1½ to 3 ounces liquor
Maraschino cherry   Slice of orange (optional)
3 or 4 ice cubes

Rub the rim of a 4-ounce cocktail glass or wineglass with lemon and dip into sugar. Put the lemon or orange rind and the cherry into the glass. Combine ice, bitters, maraschino, lemon juice and liquor in a mixing glass and stir. Strain into the prepared glass. Add a slice of orange. Serves 1.

DEAUVILLE

½ ounce brandy
½ ounce calvados or
   applejack

½ ounce Cointreau
1 tablespoon lemon juice
3 or 4 ice cubes

Combine all ingredients in a mixing glass and stir well. Strain into a cocktail glass. Serves 1.

EAST INDIA

1½ ounces brandy
¼ ounce pineapple juice
¼ ounce curaçao

Dash Angostura bitters
3 or 4 ice cubes

Combine all ingredients in a mixing glass and stir well. Strain into a cocktail glass. Serves 1.

EGG SOUR

1–1½ ounces brandy
1–1½ ounces curaçao
2 tablespoons lemon juice

1 teaspoon superfine sugar
1 egg
3 or 4 ice cubes

Combine all ingredients in a cocktail shaker and shake vigorously. Strain into a cocktail glass. Serves 1.

FANCY BRANDY

2 ounces brandy
¼ teaspoon curaçao
¼ teaspoon superfine sugar

Dash Angostura bitters
½ cup cracked ice
Twist lemon peel

Combine all ingredients except the peel in a cocktail shaker and shake vigorously. Strain into a cocktail glass and drop in the lemon peel. Serves 1.

Fancy Whiskey and **Fancy Gin** cocktails are made the same way, substituting whiskey or gin for brandy.

FANTASIO

1 ounce brandy	1 teaspoon white crème de
¾ ounce dry vermouth	menthe
1 teaspoon maraschino	3 or 4 ice cubes

Combine all ingredients in a mixing glass and stir well. Strain into a cocktail glass. Serves 1.

FROUPE

1 ounce brandy	1 teaspoon Benedictine
1 ounce sweet vermouth	3 or 4 ice cubes

Combine all ingredients in a mixing glass and stir well. Strain into a cocktail glass. Serves 1.

This drink is also known as a **Rock-a-Bye.**

GAZETTE

1 ounce brandy	1 teaspoon sugar syrup
1 ounce sweet vermouth	3 or 4 ice cubes
1 teaspoon lemon juice	

Combine all ingredients in a mixing glass and stir well. Strain into a cocktail glass. Serves 1.

HARVARD

1½ ounces brandy	1 teaspoon grenadine
¾ ounce sweet vermouth	2 teaspoons lemon juice
Dash Angostura bitters	3 or 4 ice cubes

Combine all ingredients in a mixing glass and stir well. Strain into a cocktail glass. Serves 1.

This drink is sometimes made without the grenadine and lemon juice—in which case, use 2 dashes of bitters and a dash of sugar syrup.

LADY BE GOOD

1 ounce brandy
½ ounce white crème de menthe

½ ounce sweet vermouth
½ cup cracked ice

Combine all ingredients in a cocktail shaker and shake vigorously. Strain into a cocktail glass. Serves 1.

Cold Deck: Stir with ice cubes in a mixing glass rather than shake.

LUXURY

2 3 ounces brandy
2 dashes orange bitters

3 ounces chilled champagne

Combine all ingredients in a large saucer champagne glass and stir gently. Serves 1.

MORNING

1 ounce brandy
1 ounce dry vermouth
2 dashes Pernod
2 dashes maraschino

2 dashes curaçao
2 dashes orange bitters
3 or 4 ice cubes
Maraschino cherry

Combine all ingredients except the cherry in a mixing glass and stir well. Strain into a cocktail glass and add cherry. Serves 1.

NETHERLAND

Cut of lemon
Superfine sugar
1½ ounces brandy
2 dashes curaçao

2 dashes orange bitters
3 or 4 ice cubes
Twist lemon peel

Rub the rim of a cocktail glass with lemon and dip rim into sugar to frost. Combine all ingredients except the lemon peel in a mixing glass and stir well. Strain into the prepared glass and drop in the twist of peel. Serves 1.

Mrs. Solomon: Use Angostura bitters instead of orange bitters.

NEWTON'S SPECIAL

1½ ounces brandy
½ ounce Cointreau

Dash Angostura bitters
3 or 4 ice cubes

Combine all ingredients in a mixing glass and stir well. Strain into a cocktail glass. Serves 1.

NONE BUT THE BRAVE

1½ ounces brandy
¾ ounce Pimento Dram
1 teaspoon superfine sugar

Dash Jamaica ginger
Dash lemon juice
3 or 4 ice cubes

Combine all ingredients in a cocktail shaker and shake vigorously. Strain into a cocktail glass. Serves 1.

OLYMPIC

¾ ounce brandy
¾ ounce curaçao

¾ ounce orange juice
3 or 4 ice cubes

Combine all ingredients in a mixing glass and stir well. Strain into a cocktail glass. Serves 1.

PHOEBE SNOW

1 ounce brandy
1 ounce Dubonnet

Dash Pernod
3 or 4 ice cubes

Combine all ingredients in a mixing glass and stir well. Strain into a cocktail glass. Serves 1.

PISCO SOUR

2 ounces Pisco (Peruvian brandy)
1 teaspoon superfine sugar
1 teaspoon lime or lemon juice

1 tablespoon egg white
3 or 4 ice cubes
2 or 3 dashes Angostura bitters

Combine all ingredients except the bitters in a cocktail shaker and shake very thoroughly. Strain into a sour glass and shake bitters on top. Serves 1. (For other sours, see page 130.)

POOP DECK

1 ounce brandy
½ ounce blackberry brandy

½ ounce port
3 or 4 ice cubes

Combine all ingredients in a cocktail shaker and shake vigorously. Strain into a cocktail glass. Serves 1.
This drink is also known as a **Let's Slide.**

PRESTO

1½ ounces brandy
¾ ounce sweet vermouth
Dash Pernod

Dash orange juice
3 or 4 ice cubes

Combine all ingredients in a mixing glass and stir well. Strain into a cocktail glass. Serves 1.

QUEEN ELIZABETH NO. 2

1–1½ ounces brandy
1–1½ ounces sweet
  vermouth

Dash curaçao
3 or 4 ice cubes
Maraschino cherry (optional)

Combine all ingredients except the cherry in a mixing glass. Stir well and strain into a cocktail glass. Add cherry. Serves 1.

QUELLE VIE

1½ ounces brandy
¾ ounce kümmel

3 or 4 ice cubes

Combine all ingredients in a mixing glass and stir well. Strain into a cocktail glass. Serves 1.

SARATOGA NO. 1

2–3 ounces brandy
2 dashes maraschino
2 dashes Angostura bitters
½ teaspoon pineapple syrup

or
¼ slice pineapple, coarsely
  chopped
3 or 4 ice cubes

Combine all ingredients in a cocktail shaker and shake vigorously. Strain into a cocktail glass. Serves 1.

SAUCY SUE NO. 2

1 ounce brandy
1 ounce calvados or
  applejack
Dash apricot brandy

Dash Pernod
3 or 4 ice cubes
Twist orange peel

Combine the first five ingredients in a mixing glass and stir well. Strain into a cocktail glass and twist the orange peel over the drink to release the oil, then drop peel in. Serves 1.
  Lugger: Omit Pernod.

SIDECAR

2 ounces brandy
½ ounce Cointreau or
Triple Sec

3 or 4 ice cubes
½ ounce lemon juice

Combine all ingredients in a cocktail shaker and shake vigorously. Strain into a cocktail glass. This can also be served as an after-dinner drink. Serves 1.

SIR WALTER

1½ ounces brandy
¾ ounce light rum
1 teaspoon curaçao

1 teaspoon grenadine
1 teaspoon lemon juice
3 or 4 ice cubes

Combine all ingredients in a cocktail shaker and shake vigorously. Strain into a cocktail glass. Serves 1.

THIRD RAIL NO. 2

¾ ounce brandy
¾ ounce calvados or
applejack

¾ ounce light rum
Dash Pernod
3 or 4 ice cubes

Combine all ingredients in a cocktail shaker and shake vigorously. Strain into a cocktail glass. Serves 1.

This drink, also known as a **Sledge Hammer,** is sometimes made with a darker rum.

Special Rough: Same recipe without the rum.

THUNDER

2–3 ounces brandy
1 egg yolk
1 teaspoon sugar syrup

Pinch cayenne pepper
3 or 4 ice cubes

Combine all ingredients in a cocktail shaker and shake vigorously. Strain into a cocktail glass. Serves 1.

This is sometimes called a **Thunder and Lightning.**

VANDERBILT HOTEL

1½ ounces brandy	2 dashes sugar syrup
½ ounce cherry brandy	3 or 4 ice cubes
2 dashes Angostura bitters	

Combine all ingredients in a mixing glass and stir well. Strain into a cocktail glass. Serves 1.

This is sometimes called simply a **Vanderbilt.**

WATERBURY

2–3 ounces brandy	½ teaspoon superfine sugar
1 egg white	2 dashes grenadine
1 tablespoon lemon juice	3 or 4 ice cubes

Combine all ingredients in a cocktail shaker and shake vigorously. Strain into a cocktail glass. Serves 1.

WHITE WAY NO. 1

¾ ounce brandy	¾ ounce Pernod
¾ ounce anisette	3 or 4 ice cubes

Combine all ingredients in a mixing glass and stir well. Strain into a cocktail glass. Serves 1.

WILLIAM OF ORANGE

1½ ounces brandy	¾ ounce orange bitters
¾ ounce curaçao	3 or 4 ice cubes

Combine all ingredients in a mixing glass and stir well. Strain into a cocktail glass. Serves 1.

Dream: Substitute dash of Pernod for the orange bitters.

CHAMPAGNE COCKTAILS

ALFONSO COCKTAIL

1 cube sugar	1 ounce Dubonnet
Dash Angostura bitters	4 ounces chilled champagne
1 cube ice	Twist lemon peel

Put the sugar in a large saucer champagne glass and sprinkle it with the bitters. Add ice cube and Dubonnet and fill with champagne. Drop in the lemon peel. Serves 1.

CHAMPAGNE CASSIS

1 bottle inexpensive champagne, well chilled	Crème de cassis

Pour the champagne into chilled saucer champagne glasses and add a few drops of crème de cassis to each glass. Serves 6.

CHAMPAGNE COCKTAIL NO. 1

1 lump sugar	4 ounces chilled champagne
1 or 2 dashes Angostura bitters	Twist lemon or orange peel

Place the sugar in a champagne glass and moisten with bitters. Fill glass with champagne; garnish with the peel. Serves 1.

This cocktail is sometimes called a **London Special.**

CHAMPAGNE COCKTAIL NO. 2

1 ounce Southern Comfort   4 ounces chilled champagne
Dash Angostura bitters   Twist lemon peel

Pour the Southern Comfort into a champagne glass, add bitters and champagne and garnish with the lemon peel. Serves 1.

CHAMPAGNE COCKTAIL NO. 3

1 ounce brandy   Twist orange peel
4 ounces chilled champagne

Pour brandy into a champagne glass, fill with champagne, twist the orange peel over it to release the oil, then drop the peel into the glass. Serves 1.

CHAMPAGNE COCKTAIL NO. 4

1 lump sugar   1 ounce cognac
2 to 3 dashes Angostura   4 ounces chilled champagne
  bitters

Place the sugar in a champagne glass and moisten thoroughly with bitters. Add the cognac and pour on the champagne. Serves 1.

This cocktail is sometimes called an **Ambrosia.**

CHAMPAGNE COCKTAIL NO. 5

2 small sugar cubes   1 ounce crème de cacao
1 ounce Benedictine   4 ounces champagne

Soak the sugar cubes separately, one in Benedictine, one in crème de cacao, and place them in the bottom of a champagne flute. Fill with chilled champagne, preferably brut.

MIMOSA

1 ice cube
¼ cup orange juice

4 ounces champagne

Place the ice cube in an 8-ounce wineglass, add the orange juice, pour in the champagne and stir. Serves 1.
This is sometimes called a **California Sunshine.**

PINK CALIFORNIA SUNSHINE

4 ounces chilled pink
  champagne

4 ounces chilled orange juice
Dash crème de cassis

Pour the champagne into a saucer champagne glass. Add the orange juice and cassis. Serves 1.

SOYER AU CHAMPAGNE

1 heaping tablespoon vanilla
  ice cream
2 dashes maraschino
2 dashes curaçao

2 dashes brandy
4 ounces chilled champagne
Slice orange
Maraschino cherry

Put the ice cream in the bottom of a large saucer champagne glass, add maraschino, curaçao and brandy and stir gently. Pour in the champagne and decorate with the orange and cherry. Serves 1.

GIN COCKTAILS

Without question, the Martini is the best-known gin cocktail. Some like it almost sweet, some like it very dry, some like it with a lemon peel or olive, others with neither, and still others with a tiny onion—in which case it's called a Gibson. Some want it "straight up" (poured into a cocktail glass without ice) and some want it "on the rocks" in an Old-fashioned glass. However they prefer it, Martini enthusiasts are legion. This is undoubtedly because the famed juniper-flavored spirit and the popular aromatized wine are a first-rate combination, so much so that innumerable cocktails are based on them. In fact, it soon becomes apparent that a number of key recipes calling for specific measures of gin and dry vermouth or both turn up again and again under different names, with only very minor changes in ingredients. In an effort to simplify your drink-mixing activities and also to make them more fun, all "anchor-man" recipes are followed by a list of those cocktails that are made so nearly the same way that only the briefest directions need be given for each. As a result, once you find the gin-vermouth formula you like, you can ring changes on it easily, and earn a fine reputation for bartending know-how.

Take, for example, a cocktail aptly named a Trinity, which consists of ¾ ounce each of gin and dry and sweet vermouth. Five near-relatives follow, because they require only the simple addition of a splash of this or a slice of that. Again, starting with a base of 3 parts gin and 1 part dry vermouth, you can produce nine different cocktails by dint of mere dollops and dashes. All are grouped under the recipe for a Golf. Don't be misled, however, into thinking that such slight variations cannot make enough flavor change to be worth your while. They can—and they do. Should you want more pronounced differences, the cocktail called a Favorite could be your answer. It's essentially 1 part gin, 1 part vermouth, and the third part is apricot brandy. But six variations give you as many chances to use the same measures, principally by switching the last third to rum, peach or cherry brandy, Pernod or crème de cassis. Needless to say, such changes make themselves noticed far more conspicuously than do squirts or splashes! However, where these little fillips are called for, be sure to include them.

The Bronx is yet another gin and vermouth drink, and a favorite with many, but its neighbors are quite individual. One calls for the white of an egg, for instance, and another for the yolk. This kind of shift not only changes flavor; it alters character. A drink made with any part of an egg is opaque rather than clear; its texture and substance are more pronounced; it should always be shaken vigorously rather than stirred.

Besides the numerous partnerships of gin and vermouth in cocktails, you will find others that are less familiar but perhaps more venturesome. One such is the Zaza and its satellites; all are concocted with equal parts of gin and Dubonnet. And just for a new angle on an old liquor, a handful of gin-based cocktails in this section are made with sloe gin, which is really a liqueur and only a very distant cousin of that dependable, familiar, dry gin.

ABBEY

1½ ounces gin
2 tablespoons orange juice
Dash orange bitters

2 or 3 ice cubes
Maraschino cherry

Combine all ingredients in a cocktail shaker and shake vigorously. Strain into a cocktail glass; decorate with cherry. Serves 1.

ALASKA

1½ ounces gin
¾ ounce yellow chartreuse

2 dashes orange bitters
3 or 4 ice cubes

Combine all ingredients in a mixing glass and stir well. Strain into a cocktail glass. Serves 1.

Emerald Isle: Substitute green chartreuse for yellow chartreuse.

ALEXANDER NO. 2

1 ounce gin	½ ounce heavy cream
½ ounce crème de cacao	3 or 4 ice cubes

Combine all ingredients in a cocktail shaker and shake vigorously. Strain into a cocktail glass. Serves 1.

Alexander's Sister: Substitute ½ ounce green crème de menthe for the crème de cacao.

ALLEN

1½ ounces gin	Dash lemon juice
¾ ounce maraschino	3 or 4 ice cubes

Combine all ingredients in a mixing glass and stir well. Strain into a cocktail glass. Serves 1.

ALLIES

1 ounce gin	2 dashes kümmel
1 ounce dry vermouth	3 or 4 ice cubes

Combine all ingredients in a mixing glass and stir well. Strain into a cocktail glass. Serves 1.

Elegant: Substitute Grand Marnier for kümmel.

ARTILLERY

1½ ounces gin	3 or 4 ice cubes
½ ounce sweet vermouth	Twist lemon peel
2 dashes Angostura bitters	

Combine all ingredients except lemon peel in a mixing glass and stir well. Strain into a cocktail glass and drop in the lemon peel. Serves 1.

Moulin Rouge: Substitute sloe gin for gin. Omit lemon peel.
Sunshine No. 1: Use orange peel instead of lemon peel.

BACHELOR'S BAIT

2 ounces gin
½ teaspoon grenadine
Dash orange bitters

1 egg white
3 or 4 ice cubes

Combine all ingredients in a cocktail shaker and shake vigorously. Strain into a cocktail glass. Serves 1.
Beauty Spot: Omit orange bitters.

BARBARY COAST

1 ounce gin
1 ounce Scotch whiskey
1 ounce crème de cacao

1 ounce cream
3 or 4 ice cubes

Combine all ingredients in a cocktail shaker and shake vigorously. Strain into an Old-fashioned glass. Serves 1.

BARNUM

1½ ounces gin
½ ounce apricot brandy
2 dashes Angostura bitters

1 dash lemon juice
3 or 4 ice cubes

Combine all ingredients in a cocktail shaker and shake vigorously. Strain into a cocktail glass. Serves 1.

BEE'S KNEES

1½ ounces gin
1 teaspoon honey

1 tablespoon lemon juice
3 or 4 ice cubes

Combine all ingredients in a cocktail shaker and shake vigorously. Strain into a cocktail glass. Serves 1.

BELMONT

2 ounces gin
½ ounce grenadine or
raspberry syrup

¾ ounce heavy cream
3 or 4 ice cubes

Combine all ingredients in a cocktail shaker and shake vigorously. Strain into a cocktail glass. Serves 1.

BENNETT

2 ounces gin
2 tablespoons lime juice
1 teaspoon superfine sugar

2 dashes Angostura or
orange bitters
3 or 4 ice cubes

Combine all ingredients in a cocktail shaker and shake vigorously. Strain into a cocktail glass. Serves 1.

BERMUDA ROSE

1½ ounces gin
Dash grenadine
Dash apricot brandy

1 tablespoon lime or lemon
juice
3 or 4 ice cubes

Combine all ingredients in a cocktail shaker and shake vigorously. Strain into a cocktail glass. Serves 1.

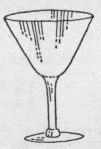

BIFFY

1½ ounces gin
¾ ounce Swedish Punch

1½ tablespoons lemon juice
3 or 4 ice cubes

Combine all ingredients in a mixing glass and stir well. Strain into a cocktail glass. Serves 1.

BISHOP'S COCKTAIL

2 ounces gin
2 ounces Stone's ginger wine

2 or 3 ice cubes

Combine all ingredients in a mixing glass and stir well. Strain into a cocktail glass. Serves 1.

BLACKTHORN NO. 2

1–1½ ounces sloe gin
1–1½ ounces sweet vermouth
2 dashes orange bitters

3 or 4 ice cubes
Twist lemon peel
Maraschino cherry

Combine all ingredients except the lemon peel and cherry in a mixing glass. Stir well and strain into a cocktail glass. Decorate with peel and cherry. Serves 1.

BLUE DEVIL

1½ ounces dry gin
¾ ounce maraschino
¾ ounce lime or lemon juice
½ teaspoon Crème Yvette
   or

Dash of blue vegetable coloring
3 or 4 ice cubes

Combine all ingredients in a cocktail shaker. Strain into a cocktail glass. Serves 1.

Blue Train No. 1: Substitute Cointreau for maraschino.

BLUEBIRD

2–3 ounces gin
4 dashes Angostura bitters
4 dashes curaçao

3 or 4 ice cubes
Twist lemon peel
Maraschino cherry

Combine all ingredients except the lemon peel and cherry in a mixing glass and stir well. Strain into a cocktail glass and decorate with the peel and cherry. Serves 1.

BRONX

1½ ounces gin
½ ounce dry vermouth
½ ounce sweet vermouth

2 tablespoons orange juice
3 or 4 ice cubes

Combine all ingredients in a mixing glass and stir well. Strain into a cocktail glass. Serves 1.

Bronx Golden: Add 1 egg yolk and shake rather than stir.

Bronx Silver or **Oriental:** Add 1 egg white and shake rather than stir.

Dry Bronx: Omit the sweet vermouth.

BUBY

2 ounces gin
2 ounces lemon juice

1 teaspoon grenadine
3 or 4 ice cubes

Combine all ingredients in a cocktail shaker and shake vigorously. Strain into a cocktail glass. Serves 1.

BULLSHOT

2 or 3 ice cubes
1½–2 ounces gin

3 ounces chilled beef bouillon

Put ice cubes in an Old-fashioned glass. Add gin and bouillon and stir gently. Serves 1.

Vodka may be used instead of gin.

BUNNY HUG OR EARTHQUAKE

¾ ounce gin	¾ ounce Pernod
¾ ounce whiskey	3 or 4 ice cubes

Combine all ingredients in a cocktail shaker and shake vigorously. Strain into a cocktail glass. Serves 1.

CABARET NO. 2

1½ ounces gin	2 dashes Angostura bitters
½ teaspoon dry vermouth	3 or 4 ice cubes
¼ teaspoon Benedictine	Maraschino cherry

Combine all ingredients except the cherry in a mixing glass and stir well. Strain into a cocktail glass and garnish with the cherry. Serves 1.

CAFE DE PARIS

2 ounces gin	1 egg white
3 dashes Pernod	3 or 4 ice cubes
1 teaspoon heavy cream	

Combine all ingredients in a cocktail shaker and shake vigorously. Strain into a cocktail glass. Serves 1.

CARUSO

1 ounce gin	1 ounce green crème de
1 ounce dry vermouth	menthe
	3 or 4 ice cubes

Combine all ingredients in a mixing glass and stir well. Strain into a cocktail glass. Serves 1.

CASINO

2 ounces gin
½ teaspoon maraschino
2 dashes orange bitters

2 dashes lemon juice
3 or 4 ice cubes

Combine all ingredients in a mixing glass and stir well. Strain into a cocktail glass. Serves 1.

CHANTICLEER

2–3 ounces gin
2 tablespoons lemon juice
1 tablespoon raspberry
syrup

1 egg white
3 or 4 ice cubes

Combine all ingredients in a cocktail shaker and shake vigorously. Strain into a cocktail glass. Serves 1.

CHAPPELLE

2 slices fresh pineapple
1 ounce gin
1 ounce sweet vermouth

2 tablespoons lime juice
3 or 4 ice cubes

Muddle the pineapple in a cocktail shaker. Add remaining ingredients and shake vigorously. Strain into a cocktail glass. Serves 1.

CHELSEA SIDECAR

1½ ounces gin
¾ ounce Triple Sec

1 tablespoon lemon juice
½ cup crushed ice

Combine all ingredients in a cocktail shaker and shake vigorously. Strain into a cocktail glass. Serves 1.

CHOCOLATE SOLDIER

1½ ounces gin
¾ ounce Dubonnet

1 tablespoon lime juice
3 or 4 ice cubes

Combine all ingredients in a cocktail shaker and shake vigorously. Strain into a cocktail glass. Serves 1.

CLOVER CLUB

1½ ounces gin
½ ounce grenadine
2 tablespoons lime juice

1 egg white
3 or 4 ice cubes

Combine all ingredients in a cocktail shaker and shake vigorously. Strain into a cocktail glass. Serves 1.

Clover Leaf: Float a mint leaf on top of the drink.

Cornell: Omit grenadine and lime juice. Add 1 teaspoon maraschino.

Froth Blower: Reduce grenadine to 1 teaspoon. Omit lime juice.

CLUB

1½ ounces gin
½ ounce sweet vermouth

3 or 4 ice cubes
Maraschino cherry or olive

Combine gin, vermouth and ice in a mixing glass and stir well. Strain into a cocktail glass and add the cherry or olive. Serves 1.

Bronx River: Add 1 tablespoon lemon juice and ¼ teaspoon superfine sugar. Omit garnish.

Homestead: Substitute slice of orange for cherry or olive.

Ideal: Add ¼ teaspoon maraschino and 1 tablespoon grapefruit juice. Shake rather than stir. Omit garnish.

Jeyplak: Add 2 dashes Pernod. Garnish with a cherry.

COLONIAL OR GRAPEFRUIT

1½ ounces gin
½ ounce grapefruit juice

1 teaspoon maraschino
3 or 4 ice cubes

Combine all ingredients in a cocktail shaker and shake vigorously. Strain into a cocktail glass. Serves 1.

Seventh Heaven No. 2: Use ½ ounce maraschino and 1 tablespoon grapefruit juice. Garnish with a sprig of fresh mint.

Southern Bride: Increase grapefruit juice to ¾ ounce.

COMMERCIAL CLUB GIN OLD FASHIONED

1½ ounces gin
2 dashes grenadine
Dash Angostura bitters
1 teaspoon coconut cream

Dash curaçao
½ cup crushed ice
3 or 4 ice cubes

Combine all ingredients except the ice cubes in a cocktail shaker and shake vigorously. Strain into an Old-fashioned glass filled with ice cubes. The coconut cream makes a delicious white foam on top of the drink and adds smoothness. Serves 1.

CRIMSON

2 ounces gin
2 teaspoons lemon juice
1 teaspoon grenadine

3 or 4 ice cubes
1 ounce port

Combine all ingredients except the port in a cocktail shaker and shake vigorously. Strain into a cocktail glass and carefully float the port on top. Serves 1.

DAMN THE WEATHER

1 ounce gin
½ ounce sweet vermouth
1 teaspoon curaçao

½ ounce orange juice
3 or 4 ice cubes

Combine all ingredients in a cocktail shaker and shake vigorously. Strain into a cocktail glass. Serves 1.

DEMPSEY

1 ounce gin
1 ounce calvados or
   applejack

2 dashes Pernod
2 dashes grenadine
3 or 4 ice cubes

Combine all ingredients in a mixing glass and stir well. Strain into a cocktail glass. Serves 1.

DERBY NO. 1

1½ ounces gin
2 dashes peach bitters

3 or 4 ice cubes
2 sprigs mint

Combine all ingredients except the mint in a cocktail shaker and shake well. Strain into a cocktail glass and garnish with mint sprigs. Serves 1.

DIXIE

¾ ounce gin
½ ounce Pernod
½ ounce dry vermouth

2 dashes grenadine
2 tablespoons orange juice
3 or 4 ice cubes

Combine all ingredients in a cocktail shaker and shake vigorously. Strain into a cocktail glass. Serves 1.

ECLIPSE

Maraschino cherry or ripe
   olive
½ ounce grenadine
   (approx.)

1½–2 ounces sloe gin
¾–1 ounce gin
3 or 4 ice cubes
Twist orange peel

Drop the cherry or olive into a cocktail glass and pour enough grenadine over it to cover. Combine the gins in a cocktail shaker with the ice and shake vigorously, then strain into the cocktail glass, pouring very carefully so that the gins do not mix with the grenadine. Twist the orange peel over the drink to release the oil before dropping the peel in. Serves 1.

ELK

1 ounce dry gin	2 dashes dry vermouth
1 ounce Prunelle	3 or 4 ice cubes

Combine all ingredients in a cocktail shaker and shake vigorously. Strain into a cocktail glass. Serves 1.

FAIRY BELLE

2 ounces gin	1 egg white
½ ounce apricot brandy	3 or 4 ice cubes
1 teaspoon grenadine	

Combine all ingredients in a cocktail shaker and shake vigorously. Strain into a cocktail glass. Serves 1.

FALLEN ANGEL

3 ounces gin	Dash Angostura bitters
4 tablespoons lemon or lime juice	Maraschino cherry
2 dashes green crème de menthe	

Combine all ingredients except the cherry in a mixing glass and stir well. Strain into a cocktail glass and decorate with cherry. Serves 1.

FARMER'S

1 ounce gin	2 dashes Angostura bitters
½ ounce dry vermouth	½ cup crushed ice
½ ounce sweet vermouth	

Combine all ingredients in a mixing glass and stir well. Strain into a cocktail glass. Serves 1.

Bloodhound: Omit bitters. Add 2 or 3 crushed strawberries.

Cooperstown: Omit bitters and garnish with a sprig of mint.

Maurice: Add 2 tablespoons orange juice.

Smiler: Add dash orange bitters.

Tago: Omit bitters. Add ½ teaspoon curaçao, 2 tablespoons orange juice.

FAVORITE

¾–1 ounce gin
¾–1 ounce dry vermouth
¾–1 ounce apricot brandy

Dash lemon juice
3 or 4 ice cubes

Combine all ingredients in a mixing glass and stir well. Strain into a cocktail glass. Serves 1.

This is also called a **Darb.**

Brown: Substitute light rum for the apricot brandy.

Judgette: Substitute peach brandy for apricot brandy; and lime juice for lemon juice. Garnish, if you like, with a maraschino cherry.

Knockout: Substitute Pernod for apricot brandy, and 1 teaspoon white crème de menthe for the lemon juice. Garnish with mint leaves.

Parisian or **Cocktail Maison:** Substitute crème de cassis for apricot brandy. Omit lemon juice.

Peter Pan: Substitute peach brandy for apricot brandy, and ¾ ounce orange juice for lemon juice. Shake rather than stir.

Royal No. 2: Substitute cherry for apricot brandy. Omit lemon juice.

FERNET BRANCA

2 ounces gin
½ ounce sweet vermouth

½ ounce Fernet Branca
3 or 4 ice cubes

Combine all ingredients in a mixing glass and stir well. Strain into a cocktail glass. Serves 1.

FIFTY-FIFTY

1–1½ ounces gin   ½ cup cracked ice or 2 or
1–1½ ounces dry vermouth   3 ice cubes
                   Olive

Combine gin, vermouth and ice in a mixing glass, stir well and strain into a cocktail glass. Drop in the olive. Serves 1.

Bronx Terrace: Add 2 tablespoons lime juice and 1 teaspoon superfine sugar. Omit olive. Shake rather than stir.

Imperial: Add a dash each maraschino and Angostura bitters.

Silver: Add a dash each maraschino and orange bitters. Substitute orange peel for olive.

Wallick: Add 4 dashes orange-flower water. Omit olive.

FINE AND DANDY

1½ ounces gin   Dash Angostura bitters
½ ounce Cointreau   3 or 4 ice cubes
½ ounce lemon juice   Maraschino cherry

Combine all ingredients except the cherry in a mixing glass and stir well. Strain into a cocktail glass; add cherry. Serves 1.

Queen Elizabeth No. 2: Substitute Pernod for Angostura bitters and omit cherry.

FRANKENJACK

1 ounce gin   ½ ounce Cointreau
1 ounce dry vermouth   3 to 4 ice cubes
½ ounce apricot brandy   Maraschino cherry

Combine all ingredients except the cherry in a mixing glass and stir well. Strain into a cocktail glass and drop in cherry. Serves 1.

This is also called a **Claridge.**

GIBSON

This drink is simply a dry Martini with a small cocktail onion added, but the recipe is given here because Gibson is the accepted name.

2½ ounces gin
Dash dry vermouth

3 or 4 ice cubes
Pickled pearl onion

Combine all ingredients except the onion in a mixing glass and stir well. Strain into a cocktail glass; drop in onion. Serves 1.

GILROY

¾ ounce gin
¾ ounce cherry brandy
½ ounce dry vermouth

½ ounce lemon juice
Dash orange bitters
3 or 4 ice cubes

Combine all ingredients in a mixing glass and stir well. Strain into a cocktail glass. Serves 1.

GIMLET

2 ounces gin
2 ounces Rose's lime juice

2 ice cubes

Combine all ingredients in a mixing glass and stir well. Strain into a cocktail glass. Serves 1.

This drink may be served un-iced, although this is unusual today. If fresh lime juice is preferred, add 1 teaspoon sugar to 2 ounces lime juice.

GIN

1½ ounces gin
Dash orange bitters

3 or 4 ice cubes
Twist lemon peel

Combine all ingredients except the peel in a mixing glass and stir well. Strain into a cocktail glass and add the peel. Serves 1.

Come Again: Use 2 dashes peach bitters instead of orange bitters and garnish with a sprig of mint instead of lemon peel.

GIN AND BITTERS

See Pink Gin, pages 179–80.

GIN AND IT

2 ounces gin

1 ounce sweet vermouth

Pour ingredients into a cocktail glass and stir. Serves 1.

Traditionally, no ice is used in this drink. For those who dislike un-iced drinks, pour the gin and vermouth over 2 or 3 ice cubes in an Old-fashioned glass. The "It" in the name refers to Italian (sweet) vermouth. The drink is sometimes called **Gin and Cin** (pronounced "sin") after Cinzano, a popular brand of Italian vermouth.

GIN COCO

This Hawaiian drink can be made wherever fresh coconuts are available—often in Latin-American markets and in tropical regions of the U.S.

Fresh coconut
2 ounces gin

2 or 3 ice cubes

Cut the top off a fresh coconut and pour 4 ounces of the coconut water into an 8-ounce wineglass. Add the gin and ice cubes and stir. Serves 1.

GOLF

1½ ounces gin
½ ounce dry vermouth
2 dashes Angostura bitters

3 or 4 ice cubes
Olive

Combine all ingredients except the olive in a mixing glass and stir well. Strain into a cocktail glass and add olive. Serves 1.

Baron: Omit Angostura bitters and olive. Add 2 dashes sweet vermouth and 6 dashes curaçao. Garnish with lemon peel.

Blenton: Omit olive and garnish with lemon peel and a maraschino cherry.

Du Barry: Add 2 dashes Pernod. Omit olive and garnish with a thin orange slice.

Fare-Thee-Well: Substitute 2 dashes sweet vermouth for Angostura bitters, add ½ teaspoon curaçao and omit olive. Shake rather than stir.

Hasty: Omit Angostura bitters and olive. Add ¼ teaspoon grenadine and a dash of Pernod. Shake rather than stir.

Martinez: Use 1 ounce dry vermouth and add 1½ teaspoons curaçao. Substitute orange bitters for Angostura bitters and omit olive. Shake rather than stir. Vodka may be used instead of gin.

Queen Elizabeth No. 1: Substitute ¼ ounce Benedictine for Angostura bitters and omit olive.

Roslyn: Substitute grenadine for bitters and a twist of lemon peel for olive.

GRAND PASSION

2 ounces gin
1 ounce passion-fruit nectar

Dash Angostura bitters
3 or 4 ice cubes

Combine all ingredients in a mixing glass and stir well. Strain into a cocktail glass. Serves 1.

GREAT SECRET

1½ ounces gin
½ ounce Lillet
Dash Angostura bitters

3 or 4 ice cubes
Twist orange peel

Combine all ingredients except the orange peel in a mixing glass and stir well. Strain into a cocktail glass and add peel. Serves 1.

Eddie Brown: Substitute 2 dashes apricot brandy for Angostura bitters, and lemon peel for orange peel.

GYPSY

1–1½ ounces gin	3 or 4 ice cubes
1–1½ ounces sweet vermouth	Maraschino cherry

Combine all ingredients except the cherry in a mixing glass and stir well. Strain into a cocktail glass and add cherry. Serves 1.

Sandmartin: Add 1 teaspoon green chartreuse and omit cherry.

Newbury: Add 3 dashes curaçao; substitute orange and lemon peel for cherry.

HAWAIIAN NO. 1

1½ ounces gin	1 egg white
¾ ounce pineapple juice	3 or 4 ice cubes
Dash orange bitters	

Combine all ingredients in a cocktail shaker and shake vigorously. Strain into a cocktail glass. Serves 1.

HAWAIIAN NO. 2

2 ounces gin	1 ounce orange juice
1 ounce curaçao	3 or 4 ice cubes

Combine all ingredients in a cocktail shaker and shake vigorously. Strain into a cocktail glass. Serves 1.

HOLLAND HOUSE

1½ ounces gin	1 slice pineapple, coarsely chopped
½ ounce dry vermouth	¼ teaspoon maraschino
1 tablespoon lemon juice	3 or 4 ice cubes

Combine all ingredients in a mixing glass and stir well. Strain into a cocktail glass. Serves 1.

Harlem: Omit vermouth and substitute pineapple juice for lemon juice.

HONOLULU

¾ ounce gin
¾ ounce Benedictine

¾ ounce maraschino
3 or 4 ice cubes

Combine all ingredients in a mixing glass and stir well. Strain into a cocktail glass. Serves 1.

HPW

1½ ounces gin
½ ounce dry vermouth
½ ounce sweet vermouth

3 or 4 ice cubes
Twist orange peel

Combine all ingredients except the peel in a mixing glass and stir well. Strain into a cocktail glass and add peel. Serves 1.

Kup's Indispensable: Add dash Angostura bitters.

JAMAICA GLOW

1½ ounces gin
1 teaspoon Jamaica rum
½ ounce dry red wine

½ ounce orange juice
3 or 4 ice cubes

Combine all ingredients in a cocktail shaker and shake vigorously. Strain into a cocktail glass. Serves 1.

JEWEL OR BIJOU

1 ounce gin
1 ounce sweet vermouth
1 ounce green chartreuse

Dash orange bitters
3 or 4 ice cubes
Twist lemon peel

Combine all ingredients except the peel in a cocktail shaker and shake vigorously. Strain into a cocktail glass. Add peel. Serves 1.

JOCKEY CLUB

2 ounces gin
2 dashes Crème de Noyau
1 dash orange bitters

1 dash Angostura bitters
1/4 teaspoon lemon juice
3 or 4 ice cubes

Combine all ingredients in a mixing glass and stir well. Strain into a large cocktail glass. Serves 1.

JOURNALIST

1 1/2 ounces dry gin
1/4 ounce dry vermouth
2 dashes curaçao

2 dashes lemon juice
Dash Angostura bitters
3 or 4 ice cubes

Combine all ingredients in a mixing glass and stir well. Strain into a cocktail glass. Serves 1.

JUDGE JR.

3/4 ounce gin
3/4 ounce light rum
3/4 ounce lemon juice

1/4 teaspoon grenadine
3 or 4 ice cubes

Combine all ingredients in a cocktail shaker and shake vigorously. Strain into a cocktail glass. Serves 1.

KCB

1 1/2 ounces gin
1/2 ounce kirsch
Dash apricot brandy

Dash lemon juice
3 or 4 ice cubes
Twist lemon peel

Combine all ingredients except the peel in a mixing glass and stir well. Strain into a cocktail glass and add the peel. Serves 1.

KNICKERBOCKER

1½ ounces gin
¾ ounce dry vermouth
Dash sweet vermouth

3 or 4 ice cubes
Twist lemon peel

Combine all ingredients except the peel in a mixing glass and stir well. Strain into a cocktail glass. Twist the peel over the glass to release the oil, then drop the peel in. Serves 1.

LADYFINGER

1 ounce gin
½ ounce kirsch

½ ounce cherry brandy
3 or 4 ice cubes

Combine all ingredients in a mixing glass and stir well. Strain into a cocktail glass. Serves 1.

LEAP YEAR

1½ ounces gin
¼ ounce sweet vermouth
¼ ounce Grand Marnier

Dash lemon juice
3 or 4 ice cubes
Twist lemon peel

Combine all ingredients except the peel in a mixing glass and stir well. Strain into a cocktail glass, twist peel over the drink to release the oil, and then drop the peel in. Serves 1.

LEAVE IT TO ME NO. 2

2 ounces gin
1 teaspoon raspberry syrup
1 teaspoon lemon juice

Dash maraschino
3 or 4 ice cubes

Combine all ingredients in a cocktail shaker and shake vigorously. Strain into a cocktail glass. Serves 1.

LITTLE DEVIL

¾ ounce gin
¾ ounce light rum
¼ ounce Cointreau or
   Triple Sec

¼ ounce lemon juice
3 or 4 ice cubes

Combine all ingredients in a mixing glass and stir well. Strain into a cocktail glass. Serves 1.
Stanley: Substitute grenadine for Cointreau.

LONDON

1½ ounces gin
2 dashes maraschino
2 dashes orange bitters

2 dashes sugar syrup
3 or 4 ice cubes
Twist lemon peel

Combine all ingredients except the lemon peel in a mixing glass and stir well. Strain into a cocktail glass. Drop in peel. Serves 1.

LOUDSPEAKER

¾ ounce gin
1 ounce brandy

¼ ounce lemon juice
3 or 4 ice cubes

Combine all ingredients in a mixing glass and stir well. Strain into a cocktail glass. Serves 1.

LOVE

2 ounces sloe gin
½ teaspoon lemon juice
½ teaspoon raspberry juice

1 egg white
3 or 4 ice cubes

Combine all ingredients in a cocktail shaker and shake vigorously. Strain into a cocktail glass. Serves 1.

MAGNOLIA

2 ounces gin
1 ounce heavy cream
2 tablespoons lemon juice

½ teaspoon grenadine
3 or 4 ice cubes

Combine all ingredients in a cocktail shaker and shake quickly. Strain into a large cocktail glass. Serves 1.
This is also called a **Magnolia Blossom.**

MAIDEN'S BLUSH NO. 1

2 ounces gin
¼ teaspoon lemon juice
1 teaspoon curaçao

1 teaspoon grenadine
3 or 4 ice cubes

Combine all ingredients in a cocktail shaker and shake vigorously. Strain into a cocktail glass. Serves 1.

MAIDEN'S BLUSH NO. 2

1½ ounces gin
¾ ounce Pernod

1 teaspoon grenadine
3 or 4 ice cubes

Combine all ingredients in a mixing glass and stir well. Strain into a cocktail glass. Serves 1.

MAIDEN'S PRAYER NO. 1

¾ ounce gin
¾ ounce Cointreau
¼ ounce lemon juice

¼ ounce orange juice
3 or 4 ice cubes

Combine all ingredients in a mixing glass and stir well. Strain into a cocktail glass. Serves 1.

MAIDEN'S PRAYER NO. 2

¾ ounce gin
¾ ounce Lillet
½ ounce calvados or applejack

½ ounce apricot brandy
3 or 4 ice cubes

Combine all ingredients in a mixing glass and stir well. Strain into a cocktail glass. Serves 1.

MAINBRACE

¾ ounce gin
¾ ounce Triple Sec

¾ ounce grape juice
3 or 4 ice cubes

Combine all ingredients in a cocktail shaker and shake vigorously. Strain into a cocktail glass. Serves 1.

Lasky: Substitute Swedish Punch for Triple Sec.

MARTINI, DRY

2–2½ ounces gin
¼–½ ounce dry vermouth

3 or 4 ice cubes
Twist lemon peel or an olive

Combine all ingredients except the lemon peel or olive in a mixing glass and stir. Strain into a well-chilled cocktail glass. Add either peel or olive. Serves 1.

Vodka may be used instead of gin, in which case the drink is called a **Vodka Martini.**

Martini, Sweet: Reduce gin to 1½ ounces, use ½ ounce dry vermouth, add ½ ounce sweet vermouth. Garnish with olive. For a

Perfect Martini, garnish with a twist of orange peel rather than an olive.

Martini on the Rocks: Put ice in an Old-fashioned glass. Pour in the gin and vermouth and stir. Add lemon peel or olive.

MAYFAIR

1 ounce gin	Dash Pimento Dram
½ ounce apricot brandy	3 or 4 ice cubes
½ ounce orange juice	

Combine all ingredients in a cocktail shaker and shake vigorously. Strain into a cocktail glass. Serves 1.

McCLELLAND

1½ ounces sloe gin	Dash orange bitters
¾ ounce curaçao	3 or 4 ice cubes

Combine all ingredients in a mixing glass and stir well. Strain into a cocktail glass. Serves 1.
Johnnie Mack: Substitute 3 dashes Pernod for orange bitters. Garnish with lemon peel.

MILLION DOLLAR

1½ ounces gin	1 egg white
¾ ounce sweet vermouth	3 or 4 ice cubes
1 teaspoon grenadine	
1 tablespoon pineapple juice	

Combine all ingredients in a cocktail shaker and shake vigorously. Strain into a cocktail glass. Serves 1.
Twin Six: Substitute orange juice for pineapple juice.

MILLIONAIRE NO. 1

1½ ounces gin	1 egg white
¾ ounce Pernod	½ cup crushed ice
Dash anisette	

Combine all ingredients in a cocktail shaker and shake vigorously. Strain into a cocktail glass. Serves 1.

MISSISSIPPI MULE

1½ ounces gin   ¼ ounce lemon juice
¼ ounce crème de cassis 3 or 4 ice cubes

Combine all ingredients in a mixing glass and stir well. Strain into a cocktail glass. Serves 1.

MODERN NO. 1

1½ ounces sloe gin   Dash orange bitters
¾ ounce Scotch whiskey   Dash grenadine
Dash Pernod   3 or 4 ice cubes

Combine all ingredients in a mixing glass and stir well. Strain into a cocktail glass. Serves 1.

MONKEY GLAND

1½ ounces gin   3 dashes grenadine
¾ ounce orange juice   3 or 4 ice cubes
3 dashes Benedictine

Combine all ingredients in a mixing glass and stir well. Strain into a cocktail glass. Serves 1.

MONTMARTRE

1½ ounces gin   3 or 4 ice cubes
½ ounce sweet vermouth   Maraschino cherry
½ ounce Triple Sec

Combine all ingredients except the cherry in a cocktail shaker and shake vigorously. Strain into a cocktail glass; add cherry. Serves 1.

MR. MANHATTAN

1 cube sugar	1 teaspoon orange juice
4 mint leaves	¼ teaspoon lemon juice
3 ounces gin	3 or 4 ice cubes

Moisten the sugar with a little water. Muddle the sugar and mint leaves in a cocktail shaker. Add all other ingredients and shake vigorously. Strain into a cocktail glass. Serves 1.

MULE'S HIND LEG

½ ounce gin	½ ounce apricot brandy
½ ounce applejack	½ ounce maple syrup
½ ounce Benedictine	3 or 4 ice cubes

Combine all ingredients in a mixing glass and stir well. Strain into a cocktail glass. Serves 1.

NAPOLEON

3 ounces gin	Dash Fernet Branca
Dash Dubonnet	3 or 4 ice cubes
Dash curaçao	Twist lemon peel

Combine all ingredients except the peel in a mixing glass and stir well. Strain into a cocktail glass. Twist the peel over the drink to release the oil and then drop the peel in. Serves 1.

NIGHTMARE

¾ ounce gin	½ ounce orange juice
¾ ounce Dubonnet	3 or 4 ice cubes
½ ounce cherry brandy	

Combine all ingredients in a cocktail shaker and shake well. Strain into a cocktail glass. Serves 1.

NINETEEN NO. 2

¾ ounce gin
¾ ounce kirsch
¾ ounce dry vermouth
Dash Angostura bitters

¼ teaspoon sugar syrup
3 or 4 ice cubes
Maraschino cherry

Combine all ingredients except the cherry in a mixing glass and stir well. Strain into a cocktail glass; add cherry. Serves 1.

OPAL

1 ounce gin
½ ounce Triple Sec
½ ounce orange juice
¼ teaspoon superfine sugar

½ teaspoon orange flower water
3 or 4 ice cubes

Combine all ingredients in a cocktail shaker and shake vigorously. Strain into a cocktail glass. Serves 1.

OPERA

1½ ounces gin
¼ ounce Dubonnet
¼ ounce maraschino

3 or 4 ice cubes
Twist orange peel

Combine all ingredients except the peel in a mixing glass and stir well. Strain into a cocktail glass. Twist the peel over the drink to release the oil and then drop the peel in. Serves 1.

ORANGE BLOOM

1 ounce gin
½ ounce sweet vermouth
½ ounce Cointreau

3 or 4 ice cubes
Maraschino cherry

Combine all ingredients except the cherry in a mixing glass and stir well. Strain into a cocktail glass and add cherry. Serves 1.

ORANGE BLOSSOM

1½ ounces gin
2 tablespoons orange juice

Pinch superfine sugar
(optional)
3 or 4 ice cubes

Combine all ingredients in a cocktail shaker and shake vigorously. Strain into a cocktail glass. Serves 1.

This is also known as a **Golden Gate.**

Abbey: Add a dash of orange bitters and garnish with a maraschino cherry.

PALM BEACH

1½ ounces gin
¼ ounce sweet vermouth
½ tablespoon grapefruit
juice

3 or 4 ice cubes

Combine all ingredients in a cocktail shaker and shake vigorously. Strain into a cocktail glass. Serves 1.

PARADISE

1 ounce gin
1 ounce apricot brandy

2 tablespoons orange juice
3 or 4 ice cubes

Combine all ingredients in a mixing glass and stir well. Strain into a cocktail glass. Serves 1.

PING-PONG

1 ounce sloe gin
1 ounce Crème Yvette

1 tablespoon lemon juice
3 or 4 ice cubes

Combine all ingredients in a cocktail shaker and shake vigorously. Strain into a cocktail glass. Serves 1.

PINK GIN

2 dashes Angostura bitters
2 ounces gin

2 ounces water, or 2 or
3 ice cubes

Pour the bitters into an 8-ounce wineglass and swill them around it. Add the gin and dilute with water or, if preferred, add the ice cubes. Serves 1.

This is also called **Gin and Bitters.**

PINK LADY NO. 1

1–1½ ounces gin
1–1½ ounces calvados or
applejack
1 tablespoon grenadine

3 tablespoons lemon juice
1 egg white
3 or 4 ice cubes

Combine all ingredients in a cocktail shaker and shake vigorously. Strain into a cocktail glass. Serves 1.

Pink Lady No. 2: Omit calvados or applejack. Reduce lemon juice to 1½ tablespoons.

PINK ROSE

1 ounce gin
1 teaspoon grenadine
1 teaspoon lemon juice

1 teaspoon cream
1 egg white
3 or 4 ice cubes

Combine ingredients in a cocktail shaker and shake vigorously. Strain into a cocktail glass. Serves 1.

POLLYANNA

3 slices orange
3 slices pineapple
3 or 4 ice cubes

2 ounces gin
½ ounce sweet vermouth
½ ounce grenadine

Muddle orange and pineapple slices in the bottom of a cocktail shaker. Add the ice and remaining ingredients. Shake vigorously. Strain into a cocktail glass. Serves 1.

POLO NO. 2

1½ ounces gin
¼ ounce grapefruit juice

¼ ounce orange juice
3 or 4 ice cubes

Combine ingredients in a cocktail shaker and shake vigorously. Strain into a cocktail glass. Serves 1.

PRINCE'S SMILE

2 ounces gin
1 ounce calvados or
   applejack

1 ounce apricot brandy
Dash lemon juice
3 or 4 ice cubes

Combine the ingredients in a mixing glass and stir well. Strain into a cocktail glass. Serves 1.

PRINCESS MARY

1½ ounces gin
1½ ounces crème de cacao

1½ ounces heavy cream
3 or 4 ice cubes

Combine all ingredients in a cocktail shaker and shake vigorously. Strain into a cocktail glass. Serves 1. The Princess Mary differs from the Alexander No. 2 only in the proportions.

PRINCETON

1½ ounces gin
½ ounce port
2 dashes orange bitters

3 or 4 ice cubes
Twist lemon peel

Combine ingredients in a mixing glass and stir well. Strain into a cocktail glass. Add twist lemon peel. Serves 1.

Crystal Slipper: Substitute Crème Yvette for port, and omit lemon peel.

RACQUET CLUB

1½ ounces gin	Dash orange bitters
¾ ounce dry vermouth	3 or 4 ice cubes

Combine ingredients in a mixing glass and stir well. Strain into a cocktail glass. Serves 1.

Hoffman House or **Astoria:** Add an olive as garnish.

Peggy: Omit orange bitters and add dash each Pernod and Dubonnet.

Piccadilly: Omit orange bitters. Add dash each Pernod and grenadine.

Society: Omit orange bitters and add ¼ teaspoon grenadine.

Three Stripes: Omit orange bitters. Add 1 tablespoon orange juice.

Van: Omit orange bitters. Add 2 dashes Grand Marnier.

Wembley No. 1: Omit orange bitters. Add 3 dashes calvados or applejack.

Yale: Add dash maraschino and 2 dashes sugar syrup.

RESOLUTE

2 ounces gin	1 tablespoon lemon juice
1 ounce apricot brandy	3 or 4 ice cubes

Combine the ingredients in a mixing glass and stir well. Strain into a cocktail glass. Serves 1.

ROYAL CLOVER CLUB

2–3 ounces gin	1 egg yolk
2 tablespoons lemon juice	3 or 4 ice cubes
1 tablespoon grenadine	

Combine ingredients in a cocktail shaker and shake vigorously. Strain into a cocktail glass. Serves 1.

ROYAL NO. 1

1½ ounces gin
2 tablespoons lemon juice
1 teaspoon superfine sugar

1 whole egg
3 or 4 ice cubes

Combine ingredients in a cocktail shaker and shake vigorously. Strain into a cocktail glass. Serves 1.

ROYAL SMILE NO. 2

1 ounce gin
1 ounce grenadine

2 dashes lemon juice
3 or 4 ice cubes

Combine ingredients in a mixing glass and stir well. Strain into a cocktail glass. Serves 1.

RUSSIAN

1 ounce gin
1 ounce vodka

1 ounce crème de cacao
3 or 4 ice cubes

Combine ingredients in a mixing glass and stir well. Strain into a cocktail glass. Serves 1.

SAN FRANCISCO

¾ ounce sloe gin
¾ ounce sweet vermouth
¾ ounce dry vermouth
Dash Angostura bitters

Dash orange bitters
3 or 4 ice cubes
Maraschino cherry

Combine all ingredients except the cherry in a cocktail shaker and shake vigorously. Strain into a cocktail glass; add cherry. Serves 1.

SCREWDRIVER

2 or 3 ice cubes   3 ounces orange juice
1½ ounces gin

Put the ice cubes in an Old-fashioned glass; add the gin and orange juice. Stir gently. Serves 1.

This drink derives from the shaken cocktail: Orange Blossom or Golden Gate. Some authorities say vodka should be used; others call the vodka drink Golden Screw or Golden Spike.

SELF-STARTER

1 ounce gin   2 dashes Pernod
½ ounce Lillet   3 to 4 ice cubes
¼ ounce apricot brandy

Combine ingredients in a mixing glass and stir well. Strain into a cocktail glass. Serves 1.

SENSATION

1½ ounces gin   3 or 4 ice cubes
1 tablespoon lemon juice   3 sprigs fresh mint
1 teaspoon maraschino

Combine all ingredients except mint in a cocktail shaker and shake vigorously. Strain into a cocktail glass and garnish with mint sprigs. Serves 1.

Melon: Reduce lemon juice to ¼ teaspoon, maraschino to ½ teaspoon. Garnish with a maraschino cherry instead of mint.

SHRINER

1 ounce sloe gin   2 dashes sugar syrup
1 ounce brandy   3 or 4 ice cubes
2 dashes Peychaud's bitters   Twist lemon peel

Combine all ingredients, except peel, in a mixing glass and stir well. Strain into a cocktail glass. Drop in peel. Serves 1.

SILVER BULLET

1 ounce gin
½ ounce kümmel

½ ounce lemon juice
3 or 4 ice cubes

Combine the ingredients in a mixing glass and stir well. Strain into a cocktail glass. Serves 1.

Silver Streak: Increase kümmel to 1 ounce; omit lemon juice.

Spring Feeling: Substitute green chartreuse for kümmel.

SILVER KING

1½ ounces gin
2 tablespoons lemon juice
2 dashes sugar syrup

2 dashes orange bitters
1 egg white
3 or 4 ice cubes

Combine ingredients in a cocktail shaker and shake vigorously. Strain into a cocktail glass. Serves 1.

SILVER STALLION

1 ounce gin
½ scoop vanilla ice cream
1½ tablespoons lime juice

2 tablespoons lemon juice
¼ cup crushed ice
Club soda

Combine ingredients in a cocktail shaker and shake vigorously. Strain into a large cocktail glass. Serves 1.

SLOE GIN

2–3 ounces sloe gin
Dash orange bitters

Dash dry vermouth
3 or 4 ice cubes

Combine the ingredients in a mixing glass and stir well. Strain into a cocktail glass. Serves 1.

Sloeberry: Use dash Angostura bitters instead of dry vermouth.

SNICKER

1½ ounces gin
¾ ounce dry vermouth
½ teaspoon maraschino
Dash orange bitters

1 teaspoon sugar syrup
1 egg white
3 or 4 ice cubes

Combine all ingredients in a cocktail shaker and shake vigorously. Strain into a cocktail glass. Serves 1.

SNOWBALL

1 ounce gin
¼ ounce crème de violette
¼ ounce white crème de menthe

¼ ounce anisette
¼ ounce heavy cream
3 or 4 ice cubes

Combine ingredients in a cocktail shaker and shake vigorously. Strain into a cocktail glass. Serves 1.

SOUTH SIDE

2–3 ounces gin
2 tablespoons lemon juice
½ tablespoon superfine sugar

2 sprigs fresh mint
3 or 4 ice cubes
Club soda (optional)

Combine all ingredients, except the club soda, in a cocktail shaker and shake vigorously. Strain into a cocktail glass. Add a splash of club soda. Serves 1.

SOUTHERN GIN

2–3 ounces gin
2 dashes orange bitters
2 dashes curaçao

3 or 4 ice cubes
Twist lemon peel

Combine all ingredients except the peel in a cocktail shaker and shake vigorously. Strain into a cocktail glass; drop in peel. Serves 1.

SPENCER

1½ ounces gin
¾ ounce apricot brandy
Dash Angostura bitters
Dash orange juice

3 or 4 ice cubes
Twist orange peel
Maraschino cherry

Combine all ingredients except the orange peel and cherry in a mixing glass and stir well. Strain into a cocktail glass. Twist the peel over the glass to release the oil and then drop it in with the cherry. Serves 1.

TRILBY NO. 1

1–1½ ounces gin
1–1½ ounces sweet
    vermouth
2 dashes orange bitters

3 or 4 ice cubes
1 teaspoon Crème Yvette

Combine all ingredients except the Crème Yvette in a cocktail shaker and shake vigorously. Strain into a cocktail glass and carefully float the Crème Yvette on top. Serves 1.

TRINITY

¾ ounce gin
¾ ounce dry vermouth

¾ ounce sweet vermouth
3 or 4 ice cubes

Combine all ingredients in a mixing glass and stir well. Strain into a cocktail glass. Serves 1.

Hotel Plaza: Add 1 slice pineapple, coarsely chopped, and shake rather than stir.

Income Tax: Add dash Angostura bitters and 2 tablespoons orange juice.

Lone Tree: Add 2 dashes orange bitters and garnish with a maraschino cherry.

Pall Mall: Add 1 teaspoon white crème de menthe and a dash of orange bitters.

Polo No. 1: Add 1 tablespoon lime juice and shake rather than stir.

TROPICAL COCKTAIL

3 or 4 ice cubes
2–3 ounces gin
1 ounce guava nectar

1 ounce frozen pineapple juice
3 or 4 ice cubes

Put the ice cubes in an Old-fashioned glass, add the rest of the ingredients and stir gently. Serves 1.

TURF OR THIRD DEGREE

1–1½ ounces gin
1–1½ ounces dry vermouth
2 dashes Pernod

3 or 4 ice cubes
Twist lemon peel

Combine all ingredients, except peel, in a mixing glass and stir well. Strain into a cocktail glass; drop in peel. Serves 1.

Deep Sea: Add ¼ teaspoon superfine sugar and a dash of orange bitters. Add an olive to garnish.

Merry Widow No. 2: Add 2 dashes Benedictine and a dash Peychaud's or orange bitters.

Tuxedo: Add dash maraschino and 2 dashes orange bitters. Add maraschino cherry to garnish.

ULANDA

1½ ounces gin
¾ ounce Cointreau

Dash Pernod
3 or 4 ice cubes

Combine all ingredients in a mixing glass and stir well. Strain into a cocktail glass. Serves 1.

UNION JACK

1½ ounces gin
¾ ounce Crème Yvette

3 or 4 ice cubes

Combine all ingredients in a mixing glass and stir well. Strain into a cocktail glass. Serves 1.

Blue Moon: Garnish with lemon peel.

Polly or **Poppy:** Substitute crème de cacao for Crème Yvette.

VIRGIN

¾ ounce gin
¾ ounce Forbidden Fruit
    liqueur

¾ ounce white crème de
    menthe
3 or 4 ice cubes

Combine all ingredients in a mixing glass and stir well. Strain into a cocktail glass. Serves 1.

WEDDING BELLE

¾ ounce gin
¾ ounce Dubonnet
¼ ounce cherry brandy

¼ ounce orange juice
3 or 4 ice cubes

Combine all ingredients in a cocktail shaker and shake vigorously. Strain into a cocktail glass. Serves 1.

WESTERN ROSE

1 ounce gin
½ ounce dry vermouth
½ ounce apricot brandy

Dash lemon juice
3 or 4 ice cubes

Combine all ingredients in a mixing glass and stir well. Strain into a cocktail glass. Serves 1.

English Rose or **Leave It to Me No. 1:** Add dash grenadine. May be shaken instead of stirred, and cocktail glass may be frosted by rubbing the rim of the glass with lemon, dipping into superfine sugar and shaking off the excess. Maraschino cherry garnish is optional.

French Rose or **French Manhattan:** Substitute cherry brandy for apricot brandy. You may use ½ ounce kirsch instead of, or in addition to, the dry vermouth.

Webster: Reduce apricot brandy to ¼ ounce, and use ¼ ounce lime juice instead of the lemon juice. Shake rather than stir.

WHITE CARGO

1 ounce gin
½ scoop vanilla ice cream

Dry white wine, if necessary

Combine first two ingredients in a cocktail shaker and shake until thoroughly blended. Pour into a cocktail glass. If the mixture is too thick, thin it with a little dry white wine. Serves 1.

WHITE LADY

2 ounces gin
1 ounce Cointreau or Triple Sec

1 ounce lemon juice
3 or 4 ice cubes

Combine all ingredients in a cocktail shaker and shake vigorously. Strain into a cocktail glass. Serves 1.

WHITE LILY

¾ ounce gin
¾ ounce light rum
¾ ounce Cointreau

Dash Pernod
3 or 4 ice cubes

Combine all ingredients in a mixing glass and stir well. Strain into a cocktail glass. Serves 1.

WHITE ROSE

1½ ounces gin	3 tablespoons lime juice
¾ ounce maraschino	1 egg white
2 tablespoons orange juice	3 or 4 ice cubes

Combine all ingredients in a cocktail shaker and shake vigorously. Strain into a cocktail glass. Serves 1.

ZAZA

1–1½ ounces gin	3 or 4 ice cubes
1–1½ ounces Dubonnet	Twist orange peel

Combine all ingredients except the peel in a mixing glass and stir well. Strain into a cocktail glass; drop in the peel. Serves 1.

Appetizer No. 2 or **Dubonnet:** Omit orange peel. Dash Angostura or orange bitters may be added.

Cabaret No. 1: Add dash each Pernod and Angostura bitters. Substitute maraschino cherry for orange peel.

Seventh Heaven No. 1: Add 2 dashes maraschino, dash Angostura bitters and a maraschino cherry.

LIQUEUR-BASED COCKTAILS

There is considerable difference of opinion about these drinks. Because they are based on liqueurs, they are, for the most part, rather sweet. Some recipes call for lemon or lime juice, either of which adds tartness. And some recipes list gin, rum, whiskey or some other liquor as an ingredient; the dryness of any of these offsets the sweetness of liqueurs to varying degrees depending on the proportions used. Drinks that include cream or egg are, of course, quite rich. Richness and sweetness are not qualities that whet the appetite, which is one of the attributes many people look for in a cocktail. There are those, however, who prefer the *flavor* of various liqueurs to that of other alcoholic drinks, and therefore they enjoy liqueur-based cocktails. Such people are usually light drinkers, which is just as well, because these particular cocktails should be sipped sparingly and savored more for their taste than anything else.

You will find another collection of mixed libations—*After-Dinner Drinks,* on pages 319–20—that are somewhat similar in character to the ones in this group. There is no rule which says that you must serve any of them at a particular time. It is entirely a matter of personal taste and local custom. If you and your friends enjoy sweet cocktails, you might experiment with various liqueur-based recipes and discover which of them are the most popular. There is one point, however, that should be remembered. Any of these drinks, if served before a meal, is correctly referred to as a *cocktail*. The same drink, if served after a meal, is an *after-dinner drink* even though it may be made in a cocktail shaker and served in a cocktail glass.

APRICOT NO. 1

2 ounces apricot brandy	Dash gin
1 ounce orange juice	3 or 4 ice cubes
1 ounce lemon juice	

Combine all ingredients in a cocktail shaker and shake vigorously. Strain into a cocktail glass. Serves 1.

APRICOT NO. 2

1½ ounces apricot brandy	1 tablespoon lemon juice
½ ounce gin	3 or 4 ice cubes
2 tablespoons orange juice	

Combine all ingredients in a cocktail shaker and shake vigorously. Strain into a cocktail glass. Serves 1.

BABBIE'S SPECIAL

1½ ounces apricot brandy   3 or 4 ice cubes
¾ ounce heavy cream
Dash gin

Combine all ingredients in a cocktail shaker and shake vigorously. Strain into a cocktail glass. Serves 1.

BENEDICTINE COCKTAIL

Cut lemon   3 ounces Benedictine
Superfine sugar   Dash Angostura bitters
Maraschino cherry   2 or 3 ice cubes

Rub the rim of a cocktail glass with lemon and then dip it in sugar. Put a cherry in the bottom of the glass. Combine the Benedictine, bitters and ice in a cocktail shaker and shake lightly. Pour into the prepared glass. Serves 1.

BLANCHE

¾ ounce Cointreau   ¾ ounce white curaçao
¾ ounce anisette   2 or 3 ice cubes

Combine all ingredients in a cocktail shaker and shake well. Strain into a cocktail glass. Serves 1.

BULLDOG NO. 1

1½ ounces cherry brandy   1½ tablespoons lime juice
¾ ounce light rum   3 or 4 ice cubes

Combine all ingredients in a cocktail shaker and shake vigorously. Strain into a cocktail glass. Serves 1.
Bulldog No. 2: Substitute gin for the light rum.

CANADIAN NO. 1

1½ ounces curaçao
3 dashes Jamaica rum
1 teaspoon superfine sugar

2 tablespoons lemon juice
3 or 4 ice cubes

Combine all ingredients in a cocktail shaker and shake vigorously. Strain into a cocktail glass. Serves 1.

CHERRY BLOSSOM

1 ounce cherry brandy
1 ounce brandy
¼ teaspoon curaçao

¼ teaspoon grenadine
¼ teaspoon lemon juice
3 or 4 ice cubes

Combine all ingredients in a cocktail shaker and shake thoroughly. Strain into a cocktail glass. Serves 1.

CULROSS

¾ ounce apricot brandy
¾ ounce Lillet
¾ ounce light rum

1 tablespoon lemon juice
3 or 4 ice cubes

Combine all ingredients in a mixing glass and stir well. Strain into a cocktail glass. Serves 1.

DOCTOR

1½ ounces Swedish Punch   3 or 4 ice cubes
3 tablespoons lime juice

Combine all ingredients in a mixing glass and stir well. Strain into a cocktail glass. Serves 1.

FESTIVAL

¾ ounce apricot brandy   1 teaspoon grenadine
¾ ounce crème de cacao   3 or 4 ice cubes
¾ ounce heavy cream

Combine all ingredients in a cocktail shaker and shake vigorously. Strain into a cocktail glass. Serves 1.

FLAG

1 teaspoon Crème Yvette   4 dashes curaçao
½ cup crushed ice   1 ounce claret (or other dry
1½ ounces apricot brandy   red wine)

Put the Crème Yvette in a cocktail glass. Combine ice, apricot brandy and curaçao in a cocktail shaker and shake vigorously. Carefully pour into the cocktail glass so as not to mix with the Crème Yvette. Top with the claret, using a little more than an ounce if necessary. Serves 1.

GOLDEN SLIPPER

¾ ounce yellow chartreuse   1 egg yolk
¾ ounce apricot brandy   3 or 4 ice cubes

Combine all ingredients in a cocktail shaker and shake vigorously. Strain into a cocktail glass. Serves 1.

GRAND SLAM

2 ounces Swedish Punch
½ ounce sweet vermouth

½ ounce dry vermouth
3 or 4 ice cubes

Combine all ingredients in a mixing glass and stir well. Strain into a cocktail glass. Serves 1.

HAVANA NO. 1

1 ounce apricot brandy
½ ounce Swedish Punch
½ ounce gin

Dash lemon juice
3 or 4 ice cubes

Combine all ingredients in a mixing glass and stir well. Strain into a cocktail glass. Serves 1.

HESITATION

1½ ounces Swedish Punch
½ ounce rye whiskey

Dash lemon juice
3 or 4 ice cubes

Combine all ingredients in a mixing glass and stir well. Strain into a cocktail glass. Serves 1.

HUNDRED PERCENT

1½ ounces Swedish Punch
½ tablespoon lemon juice
½ tablespoon orange juice

2 dashes grenadine
3 or 4 ice cubes

Combine all ingredients in a mixing glass and stir well. Strain into a cocktail glass. Serves 1.

MARGARET DUFFY

1½ ounces Swedish Punch
½ ounce brandy

2 dashes Angostura or other
bitters
3 or 4 ice cubes

Combine ingredients in a mixing glass and stir well. Strain into a cocktail glass. Serves 1.

MERRY WIDOW NO. 3

1 ounce cherry brandy
1 ounce maraschino

3 or 4 ice cubes
Maraschino cherry

Combine all ingredients except the cherry in a cocktail shaker and shake vigorously. Strain into a cocktail glass and drop in the cherry. Serves 1.

MOTHER SHERMAN

2 ounces apricot brandy
1 ounce orange juice

4 dashes orange bitters
½ cup crushed ice

Combine all ingredients in a cocktail shaker and shake vigorously. Strain into a cocktail glass. Serves 1.

PINK WHISKERS

¾ ounce apricot brandy
¾ ounce dry vermouth
2 dashes white crème de
   menthe

1 teaspoon grenadine
2 tablespoons orange juice
3 or 4 ice cubes
1 ounce port

Combine all ingredients except the port in a cocktail shaker and shake vigorously. Strain into a cocktail glass. Carefully float the port on top. Serves 1.

RED LION

2 ounces Grand Marnier
1 ounce gin
1 tablespoon orange juice

1 tablespoon lemon juice
3 or 4 ice cubes
Twist lemon peel

Combine all ingredients except the lemon peel in a cocktail shaker and shake vigorously. Strain into a cocktail glass, and drop in the peel. Serves 1.

RHETT BUTLER

1½ ounces Southern
   Comfort
2 teaspoons lime juice
1 tablespoon lemon juice

1 teaspoon curaçao
½ teaspoon superfine sugar
3 or 4 ice cubes

Combine all ingredients in a cocktail shaker and shake vigorously. Strain into a cocktail glass. Serves 1.

SCAFFAS

These are short drinks served unchilled and undiluted in cocktail glasses. They are probably best enjoyed before or after a meal during cold weather. All are made with equal amounts of a liquor and a liqueur. Gin, Rum and Whiskey Scaffas call for Benedictine. Brandy Scaffas call for maraschino.

Basic Recipe

Dash Angostura bitters
1½ ounces liquor

1½ ounces liqueur

Combine all ingredients in a cocktail glass, and stir. Serves 1.

SCARLETT O'HARA

2 ounces Southern Comfort
2 ounces cranberry juice

2 teaspoons lime juice
3 or 4 ice cubes

Combine all ingredients in a mixing glass and stir well. Strain into a cocktail glass. Serves 1.

VODKA GRASSHOPPER

¾ ounce green crème de
   menthe
¾ ounce white crème de
   cacao

¾ ounce vodka
3 or 4 ice cubes

Combine all ingredients in a mixing glass and stir well. Strain into a cocktail glass. Serves 1.

WALDORF NO. 1

2 ounces Swedish Punch
½ ounce dry gin

½ ounce lemon or lime juice
3 or 4 ice cubes

Combine all ingredients in a mixing glass and stir well. Strain into a cocktail glass. Serves 1.

WIDOW'S DREAM

3 ounces Benedictine
1 whole egg

1½ ounces heavy cream
3 or 4 ice cubes

Combine all ingredients in a cocktail shaker and shake vigorously. Strain into a cocktail glass. Serves 1.

WINDY CORNER

3 ounces blackberry brandy
½ cup crushed ice

Nutmeg

Combine the brandy and ice in a cocktail shaker and shake vigorously. Strain into a cocktail glass and grate a little nutmeg on top. Serves 1.

XANTHIA

¾ ounce yellow chartreuse
¾ ounce cherry brandy

¾ ounce gin
3 or 4 ice cubes

Combine all ingredients in a mixing glass and stir well. Strain into a cocktail glass. Serves 1.

YELLOW PARROT

¾ ounce apricot brandy ¾ ounce Pernod
¾ ounce yellow chartreuse 3 or 4 ice cubes

Combine all ingredients in a cocktail shaker and shake vigorously. Strain into a cocktail glass. Serves 1.

RUM COCKTAILS

APPLE PIE

¾ ounce light rum 2 dashes grenadine
¾ ounce sweet vermouth 1 teaspoon lemon juice
4 dashes apricot brandy 3 or 4 ice cubes

Combine all ingredients in a cocktail shaker and shake vigorously. Strain into a cocktail glass. Serves 1.

AUNT AGATHA

2 ice cubes 3–4 ounces chilled orange
2 ounces light rum juice
Dash Angostura bitters

Put the ice cubes in an Old-fashioned glass, add the rum and orange juice and stir gently. Add the bitters. Serves 1.

BACARDI SPECIAL

1½ ounces light rum 1 teaspoon grenadine
¾ ounce gin 3 or 4 ice cubes
1½ tablespoons lime juice

Combine all ingredients in a cocktail shaker and shake vigorously. Strain into a cocktail glass. Serves 1.
Kingston No. 2: Substitute dark rum for light rum.

BANANA DAIQUIRI

2 ounces light rum
½ ounce banana liqueur
½ ounce lime juice

½ small banana, peeled and
coarsely chopped
½ cup crushed ice

Combine all ingredients in an electric blender and blend at high speed until smooth. Pour into a large saucer champagne or similar glass. Serves 1.

BATIDO DE PINA

2–3 ounces light rum
⅔ cup fresh pineapple,
coarsely chopped

Superfine sugar to taste
½ cup crushed ice
Sprig fresh mint

Combine the rum, pineapple and sugar in an electric blender and blend on high speed until smooth. Put the ice into a goblet and add the liquor. Decorate with the mint. Serves 1.

BEACHCOMBER

2 ounces light rum
¾ ounce Cointreau
1½ tablespoons lime juice

2 dashes maraschino
½ cup crushed ice

Combine all ingredients in a cocktail shaker and shake vigorously. Strain into a large cocktail glass or wineglass. Serves 1.

BEE'S KISS

1½ ounces light rum
1 teaspoon honey

1 teaspoon heavy cream
3 or 4 ice cubes

Combine all ingredients in a cocktail shaker and shake vigorously. Strain into a cocktail glass. Serves 1.

BLACK STRIPE NO. 1

2 ounces dark rum   1 cup crushed ice
1 tablespoon molasses

Combine all ingredients in a cocktail shaker and shake vigorously. Strain into a cocktail glass. Serves 1.

BLUE MOUNTAIN

1½ ounces dark rum   2 tablespoons orange juice
¾ ounce vodka   3 or 4 ice cubes
¾ ounce Tia Maria

Combine all ingredients in a cocktail shaker and shake vigorously. Strain into a large cocktail glass. Serves 1.

BOLO

3 ounces light rum   1 teaspoon superfine sugar
1½ tablespoons lime juice   3 or 4 ice cubes
2 tablespoons orange juice

Combine all ingredients in a cocktail shaker and shake vigorously. Strain into a cocktail glass. Serves 1.

CHINESE COCKTAIL

1½ ounces dark rum
¾ ounce grenadine
3 dashes curaçao

3 dashes maraschino
Dash Angostura bitters
3 or 4 ice cubes

Combine all ingredients in a cocktail shaker and shake vigorously. Strain into a cocktail glass. Serves 1.
This drink is also known as a **Jamaica Ginger.**

CUBAN NO. 3

2–3 ounces light rum
¾ ounce apricot brandy

1½ tablespoons lime juice
3 or 4 ice cubes

Combine all ingredients in a cocktail shaker and shake vigorously. Strain into a cocktail glass. Serves 1.
Paradise No. 1: Omit lime juice.

CUBAN SPECIAL

1 ounce light rum
½ teaspoon curaçao
1 tablespoon pineapple juice
1 tablespoon lime juice

3 or 4 ice cubes
Stick pineapple
Maraschino cherry

Combine all ingredients except the pineapple and cherry in a cocktail shaker and shake vigorously. Strain into a cocktail glass and garnish with the fruit. Serves 1.

DAIQUIRI

2 ounces light rum
1½ tablespoons lime juice

½ teaspoon superfine sugar
3 or 4 ice cubes

Combine all ingredients in a cocktail shaker and shake vigorously. Strain into a cocktail glass. Serves 1.
Although most often referred to as a Daiquiri, this drink is sometimes called a **Cuban No. 2,** or **Bacardi No. 1.**

Bacardi No. 2: Use grenadine instead of sugar.

Frozen Daiquiri: Use 1 cup crushed ice instead of ice cubes. Put all ingredients in a blender and blend until the mixture has the consistency of snow. Serve immediately in a large saucer champage or similar glass, with a short straw. Serves 1.

DAVIS

1½ ounces dark rum
1½ ounces dry vermouth
2 dashes raspberry syrup

3 tablespoons lime juice
3 or 4 ice cubes

Combine all ingredients in a cocktail shaker and shake vigorously. Strain into a cocktail glass. Serves 1.

Coctel Veracruzana: Substitute 1½ ounces pineapple juice for raspberry syrup and lime juice.

EL PRESIDENTE NO. 1

1½ ounces light rum
½ ounce curaçao
½ ounce dry vermouth

Dash grenadine
3 or 4 ice cubes

Combine all ingredients in a cocktail shaker and shake vigorously. Strain into a cocktail glass. Serves 1.

If preferred, pineapple juice may be used instead of dry vermouth.

EYE-OPENER NO. 1

1½ ounces light rum
1 teaspoon curaçao
1 teaspoon crème de cacao
1 teaspoon Pernod

½ teaspoon superfine sugar
1 egg yolk
3 or 4 ice cubes

Combine all ingredients in a cocktail shaker and shake vigorously. Strain into a cocktail glass. Serves 1.

FAIR AND WARMER

1½ ounces light rum
¾ ounce sweet vermouth
2 dashes curaçao

3 or 4 ice cubes
Twist lemon peel

Combine all ingredients except the peel in a mixing glass and stir well. Strain into a cocktail glass, add the peel. Serves 1.

FIREMAN'S SOUR

1½ ounces light rum
½ teaspoon superfine sugar
3 tablespoons lime juice

½ ounce grenadine
3 or 4 ice cubes
Club soda (optional)

Combine all ingredients except the club soda in a cocktail shaker and shake vigorously. Strain into a Delmonico glass. Fill up with club soda. Serves 1.

HAPPY APPLE RUM TWIST

1½ ounces light or dark rum
3 ounces apple juice or cider
1½ tablespoons lime juice

½ cup crushed ice
Twist lime peel

Combine all ingredients except the peel in a cocktail shaker and shake vigorously. Strain into a cocktail glass and drop in the peel. Serves 1.

HAVANA CLUB

1½ ounces light rum
¾ ounce dry vermouth

3 or 4 ice cubes

Combine all ingredients in a mixing glass and stir well. Strain into a cocktail glass. Serves 1.

El Presidente No. 2: Add dash Angostura bitters and shake rather than stir.

HONEYBEE

2 ounces light rum
½ ounce lemon juice

1 tablespoon honey
3 or 4 ice cubes

Combine all ingredients in a cocktail shaker and shake vigorously. Strain into a cocktail glass. Serves 1.

HONEYSUCKLE

1½ ounces golden rum
1 teaspoon honey

1½ tablespoons lime juice
3 or 4 ice cubes

Combine all ingredients in a cocktail shaker and shake vigorously. Strain into a cocktail glass. Serves 1.

HOPTOAD

¾ ounce light rum
¾ ounce apricot brandy

¾ ounce lime juice
3 or 4 ice cubes

Combine all ingredients in a mixing glass and stir well. Strain into a cocktail glass. Serves 1.

JO'BURG

1–1½ ounces light rum
1–1½ ounces Dubonnet

4 dashes orange bitters
3 or 4 ice cubes

Combine all ingredients in a cocktail shaker and shake vigorously. Strain into a cocktail glass. Serves 1.

Bushranger: Use 2 dashes Angostura instead of orange bitters.

KE KALI NEI AU

½ cup crushed ice
1½ ounces light rum
1½ ounces passion-fruit
  juice (lilikoi)
½ ounce kirsch
2 tablespoons lemon juice

1 ounce sugar syrup
Green coconut with top cut
  off, drained
1 ounce dark rum
Fruit for garnish
Red hibiscus

Put crushed ice in a mixing glass and add the light rum, passion-fruit juice, kirsch, lemon juice, and sugar syrup. Stir well. Pour into the green coconut. Float the dark rum on top and decorate with fruit and hibiscus. Serve with a straw. Serves 1.

This is a Hawaiian drink and green coconuts may not be available in all regions. If not, an Old-fashioned glass will do very nearly as well.

KINGSTON NO. 1

1 ounce dark rum
½ ounce kümmel
½ ounce orange juice

Dash Pimento Dram
3 or 4 ice cubes

Combine all ingredients in a cocktail shaker and shake vigorously. Strain into a cocktail glass. Serves 1.

MAI-TAI NO. 1

2 ounces dark rum
½ ounce curaçao
½ ounce apricot brandy

1½ tablespoons lime juice
3 or 4 ice cubes
Pineapple stick

Combine all ingredients, except the pineapple, in a cocktail shaker and shake vigorously. Strain into a cocktail glass, decorate with the pineapple. Serves 1.

MANGO DAIQUIRI

2 ounces light rum
1 ounce curaçao
½ cup mango puree

2 tablespoons lime juice
1 tablespoon superfine sugar
1 cup crushed ice

Combine all ingredients in an electric blender and blend until the contents have the consistency of snow. Serve immediately in a large saucer champagne or similar glass, with short straws. Serves 1.

MARY PICKFORD

1½ ounces light rum
1½ ounces pineapple juice
½ teaspoon grenadine

½ teaspoon maraschino
3 or 4 ice cubes

Combine all ingredients in a mixing glass and stir well. Strain into a cocktail glass. Serves 1.
This is also called a **Cuban No. 4.**

MEXICANO

2 ounces light rum
½ ounce kümmel
½ ounce orange juice

Dash Angostura bitters
½ cup crushed ice

Combine all ingredients in a cocktail shaker and shake vigorously. Strain into a cocktail glass. Serves 1.

PALMETTO

1½ ounces light rum
1½ ounces sweet vermouth
2 dashes orange bitters

3 or 4 ice cubes
Twist lemon peel

Combine all ingredients except the lemon peel in a mixing glass and stir well. Strain into a cocktail glass, drop in the peel. Serves 1.

Flanagan: Use dark instead of light rum. Substitute Angostura for orange bitters, and shake instead of stirring.

PANAMA NO. 1

1½ ounces dark rum
¾ ounce crème de cacao

¾ ounce heavy cream
3 or 4 ice cubes

Combine all ingredients in a cocktail shaker and shake vigorously. Strain into a cocktail glass. Serves 1.

PANCHO VILLA

1 ounce light rum
1 ounce gin
1 ounce apricot brandy

1 teaspoon cherry brandy
1 teaspoon pineapple juice
½ cup crushed ice

Combine all ingredients in a cocktail shaker and shake vigorously. Strain into a champagne saucer glass. Serves 1.

PARISIAN BLONDE

¾ ounce dark rum
¾ ounce curaçao

¾ ounce heavy cream
3 or 4 ice cubes

Combine all ingredients in a cocktail shaker and shake vigorously. Strain into a cocktail glass. Serves 1.

PASSION DAIQUIRI

1½ ounces light rum
½ ounce passion-fruit juice
2 tablespoons lime juice

1 teaspoon superfine sugar
3 or 4 ice cubes

Combine all ingredients in a cocktail shaker and shake vigorously. Strain into a cocktail glass. Serves 1.

PEACH DAIQUIRI

2 ounces light rum
½ peach, fresh, peeled or
  canned

1 tablespoon lime juice
1 teaspoon superfine sugar
1 cup crushed ice

Combine all ingredients in an electric blender and blend until the contents have the consistency of snow. Serve immediately in a large saucer champagne or similar glass, with short straws. Serves 1.

PINEAPPLE

1½ ounces light rum
¾ ounce pineapple juice

½ teaspoon lime or lemon
  juice
3 or 4 ice cubes

Combine all ingredients in a cocktail shaker and shake vigorously. Strain into a cocktail glass. Serves 1.

This is also called a **Havana No. 2.**

PINEAPPLE DAIQUIRI

2 ounces light rum
½ ounce Cointreau
½ cup pineapple juice

1 teaspoon lime juice
1 cup crushed ice

Combine all ingredients in an electric blender and blend quickly on high speed. Pour into a large saucer champagne or similar glass. Serves 1.

PINEAPPLE MIST

2 ounces crushed pineapple
2 ounces crushed ice

1½ ounces light rum
Maraschino cherry

Put the pineapple and ice in an Old-fashioned glass and mix lightly. Pour in the rum and decorate with the cherry. Serves 1.

PIRATE'S

1½ ounces dark rum   Dash Angostura bitters
¾ ounce sweet vermouth   3 or 4 ice cubes

Combine all ingredients in a mixing glass and stir well. Strain into a cocktail glass. Serves 1.

PLANTER'S NO. 1

1½ ounces light or golden   Dash lemon juice
    rum   3 or 4 ice cubes
1½ ounces orange juice

Combine all ingredients in a cocktail shaker and shake vigorously. Strain into a cocktail glass. Serves 1.

PLANTER'S NO. 2

1½ ounces dark rum   ¾ ounce sugar syrup
¾ ounce lemon juice   3 or 4 ice cubes

Combine all ingredients in a mixing glass and stir well. Strain into a cocktail glass. Serves 1.

QUAKER NO. 1

¾ ounce light rum   2 teaspoons raspberry syrup
¾ ounce brandy   3 or 4 ice cubes
1 tablespoon lemon juice

Combine all ingredients in a cocktail shaker and shake vigorously. Strain into a cocktail glass. Serves 1.

QUARTERDECK

1½ ounces dark rum   1 teaspoon lime juice
¾ ounce sherry   3 or 4 ice cubes

Combine all ingredients in a mixing glass and stir well. Strain into a cocktail glass. Serves 1.

ROBSON

1 ounce dark rum
½ ounce grenadine
¼ ounce orange juice

¼ ounce lemon juice
3 or 4 ice cubes

Combine all ingredients in a cocktail shaker and shake vigorously. Strain into a cocktail glass. Serves 1.

RUM DUBONNET

¾ ounce light rum
¾ ounce Dubonnet

1½ tablespoons lime juice
3 or 4 ice cubes

Combine all ingredients in a mixing glass and stir well. Strain into a cocktail glass. Serves 1.

RUM OLD-FASHIONED

1 cube sugar
2 or 3 dashes Angostura or
  orange bitters
Twist lemon peel

2 or 3 ice cubes
2 ounces light rum
Slice orange
Maraschino cherry

Place the sugar cube in an Old-fashioned glass and sprinkle with bitters. Add lemon peel, ice cubes and rum. Garnish with orange slice and cherry. Serves 1.

RUM ON THE ROCKS

2 or 3 ice cubes
2 ounces light rum

Twist lemon peel

Put the ice into an Old-fashioned glass, pour on the rum and drop in the lemon peel. Serves 1.

RUM SOUR

3 ounces dark rum	½ cup crushed ice
3 tablespoons lime juice	Slice of orange
Sugar syrup to taste	Maraschino cherry

Combine the rum, lime juice, sugar syrup and crushed ice in a cocktail shaker and shake vigorously. Strain into a Delmonico glass and decorate with the orange slice and cherry. Serves 1.

SANTIAGO

3 ounces light rum	4 dashes lime juice
2 dashes grenadine	3 or 4 ice cubes

Combine all ingredients in a mixing glass and stir well. Strain into a cocktail glass. Serves 1.

SEPTEMBER MORN

3 ounces light rum	1 egg white
1 teaspoon grenadine	3 or 4 ice cubes
1½ tablespoons lime juice	

Combine all ingredients in a cocktail shaker and shake vigorously. Strain into a cocktail glass. Serves 1.

SEVILLA NO. 1

1 ounce dark rum	Twist orange peel
1 ounce sweet vermouth	3 or 4 ice cubes

Combine all ingredients in a mixing glass and stir well. Strain into a cocktail glass. Serves 1.

Little Princess: Use light instead of dark rum and omit orange peel. This cocktail is sometimes called a **Poker.**

SEVILLA NO. 2

1 ounce light rum
1 ounce port
½ teaspoon superfine sugar

1 whole egg
3 or 4 ice cubes

Combine all ingredients in a cocktail shaker and shake vigorously. Strain into a cocktail glass. Serves 1.

SHANGHAI

1½ ounces dark rum
½ ounce anisette
¾ ounce lemon juice

2 dashes grenadine
3 or 4 ice cubes

Combine all ingredients in a mixing glass and stir well. Strain into a cocktail glass. Serves 1.

SLOPPY JOE'S NO. 1

¾ ounce light rum
¾ ounce dry vermouth
¼ teaspoon curaçao

¼ teaspoon grenadine
3 tablespoons lime juice
3 or 4 ice cubes

Combine all ingredients in a cocktail shaker and shake vigorously. Strain into a cocktail glass. Serves 1.

SPANISH TOWN

1½ ounces light rum
2 dashes curaçao

½ cup crushed Ice
Nutmeg

Combine all ingredients except the nutmeg in a cocktail shaker and shake vigorously. Strain into a cocktail glass and grate a little nutmeg on top. Serves 1.

THREE MILLER

1½ ounces light rum
¾ ounce brandy
1 teaspoon grenadine

¼ teaspoon lemon juice
3 or 4 ice cubes

Combine all ingredients in a cocktail shaker and shake vigorously. Strain into a cocktail glass. Serves 1.

WHITE LION

1½ ounces dark rum
2 tablespoons lemon juice
1 teaspoon superfine sugar

3 dashes raspberry syrup
3 dashes Angostura bitters
3 or 4 ice cubes

Combine all ingredients in a cocktail shaker and shake vigorously. Strain into a cocktail glass. Serves 1.

XYZ

1 ounce dark rum
¾ ounce Cointreau

¾ ounce lemon juice
3 or 4 ice cubes

Combine all ingredients in a cocktail shaker and shake vigorously. Strain into a cocktail glass. Serves 1.

SOURS

These drinks are usually served as cocktails before a meal. They are tart, as their name implies, and therefore do not spoil one's appetite for food. Although the most popular version is a Whiskey Sour based on blended whiskey, sours may be made with any other type of whiskey— bourbon, rye, Scotch, Irish or Canadian. Less frequently, they are made with applejack, apricot brandy, brandy, gin, rum, tequila or vodka. All except the first and last are made as follows:

SOUR (*Basic Recipe*)

2–3 ounces liquor
2 tablespoons lemon juice
½–1 teaspoon superfine
    sugar

3 or 4 ice cubes
1 orange or lemon slice or
    peel
Maraschino cherry

Combine all ingredients except the fruit slice or peel and cherry in a cocktail shaker and shake vigorously. Strain into a sour or Delmonico glass, and garnish with the fruit and cherry. Serves 1.

A 6-ounce wineglass may be used if you do not have the traditional sour glass.

Applejack Sour: Add 1½ tablespoons lime juice and a dash of grenadine.

Vodka Sour: Add soda to fill.

TEQUILA COCKTAILS

BLOODY MARIA

1½ ounces tequila
3 ounces tomato juice
1 tablespoon lemon juice
Dash Worcestershire sauce

Dash Tabasco
Salt, freshly ground pepper
   to taste
3 or 4 ice cubes

Combine all ingredients in a cocktail shaker and shake vigorously. Strain into a sour or Old-fashioned glass with a cube of ice in it. Serves 1.

DORADO COCKTAIL

2 ounces tequila
1 tablespoon honey

2 tablespoons lemon juice
½ cup crushed ice

Combine all ingredients in a cocktail shaker and shake vigorously. Strain into a cocktail glass. Serves 1.

MARGARITA

Cut lime
Salt
2 ounces tequila
½ ounce Cointreau or
   Triple Sec

1 tablespoon lime juice
3 or 4 ice cubes

Rub the rim of a cocktail glass with lime, then dip in salt to frost. Combine remaining ingredients in a mixing glass and stir well. Strain into the prepared cocktail glass. Serves 1.

PICADOR

2 ounces tequila
1 ounce Kahlúa

½ cup crushed ice
Twist lemon peel

Combine all ingredients except the lemon peel in a mixing glass and stir well. Strain into a cocktail glass and drop in the peel. Serves 1.

TEQUILA COCKTAIL NO. 1

2 ounces tequila
1 ounce dry vermouth

Few drops vanilla extract
3 or 4 ice cubes

Combine all ingredients in a mixing glass and stir well. Strain into a cocktail glass. Serves 1.

TEQUILA COCKTAIL NO. 2

½ cup grapefruit juice
1 tablespoon grenadine
2 teaspoons lime juice

2 dashes orange bitters
2–3 ounces tequila
3 or 4 ice cubes

Combine all ingredients and chill thoroughly. Serve in an Old-fashioned glass over ice cubes. Serves 1.

TEQUINI

1½ ounces tequila
½ ounce dry vermouth
Dash Angostura bitters
  (optional)

3 or 4 ice cubes
Twist of lemon peel

Put all ingredients except lemon peel in a mixing glass, stir well and strain into a 4-ounce cocktail glass. Drop in the lemon peel. Serves 1.

VODKA COCKTAILS

BLOODY BULLSHOT

1½ ounces vodka
1½ ounces tomato juice
1½ ounces chilled beef
    bouillon
1 teaspoon lemon juice

Dash salt
Dash Worcestershire sauce
Dash Tabasco
½ cup crushed ice

Combine all ingredients in a cocktail shaker and shake vigorously. Strain into a sour glass. Serves 1.

Barnacle Bill: Substitute clam juice for bouillon.

Krauter: Substitute sauerkraut juice for bouillon.

Geisha Whirl: Increase tomato juice to 3 ounces, eliminate the bouillon and Worcestershire sauce and add a dash of soy sauce.

BLOODY MARY

1½ ounces vodka
3 ounces tomato juice
1 tablespoon lemon juice
Dash Worcestershire sauce

Dash Tabasco
Salt, freshly ground pepper
    to taste
3 or 4 ice cubes

Combine all ingredients in a cocktail shaker and shake vigorously. Strain into a sour glass, or, if preferred, into an Old-fashioned glass with a cube of ice in it. Serves 1.

Bloody Marie: Reduce the lemon juice to 1 teaspoon and add a dash of Pernod.

Bloody Maria: Use tequila instead of vodka.

BLOODY MARY

46-ounce can tomato juice
4 ounces lemon juice
2 tablespoons
    Worcestershire sauce
Salt

Freshly ground pepper
1½ ounces vodka per
    serving
20 ice cubes
10 thin slices lemon

Combine the tomato juice, lemon juice, Worcestershire sauce, salt and pepper. Stir to mix well. Pour into bottles and refrigerate until thoroughly chilled. Put 2 ice cubes in each 8-ounce glass, add 1½ ounces vodka and 5 ounces tomato juice mixture. Garnish with a slice of lemon. Serves 10.

BLUE MONDAY

1½ ounces vodka   Dash blue vegetable coloring
½ ounce Cointreau   3 or 4 ice cubes

Combine all ingredients in a mixing glass and stir well. Strain into a cocktail glass. Serves 1.
This is sometimes called a **Caucasian.**

BULLSHOT

2 ounces vodka   Salt
4 ounces chilled beef   Freshly ground pepper
  bouillon   3 or 4 ice cubes

Combine all ingredients in a mixing glass and stir well. Strain into an 8-ounce wineglass, or over 2 ice cubes in an Old-fashioned glass. Serves 1.

CHERRY VODKA

1½ ounces vodka   1 ounce lemon juice
¾ ounce cherry brandy   3 or 4 ice cubes

Combine all ingredients in a cocktail shaker and shake vigorously. Strain into a cocktail glass. Serves 1.

COOCH BEHAR

2 or 3 ice cubes   3 ounces tomato juice
1½ ounces pepper vodka

If pepper vodka is not available, make your own. Place a very hot, fresh or dried chili pepper in a bottle of vodka and let it stand for a week to ten days, by which time the vodka will have taken on the heat of the pepper.

Put ice cubes in an Old-fashioned glass, add the vodka and tomato juice, and stir gently. Serves 1.

GINGERSNAP

3 or 4 ice cubes	1 ounce Stone's ginger wine
3 ounces vodka	Club soda

Put the ice cubes in an Old-fashioned glass and pour in the vodka and ginger wine. Stir gently. Add club soda to taste. Serves 1.

GOLDEN SCREW

1½ ounces vodka	3 or 4 ice cubes
3 ounces orange juice	Dash Angostura bitters

Combine ingredients in a cocktail shaker and shake vigorously. Strain into a cocktail glass. Serves 1.

If preferred, place 2 or 3 ice cubes in an Old-fashioned glass and pour in the vodka and orange juice. Stir lightly; add a dash of Angostura bitters. Note: This is also called a **Golden Spike,** and some people insist that this version of the drink is called a **Screwdriver;** see below.

Orange Blossom or **Golden Gate:** Use gin instead of vodka, and shake.

Screwdriver: Use gin instead of vodka, and stir. (There is some confusion about whether this name applies to a gin-based or vodka-based drink.)

KANGAROO

1½ ounces vodka	½ cup crushed ice
¾ ounce dry vermouth	Twist lemon peel

Combine all ingredients except the peel in a mixing glass and stir well. Strain into a cocktail glass and decorate with the lemon peel. Serves 1.

RUSSIAN

1 ounce vodka	1 ounce crème de cacao
1 ounce gin	3 or 4 ice cubes

Combine all ingredients in a mixing glass and stir well. Strain into a cocktail glass. Serves 1.

SALTY DOG NO. 1

Cut lemon	2 ounces vodka
Salt	4 ounces grapefruit juice
2 or 3 ice cubes	

Rub the rim of an Old-fashioned glass or 8-ounce wineglass with lemon, then spin in salt. Add the ice cubes, vodka and grapefruit juice and stir gently to mix. Serves 1.

SPANISH VODKA MARTINı

2–3 ounces vodka	3 or 4 ice cubes
½–1 ounce dry sherry	Twist lemon peel

Combine the vodka and sherry in a mixing glass with ice cubes and stir well. Strain into a cocktail glass. Twist the lemon peel over the glass to release the oil and then drop peel in. Serves 1.

TOVARICH

1½ ounces vodka	1½ tablespoons lime juice
1 ounce kümmel	½ cup crushed ice

Combine all ingredients in a cocktail shaker and shake vigorously. Strain into a cocktail glass. Serves 1.

VODKA GIBSON

2–3 ounces vodka
½–¾ ounce dry vermouth

3 or 4 ice cubes
Pickled pearl onion

Combine all ingredients in a mixing glass and stir well. Strain into a cocktail glass. Serves 1.

VODKA GIMLET

1½ ounces vodka
1 teaspoon superfine sugar

1½ tablespoons lime juice
½ cup crushed ice

Combine all ingredients in a mixing glass and stir well. Strain into a cocktail glass. Serves 1.

VODKA GYPSY

1½ ounces vodka
¾ ounce Benedictine

Dash orange bitters
3 or 4 ice cubes

Combine all ingredients in a mixing glass and stir well. Strain into a cocktail glass. Serves 1.

VODKA MARTINI

2½ ounces vodka
½ ounce dry vermouth

3 or 4 ice cubes
Twist lemon peel

Combine all ingredients except the peel in a mixing glass and stir well. Strain into a cocktail glass and drop in the peel. Serves 1.

VODKA SOUR

See "Sours," page 216.

VOLGA BOATMAN

1½ ounces vodka　　　　1½ ounces orange juice
1½ ounces cherry brandy　3 or 4 ice cubes

Combine all ingredients in a mixing glass and stir well. Strain into a cocktail glass. Serves 1.

WHISKEY COCKTAILS

AFFINITY

¾ ounce Scotch whiskey　　3 or 4 ice cubes
¾ ounce dry vermouth　　　Twist lemon peel
¾ ounce sweet vermouth　　Maraschino cherry
2 dashes Angostura bitters

Combine all ingredients except the peel and cherry in a mixing glass and stir well. Strain into a cocktail glass and garnish with the peel and cherry. Serves 1.

This drink is sometimes made with orange bitters instead of Angostura bitters, and the peel and cherry are omitted.

Whisper: Omit bitters and garnish and shake rather than stir.

Whispers of the Forest: Use ¾ ounce dry sherry and ¾ ounce port in place of the vermouths.

ALEXANDER YOUNG

½ ounce pineapple juice
½ ounce orange juice
½ ounce lemon juice
1½ ounces bourbon

Dash grenadine
Dash Angostura bitters
½ cup crushed ice

Combine all ingredients in a cocktail shaker and shake vigorously. Strain into a cocktail glass. Serves 1.

In Hawaii, okolehao is used instead of bourbon.

BLACKTHORN

1 ounce Irish whiskey
1 ounce dry vermouth
3 dashes Pernod

3 dashes Angostura bitters
3 or 4 ice cubes

Combine all ingredients in a mixing glass and stir well. Strain into a cocktail glass. Serves 1.

Sloe gin is sometimes used in place of Irish whiskey in this drink.

BLARNEY STONE

1½–2 ounces Irish whiskey
½ teaspoon Pernod
½ teaspoon curaçao
½ teaspoon maraschino

Dash Angostura bitters
½ cup crushed ice
Twist orange peel
Olive (optional)

Combine all ingredients except the orange peel and olive in a cocktail shaker and shake vigorously. Strain into a cocktail glass and add the peel and the olive. Serves 1.

Irish: Stir with 3 or 4 ice cubes in a mixing glass, rather than shake. Omit olive.

BLINKER

1½ ounces rye whiskey
2 ounces grapefruit juice

¾ ounce grenadine
3 or 4 ice cubes

Combine all ingredients in a cocktail shaker and shake vigorously. Strain into a cocktail glass. Serves 1.

Beehive: Use bourbon instead of rye, and a teaspoon of honey instead of grenadine.

BLOOD AND SAND

½ ounce Scotch whiskey	½ ounce orange juice
½ ounce cherry brandy	3 or 4 ice cubes
½ ounce sweet vermouth	

Combine all ingredients in a mixing glass and stir well. Strain into a cocktail glass. Serves 1.

BOBBY BURNS

1 ounce Scotch whiskey	Dash Benedictine
½ ounce sweet vermouth	3 or 4 ice cubes
½ ounce dry vermouth	

Combine all ingredients in a mixing glass and stir well. Strain into a cocktail glass. Serves 1.

This is sometimes made with 1 ounce sweet vermouth, no dry vermouth, and the Benedictine increased to 1 teaspoon.

CABLEGRAM

3 ounces rye whiskey	3 or 4 ice cubes
2 tablespoons lemon juice	Ginger ale
1 teaspoon superfine sugar	

Combine all ingredients except the ginger ale in a mixing glass and stir well. Strain into a large cocktail glass and fill with a little ginger ale. Serves 1.

CAMERON'S KICK

¾ ounce Scotch whiskey	½ tablespoon orgeat syrup
¾ ounce Irish whiskey	3 or 4 ice cubes
½ tablespoon lemon juice	

Combine all ingredients in a mixing glass and stir well. Strain into a cocktail glass. Serves 1.

Two dashes of orange bitters are sometimes used instead of orgeat syrup in this drink.

COMMODORE

3 ounces rye whiskey	2 dashes orange bitters
1 tablespoon lime or lemon juice	1 teaspoon sugar syrup
	3 or 4 ice cubes

Combine all ingredients in a cocktail shaker and shake vigorously. Strain into a cocktail glass. Serves 1.

COWBOY

1½ ounces whiskey	½ cup crushed ice
¾ ounce heavy cream	

Combine all ingredients in a cocktail shaker and shake vigorously. Strain into a cocktail glass. Serves 1.

When made with bourbon, this drink is sometimes called **Bourbon Crème** or **Cream.**

CREOLE

1 ounce whiskey	2 dashes Amer Picon
1 ounce sweet vermouth	3 or 4 ice cubes
2 dashes Benedictine	Twist lemon peel

Combine all ingredients in a mixing glass and stir well. Strain into a cocktail glass and drop in the peel. Serves 1.

DE RIGUEUR

1 ounce whiskey	½ ounce honey
½ ounce grapefruit juice	3 or 4 ice cubes

Combine all ingredients in a cocktail shaker and shake vigorously. Strain into a cocktail glass. Serves 1.

DERBY NO. 2

1 ounce whiskey	1½ tablespoons lime juice
½ ounce sweet vermouth	3 or 4 ice cubes
½ ounce white curaçao	Mint leaf

Combine all ingredients except the mint leaf in a cocktail shaker and shake vigorously. Strain into a cocktail glass and garnish with mint leaf. Serves 1.

This drink is sometimes called an **Oriental Cocktail.**

DINAH

1½ ounces whiskey	2 or 3 sprigs fresh mint
1 tablespoon lemon juice	½ cup crushed ice
½ teaspoon superfine sugar	

Put all ingredients in a cocktail shaker, reserving one mint leaf, and shake vigorously. Strain into a cocktail glass, float the mint leaf on top. Serves 1.

DIXIE WHISKEY

2 ounces whiskey	½ teaspoon superfine sugar
¼ teaspoon curaçao	1 teaspoon lemon juice
½ teaspoon white crème de menthe	Dash Angostura bitters
	3 or 4 ice cubes

Combine all ingredients in a cocktail shaker and shake vigorously. Strain into a cocktail glass. Serves 1.

ELK'S OWN

1½ ounces rye whiskey	1 teaspoon superfine sugar
¾ ounce port	3 or 4 ice cubes
1 egg white	Small pineapple stick
1 tablespoon lemon juice	

Combine all ingredients except pineapple in a cocktail shaker and shake vigorously. Strain into a cocktail glass, and garnish with a pineapple stick. Serves 1.

EVERYBODY'S IRISH

1½ ounces Irish whiskey
6 dashes green chartreuse
3 dashes crème de menthe

3 or 4 ice cubes
Olive

Combine all the ingredients except the olive in a cocktail shaker and shake vigorously. Strain into a cocktail glass and drop in the olive. Serves 1.

FOX RIVER

1½ ounces rye whiskey
½ ounce crème de cacao
4 dashes peach bitters

1 or 2 ice cubes
Twist lemon peel

Combine all ingredients except the peel in a mixing glass and stir gently. Strain into a cocktail glass, twist the peel over the glass to release the oil, then drop it in. Serves 1.

FRISCO

1½ ounces bourbon
1½ ounces Benedictine

½ cup crushed ice
Twist lemon peel

Combine all ingredients except the peel in a mixing glass and stir well. Strain into a cocktail glass and drop in the peel. Serves 1.

FRISCO SOUR

2 ounces whiskey
1 tablespoon lemon juice
1 tablespoon lime juice
½ ounce raspberry syrup or
  grenadine

½ cup crushed ice
Chilled club soda
Slice lemon, slice lime

Combine all ingredients except soda and fruit slices in a cocktail shaker and shake vigorously. Strain into a sour or Delmonico glass, fill with club soda and decorate with fruit. Serves 1.

HIGHLAND FLING NO. 1

1½ ounces Scotch whiskey	3 or 4 ice cubes
1 teaspoon superfine sugar	Nutmeg
3 ounces milk	

Combine all ingredients except the nutmeg in a cocktail shaker and shake very thoroughly. Strain into a cocktail glass and grate a little nutmeg on top. Serves 1.

HIGHLAND FLING NO. 2

1½ ounces Scotch whiskey	½ cup crushed ice
¾ ounce sweet vermouth	Olive
2 dashes orange bitters	

Combine all the ingredients except the olive in a cocktail shaker and shake vigorously. Strain into a cocktail glass. Add the olive. Serves 1.

Hole-in-One: Substitute dry vermouth for sweet, and add ¼ teaspoon lemon juice.

HOOT MON

1 ounce Scotch whiskey	½ ounce sweet vermouth
½ ounce Lillet	3 or 4 ice cubes

Combine all ingredients in a mixing glass and stir well. Strain into a cocktail glass. Serves 1.

IRISH CRESTA

1 ounce Irish whiskey	1 egg white
½ ounce Irish Mist liqueur	3 or 4 ice cubes
½ ounce orange juice	

Combine all ingredients in a cocktail shaker and shake vigorously. Strain into a cocktail glass. Serves 1.

IRISH SHILLELAGH

1½ ounces Irish whiskey
½ ounce sloe gin
½ ounce light rum
2 tablespoons lemon juice
1 teaspoon superfine sugar
2 slices fresh peach,
   coarsely chopped

½ cup crushed ice
2 fresh raspberries
1 strawberry
1 cherry

Combine all ingredients except the berries and cherry in a cocktail shaker and shake vigorously. Strain into a cocktail glass and garnish with the fruit. Serves 1.

KENTUCKY

¾ ounce bourbon
1½ ounces pineapple juice

½ cup crushed ice

Combine all ingredients in a mixing glass and stir well. Strain into a cocktail glass. Serves 1.

KENTUCKY COLONEL

1½ ounces bourbon
½ ounce Benedictine

½ cup crushed ice
Twist lemon peel

Combine all ingredients except the peel in a mixing glass and stir well. Strain into a cocktail glass and drop in the peel. Serves 1.

KING COLE

2 ounces bourbon
Dash Fernet Branca
2 dashes sugar syrup

1 slice orange
1 slice pineapple
1 ice cube

Muddle all the ingredients well in an Old-fashioned glass.
Serves 1.

LADIES'

1½ ounces whiskey	Dash Angostura bitters
2 dashes Pernod	3 or 4 ice cubes
3 dashes anisette	Small stick pineapple

Combine all ingredients except the pineapple in a mixing
glass and stir well. Strain into a cocktail glass and add the
pineapple stick. Serves 1.

LAWHILL

1½ ounces rye whiskey	Dash maraschino
¾ ounce dry vermouth	Dash Angostura bitters
Dash Pernod	3 or 4 ice cubes

Combine all ingredients in a mixing glass and stir well. Strain
into a cocktail glass. Serves 1.

LEPRECHAUN

2 ounces Irish whiskey	3 or 4 ice cubes
3 ounces tonic water	Twist lemon peel

Put whiskey and tonic water in an Old-fashioned glass, add
ice cubes and stir gently. Drop in the lemon peel. Serves 1.
  This drink, which is usually just called Irish whiskey and
tonic, is served by Aer Lingus on its flights under the name
given above.

LINSTEAD

1½ ounces whiskey	¼ teaspoon superfine sugar
1½ ounces pineapple juice	Dash Angostura bitters
¼ teaspoon Pernod	3 or 4 ice cubes
½ teaspoon lemon juice	Twist lemon peel

Combine all ingredients except the peel in a cocktail shaker and shake vigorously. Strain into a cocktail glass. Serves 1.

LOCH LOMOND

1½ ounces Scotch whiskey
1 teaspoon superfine sugar
3 dashes Angostura bitters
3 or 4 ice cubes

Combine all ingredients in a cocktail shaker and shake vigorously. Strain into a cocktail glass. Serves 1.

Canadian No. 2: Use Canadian whiskey and add a dash of curaçao.

Palmer: Use rye whiskey, add a dash of lemon juice and omit sugar. Stir rather than shake.

Paddy: Use Irish whiskey, add 1½ ounces sweet vermouth and omit sugar. Stir rather than shake.

MANHATTAN

2½ ounces blended whiskey
¾ ounce sweet vermouth
Dash Angostura bitters
3 or 4 ice cubes
Maraschino cherry

Combine the whiskey, vermouth and ice cubes in a mixing glass and stir well. Strain into a cocktail glass. Garnish with the cherry. Serves 1.

Dry Manhattan: Use dry vermouth in place of sweet, and omit cherry. Add lemon peel, twisting over the drink to release the oil before dropping in; or garnish with an olive.

Spanish Manhattan: Use dry sherry in place of vermouth.

MIAMI BEACH

1 ounce Scotch whiskey
1 ounce dry vermouth
1 ounce grapefruit juice
3 or 4 ice cubes

Combine all ingredients in a mixing glass and stir well. Strain into a cocktail glass. Serves 1.

MILLIONAIRE NO. 2

1½ ounces bourbon
½ ounce curaçao
1 egg white

Dash grenadine
½ cup crushed ice

Combine all ingredients in a cocktail shaker and shake vigorously. Strain into a cocktail glass. Serves 1.

MODERN NO. 2

3 ounces Scotch whiskey
Dash Pernod
2 dashes Jamaica rum
Dash orange bitters

Dash lemon juice
3 or 4 ice cubes
Maraschino cherry

Combine all ingredients except the cherry in a mixing glass and stir well. Strain into a cocktail glass, and drop in the cherry. Serves 1.

MORNING GLORY

1 ounce blended or Scotch
    whiskey
1 ounce brandy
1 dash Pernod
2 dashes curaçao

2 dashes Angostura bitters
3 dashes sugar syrup
1 or 2 ice cubes
Chilled club soda
Superfine sugar

Place all ingredients except the soda and sugar in a mixing glass and stir well. Strain into a 6-ounce glass. Fill with soda water. Wet a spoon, dip it in sugar and stir into the cocktail. Serves 1.

NEW ORLEANS

1½ ounces bourbon
1 dash anisette
2 dashes Pernod
2 dashes Angostura bitters

1 dash orange bitters
½ teaspoon superfine sugar
3 or 4 ice cubes
Twist lemon peel

Combine all ingredients except the peel in a mixing glass and stir well. Strain into a cocktail glass and drop in the peel. Serves 1.

NEW YORK

2 ounces rye whiskey	1½ tablespoons lime juice
½ teaspoon superfine sugar	3 or 4 ice cubes
Dash grenadine	Twist orange peel

Combine all ingredients except the peel in a cocktail shaker and shake vigorously. Strain into a cocktail glass and drop in the peel. Serves 1.

NEW YORK SOUR

2 ounces whiskey	1 tablespoon claret
2 tablespoons lemon juice	Half slice lemon
1 teaspoon superfine sugar	Maraschino cherry
½ cup cracked ice	

Combine whiskey, lemon juice, sugar and ice in a cocktail shaker and shake vigorously. Strain into a sour or Delmonico glass. Float the claret on top and decorate with lemon slice and cherry. Serves 1.

OLD-FASHIONED

The bartender at the Pendennis Club in Louisville, Kentucky, is credited with the creation of the Old-fashioned, one of the most popular of the bourbon drinks.

1 lump sugar	2–3 ounces bourbon
Dash Angostura bitters	Twist lemon peel
1–2 drops cold water	Slice orange (optional)
2 or 3 ice cubes	Maraschino cherry (optional)

Put the sugar into an Old-fashioned glass with bitters and water, and muddle to dissolve the sugar. Add the ice cubes and bourbon and stir. Twist lemon peel over the drink to release the oil and then drop it in. Garnish with orange slice and cherry. Serve with muddler. Serves 1.

Any whiskey, including Scotch, may be used for this drink. If a drier drink is preferred, reduce the sugar to half a lump.

OPENING

1 ounce rye whiskey
½ ounce sweet vermouth

½ ounce grenadine
3 or 4 ice cubes

Combine all ingredients in a mixing glass and stir well. Strain into a cocktail glass. Serves 1.

PREAKNESS

1½ ounces whiskey
¾ ounce sweet vermouth
½ teaspoon Benedictine

Dash Angostura bitters
3 or 4 ice cubes
Twist lemon peel

Combine all ingredients except the lemon peel in a mixing glass and stir well. Strain into a cocktail glass and drop in the lemon peel. Serves 1.

QUAKER NO. 2

1 ounce rye whiskey
1 ounce brandy
1 teaspoon raspberry syrup

1 tablespoon lime juice
3 or 4 ice cubes

Combine all ingredients in a cocktail shaker and shake vigorously. Strain into a cocktail glass. Serves 1.

ROB ROY

3 ounces Scotch whiskey
1 ounce sweet vermouth
2 dashes Angostura bitters

5 or 6 ice cubes
Twist orange or lemon peel

Combine all ingredients except the peel in a mixing glass and stir gently to chill as well as dilute the drink. Strain into a cocktail glass, twist the peel over the drink to release the oil and then drop it in. Serves 1.

For a less strong drink, reduce the Scotch to 1½ ounces, the vermouth to ½ ounce.

Sometimes the bitters are omitted, or orange bitters are used instead.

Dry Rob Roy: Reduce the vermouth to ½ ounce.

ROCK AND RYE

1 piece rock candy
3 ounces rye whiskey

½ teaspoon lemon juice
(optional)

Dissolve the rock candy in the whiskey, add lemon juice and serve in a cocktail glass. Serves 1.

SAZERAC

1 cube sugar
1 teaspoon cold water
2 ounces rye whiskey
Dash Pernod

Dash Peychaud's bitters
3 or 4 ice cubes
Twist lemon peel

Dissolve the sugar in cold water in a mixing glass. Add the whiskey, Pernod, bitters and ice cubes and stir well. Strain into a well-chilled cocktail glass, twist the lemon peel over the drink to release the oil, then drop it in. Serves 1.

This drink is sometimes spelled **Zazarac,** in which case ¼ ounce light rum should be added, and a dash each of orange and Angostura bitters used instead of Peychaud's bitters.

SCOTCH ON THE ROCKS

3 or 4 ice cubes
2 ounces Scotch or any
other whiskey

Twist lemon peel
Cold water (optional)

Put the ice cubes into an Old-fashioned glass, pour in the Scotch or other whiskey and drop in the lemon peel. Add a little cold water. Serves 1.

This method of serving liquor has become extremely popular. Any liquor may be used and many mixed drinks are now poured over ice cubes instead of being strained into a cocktail glass.

SCOTCH SIDECAR

1½ ounces Scotch or any   ¾ ounce lemon juice
  other whiskey   3 or 4 ice cubes
¾ ounce Cointreau

Combine all ingredients in a cocktail shaker and shake vigorously. Strain into a cocktail glass. Serves 1.

SECRET

1½ ounces Scotch whiskey   3 or 4 ice cubes
3 dashes white crème de   Chilled club soda
  menthe

Combine all ingredients except the soda in a mixing glass and stir well. Strain into a cocktail glass and fill with soda. Serves 1.

SERPENT'S TOOTH

1 ounce Irish whiskey   ½ ounce kümmel
2 ounces sweet vermouth   Dash Angostura bitters
2 ounces lemon juice   3 or 4 ice cubes

Combine all ingredients in a mixing glass and stir well. Strain into a cocktail glass. Serves 1.

This drink is also known as a **John Wood.**

SHAMROCK

1 ounce Irish whiskey
1 ounce dry vermouth
3 dashes green chartreuse
3 dashes green crème de
  menthe

3 or 4 ice cubes
Olive

Combine all ingredients in a mixing glass and stir well. Strain
into a cocktail glass. Add an olive. Serves 1.
  This drink is also known as the **Friendly Sons of St. Patrick.**

SUMMER BOURBON

1½ ounces bourbon
3 ounces orange jjuice

Pinch salt
½ cup crushed ice

Mix whiskey, orange juice and salt together and pour into an
8-ounce goblet or wineglass half-filled with the ice. Serves 1.

THISTLE

1½ ounces Scotch whiskey
1½ ounces sweet vermouth

2 dashes Angostura bitters
3 or 4 ice cubes

Combine all ingredients in a mixing glass and stir well. Strain
into a cocktail glass. Serves 1.
  Beadlestone: Omit bitters.

Beals: Use ½ ounce each sweet and dry vermouth instead of 1½ ounces sweet vermouth. Omit bitters.

Flying Scotsman: Add ½ teaspoon superfine sugar.

Harry Lauder: Add 2 dashes sugar syrup. Omit bitters.

TIPPERARY

¾ ounce Irish whiskey
¾ ounce chartreuse
¾ ounce sweet vermouth
3 or 4 ice cubes

Combine all ingredients in a mixing glass and stir well. Strain into a cocktail glass. Serves 1.

TNT

1 ounce rye whiskey
1 ounce Pernod
3 or 4 ice cubes

Combine all ingredients in a cocktail shaker and shake vigorously. Strain into a cocktail glass. Serves 1.

TRILBY NO. 2

¾ ounce Scotch whiskey
¾ ounce sweet vermouth
¾ ounce Parfait Amour
    liqueur
2 dashes Pernod
2 dashes Angostura bitters
3 or 4 ice cubes

Combine all ingredients in a mixing glass and stir well. Strain into a cocktail glass. Serves 1.

This drink is sometimes made without the Parfait Amour liqueur and the Pernod, and with orange bitters instead of Angostura bitters.

WARD EIGHT

1½ ounces rye or bourbon
    whiskey
3 dashes grenadine
3 or 4 ice cubes
Slice each orange and lemon
Maraschino cherry

Combine whiskey, grenadine and 1 or 2 ice cubes in a cocktail shaker and shake vigorously. Strain into an 8-ounce goblet, drop in 2 ice cubes and garnish with the fruit slices and cherry. Serve with straws. Serves 1.

WHISKEY COCKTAIL

1½–3 ounces rye or   ½ teaspoon sugar syrup
    bourbon whiskey   3 or 4 ice cubes
Dash Angostura bitters

Combine all ingredients in a mixing glass and stir well. Strain into a cocktail glass. Serves 1.

When rye whiskey is used, the drink is sometimes called **Rye Whiskey Cocktail,** and a maraschino cherry is added.

Whiskey and Bitters: Omit sugar syrup and add an ice cube to the glass.

WHISKEY AND HONEY

1 teaspoon honey   Twist lemon peel
2 or 3 ice cubes   3 ounces whiskey

Put the honey in an Old-fashioned glass with the ice cubes and lemon peel. Add the whiskey and stir. Serve with muddler. Serves 1.

WHISKEY MAC

2 ounces Scotch whiskey   2 or 3 ice cubes
2 ounces Stone's ginger wine

Combine the Scotch whiskey and ginger wine in a mixing glass with ice cubes and stir well. Strain into a cocktail glass. If preferred, pour the whiskey and ginger wine over ice cubes in an Old-fashioned glass, or serve neat in a stemmed cocktail glass. Serves 1.

WHISKEY SOUR

This drink may be made with any kind of whiskey. See "Sours," page 216.

YASHMAK

¾ ounce rye whiskey	Dash Angostura bitters
¾ ounce Pernod	⅛ teaspoon superfine sugar
¾ ounce dry vermouth	3 or 4 ice cubes

Combine all ingredients in a mixing glass and stir well. Strain into a cocktail glass. Serves 1.

Old Pal: Use Campari instead of Pernod. Omit bitters and sugar.

Companionable Drinks for Round-the-Clock Hospitality

Some drinks, such as cocktails, party punches and those short after-dinner mixtures of brandy and liqueurs, belong to clearly defined categories. A host has little doubt about when and how they should be served. But there is a large assortment of potables so varied in character that no specific overall rules about suitability of time and occasion apply. These drinks range from mild to potent, from sweet to tart, from long to quite short. Most are made with crushed ice or ice cubes, but one group is served hot. Some are exotic, others are robust; a few are rich and creamy, and a number of them are truly elegant.

Nobody but a professional and highly experienced bartender can or should be familiar with all of them, but it will be helpful to you if you learn to recognize the separate characteristics of these drinks, simply by reading the recipes. Having found several that appear to fit into your way of life and your particular patterns of entertaining, you can then test your selections for *taste* over a period of time. Once you learn how to properly prepare those you like best, you will never be at a loss about what drink to serve at any hour to any person—from your most conservative acquaintances to your most imaginative friends. You will always be able to offer appropriate drinks and, when you wish, unusual and memorable ones.

The alcoholic strength of a drink is the first point to consider. This is affected not only by the type and quantity of the alcoholic ingredients but by the amount of dilutants—ice and soda or other mixer—that the recipe calls for. Liquor such as gin, rum, whiskey or vodka has a high alcoholic content; 2 ounces are a good measure in a drink, 1½ a conservative measure, 3 a potent measure. Aperitifs and wines have a much lower percentage of alcohol. The more ice you use in a glass, the more nearly a short drink will fill it; it is much wiser to increase the quantity of ice than the amount of alcohol. Crushed ice both cools and melts (therefore dilutes) more quickly than ice cubes. As a general rule of thumb, the instruction ". . . and fill up with soda" (or tonic, etc.) should be considered in relation to the size of the glass; the bigger it is, the more mixer is needed to fill it and the weaker the drink winds up.

Sizable quantities of non-alcoholic ingredients such as fruit juice or milk definitely affect a drink's character and taste. Small amounts—spoonfuls and dashes—of almost anything from liqueurs to fruit juice and bitters—are essentially for flavor. Egg, molasses, cream or anything else that is thick in substance gives a drink a creamy richness. Of course, honey, sugar, sugar- or fruit-flavored syrup, and sweet liqueurs like Grand Marnier or maraschino add sweetness. Lemon or lime adds tartness.

Creamy or sweet drinks don't sharpen the appetite as much as dry or tart ones, but they often have little alcoholic taste to them, which is one reason why they are popular with people who arc light or inexperienced drinkers.

Very long drinks are excellent thirst quenchers but filling and therefore best suited to midmorning, midafternoon or late evening quaffing.

Drinks made with milk are soothing and for this reason very pleasant in the late morning or at bedtime.

Rather strong drinks of short length that are served in goblets, Old-fashioned glasses or small tumblers are not a good choice when people have a lot of time on their hands, because more than two rounds can be more than enough. It's a good idea to serve appetizing snacks with them unless a meal is in the offing.

Enthusiastic beer drinkers may enjoy some of the drinks based on wine or liquor with beer or one of its near relatives, but always offer an alternative unless you are very sure of your friends' preferences. The same liquor or wine mixed with soda, for example, makes a simple and satisfactory second choice.

Many potables in this section can be easily mixed right in the living room, on the porch, by the swimming pool or wherever your guests are assembled. Simply set up a tray with the necessary ingredients and glasses, fill an ice bucket and place both on a nearby table so you can handle the bartending without having to miss a word of the conversation. (The table should be in the shade if it is outside the house.) It is a wise precaution, however, to make certain drinks alone and bring them to your guests on a tray. The drinks that are complicated and require concentration to put together tend to turn out better if you have no audience. When eggs must be separated, ice crushed, etc., perform these chores in the kitchen, and ahead of time if possible. Potent drinks should be whipped up in private for a less obvious reason: People do not ask for refills as readily if making them appears to involve any effort. Therefore you can control consumption by spacing your servings or, when necessary, stopping them.

Drinks based on beer, champagne or other ingredients that should be kept very cold until serving time are easier to make on a counter by the refrigerator than anywhere else. This avoids setting out wine buckets or tubs of ice and risking messiness.

Whether the day is hot and sunny or cold and snowy, whether friends drop in or are invited at any odd time in the day, whether you sit around the living room or patio or go off on a picnic, the drinks you offer are indicative of your flair for hospitality. Here are some suggestions and ideas that can put you at ease as a bartender-host; with them you can delight your guests with the delicious products of a seemingly effortless skill.

Curtain Raisers on the Late Morning Scene

The drinks you serve your guests before brunch can vary widely. They run the appetizing gamut from non-alcoholic juices and mixtures through the white wines that make fine aperitifs, to such hearty eye-openers as Bloody Marys. And, of course, some purists feel that the only truly suitable drink for a sociable late breakfast is champagne in one form or another. For sheer elegance, it's hard to beat a champagne cocktail. For panache cum practicality, serve champagne alone—as an aperitif and then throughout the meal. This requires only one set of glasses and no ice cubes or mixing. *Blanc de blancs* and brut—the driest of the champagnes—make marvelously brisk eye-openers. Or you might offer your brunch guests a choice of simpler drinks. For example, you could set out one pitcher of iced pineapple juice mixed with lime, and another of sangría, and let everyone help himself. Both are light and a pleasure to drink; one is non-alcoholic and the other only mildly alcoholic. The most thoughtful host provides a choice of potions that vary enough in strength and appeal so that each guest can choose one to suit his particular morning mood.

Mixed drinks: Many delectable mixed drinks are appropriate for the morning hours, although not necessarily limited to them. Two of the simplest are based on well-chilled champagne. One is a California Sunshine, a smooth blend of pink champagne and icy orange juice with a dash of cassis syrup. Another, richer and heavier, is a Black Velvet, an English standby that combines champagne with chilled stout (the dark stout gives the drink its name), served in silver tankards or tall glasses. Should you prefer your morning champagne in an even more memorable form, try a drink that comes from Harry's Bar in Venice, one of the really fascinating eating and drinking establishments in Europe. It is called a Bellini in honor of the composer and is a highly successful merger of peach puree and champagne.

If it's fortification you're looking for, consider such uniquely flavorful drinks as a Pisco Sour, made with Peruvian brandy, or a Tequila Sour, based on south-of-the-border tequila. There are also times when Pernod seems the best morning drink of all. Its anise flavor is especially refreshing for a leisurely breakfast outdoors on a hot day. Most people like to drink Pernod with ice and water or use it as an ingredient in certain pick-me-ups.

Flips are highly satisfactory drinks to serve on a cold morning. They are made with various liquors or wines and always with egg. They are shaken like a cocktail or mixed in a blender until creamy smooth. A Brandy Flip is full of character; a Sherry Flip is gently soothing. Each is an excellent noontime drink, as are the other flips.

Among the many midday cocktails that are popular, the Bloody Mary seems particularly so, perhaps because its basic ingredient is vodka, that near-flavorless liquor. But guests often enjoy variations that are more provocative because less familiar. To list a few: Barnacle Bill, Bloody Marie, Bloody Bullshot and Geisha Whirl.

Mild drinks: The delicately flavored aperitif wines, because of their relatively low alcoholic content and pleasant taste, make ideal drinks in the morning. (For more about them, see page 42.) Serve them well chilled and have soda or ginger ale, fresh lemons and oranges ready for guests who wish to dilute or dress up their aperitif.

Any light, wine-based mixture, provided it is not too

sweet, is an excellent curtain raiser during the morning. Just before brunch or lunch, a cobbler made with dry, rather than sweet, wine is often preferable to a long drink because it leaves more room for the food.

Milk-based drinks: A number of people swear that their favorite of these, to paraphrase Tennyson's famous line, "gentlier on the stomach lies, than tired eyelids upon tired eyes." Some feel that Alexanders made with milk rather than cream are dependable restorers of good health and good temper in spite of their sweetness. Others prefer a Milk Punch made with brandy or whiskey in a tall glass. They drink it cold in summer, gently warmed in winter. Puffs may not be familiar to your friends, but it is likely that they will meet with instant success. They are simply a combination of liquor and milk with ice and soda. The most popular one is based on brandy, but you can also concoct them with gin, rum or almost any type of whiskey. Medium in length and fine in flavor, they are good pre-luncheon drinks and rather dependable pick-me-ups.

Pick-me-ups: These are specifically designed for the "morning-after" sufferer who wants to bolster his flagging spirits, calm his nerves and digestive tract and develop strength in his knees. Obviously, such a cure-all requires a combination of uplifting, body-building and soothing ingredients. Many trenchermen swear by champagne as the only antidote for a queasy stomach, and certainly it has long been regarded as a panacea for seasickness. With such a reputation, a Champagne Pick-Me-Up may indeed work miracles. It also includes a goodly measure of brandy for strength and some dashes of Fernet Branca, the well-known Italian digestive. Harry's Pick-Me-Up consists almost entirely of champagne and brandy.

An unbroken egg yolk or whole egg is a time-honored remedy and is customarily swallowed whole, probably because it is not generally considered a highly palatable morsel. When teamed with brandy and pepped up with Worcestershire sauce, however, as in a Prairie Oyster No. 1, or with port in a No. 2, or with sherry in Sherry and Egg, even a raw egg becomes quite easy to cope with. Those more cautious souls who want non-alcoholic pick-me-ups will find them among the Non-Alcoholic Drinks (page 390).

Drinks for Idle Afternoons

We've all known and loved them—those long, leisurely weekend afternoons when nothing seems more important —or desirable—than to sit around and loaf in the company of friends. In warm weather, the gathering place often is the patio, lawn, swimming pool or shaded front porch. On bleak, wintry days it is apt to be the living room or den. The invitation is casual: "Why don't you come over after lunch on Sunday?" No schedule, no formalities, no spelled-out entertainment. Whether you are host to one or two guests or several, for a couple of hours or longer, the basic need—in terms of a potable—is the same: drinks that can be sipped and enjoyed slowly and that you can mix in batches or in tall glasses with a minimum of effort.

A cup of one sort or another can be a good solution (page 371). This is a wine-based, punchlike drink that is made in a pitcher. Some cups are stronger than others, so study the recipes and pick out one that will best please your particular guests. Another excellent accompaniment for idle hours, particularly in summer, is sangría, which is also made with wine.

If your friends don't want anything very alcoholic—and this can happen to the bravest and boldest—consider offering them Angostura Highballs, essentially nothing but ginger ale, or, for something a little zestier, Americanos based on sweet vermouth and Campari, both of which are low in alcoholic content.

Look into the sizable group of coolers, ranging from mild to fairly potent. Don't let the group name mislead you; these drinks can be enjoyed the year round. They're based on wine or liquor, and almost all of them call for an effervescent mixer—soda, ginger ale or, in one recipe, champagne. Test and taste on your own in advance so you will know which to serve to any particular crowd—an invaluable asset.

The most uncomplicated thing you can do is offer long drinks such as one of the simpler fizzes, collinses or high-balls. Fizzes are shaken, but the other two are made in tall glasses, and all are a cinch to concoct. Because any of these drinks can be based on one of a number of liquors, although the setups remain the same, you may be tempted to offer guests alternatives, depending upon the extent of your bar supplies. If tempted, limit yourself to a choice of two. Always remember that you're not running a public bar but simply trying to be a good host and make your guests happy.

There is an impressive assortment of middle-sized drinks that may tempt you. Some are well known; others are un-usual. They are served in small tumblers, goblets, Old-fashioned glasses or large wineglasses. Although there is no rule about them, these potables, owing to their size, tend to be drunk more quickly than long ones, which usually means that glasses need to be refilled more often. This may turn out to be hard on you as a host and your guests as imbibers, unless the drink is based on a wine or aperitif. For most people, long hours and long drinks are probably the most satisfactory partners.

Portable Potables

Picnics can stick in your memory when three-star restaurants have all merged into one great ruinous excess. Pâté and crackers in the hills, sandy sandwiches on the beaches, mugs of soup in the cockpits of boats, wine and peaches among the boulders of a dried-up creek, apples and cheese by a river, even a can of consommé by the roadside, with a flat tire and night falling—all these snacks or meals, little-planned or not planned at all—have that great element of a picnic, the open air, and they can be unforget-table.

A bar away from home is simple to set up if you keep your choice of drinks to a suitable minimum and have adequate equipment for transporting and producing them at a properly low temperature. Too much variety complicates the preparing, packing, unpacking and serving procedures, so plan easy-to-make drinks and no more than two or three kinds.

Chilling techniques: Cold liquids save on ice cubes, so chill all ingredients well in your refrigerator before leaving home. If you have room in your freezer, use it to do an arctic job on thermos bottles and jugs, unzippered insulated bags and, if possible, a large ice chest too. Or put plastic bags of regular or dry ice in such containers for a few hours beforehand. By taking these simple precautions, you can ensure that your drinks won't be lukewarm when you're ready to serve them. Always refrigerate whatever liquors and mixers you plan to take along, for the colder everything is to begin with, the longer it will stay that way, including the ice itself. At freezer temperature (0° F.) ice will last longer than at freezing temperature (32° F.), and dry ice (−109° F.) is very long-lived indeed. Extremely low temperatures, of course, are not good for wine or beer, or for mixers or foods that are going on a picnic. (Spirits, however, will not freeze.) Ice cubes can be neatly transported in plastic bags stored in insulated containers. Open containers designed for sending bon voyage presents of iced champagne, or galvanized metal buckets, can be packed with ice and will hold up to twelve bottles, depending on size. You might even choose to revive the old, dependable method used for toting cold drinks forty or fifty years ago: put a good-sized washtub in the trunk of your car (or on the boat), add plenty of ice, the bottles of drinks, and cover with a wet gunnysack. If you are picnicking by or on the water, nature can do the cooling of wine. You can wedge a bottle or two between stones in a running stream or make a cradle for the bottles over the side of a boat (a string shopping bag is ideal). Ten minutes' immersion in cold running water is usually enough. Another, slower method, and remarkably successful, is to wrap a standing bottle in a wet cloth. If there is any sort of breeze or draft, the evaporation from the drying cloth cools the wine quite efficiently. The cloth needs rewetting from time to time, but an hour of this treatment should do it.

Unbreakable glasses: No drink is at its best out of a paper cup or enamel mug. If your potable is worth drinking at all, it is worth taking glasses along. You can pack up the standard type, but satisfying one's thirst alfresco has become much more enjoyable since the development of excellent throwaway plastic glasses—good-looking, thin, tasteless, odorless, light and virtually unbreakable. These glasses are inexpensive enough to be used once and discarded; sturdy enough to be carried home, washed and used over and over. Stick to the colorless variety; they're the most satisfactory.

Some good traveling companions: Drinks, like people, have their individual talents and drawbacks. When you're planning an excursion to some picnic purlieu, you'll be grateful later if you've considered in advance which drinks will be most cooperative on such a jaunt, which will best complement the food you'll be taking and best please the people you'll be leading on the particular safari. Given enough planning, equipment and efficiency, there are dozens of libations that can be served almost anywhere on land or sea or in the air, but the wise hostess concentrates on the most effect at the lowest risk.

Oddly enough, a large batch of certain cocktails is easy to prepare in advance for a picnic if you know the trick. In each case, the cocktails, listed below, are mixed in a quart-size bottle that contains the basic liquor. When the blending has been done, recork the bottle firmly and store it in the refrigerator until the time comes to transport it; then nestle it in ice for the trip. Serve the cocktails over plenty of ice in Old-fashioned glasses, which are excellent for the purpose and more practical, of course, if made of plastic. Each quart bottle holds about eight 4-ounce drinks.

Martinis: Pour out 4 ounces from a quart bottle of gin

and replace with dry vermouth. (This will make a very dry Martini—about 7 to 1; if you prefer yours less potent, increase the amount of vermouth.) Remove the peel from a lemon in one long continuous spiral and put it in the bottle.

Manhattans: For a dry Manhattan, pour out 6 ounces of bourbon or rye from a quart bottle and replace it with dry vermouth. Peel a lemon in a single spiral and put the peel in the bottle. When serving, add a dash of bitters to each glass.

For a sweet Manhattan, use sweet vermouth. Omit the lemon peel, but add a dash of bitters and a maraschino cherry to each glass at serving time.

Daiquiris: Pour out 6 ounces of rum (light or dark) from a quart bottle and replace it with a defrosted 6-ounce can of frozen Daiquiri mix or the juice of about 8 limes mixed with 3 tablespoons of fine sugar or simple sugar syrup (to prepare the syrup, see page 18). Shake the bottle of Daiquiris thoroughly before storing in the refrigerator.

Margaritas: Pour out 6 or 7 ounces of tequila from a quart bottle and replace it with 4 or 5 ounces of Cointreau and 1 or 2 ounces of lime juice. Shake the mix well before storing. When serving, rub the rims of Old-fashioned glasses with pre-cut lime quarters, then spin the rims in salt to frost them. A small slice of lime may be added to each drink for decoration.

Ready-made, bottled cocktails may be frozen in a block of ice, as may aquavit, vodka and other liquors. (For how to do this, see page 20.) On the way to the picnic, keep the bottles very cold, and do not remove the outer containers that surround the iced bottles until serving time.

Cocktails in cans should be thoroughly chilled ahead of time and packed in ice in insulated bags.

Your pet cocktails can always be made according to the standard recipes without using ice and then chilled thoroughly before packing in an insulated bag. Add ice before serving.

Long drinks: Many people prefer the long standbys to

cocktails. Some of these can be made in advance, and any simple ones can be put together at the picnic spot with very little effort. All you have to do is chill the liquor and the mixers and pack them with bags of ice cubes. Use plenty of ice and, if fruit juices are among the ingredients, bring them along ready-squeezed and chilled. Such old reliables as Scotch on the rocks or with water, bourbon with water or soda, or gin and tonic are easy to cope with. Or you might choose from a variety of collinses or bucks. If you're in the mood for something more unusual and quite British in tone, you can make long drinks based on one of the three varieties of Pimm's Cup. Or you can pre-mix the tomato juice base for Bloody Marys, chill it thoroughly and complete the drinks when you reach your picnic spot. Ginger beer, much neglected in this country, blends well with vodka, gin or rum for a long drink.

Dieters and non-drinkers may relish the afore-mentioned ginger beer on its own, as it is briskly refreshing. Or they may like something as simple as plain tonic water, chilled Perrier or cola. Any of the fruit-based non-alcoholic drinks (pages 386–402) are also excellent candidates.

Drinks with a fruit flavor: There are times on a lazy summer day when nothing tastes better than a long, cooling draft of fruit juice, with or without alcohol. If you pack frozen concentrated juices in insulated bags, they will save on space and also help to keep bottles cold. Don't forget water for dilution. Also take along chilled vodka, gin or rum. Children can enjoy the plain fruit juice; adults may add a jigger of liquor and some ice cubes if they wish.

A summer punch is another good choice for a family party. Pack your favorite concentrated juices, a jar of instant tea, a supply of chilled water, plain or carbonated, and some fruit to add to the punch: cherries, orange slices, berries, pineapple cubes are all good additions. Take two bowls (you can pack the fruit in them) and mix the punch at the picnic—one bowl for children and the second, spiked with liquor, for adults. For the spiking, you can choose from a large list: vodka, pisco (Peruvian brandy), tequila, cognac, whiskey, kirsch, rum, vermouth, champagne, white or red wine. Whatever you select, be sure to chill the bottles and pack them in insulated bags. You will need some ice, but a little goes a long way in punch. Two cautions: Because of the many ingredients and open bowls, punch is best made on a sturdy picnic table. Also, the open bowls are a hazard if the wind is blowing and you're going to a beach; a sandy drink is nobody's treat.

A jug of wine beneath the bough: The joys of picnicking are not the joys of the exquisite, the rarefied, of rich sauces and great growths of wine, but the simple pleasures of refreshment. Bread, cheese and beer make a perfect meal under a hayrick at harvest time if the bread be warm and crusty, the cheese creamy and strong and the beer as cold as a stone. So, suitable picnic wines are not wines to hold up to the light, to nose and ponder over. Rather, they're the friendly, unassuming and accommodating ones.

Ideally, a picnic wine should be definitely *cold*. Not icy, but like spring water. Many people feel that this goes for red wine at picnics as well as white or rosé. You don't want to drink anything, not even red Burgundy, that's the temperature of the inside of a car on a hot day. All wine should be brought down to a coolness that refreshes your mouth, and white wines should be a bit colder than that. For various ways to accomplish this chilling, see "Chilling Techniques," above.

A bone-dry sherry, chilled and served as an aperitif, is a welcome change from stronger drinks on a summer picnic. Some people even like it right through the meal.

Vermouth, sweet or dry, is also popular with many as an aperitif. Or you may blend the two, and add a drop or so of bitters and a twist of lemon peel. Or add a dash of soda and a little Campari. (This is one drink that does not require ice; another is the English brandy and soda: cognac with splash of Perrier.)

The virtues of champagne for a picnic are too obvious to mention. Its disadvantages are the care you must take not to shake it up so that it behaves like a geyser when you open it, and the cooling problem. Warm champagne is a terrible thing. But for lunch in sunlight or dinner in moonlight, on terrace, backyard, quarterdeck or coral reef, cold dry, sparkling champagne is the essence of fresh-air celebration. For a tall drink with an iced champagne base, you might consider a French "75," a King's Peg or a Queen's Peg.

Still white wines, sufficiently chilled, go well with outdoor meals. Add a dash of crème de cassis to the first glass of wine for an aperitif and drink the rest plain with the food. Make your selection from California Rieslings or the pleasant light wines from Alsace, the Loire Valley, or the Rhine and Moselle regions of Germany. Save the great white Burgundies and German wines for at-home entertaining—such outstanding wines do not take kindly to the jiggling they would suffer on a picnic excursion. The same is true of red wines; never try to tote fine château-bottled Bordeaux or one of the famous Burgundies. Stick to the lighter, simpler red wines that go excellently with alfresco food—a good Beaujolais, some of the reds from the Rhône valley, Italian reds and the California Gamays and Mountain Reds. Several of the French and American rosés are also splendid picnic troupers.

If you prefer serving wine in a mixed drink, spritzers make delightfully refreshing aperitifs. And sangría is a delicious thirst quencher with a red wine base. Bring the chilled ingredients with you, including ice, and combine in a large pitcher at the picnic table. *Remember:* Don't forget to include a corkscrew and, if required, a bottle and can opener. Such small and homely tools are essential open sesames to thirst quenching.

How to Bring Home the Best of Café Life

All across Europe, cafés are an integral part of daily living. From the biggest cities to the smallest villages, "Everyman's club" prospers. When the weather is warm, tables and chairs are set out on the sidewalk. When it's cold, glass window walls are put around them, or the customers congregate inside. Thousands of American tourists have savored the simple enjoyment of sitting at a café table and sipping mild drinks without watching the clock. Until quite recently, however, this mode of relaxation remained an ocean removed, psychologically as well as geographically, from our own country's popular concept of drinking. The easy-do-it approach was never our forte, but there are signs that we are beginning to cultivate and appreciate it. Since the atmosphere and attitude in public bars here do not exactly encourage it, more and more people are practicing the principles of café life in their own homes.

If you want to establish the civilized and delightful ambience that so many Europeans find rewarding, nothing could be easier. All you need do is have a comfortably furnished living room, porch or patio, depending on the season, become familiar with some of the better known aperitifs and aperitif-based mixed drinks, and gather kindred souls around you.

Investigate the favorite drink of Spain—sherry (page 63). Try the different types and various brands. Look at dry and sweet vermouth in the European way—not as cocktail ingredients but as drinks you can enjoy on their own (page 66). And seriously sample aperitifs such as Dubonnet, Campari, Punt e Mes and Byrrh.

Once you get to know the individual characteristics of these assorted potables, you will be well prepared to start using your favorites in interesting mixed drinks. Almost all of them can be the base for delicious concoctions—long, short or goblet-size.

For aperitif-based cocktails, see page 107.

But what of those midafternoon hours, even midmorning times, when one wants a *tall* drink that is delicious but only mildly alcoholic? Some of the coolers fail into this category. The Country Club Cooler, for example, although so American in name, is simply dry vermouth, a little grenadine and plenty of soda in a tall glass with ice.

Substitute a sizable measure of raspberry syrup for the grenadine and you have a Vermouth Cooler. Or you might try a Dubonnet Fizz, which is made a little differently from the run of fizzes because it calls for a generous amount of orange juice and a flavorful spoon of cherry brandy along with the Dubonnet and soda. This is a fine drink and not encountered at every turn.

Look through the group of long drinks if real thirst quenching is an important requisite—as on a hot day or after some exercise. The Americano, invented by an Italian, is made with sweet vermouth, Campari and soda. A Byrrh Cassis is, of course, based on the popular French aperitif, and a Vermouth Cassis on dry vermouth. The crème de cassis adds a tang of black currants and is, by the way, one of those inspired liqueurs that has dozens of uses.

Although you may think of a highball as an American teaming of hard liquor and soda, you can give it a French interpretation by basing it on Dubonnet! Here is a drink that is pleasantly pink to look at, delightful to sip and so easy to make that producing "seconds" scarcely interrupts a conversation. This is particularly true when you have the ingredients set out on a handy cocktail tray.

If you want to switch the mood from Continental to British and the inspiration from café to pub, all you need do is serve Shandygaff, which is popular throughout England. Most usually a happy merger of beer and ginger beer, other versions call for ale and ginger ale, or lager beer and tart lemonade. Just be sure the ingredients are well chilled because you don't even have to break out a tray of ice cubes for this one.

It is fun to find an appropriate drink for a particular season or hour, a drink that is not altogether usual. If you live in apple country, for example, and the nip of autumn is in the air, you might enjoy serving cider-diluted Stone Fences after a few hours in the open. Or if it's nourishment that guests desire as well as good cheer, consider Tiger's Milk, with its two liquors and heavy cream. Should you want to summon up the "green hour" (l'heure verte), as before-dinnertime used to be called in Paris in the days when absinthe was *the* drink of the daring, try a Tomate based on Pernod, today's less lethal potion but with the same flavor and character as now-illegal absinthe.

The best of café life is its relaxed, permissive easiness. True, the most typical café drinks are wines, aperitifs and mixtures based on them. But many a café habitué in Europe orders a bottle of mineral water or an espresso. At the other end of the favorite drinks are small glasses of straight liquor—brandy, Holland gin in its own country, and so on. So concentrate on evoking a *mood* and encourage it with whatever drinks you think fitting.

The Bubbly Reliables

Just before a meal, tall effervescent drinks may be too filling, and just after a meal people may be too full for them, but at almost any other time they are both suitable and satisfactory. As a host, you will find them most cooperative. They won't trip you up with demands for out-of-the-ordinary ingredients that you don't have on hand, or with complicated instructions. Many of them are extremely similar, with little but their names to distinguish them from one another. Begin by experimenting with some of the basic recipes in which you can use almost any liquor. For bucks, you add ginger ale. For collinses, fizzes, rickeys, slings and swizzles, you add soda (although traditional rickeys are made with water and swizzles require swizzle sticks to give them a right to their name). Any of these drinks can be put together, without bother, at a serving table in the living room or on the terrace, or made in the kitchen and brought in on a tray. All you need is tall, sturdy glasses, plenty of ice and the simple ingredients.

While it is quite true that the above-mentioned drink "families" could be included among the coolers or long drinks, you won't find basic recipes within these two groups, but you will notice a lot of variety. Many is the time, for example, when a mild quaff seems more desirable than a stronger one, and a Red or White Wine Cooler might be the ideal libation to offer. For clean-tasting refreshment, the dash of crème de menthe in a Scotch Cooler is hard to beat and very apt to earn you compliments.

If your friends and the hour call for substantial drinks, and you know that they like beer, offer them Boilermakers—nothing more nor less than beer spiked with whiskey or used as a chaser for straight whiskey. Another hearty thirst quencher is a Foghorn, made with gin and ginger beer. These are essentially earthy, masculine drinks that encourage good talk, tall stories, and perhaps a few hands of poker. A French "75" is something else again. Gin gives it power and champagne gives it style. This is a great potable to serve when you want to celebrate on the spur of the moment and happen to have some champagne in the refrigerator. It is definitely not for the long haul. There are less overpowering drinks made with champagne, and of course all of them sparkle with a bright horde of bubbles. Take a look at the recipes for a Champagne Cooler, Buck Fizzes No. 1 and No. 2, a Champagne Fizz, the totally non-traditional Champagne Julep, and a raft of other long drinks such as the rather fabulous American Rose that includes brandy, half a mashed ripe peach and a dash of Pernod along with the champagne. Don't pass over a Champagne Cassis Highball, Prince of Wales and additional tempters without stopping to consider.

If you think that hearty flavor but low alcoholic content is indicated, consider a Shandygaff or a Gingerade. If you're looking for a more subtle brew, there is Byrrh or Vermouth Cassis, Claret Lemonade, Soda Aperitif or a spritzer. All are made with an aperitif or wine base, and no guest need worry about whether or not she should have a second.

Three much-liked effervescent mixers to which many are devoted are cola, tonic water and bitter lemon. Tonic water, because of its quinine content and the fact that quinine has long been used in tropical countries to combat malaria, is invariably associated with hot-weather drinks. It is most often teamed with gin or vodka, as is bitter lemon, and any of these is as easy as a highball to make. Cola complements rum so well that the combination has even been incorporated in a popular song! The name of the best-known variation is Cuba Libre.

Most of us like the tangy taste of bubbles and the playful look of them. And it is one of the happier facts of life that so many drinks made with effervescent mixers require a minimum of effort to produce. There are only a few bits of general bubble knowledge that you should be familiar with. For one thing, the more chilled your mixer the more slowly it will dilute ice in a drink. So take the precaution of keeping emergency bottles of popular types in the refrigerator. The second point: Open any bottle or can of effervescent liquid gently or it may overflow and be messy. Note that the colder it is, the better it is apt to behave. Three: Always add the bubbly ingredient last, after the others and after the ice. Four: Although a long drink requires stirring, do this very gently and briefly when bubbles are involved, to preserve as many of them as possible. Then add any garnish, and serve promptly. Five: Partly used bottles of soda and so on can be kept for a reasonable length of time if properly recapped, but make sure that the liquid hasn't gone flat before you pour it into a drink. Test by holding your thumb over the open bottle while shaking it once or twice quickly. If you see no bubbles or very few, open a fresh bottle. Nothing—but nothing—is flatter than a flat mixer that is supposed to be lively.

Winter Warm-ups

There are times when a well-made hot drink is the most satisfactory potable in the world. It warms blood that's chilled from wind and weather and lifts spirits that are dampened by storms and icy roads.

All the recipes given in this section are for one serving,

but it is a simple matter to multiply quantities by whatever number you want. For hot drinks designed to serve four or more, however, you should also consider the Hot Punches (page 376).

Here are a few tips that may be helpful when you make hot drinks. For one thing, be sure of what you're doing, because a hot drink must be made immediately before serving, and with a minimum of fussing around. If it requires boiling water, have this ingredient at the ready. When a drink is long enough to almost fill a mug, be considerate of your guest's comfort and use one. Mugs with handles are easy to hold and friendly to drink from. If you serve a hot drink in glass, put a silver demitasse spoon or teaspoon in it before you pour in any hot liquid. This will prevent your glass from cracking. To pre-warm a glass or mug, rinse it out with hot water. Do not get careless about measurements when making a hot drink. Heat increases the headiness of the liquor and intensifies the taste of flavorings, so what may seem a small increase in quantity may turn out to be too much of a good thing. Furthermore, any "dividend" will be wasted because a lukewarm second serving is worse than no second at all. Each round should be made fresh (with the exception of warm punches).

Brandy, whiskey and rum are the most popular bases for a hot drink made with liquor. If you wish to serve something milder, use a recipe based on wine.

There are several occasions when hot drinks can be most welcome, but only one season—and cold winter, at that! After skiing, skating, sledding, a long walk or any other vigorous exercise when it's cold enough to see your breath, such ingredients as the molasses in a Black Stripe No. 2, or the butter in a mug of Hot Buttered Rum give the liquor a fine fillip. The choice of hot drinks is wide and in some instances the service is spectacular. If you learn, for instance, to make a Blue Blazer with casual deftness, you will never lack an audience, but be content to keep the audience small. It takes too long to turn out Blazers in quantity—and besides, repetition undermines showmanship!

Just before the party breaks up to go home on a snowy night or off to bed, warm and soothe everyone with an Irish Cow based—you guessed it—on Irish whiskey, or use rum instead, for a simple Nightcap.

Toddies are simplicity itself to brew. The cold ones are all made alike, with liquor, a little sugar and ice cubes. They're served in small tumblers or Old-fashioned glasses. Hot toddies are something else again. Some are as easy to put together as the cold kind, but there is one delicious recipe that calls for a baked apple; another for sweet butter and flavorings, and so on. All are at their best when served in warmed mugs.

Nourishing and fortifying potions come into their own when there is a sharp nip to the air. Many of these include egg or milk or both. Sometimes cream is an ingredient. Although not usually hot, individual milk punches are excellent candidates, as are flips made with eggs and puffs made with milk.

All of us are accustomed to iced drinks at every season, but you might break with American tradition and serve scaffas for a change when the snow is flying. These are unusual and a cinch to make. They consist of one part liquor and one part liqueur in a cocktail glass with a dash of bitters, served at room temperature. No ice; no shaking. Try them out on friends who enjoy new ideas and tastes. Scaffas are good cocktails before a meal or fine short drinks after dinner with coffee.

It's always more fun to be with your friends when you're making drinks than to whip them up alone in the kitchen. In the case of hot brews, you can use a saucepan or keep a kettle boiling over a spirit lamp or on an electric plate right in the living room. Place it on the hearth or a side table where it won't get knocked over, and where your friends can enjoy watching your performance. And in the excitement of trying out delectable recipes, don't forget that old-time favorite, a cup of hot tea laced with rum.

Everyone's appetite is keener in winter, so be sure to serve some food with your drinks, whatever the time of day. Sandwiches, cheese, apples, raisins and nuts are all good with winter drinks.

If you have a dependable thermos bottle, you can enjoy hot drinks along with a tailgate lunch before a football game or on the deck of a house in the mountains or when picnicking by the skating rink. Grog, Port or Sherry Wine Negus, or hot toddies made with whiskey, rum or brandy are good travelers. Bring lemon slices separately to add at the last moment, and grated nutmeg in a small shaker. But switch to cold drinks if the day isn't cold and crisp.

Specialties of the House

Many women have discovered that it is first-rate hostess strategy to become known for a particular dish they cook superbly and that their friends always associate with them. It might be something as sophisticated as a caviar mousse served with cocktails before dinner, or as substantial as a pork tenderloin casserole, but it is never run-of-the-mill. By the same token, a host can establish an enviable reputation by serving a particular drink that is delicious, a little unusual and something of a specialty with him. This is not to say that he offers no alternatives. Tastes differ and occasions vary. But it is fun to develop a "specialty of the house," and to become more or less famous for it.

If you want to make a cocktail your house specialty, look for a winner in that section (page 92). If after-dinner drinks tempt you, turn to them (page 319). But if you prefer to depart from the pre- and post-prandial brews and concentrate on those that adapt themselves to many times of day, read on.

It is wise to do some experimenting in order to find a particular mixed drink that is not only a standout but also suited to your way of life, the place where you live, and the taste of your friends as well as your own. Superb Mint Juleps, for example, can be real reputation builders. But they require lots of mint (do you have a mint patch?), masses of crushed ice (have you got an automatic ice crusher?), ideally a hot day (where do you live?), and considerable effort. In short, Mint Juleps are excellent drinks to serve to a few people on your porch or lawn in the late morning or midafternoon of very warm days, provided—of course—that you have the ingredients and facilities at hand. Ask yourself if such times occur often enough to warrant your becoming a julep connoisseur. You might also consider smashes, which are miniature juleps served in small tumblers or Old-fashioned glasses. Although bourbon is the traditional base, you can use another liquor to give your juleps a personal flair.

Almost any drink based on champagne can earn plaudits and an enviable reputation for a host if he makes and serves it properly. Consider having Peach or Pear Bowls in lieu of a snack or dessert. Guests will drink the champagne, eat the fruit and compliment you. Black Velvet, that satin-smooth teaming of stout and champagne, both well chilled, is a very special, all-seasons mixture that you might base your claim to fame on. So is a King's Peg or Queen's Peg, provided your friends like their champagne spiked with liquor. For these and other mixed drinks based on champagne, you need not use the finest brand, but do choose a good, dependable one that is very dry, or brut. Be sure it is refreshingly cold. And recognize that champagne evokes an aura of festive elegance which is usually wasted on earthy souls who favor such elementary thirst quenchers as gin and ginger ale or rum and Coca-Cola.

If you live in a part of the country where fresh green coconuts are available, and if the people you know like them, you might go in for one version or another of the Coco Loco. Or, if your friends tend to favor things British, Pimm's Cup may strike a responsive chord.

Cobblers are definitely round-the-clock drinks, because they range from mild to strong, depending on the base ingredient used. This can run the gamut from fiery applejack to mellow port (page 265). The only other components required are crushed ice, sugar—and a garnish of fruit and mint if you feel so inclined. These drinks look most inviting when served in large, clear glass goblets. Try your hand at a few, varying the quantities of liquor or wine and sugar. You might become known for two cobblers—one gentle and the other powerful. And if you have a collection of good-looking goblets, you couldn't use them to better advantage than for serving cobblers.

Among the pre-mixed, homemade, bottled drinks, Brandy or Rum Shrub or Hippocras is a likely candidate for a house specialty. All are made ahead, bottled and allowed to stand for awhile—which is good news for a host. All are rather sweet—which is good news for those people who don't really enjoy dry drinks. They are served over ice cubes in tall glasses, and Hippocras calls for soda or Perrier water as well. Shrubs are not encountered everywhere and they are not everyone's tipple, but those who like them tend to love them—and they are always conversation makers.

BUCKS

Bucks are long drinks made with liquor and ginger ale. In recent years, bucks have declined in popularity, but they are excellent hot-weather drinks. Like a collins, a buck may be made with applejack, brandy, gin, rum, sloe gin, tequila, vodka or whiskey. Originally, only gin was used, but the Gin Buck recipe below may be followed when making any buck. Simply substitute the liquor of your choice for the gin.

GIN BUCK

3 or 4 ice cubes	2–3 ounces gin
2 tablespoons lemon or lime juice	Ginger ale
Large twist lemon or lime peel	

Put the ice cubes in a 10-ounce highball glass, add the lemon or lime juice, peel and gin. Fill up with ginger ale and stir gently. Serves 1.

COBBLERS

Like juleps, cobblers are an American invention. They are based on wine or liquor and crushed ice. Those made with applejack, gin, rum, white wine, vodka or whiskey are prepared as follows:

Basic Recipe

Crushed ice
1 teaspoon superfine sugar
1½–3 ounces liquor or wine, according to taste

Fruit and mint garnish

Fill two-thirds of a large goblet with crushed ice. Sprinkle sugar over the ice and add the liquor or wine. Garnish with a slice of orange, a pineapple stick and, if you like, a sprig of fresh mint. Serves 1.

Some cobblers are not made as above. Following are individual recipes for those based on brandy, champagne, claret, port, Rhine wine, sherry, and vermouth, both dry and sweet.

BRANDY COBBLER

Crushed ice
2 or 3 ounces brandy
1 teaspoon curaçao

½ teaspoon superfine sugar
Slice orange
Small pineapple stick

Fill a tumbler three-quarters full with crushed ice. Add brandy, curaçao and sugar. Stir. Decorate with the orange slice and pineapple stick. Serves 1.

CHAMPAGNE COBBLER

Crushed ice
½ teaspoon lemon juice
½ teaspoon curaçao

Thin slice orange
Small pineapple stick
4 ounces chilled champagne

Fill a 10-ounce goblet two-thirds full with crushed ice. Add lemon juice and curaçao, stir and add the orange slice and pineapple stick. Fill with champagne. Serves 1.

CLARET COBBLER

Crushed ice
Dash maraschino
1 teaspoon superfine sugar
1 teaspoon lemon juice

4 ounces claret (approx.)
Orange slice
Pineapple stick

Half-fill a tumbler with crushed ice; add maraschino, sugar and lemon juice and stir. Pour in the claret. Decorate with orange and pineapple garnish. Serves 1.

Rhine Wine Cobbler: Use Rhine wine instead of claret. Omit the dash of maraschino and garnish with lemon peel and a sprig of mint.

DRY VERMOUTH COBBLER

Crushed ice
3 ounces dry vermouth

3 ounces club soda
Twist lemon peel

Fill a goblet or highball glass three-quarters full with crushed ice; pour on the vermouth and club soda. Garnish with lemon peel. Serves 1.

Sweet Vermouth Cobbler: Use sweet vermouth instead of dry. Garnish with orange peel and an orange slice instead of lemon peel.

PORT COBBLER

Crushed ice
1 teaspoon orange juice
1 teaspoon curaçao

4 ounces port (approx.)
Orange slice
Pineapple stick

Fill two-thirds of a tumbler with crushed ice, add orange juice and curaçao, and stir. Pour in the port and decorate with orange slice and pineapple stick. Serves 1.

SHERRY COBBLER

Crushed ice
1 teaspoon superfine sugar
1 teaspoon orange juice
3 ounces sherry

Slice of orange
Small pineapple stick
Mint sprig (optional)

Fill a large (about 9-ounce) goblet two-thirds full with crushed ice. Add sugar, orange juice and sherry. Decorate with fruit and a sprig of mint. Serves 1.

COLLINSES

All the collinses are long drinks. The best-known of them are the Tom Collins, a dry gin drink, and the John Collins, which is made with Holland gin. Any other liquor can be used as a base, however: applejack, brandy, rum, sloe gin, tequila, vodka or whiskey. All collinses are made the same way as a Tom Collins.

TOM COLLINS

2 tablespoons lemon juice
1 teaspoon superfine sugar
2 ounces dry gin
3 or 4 ice cubes

Chilled club soda
Slice each of lemon and
  orange (optional)
Maraschino cherry (optional)

Put the lemon juice and sugar in a collins glass and stir to dissolve the sugar. Add the gin and ice cubes and fill with club soda. Stir quickly. Garnish the drink with fruit slices and cherry. Serves 1.

COOLERS

Coolers are long drinks resembling individual punches except that they usually contain little or no fruit juice. Most coolers are made with liquor or wine, ice and a carbonated mixer. They should be stirred gently so that the bubbles will not be dispersed.

APRICOT COOLER

1 cup crushed ice	Club soda or ginger ale
2 ounces apricot brandy	Twist each orange and lemon
2 dashes grenadine	peel

Put the ice in a highball glass; add the brandy and grenadine and stir. Fill with soda or ginger ale and decorate with fruit peel. Serves 1.

CHAMPAGNE COOLER

Crushed ice	6 ounces chilled champagne
1 ounce brandy	Mint sprigs
1 ounce Cointreau	

Half-fill a 12-ounce highball glass with crushed ice. Pour in the brandy and Cointreau and fill with champagne. Garnish with mint. Serves 1.

COUNTRY-CLUB COOLER

3 ounces dry vermouth	3 or 4 ice cubes
1 teaspoon grenadine	Chilled club soda

Pour the vermouth and grenadine into a highball glass, add ice cubes and fill with club soda. Serves 1.

CUBAN COOLER

3 or 4 ice cubes
3 ounces rum
Ginger ale
Twist lemon peel

Put the ice cubes in a tall highball glass, add the rum and fill with ginger ale. Garnish with lemon peel. Serves 1.

FLORADORA

1 cup crushed ice
2 ounces gin
3 tablespoons lime juice
½ teaspoon superfine sugar
1 tablespoon grenadine or raspberry syrup
2 ounces club soda or ginger ale

Put the ice into a 12-ounce collins glass, add remaining ingredients and stir gently. Serves 1.

HARVARD COOLER

1 tablespoon sugar syrup
2 tablespoons lemon juice
3 ounces applejack
3 or 4 ice cubes
Club soda

Combine all ingredients except the soda in a cocktail shaker and shake vigorously. Strain into a 12-ounce collins glass and fill with soda. Serves 1.

HIGHLAND COOLER

3 or 4 ice cubes
2–3 ounces Scotch whiskey
2 dashes Angostura bitters
2 tablespoons lemon juice
1 teaspoon superfine sugar
Ginger ale

Put the ice cubes in a 12-ounce collins glass and add all ingredients except the ginger ale. Stir gently, then fill up with ginger ale. Serves 1.

IRISH COOLER

3 or 4 ice cubes
Peel from 1 lemon

3 ounces Irish whiskey
Club soda

Put the ice cubes in a highball glass, add lemon peel and whiskey and fill up with soda. Serves 1.

MANHATTAN COOLER

4 ounces claret
3 dashes rum
2 tablespoons lemon juice
1 or 2 teaspoons superfine
  sugar

3 or 4 ice cubes
Fruit for garnish (optional)

Combine all ingredients except the fruit in a highball glass and stir. Garnish with citrus fruit slices, if you like. Serves 1.

NEGRONI COOLER

3 or 4 ice cubes
1½ ounces sweet vermouth
1½ ounces Campari

1½ ounces gin
Chilled club soda
Slice of orange

Put the ice cubes in a highball glass and pour in the vermouth, Campari and gin. Fill with club soda and garnish with slice of orange. Serves 1.

RED OR WHITE WINE COOLER

2 teaspoons superfine sugar
1 teaspoon cold water
1 tablespoon orange juice

3 or 4 ice cubes
Chilled red or white wine
Lemon or orange slice

Put the sugar and water in a 10-ounce highball glass and stir until the sugar is dissolved. Add the orange juice and ice cubes and fill with any chilled red or white wine. Garnish a Red Wine Cooler with a slice of lemon, a White Wine Cooler with a slice of orange. Serves 1.

REMSEN COOLER

½ teaspoon superfine sugar
2 ounces club soda
3 or 4 ice cubes
2–3 ounces Scotch whiskey
    or gin

Club soda or ginger ale
Peel of 1 lemon

Put sugar and club soda in a 12-ounce collins glass and stir to dissolve the sugar. Add the ice, Scotch or gin, and stir. Fill up with soda or ginger ale. Garnish with lemon peel. Serves 1.

SCOTCH COOLER

3 ounces Scotch whiskey
3 dashes white crème de
    menthe

3 or 4 ice cubes
Chilled club soda

Put the Scotch, crème de menthe and ice cubes in a highball glass. Fill with soda. Serves 1.

This drink is also known as a **Mint Cooler.**

VERMOUTH COOLER

3 or 4 ice cubes
2 ounces dry vermouth
2 tablespoons raspberry
    syrup

Club soda
Slice of orange

Put the ice cubes in a highball glass, add the vermouth and raspberry syrup and fill with club soda. Garnish with orange slice. Serves 1.

ZENITH

3 or 4 ice cubes
2–3 ounces gin
1 tablespoon pineapple juice

Chilled club soda
Pineapple stick

Put the ice cubes in a 10-ounce highball glass and pour in the gin and pineapple juice. Fill up with club soda and stir. Decorate with pineapple stick. Serves 1.

DAISIES

Daisies are overgrown cocktails and should be served in goblets, large cocktail glasses or Old-fashioned glasses. Daisies may be based on applejack, brandy, gin, rum, tequila or whiskey.

Basic Recipe

2 tablespoons lemon juice
½ teaspoon superfine sugar
1 teaspoon grenadine or
  raspberry syrup

1½–3 ounces liquor
½ cup crushed ice
Chilled club soda
Fruit for garnish (optional)

Combine all ingredients except the club soda and garnish in a cocktail shaker and shake vigorously. Strain into a glass and fill with soda. Garnish with fruit. Serves 1.

Following are recipes for daisies that differ a little from the standard drink.

SANTA CRUZ RUM DAISY

Crushed ice
3 dashes sugar syrup
3 dashes maraschino or
  curaçao

2 tablespoons lemon juice
3 ounces rum

Fill a goblet one-third full with ice, add the syrup, maraschino or curaçao, and lemon juice, then pour in the rum. Stir gently. Serves 1.

Star Daisy: Use 1 ounce each gin and applejack instead of the rum.

Chocolate Daisy: Use 1½ ounces each brandy and port instead of the rum.

FIXES

The ingredients for a fix are put in a small tumbler with crushed ice and stirred gently. The drink may be based on brandy, gin, rum or whiskey, and no dilutant is ever used.

Basic Recipe

1 teaspoon superfine sugar	2 tablespoons lemon juice
1 teaspoon water	Crushed ice
2–3 ounces liquor	

Put the sugar and water in an 8-ounce tumbler and stir to dissolve the sugar. Add the liquor and lemon juice, and fill with crushed ice. Stir gently again. Serve with a straw. Serves 1.

Brandy Fix: Combine brandy and cherry brandy half and half.

Santa Cruz Fix: Combine rum and cherry brandy half and half.

FIZZES

Fizzes, which are popular drinks in the late morning and afternoon, are usually served in highball glasses. They are made from liquor, citrus juices and sugar, shaken with ice. The mixture is strained into glasses which are then filled with club soda or other carbonated drink, including champagne. Egg, both yolk and white, is used in some fizzes.

Perhaps the best-known of these drinks is the Gin Fizz. There are many versions of it, but following is the classic recipe.

GIN FIZZ

3 ounces gin	1 tablespoon lime juice
1 tablespoon superfine sugar	3 or 4 ice cubes
2 tablespoons lemon juice	Club soda

Combine all ingredients except the soda in a cocktail shaker and shake vigorously. Strain into a highball glass and fill with soda. Serves 1.

Brandy Fizz: Use brandy instead of gin.

Holland Gin Fizz: Substitute Holland gin for standard dry gin.

Scotch Fizz: Use Scotch instead of gin.

Silver Fizz: Add the white of an egg.

Golden Fizz: Add the yolk of an egg.

Bootleg Fizz: Add the white of an egg and a sprig of mint.

Cream Fizz: Add 2 teaspoons heavy cream.

Alabama Fizz: Add a sprig of mint.

APPLE BLOW

3 ounces applejack	1 egg white
4 dashes lemon juice	3 or 4 ice cubes
1 teaspoon sugar	Club soda

Combine all ingredients except the club soda in a cocktail shaker and shake vigorously. Strain into a highball glass and fill with soda. Serves 1.

BIRD-OF-PARADISE FIZZ

2 ounces gin
2 tablespoons lemon juice
1 teaspoon superfine sugar
1 teaspoon grenadine

1 egg white
3 or 4 ice cubes
Club soda

Put all ingredients except the club soda in a cocktail shaker and shake vigorously. Strain into an 8-ounce highball glass. Fill with club soda. Serves 1.

Royal Fizz: Omit grenadine and use a whole egg instead of just the white.

BUCKS FIZZ NO. 1

1½ ounces gin
½ teaspoon sugar
¼ cup orange juice

3 or 4 ice cubes
Chilled champagne

Combine all ingredients except the champagne in a cocktail shaker and shake vigorously. Strain into a highball glass. Fill with champagne. Serves 1.

BUCKS FIZZ NO. 2

3 ounces fresh orange juice   8 ounces chilled champagne

Pour orange juice into a 12-ounce collins glass, add the champagne and stir gently to mix. Serves 1.

CHAMPAGNE FIZZ

½ cup orange juice
3 or 4 ice cubes

4 ounces chilled champagne

Pour the orange juice into a 10-ounce highball glass, add ice cubes and fill with champagne. Serves 1.

CREAM GIN FIZZ

1½ ounces gin	3 or 4 ice cubes
1½ ounces milk	½ cup crushed ice
3 teaspoons sugar	Club soda
4 tablespoons lime juice	

Combine all ingredients except the crushed ice and soda in a cocktail shaker and shake vigorously. Put the crushed ice in a highball glass, and strain in the mixture. Add soda to fill and stir quickly to make it foam up. Serves 1.

DERBY FIZZ

1½ ounces whiskey	3 dashes curaçao
1 teaspoon lemon juice	3 or 4 ice cubes
1 teaspoon sugar	Club soda
1 whole egg	

Combine all ingredients except the club soda in a cocktail shaker and shake vigorously. Strain into a highball glass and fill with club soda. Serves 1.

DIAMOND FIZZ

1½ ounces gin	3 or 4 ice cubes
2 tablespoons lemon juice	Club soda
1 teaspoon superfine sugar (or less, to taste)	

Put all ingredients except the club soda in a cocktail shaker and shake vigorously. Strain into an 8-ounce highball glass and fill with club soda. Serves 1.

DUBONNET FIZZ

3 ounces Dubonnet
1 teaspoon cherry brandy
¼ cup orange juice

1 tablespoon lemon juice
3 or 4 ice cubes
Club soda

Combine all ingredients except the soda in a cocktail shaker and shake vigorously. Strain into a highball glass and fill with soda. Serves 1.

GRAND ROYAL FIZZ

3 ounces gin
2 tablespoons orange juice
2 tablespoons lemon juice
1 teaspoon superfine sugar

½ teaspoon maraschino
2 teaspoons heavy cream
3 or 4 ice cubes
Club soda

Combine all ingredients except the club soda in a cocktail shaker and shake vigorously. Strain into a highball glass and fill with soda. Serves 1.

IMPERIAL FIZZ

1½ ounces rye or bourbon
2 tablespoons lemon juice
½ teaspoon superfine sugar

3 or 4 ice cubes
Chilled champagne

Combine all ingredients except the champagne in a cocktail shaker and shake vigorously. Strain into a highball glass and fill with champagne. Serves 1.

IMPERIAL HOTEL FIZZ

1½ ounces whiskey
¾ ounce light rum
1 teaspoon lemon juice
1½ tablespoons lime juice

1 teaspoon superfine sugar
3 or 4 ice cubes
Club soda

Combine all ingredients except the soda in a cocktail shaker and shake vigorously. Strain into a highball glass and fill with soda. Serves 1.

MAY BLOSSOM FIZZ

1½ ounces Swedish Punch
1 teaspoon grenadine
2 tablespoons lemon juice

3 or 4 ice cubes
Club soda

Combine all ingredients except the soda in a cocktail shaker and shake vigorously. Strain into a highball glass and fill with soda. Serves 1.

MORNING-GLORY FIZZ

3 ounces Scotch whiskey
2 dashes Pernod
1 egg white
1 teaspoon superfine sugar

2 tablespoons lemon juice
1½ tablespoons lime juice
3 or 4 ice cubes
Club soda

Combine all ingredients except the soda in a cocktail shaker and shake vigorously. Strain into a highball glass and fill with soda. Serves 1.

NEW ORLEANS FIZZ

3 ounces gin
1 egg white
2 tablespoons lemon juice
1 teaspoon superfine sugar

1 teaspoon heavy cream
Dash orange-flower water
3 or 4 ice cubes
Club soda

Combine all ingredients except the soda in a cocktail shaker and shake vigorously. Strain into a highball glass and fill with soda. Serves 1.

ORANGE GIN FIZZ

3 ounces gin
¼ cup orange juice
Dash grenadine

3 or 4 ice cubes
Club soda

Combine all ingredients except the soda in a cocktail shaker and shake vigorously. Strain into a highball glass and fill with soda. Serves 1.

PEACH BLOW FIZZ

3 ounces gin
1 ounce heavy cream
1 teaspoon superfine sugar
4 strawberries, mashed

2 tablespoons lemon juice
1½ tablespoons lime juice
3 or 4 ice cubes
Club soda

Combine all ingredients except the club soda and shake vigorously. Strain into a highball glass and fill with soda. Serves 1.

PINA FIZZ

1 cup crushed ice
1½ ounces light rum
½ ounce dark rum
2 ounces pineapple juice

3 tablespoons lime juice
½ ounce orgeat syrup
½ ounce falernum
Pineapple stick

Put the ice into an electric blender. Add all other ingredients except pineapple and blend on high speed. Serve in a 14-ounce collins glass garnished with pineapple stick. Serves 1.

PINEAPPLE FIZZ

3 ounces light rum or gin
½ teaspoon superfine sugar
2 tablespoons pineapple
   juice

Dash lime juice
3 or 4 ice cubes
Club soda

Combine all ingredients except the soda in a cocktail shaker and shake vigorously. Strain into a highball glass and fill with soda. Serves 1.

RAMOS GIN FIZZ

This Fizz, named after Henry C. Ramos who served it in the Imperial Cabinet Saloon which he bought in New Orleans in 1888, needs a great deal of shaking. Mr. Ramos hired young boys who did nothing but shake the fizzes for his clients, something like five minutes per drink. It is said that the staff of shakers reached its peak of thirty-five boys during the Mardi Gras of 1915.

Cut lemon
Superfine sugar
2 ounces gin
1 egg white
2 tablespoons cream
½ teaspoon orange-flower water

2 tablespoons lemon juice
1½ tablespoons lime juice
½ cup crushed ice
Club soda (optional)

Rub the rim of a highball glass with lemon and dip into sugar to frost. Combine all the ingredients, except the soda, in a cocktail shaker and shake long and steadily until the mixture is thick and frothy. Strain into the prepared glass. Fill with soda. Serves 1.

For those who find long and steady shaking tiresome, put ingredients in a blender and blend at high speed for about a minute. Pour into the prepared glass and top with a dash of soda.

ROSE IN JUNE FIZZ

1½ ounces gin
1½ ounces framboise
½ cup orange juice

4 tablespoons lime juice
3 or 4 ice cubes
Club soda

Combine all ingredients except the soda in a cocktail shaker and shake vigorously. Strain into a 10-ounce highball glass. Top with several dashes of soda. Serves 1.

RUBY FIZZ

3 ounces sloe gin
1 egg white
1 teaspoon raspberry syrup

2 tablespoons lemon juice
3 or 4 ice cubes
Club soda

Combine all ingredients except the soda in a cocktail shaker and shake vigorously. Strain into a highball glass and fill with soda. Serves 1.

RUM FIZZ

1½ ounces rum
¾ ounce cherry brandy
½ teaspoon sugar

2 tablespoons lemon juice
3 or 4 ice cubes
Club soda

Combine all ingredients except the soda in a cocktail shaker and shake vigorously. Strain into a highball glass and fill with soda. Serves 1.

TAXCO FIZZ

2 ounces tequila
1½ tablespoons lime juice
½ teaspoon sugar

2 dashes orange bitters
3 or 4 ice cubes
Club soda

Combine all ingredients except the soda in a cocktail shaker and shake vigorously. Strain into a highball glass and fill with soda. Serves 1.

VIOLET FIZZ

1½ ounces gin
½ ounce crème Yvette
2 tablespoons lemon juice

½ teaspoon superfine sugar
3 or 4 ice cubes
Club soda

Combine all ingredients except the soda in a cocktail shaker and shake vigorously. Strain into a highball glass and fill with soda. Serves 1.

FLIPS

These were originally hot drinks made with egg and a variety of liquors and wines. They were warmed up by means of a loggerhead, an iron tool with a long handle and bulbous end that could be heated and plunged, like a poker, into the drink. Today, however, flips are served cold, with the exception of that old-time one, the Yard of Flannel. They are most often served in the morning or at bedtime, because of their soothing character.

APPLEJACK FLIP

4 ounces applejack	½ cup crushed ice
1 whole egg	Nutmeg
2 teaspoons superfine sugar	

Put all ingredients except the nutmeg into an electric blender and blend on high speed for 30 seconds. Pour into 6-ounce stemmed glasses, and grate a little nutmeg on top. Serves 2.

BOSTON FLIP

1½ ounces rye whiskey	1 whole egg
1½ ounces Madeira	3 or 4 ice cubes
1 teaspoon sugar	Nutmeg

Combine all ingredients except the nutmeg in a cocktail shaker and shake vigorously. Strain into a 5-ounce stemmed glass and grate a little nutmeg on top. Serves 1.

BRANDY FLIP

Any of the fruit brandies (such as cherry or blackberry), rum, sherry or whiskey may be substituted for the brandy in this recipe.

3 ounces brandy
1 whole egg
1 teaspoon superfine sugar

2 teaspoons heavy cream
(optional)
½ cup crushed ice
Nutmeg

Combine all ingredients except the nutmeg in a cocktail shaker and shake vigorously. Strain into a 5-ounce stemmed glass, and grate a little nutmeg on top. Serves 1.

Whiskey Flip: 2 or 3 dashes rum are sometimes added to the whiskey.

Whiskey Peppermint Flip: Omit rum, and add ½ ounce white crème de menthe to the whiskey.

MUSCATEL FLIP

2 ounces brandy
¼ cup muscatel
1 whole egg
1 teaspoon superfine sugar

1 tablespoon heavy cream
½ cup crushed ice
Nutmeg

Combine all ingredients except the nutmeg in an electric blender and blend on high speed for 30 seconds. Pour into 6-ounce stemmed glasses, and grate a little nutmeg on top. Serves 2.

YARD OF FLANNEL

This was a popular warm drink in the eighteenth century.

1 quart ale
4 whole eggs
4 tablespoons superfine
sugar

½ teaspoon grated nutmeg
½ teaspoon ground ginger
½ cup dark rum

Heat the ale in a heavy saucepan. Beat the eggs with the sugar, add nutmeg, ginger and rum and pour into a pitcher. When ale is hot but not boiling, pour it into a second pitcher and then add it, a little at a time, to egg mixture, stirring constantly to keep it from curdling. When the mixing is complete, pour the contents from one pitcher to the other until the drink is smooth and creamy. Serve in warmed 6-ounce mugs or glasses. Serves 4.

HOT DRINKS

These recipes might just as correctly be included in the section "Hot Punches" (page 376). The basic difference: All the ones given here are for one serving, but it is a simple matter to multiply quantities by whatever number you wish. For additional hot drinks to serve four or more, however, you should also look over the hot punches.

Brandy, rum and whiskey are the most popular bases for hot drinks made with liquor. For a milder drink, use a recipe based on wine.

BLACK STRIPE NO. 2

1 teaspoon molasses   Twist lemon peel
3 ounces dark rum

Put the molasses, rum and lemon peel in an 8-ounce mug and fill with boiling water. Stir. Serves 1.

BLUE BLAZER

2 large mugs with handles   3 ounces boiling water
3 ounces Scotch or any   1 teaspoon superfine sugar
  other whiskey   Twist lemon peel

Put the Scotch in one mug, the boiling water in the other. Ignite the whiskey and, while it is blazing, pour it and the water back and forth from one mug to the other. Properly done, this looks like a stream of fire. Add the sugar and serve with lemon peel in a warmed mug. Serves 1.

BRANDY BLAZER NO. 1

2–3 ounces brandy   Twist orange peel
1 cube sugar

Combine brandy, sugar and orange peel in a small, thick glass. Blaze brandy and stir, using a long spoon. Strain into a cocktail glass. Serves 1.

COLUMBIA SKIN NO. 2

1 tablespoon water
2 cubes sugar
2 tablespoons lemon juice

1 teaspoon curaçao
3 ounces rum

Combine all ingredients in a small, heavy saucepan and heat until the contents foam; do not let boil. Serve in a warmed wineglass. Serves 1.

Brandy, gin or whiskey may be used instead of rum.

GROG

2 ounces dark rum
1 cube sugar
3 cloves
1″ piece cinnamon stick

1 tablespoon lemon juice
Slice lemon
Boiling water

Place all ingredients except the boiling water in an 8-ounce mug. Stir to dissolve the sugar, leaving the spoon in the mug. Pour in boiling water to fill, and stir. Serves 1.

HOT BUTTERED RUM

2–3 ounces dark rum
Twist lemon peel
Stick cinnamon
2 cloves

Sweet cider or water
1 tablespoon sweet butter
Nutmeg

Put the rum, lemon peel, cinnamon and cloves in a pewter tankard or any heavy 12-ounce mug that has been rinsed out in very hot water to warm it. Heat the cider or water to the boiling point and pour into the spiced rum. Add the pat of butter and stir well. Grate a little nutmeg on top. Serves 1.

A cube of sugar may be added, if you like.

IRISH COW

1 cup hot milk   1½ ounces Irish whiskey
1 teaspoon superfine sugar

Pour the hot milk into a highball glass, stir in the sugar until dissolved and add the whiskey. Stir gently. Serves 1.

Nightcap: Use 2 ounces rum instead of the whiskey, and grate a little nutmeg on top.

MULLED WINE

This is also known as **Vin Chaud** and **Glühwein.** In the past, the drink was usually served in a pewter mug and often heated with a red-hot poker.

8 ounces claret or other dry   Small piece cinnamon stick
   red wine   Twist lemon peel
Dash Angostura bitters   1 teaspoon superfine sugar
2 or 3 cloves   Pinch allspice

Combine all ingredients in a small, heavy saucepan and heat but do not allow to boil. Strain into an 8-ounce mug. Serves 1.

Mulled Cider: Use cider instead of claret, and add a dash of rum, calvados or applejack.

PORT WINE NEGUS

1 teaspoon superfine sugar   Boiling water
3 ounces port   Nutmeg
Twist lemon peel

Put the sugar in a small, heavy saucepan and add just enough water to dissolve it. Add the port and lemon peel and heat through. Pour into a warmed mug or punch glass, fill with boiling water and stir. Grate a little nutmeg on top. Serves 1.

Sherry Wine Negus: Use sherry instead of port.

TOM AND JERRY

1 egg, separated
1 teaspoon superfine sugar
1½ ounces brandy

1½ ounces dark rum
⅓ cup hot milk
Nutmeg

Beat the egg white until it is stiff; beat the yolk until thick and lemon-colored. Combine them and beat in the sugar. Have ready a warmed 8-ounce mug. Add the egg mixture, brandy and rum, then fill with hot milk. Stir and top with a little grated nutmeg. Serves 1.

JULEPS

The Mint Julep comes from Kentucky and is traditionally made with Kentucky bourbon and fresh mint leaves. It is a controversial drink, each maker insisting on a particular method with seldom any agreement. Although the classic Mint Julep is the most famous, juleps may also be made with applejack, brandy, gin, rum or rye whiskey. The Mint Julep recipe that follows may be used for any type of julep by substituting another liquor for bourbon.

MINT JULEP

Crushed ice
4 sprigs fresh mint

1 teaspoon superfine sugar
3 ounces bourbon

Fill a collins glass with crushed ice. In a small glass, muddle the leaves from two mint sprigs with sugar and a dash of club soda or water. Add the bourbon, stir, and strain into the collins glass. Stir again with a long-handled spoon until the glass frosts. Decorate with the remaining mint sprigs. Serve with a straw. Serves 1.

Silver mugs are often used for juleps, as some people think they frost better than glass. A glass mug with a handle may also be used so that the hands need not touch the frosted surface. A slice each of orange and lemon, a pineapple stick and a maraschino cherry are sometimes used for garnish, and a splash of rum or brandy may be added to the drink.

CHAMPAGNE JULEP

This is the only julep based on wine rather than liquor, and it is made differently from other juleps.

4 sprigs fresh mint	1½ ounces brandy
1 lump sugar	6 ounces chilled champagne
Crushed ice	Mint to garnish

In the bottom of a 12-ounce highball glass crush the mint with the sugar and a teaspoon or so of water. Half-fill the glass with crushed ice, add the brandy and fill up with champagne. Decorate with extra mint and serve with a straw. Serves 1.

LONG DRINKS

Although such drinks as collinses, fizzes, rickeys and swizzles are long drinks, they all begin with a basic recipe that may be varied by using a choice of liquors and, in the case of fizzes, assorted other ingredients. The group called coolers consists of assorted recipes, but each is traditionally known as a cooler of some sort or another. The long drinks included here are simply a collection of individual potables, most of which are served in tall glasses and diluted with some mixer such as club soda. A small percentage, however, are served in good-size wineglasses, goblets or small tumblers and are not, strictly speaking, long. This is true of the champagne-based drinks, a few that are Hawaiian in origin, and perhaps half-a-dozen others. But for simplicity's sake, it seems better to include them here than to group them separately under a vague heading such as "Miscellaneous."

AMERICAN ROSE

1½ ounces brandy
Dash Pernod
1 teaspoon grenadine

Half a ripe peach, mashed
½ cup crushed ice
Chilled champagne

Combine all ingredients except the champagne in a cocktail shaker and shake vigorously. Strain into a 10-ounce goblet and fill with champagne. Serves 1.

AMERICANO

3 ounces sweet vermouth
1½ ounces Campari
2 ice cubes

Twist lemon peel
Club soda

Pour the vermouth and Campari into a tumbler, add ice cubes and lemon peel and fill with club soda. Serves 1.

The proportions may be varied to 2 ounces each of sweet vermouth and Campari.

BARBOTAGE OF CHAMPAGNE

Crushed ice
Dash Angostura bitters
1 teaspoon sugar syrup

1 teaspoon lemon juice
6 ounces chilled champagne
Twist orange peel

Half-fill a large goblet with crushed ice. Add Angostura bitters, sugar syrup, lemon juice—and fill up with champagne. Garnish with orange peel. Serves 1.

BERMUDA HIGHBALL

2 ice cubes
¾ ounce gin
¾ ounce brandy

¾ ounce dry vermouth
Ginger ale or club soda

Put ice cubes, gin, brandy and dry vermouth in a highball glass and fill with ginger ale or club soda. Serves 1.

BILLY TAYLOR

2 ounces gin
2 tablespoons lime juice
1 teaspoon superfine sugar

3 or 4 ice cubes
Club soda

Combine all ingredients except club soda in a collins glass and fill up with soda. Serves 1.

BISHOP

½ cup crushed ice
1 teaspoon superfine sugar
2 tablespoons lemon juice
¼ cup orange juice

4 ounces Burgundy or claret
  (approx.)
1 slice orange
1 teaspoon rum

Put ice, sugar, lemon and orange juice in a 12-ounce highball glass. Add enough Burgundy or claret to fill. Decorate with orange slice and float the rum on top. Serves 1.

BLACK VELVET

6 ounces chilled stout

6 ounces chilled champagne

Pour the stout slowly into a tall glass, and then simply add the champagne. Serves 1.

This drink is sometimes called **Champagne Velvet,** and in certain quarters is known as the **Friendly Sons of St. Patrick Shandygaff,** a fine euphoric title.

BLUE TRAIN NO. 2

½ cup crushed ice	2 ounces pineapple juice
2 ounces brandy	Chilled champagne

Place the crushed ice in a cocktail shaker with the brandy and pineapple juice, and shake vigorously. Pour the contents of the shaker into a 10-ounce goblet and fill with champagne. Serves 1.

BOILERMAKER

2 ounces whiskey   8 ounces chilled beer

Serve the whiskey straight and follow with a beer chaser, or combine the ingredients in a 10-ounce highball glass, pouring the whiskey into the beer without stirring. Serves 1.

Scotch whiskey may be used for this drink instead of blended whiskey.

Dog's Nose: Use gin instead of the whiskey, with chilled beer or stout as a mixer, not a chaser.

BOSTON SOUR

2 ounces whiskey	1 ice cube
2 tablespoons lemon juice	Chilled club soda
1 teaspoon superfine sugar	Lemon slice
1 egg white	Maraschino cherry
½ cup crushed ice	

Combine whiskey, lemon juice, sugar, egg white and crushed ice in a cocktail shaker and shake vigorously. Strain into a highball glass, add ice cube, and fill with soda. Decorate with the lemon slice and cherry. Serves 1.

BYRRH CASSIS

2 or 3 ice cubes   3 ounces Byrrh
1 teaspoon crème de cassis Chilled club soda

Put the ice cubes in a highball glass, add cassis and Byrrh, and fill with club soda. Stir gently. Serves 1.

BULLDOG HIGHBALL

2 or 3 ice cubes   ½ cup orange juice
2–3 ounces gin   Ginger ale

Put the ice cubes in a highball glass or double Old-fashioned glass, add the gin and orange juice and fill up with ginger ale. Stir gently. Serves 1.

CASEY'S CANNONBALL
(From the Gaslight Club)

3 or 4 ice cubes   Dash curaçao
1½ ounces okolehao Black olive

Put ice cubes in a goblet or Old-fashioned glass and add the okolehao and curaçao. Stir lightly and garnish with olive. Serves 1.

CHAMPAGNE CASSIS HIGHBALL

3 or 4 ice cubes   2 dashes kirsch
Dash crème de cassis 6 ounces chilled champagne

Place ice cubes in a 10-ounce highball glass, add the crème de cassis and kirsch, and fill up with champagne. Serves 1.

CHIEF'S CALABASH
(From The Gourmet)

1 cup crushed ice
2 ounces okolehao
3 ounces coconut milk

1 tablespoon orgeat syrup
Pineapple stick

Put all ingredients except the pineapple stick in an electric blender and blend quickly on high speed. Pour into a 10-ounce double Old-fashioned glass or goblet and garnish with pineapple stick. Serves 1.

CLARET LEMONADE

4 tablespoons lemon juice
2 teaspoons superfine sugar
6 ounces crushed ice

8 ounces chilled claret or other dry red wine
Slice lemon

Combine lemon juice and sugar in a tall collins glass and stir until sugar is dissolved. Add ice, pour in claret, and garnish with lemon slice. Serve with a straw. Serves 1.

COCO LOCO (CRAZY COCONUT)

Fresh green coconut

2 ounces tequila

Cut the top off a green coconut with a large knife or machete and pour in the tequila. Sip through a straw. If the coconut has abundant liquid, add more tequila. Serves 1.

This popular drink originated in Acapulco, Mexico. Fresh green coconuts are available in Latin-American markets and in tropical regions of the U.S.

Gin, rum or vodka may be substituted for tequila.

CUBA LIBRE

2 or 3 ice cubes
3 ounces rum
1½ tablespoons lime juice

Chilled cola
Slice lime

Put ice cubes in a highball glass, add the rum and lime juice, fill with cola and garnish with a slice of lime. Serves 1.

DOCTOR FUNK

1 small lime	1 tablespoon lemon juice
3 ounces dark rum	1 teaspoon superfine sugar
1 teaspoon Pernod	½ cup crushed ice
1 teaspoon grenadine	Club soda

Squeeze the lime into a cocktail shaker and then drop in the shell. Add all the other ingredients except the soda and shake vigorously. Pour into a tall highball or collins glass and fill with club soda. Serves 1.

EL DIABLO

½ lime	3 or 4 ice cubes
1½ ounces tequila	Ginger ale
½ ounce crème de cassis	

Squeeze juice of ½ lime into a highball glass and then drop in the peel. Add the tequila, cassis and ice cubes, fill with ginger ale and stir gently. Serves 1.

FOGHORN

2 or 3 ice cubes	Ginger beer
3 ounces gin	Slice lemon

Put the ice cubes in a highball glass, add the gin, fill up with ginger beer and garnish with lemon slice. Serves 1.

Moscow Mule: Use vodka instead of gin, add a teaspoon of lime juice, and garnish with a slice of lime rather than lemon.

FRENCH "75"

Crushed ice	1 teaspoon superfine sugar
1½ ounces dry gin	6 ounces chilled champagne
1 tablespoon lemon juice	

Half-fill a 14-ounce collins glass with crushed ice. Pour in the gin and lemon juice and stir in the sugar. Pour in the champagne. Serves 1.

French "95": Use bourbon instead of gin.
French "125": Use brandy instead of gin.

GIN AND TONIC

The popularity of drinks such as this one, especially during the summer, has led to the invention of a great many similar ones. Some variations are given, but the list is too long to enumerate and must be left to the imagination of the drink mixer.

2–3 ounces gin	Slice of lemon
2 or 3 ice cubes	Tonic water

Put the gin in a highball glass or goblet with the ice cubes and slice of lemon. Fill up with tonic water. Serves 1.

Gin and Bitter Lemon: Use bitter lemon in place of tonic.
Sherry and Tonic: For this milder drink, use sherry instead of gin. Add a squeeze of lemon or lime juice.
Tequonic: Substitute tequila for gin, and a lime slice for a lemon slice.

GINGERADE

3 ice cubes	8 ounces tonic
3 ounces Stone's ginger wine	

Put ice cubes in a 12-ounce highball glass, pour in the ginger wine, fill with tonic and stir gently. Serves 1.

HIGHBALLS

A highball is simplicity itself to make. Any of the following liquors may be used: applejack, bourbon, brandy, gin, Irish whiskey, rum, rye, Scotch or a blended whiskey. Aperitif wines such as Dubonnet are also sometimes used in highballs.

Basic Recipe

3 or 4 ice cubes	Club soda or water
1½–3 ounces liquor or wine	

Put the ice cubes in an 8–10-ounce highball glass, add to liquor and fill up with club soda or plain water.

A twist of lemon peel is sometimes used for garnish.

HORSE'S NECK

1 lemon	3 or 4 ice cubes
2–3 ounces whiskey	Ginger ale

Carefully peel the rind from a lemon in an unbroken spiral and put it in a highball glass with one end hooked over the rim. Add the whiskey and ice cubes and fill with ginger ale. Serves 1.

For non-alcoholic version see page 390

ICED COFFEE FILLIP

3 or 4 ice cubes	1 teaspoon, or more to
8 ounces strong black	taste, Tia Maria or other
coffee	coffee liqueur

Pour the coffee over ice cubes in a tall glass. Stir in the Tia Maria. Serves 1.

JAMES A. BEARD'S CHILLED IRISH COFFEE

This is a long, iced, summer version of Irish Coffee.

1 cup freshly brewed hot	2 tablespoons whipped
coffee	cream
¼ cup heavy cream	3 ice cubes
1 teaspoon superfine sugar	2 ounces Irish whiskey
	Nutmeg or cinnamon

Combine coffee, cream and sugar, stir to dissolve the sugar, and chill thoroughly. Put 1 tablespoon of whipped cream in a 14-ounce highball glass, fill with the coffee mixture, add ice cubes and whiskey. Top with the remaining tablespoon of whipped cream and dust with grated nutmeg or ground cinnamon. Serves 1.

Iced Irish: Use iced instead of hot coffee, and omit the heavy cream, ice cubes and nutmeg or cinnamon.

KING'S PEG

1 ice cube   6 ounces chilled champagne
2 ounces brandy

Place the ice cube in a 10-ounce wineglass or goblet, add the brandy and champagne. Serves 1.

This drink is sometimes known as a **Napoleon.**

Queen's Peg: Substitute ¾ ounce dry gin for the brandy.

LEAPFROG

1½ ounces gin   ½ cup cracked ice
2 tablespoons lemon juice   Ginger ale

Place the gin, lemon juice and cracked ice in a large cocktail glass, or an 8-ounce wine or highball glass, and fill up with ginger ale. Stir gently. Serves 1.

This is sometimes known as **London Buck.**

LONDON SPECIAL

1 cube sugar   2 dashes Peychaud's bitters
Twist orange peel   8 ounces chilled champagne
1 ice cube

Drop the sugar cube into a 10-ounce goblet, add the orange peel, ice cube and bitters, and fill up with champagne. Serves 1.

MAMIE TAYLOR

3 ounces Scotch whiskey
1 tablespoon lime juice
2 or 3 ice cubes

Ginger ale
Slice lemon

Pour the Scotch and lime juice into a 12-ounce collins glass, add ice cubes, fill with ginger ale, stir and garnish with slice of lemon. Serves 1.

MODERN LEMONADE

1½ ounces sherry
1½ ounces sloe gin
2 tablespoons superfine
    sugar

4 tablespoons lemon juice
3 or 4 ice cubes
Twist lemon peel
Chilled club soda

Combine sherry, sloe gin, sugar, lemon juice and ice cubes in a mixing glass and stir well. Strain into a highball glass, add the lemon peel and fill up with soda. Serves 1.

MOJITO

2 ounces light rum
½ lime
1 teaspoon superfine sugar

Crushed ice
Chilled club soda
Mint leaves

Pour rum into a 10-ounce highball glass, squeeze in the lime juice, drop in the peel. Add sugar and enough crushed ice to fill the glass two-thirds full. Fill up with club soda, stir gently and garnish with mint leaves. Serves 1.

MONTE CARLO IMPERIAL

1 ounce gin
½ ounce white crème de
    menthe

½ ounce lemon juice
3 or 4 ice cubes
4 ounces chilled champagne

Pour all ingredients except the champagne into a cocktail shaker and shake vigorously. Strain into an 8-ounce wineglass. Fill with champagne. Serves 1.

PEACH BOWL NO. 1

1 medium-sized fresh peach   6 ounces chilled champagne

Place the peach in an 8–10-ounce goblet, prick several times to release the flavor, and cover with chilled champagne. The peach may be eaten after the drink is finished. Serves 1.

Peach Bowl No. 2: Use a brandied peach instead of a fresh one, and pour 1 or 2 tablespoons of peach syrup over it.

Pear Bowl: Substitute a fresh pear for the peach.

PIMM'S CUP

This is a drink made with one of Pimm's three mixtures: Pimm's No. 1 (with a gin base), Pimm's No. 2 (with a Scotch base) and Pimm's No. 3 (with a brandy base). The most popular and best known is Pimm's No. 1, but all three are available in this country.

2 or 3 ice cubes
1 thin slice lemon
Small piece cucumber peel

2 ounces Pimm's No. 1, 2 or 3
Lemon soda, Tom Collins mix or club soda

Put ice, lemon slice and cucumber peel in a highball glass. Add the Pimm's mixture; fill with one of the three mixers and stir gently. Serves 1.

If you use club soda, add 2 tablespoons lemon juice and a teaspoon of sugar syrup. Should a stronger drink be preferred, add ½ to 1 ounce more of the basic liquor.

PIÑA COLADA

2 ounces golden rum
2 ounces coconut cream
4 ounces pineapple juice

2 or 3 ice cubes
Pineapple stick
Maraschino cherry

Combine the rum, coconut cream and pineapple juice in a cocktail shaker and shake vigorously, or whirl quickly in an electric blender. Put the ice cubes in a highball glass, add the liquid and garnish with the pineapple and cherry. Serves 1.

PINEAPPLE LEMONADE

2 slices pineapple, coarsely chopped
1 teaspoon superfine sugar
1½ ounces brandy
Dash raspberry syrup

½ cup crushed ice
Club soda
Twist lemon peel
Pineapple stick

Muddle the pineapple and sugar thoroughly in a cocktail shaker. Add the brandy, raspberry syrup and ice. Shake vigorously. Strain into a highball glass, fill up with soda and decorate with lemon peel and pineapple stick. Serves 1.

PRESBYTERIAN

2–3 ounces bourbon
2 ounces chilled ginger ale
2 ounces chilled club soda

3 or 4 ice cubes
Twist lemon peel

Combine all ingredients except the peel in a 10-ounce highball glass and stir gently. Twist lemon peel over the drink to release the oil, then drop it in. Serves 1.

PRINCE OF WALES

Dash Angostura bitters
1 teaspoon curaçao
1 ounce Madeira
1 ounce brandy

3 or 4 ice cubes
6 ounces chilled champagne
Slice orange

Put the bitters in a shaker with the curaçao, Madeira, brandy and ice cubes and shake vigorously. Strain into a large goblet or wineglass and pour in the champagne. Decorate with the orange slice. Serves 1.

ROYAL HAWAIIAN

1½ ounces gin
1½ ounces pineapple juice
½ ounce lime juice

1 teaspoon Cointreau
½ cup crushed ice
Fresh pineapple

Combine all ingredients except the pineapple in a cocktail shaker and shake vigorously. Cut the top off a pineapple, hollow it out and pour in the drink. Serve with a straw. Serves 1.

This drink may, of course, be served in a goblet or other glass.

SALTY DOG NO. 2

4 to 6 ice cubes
3 ounces gin

4 ounces grapefruit juice
Pinch salt

Put the ice cubes in a 12-ounce collins glass and pour in the gin and grapefruit juice. Add salt and stir gently. Serves 1.

SALUTE

1 ice cube
1 tablespoon Campari

6 ounces chilled champagne

Place the ice cube in a 10-ounce wineglass or goblet and pour the Campari over it. Fill slowly with champagne. Serves 1.

SHANDYGAFF

6 ounces chilled beer

6 ounces chilled ginger beer

Pour the beer and ginger beer into a 12-ounce highball glass and stir lightly. Serves 1.

Chilled ale and chilled ginger ale are also used for this drink.

Shandy: Use chilled lager beer and chilled tart lemonade instead of the ingredients given above.

SODA APERITIF

3 ounces dry vermouth
2 or 3 ice cubes
Club soda

¾ ounce Campari
¾ ounce crème de cassis

Pour the vermouth into a goblet or tumbler, add the ice and fill three-quarters full with club soda. Add the Campari and crème de cassis, and stir gently. Serves 1.

SPRITZER

4–6 ounces chilled Rhine
wine or other dry white
wine

2 or 3 ice cubes
Chilled club soda

Pour the wine into a collins glass or large goblet, add the ice cubes and fill with soda. Stir gently. Serves 1.

For a more festive drink, carefully peel the rind from a lemon in an unbroken spiral, drip into a collins glass and add the wine and soda as above.

STONE FENCE NO. 1

2–3 ounces applejack
2 dashes Angostura bitters

2 or 3 ice cubes
Sweet cider

Pour the applejack into a 10-ounce highball glass, add the bitters and ice cubes and fill with cider. Serves 1.

Stone Fence No. 2: Use Scotch instead of applejack and soda in place of cider.

Swedish Highball: Use Swedish Punch instead of applejack and soda in place of cider.

TEQUILA SUNRISE

2 ounces tequila
3 dashes grenadine
1 tablespoon lime juice
Peel from ½ lime

½ teaspoon crème de cassis
3 or 4 ice cubes
Chilled club soda

Put all ingredients except the soda in an 8-ounce highball glass. Fill with soda and stir gently. Serves 1.

TIGER'S MILK

1–1½ ounces dark rum	2 teaspoons superfine sugar
1–1½ ounces brandy	1 cup cracked ice
4 ounces heavy cream	

Combine all ingredients in a cocktail shaker and shake vigorously. Strain into a highball glass. Serves 1.

TIJUANA SUNRISE

2 ounces tequila	Dash Angostura bitters
4 ounces orange juice	3 or 4 ice cubes

Combine all ingredients in a cocktail shaker and shake vigorously. Strain into a sour glass or a stemmed wineglass. Serves 1.

A few drops of crème de cassis or grenadine may be used instead of bitters.

TOMATE

2 ice cubes	1 teaspoon grenadine
2 ounces Pernod	Cold water

Put ice cubes in a goblet or highball glass, add the Pernod and grenadine, fill with water and stir. Serves 1.

VERMOUTH CASSIS

3 ounces dry vermouth	3 or 4 ice cubes
1 ounce crème de cassis	Chilled club soda

Pour the vermouth and cassis into a large goblet or highball glass, add ice cubes and fill with soda. Stir gently. Serves 1.

VIENNESE ICED TEA

Crushed ice
Slice lemon
Superfine sugar to taste

1½ ounces rum or brandy
Freshly brewed, hot tea
Fresh mint sprigs

Fill a 14-ounce collins glass three-quarters full with crushed ice. Add the lemon slice, sugar, and rum or brandy. Fill up with tea and stir gently. Garnish with mint. Serves 1.

VODKA AND BITTER LEMON

2 or 3 ice cubes
2 ounces vodka

4–6 ounces chilled bitter
lemon

Put ice cubes in a highball glass, add the vodka, and fill up with bitter lemon. Stir lightly. Serves 1.

Vodka and Tonic: Use tonic water instead of bitter lemon.

ZOMBIE

¾ ounce 90-proof rum
1½ ounces golden rum,
    86-proof
¾ ounce light rum, 86-proof
¾ ounce pineapple juice
¾ ounce papaya juice
3 tablespoons lime juice

1 teaspoon superfine sugar
3 or 4 ice cubes
Stick pineapple
Maraschino cherry
1 tablespoon 151-proof
    Demerara rum
Superfine sugar

Combine all ingredients except the pineapple stick, cherry, Demerara rum and sugar in a cocktail shaker. Shake very thoroughly and strain into a highball glass. Garnish with pineapple stick and cherry. Carefully float the Demerara rum on top (see pp. 37–38 for directions on how to float one liquid on another), and lightly sprinkle with a little sugar. Serves 1.

PICK-ME-UPS

These drinks are, first and foremost, what they say they are. Champagne and brandy are the two most popular alcoholic ingredients, although there are others that some people prefer. A Pousse l'Amour is quite sweet and made like a Pousse-Café, in layers. It contains, as do several other pick-me-ups, an unbroken egg yolk, which should be swallowed whole by the sufferer. Sometimes an entire egg is used in a recipe, and milk is a favorite component.

In addition to the recipes that follow, you might consider some type of milk punch (page 397), which is a prime remedy for morning-after problems. There are also non-alcoholic pick-me-ups for those who wish them (pages 388–89).

BETSY ROSS

1½ ounces brandy	1 egg yolk
1½ ounces port	1 teaspoon sugar
1 dash curaçao	3 or 4 ice cubes
2 dashes Angostura bitters	Nutmeg

Combine all ingredients except the nutmeg in a cocktail shaker and shake vigorously. Strain into a large cocktail glass and top with a grating of nutmeg. Serves 1.

CECIL PICK-ME-UP

2–3 ounces brandy	3 or 4 ice cubes
1 teaspoon superfine sugar	4 ounces chilled champagne
1 egg yolk	

Combine all ingredients except the champagne in a cocktail shaker and shake vigorously. Strain into an 8-ounce wineglass and fill with champagne. Serves 1.

CHAMPAGNE PICK-ME-UP

1½ ounces brandy
3 dashes curaçao
3 dashes Fernet Branca

1 ice cube
4 ounces chilled champagne

Pour the brandy into a large saucer champagne glass or big wineglass, add the curaçao and Fernet Branca and drop in an ice cube. Stir gently. Pour in the champagne. Serves 1.

EYE OPENER NO. 2

2 ounces rum
1 teaspoon crème de cacao
1 teaspoon curaçao

1 teaspoon Pernod
1 egg yolk
½ cup crushed ice

Combine all ingredients in a cocktail shaker and shake vigorously. Strain into a cocktail glass. Serves 1.

HARRY'S PICK-ME-UP

3 ounces brandy
1 teaspoon grenadine
2 tablespoons lemon juice

3 or 4 ice cubes
6 ounces chilled champagne

Combine all ingredients except the champagne in a cocktail shaker and shake vigorously. Strain into a 10-ounce goblet and fill with champagne. Serves 1.

ICHBIEN

1½ ounces brandy   4 ounces milk
½ ounce curaçao   3 or 4 ice cubes
1 egg yolk   Nutmeg

Combine all ingredients except the nutmeg in a cocktail shaker and shake vigorously. Strain into an 8-ounce goblet, and grate a little nutmeg on top. Serves 1.

PICKUP

1½ ounces rye whiskey   2 or 3 ice cubes
¾ ounce Fernet Branca   Slice lemon
3 dashes Pernod

Combine all ingredients except the lemon slice in a mixing glass and stir gently. Strain into a cocktail glass and drop in the lemon slice. Serves 1.

POUSSE L'AMOUR

⅓ ounce maraschino   ⅓ ounce Benedictine
1 egg yolk   ⅓ ounce brandy

Pour the maraschino into a straight-sided 2-ounce liqueur glass and carefully slide in the unbroken egg yolk. Gently pour in the Benedictine, letting it trickle down the side of the slightly tilted glass, or pouring it over the back of a teaspoon held just above the glass. Add the brandy in the same way, making sure that the ingredients don't mix. Serves 1.

PRAIRIE OYSTER NO. 1

1 whole egg   Dash Worcestershire sauce
1½ ounces brandy   Salt to taste.

Carefully crack the eggshell and put the unbroken egg into a 4–6-ounce wineglass, sour glass, or champagne saucer glass.

Add the brandy, Worcestershire sauce and salt to taste. Serves 1.

When drinking this prairie oyster, the egg should be swallowed whole.

For non-alcoholic prairie oysters, see page 389.

PRAIRIE OYSTER NO. 4

1 egg yolk	1½ ounces port
2 or 3 grinds black pepper	Celery salt to taste
1 tablespoon Worcestershire sauce	

Slip the unbroken egg yolk into a 4–6-ounce wineglass, sour glass or champagne saucer glass. Season with pepper, add the Worcestershire sauce, and pour in the port. Season to taste with celery salt. Serves 1.

When drinking, the egg yolk should be swallowed whole.

RUM COW

1½ ounces light rum	1 cup milk
2 drops vanilla	Nutmeg
Dash Angostura bitters	3 or 4 ice cubes
2 teaspoons sugar	

Combine rum, vanilla, bitters, sugar and milk in a cocktail shaker. Grate a little nutmeg on top and add ice. Shake vigorously and pour into a 10-ounce highball glass. Serves 1.

SHERRY AND EGG

1 whole egg	2–3 ounces sherry

Crack the shell and put the unbroken whole egg in a cocktail glass; fill with sherry—2 or 3 ounces according to the size of the egg. Serves 1.

SPUTNIK

1½ ounces vodka
¾ ounce Fernet Branca
1 teaspoon lemon juice

½ teaspoon superfine sugar
3 or 4 ice cubes

Combine all ingredients in a cocktail shaker and shake vigorously. Strain into a cocktail glass. Serves 1.

PUFFS

A Puff is a good pick-me-up to serve before lunch. It may be made with any of the following liquors: bourbon, brandy, gin, rum, rye or Scotch, but the Brandy Puff is the most popular. However, you can substitute the liquor of your choice for the brandy in the recipe below.

BRANDY PUFF

1 or 2 ice cubes
1½–3 ounces brandy

1½–3 ounces milk
Chilled club soda

Put ice cubes in a small tumbler, add the brandy and milk, and fill up with soda. Stir gently. Serves 1.

RICKEYS

A rickey can be described as a cross between a collins and a sour. It can be made from applejack, calvados, gin, rum, or any whiskey including bourbon and Scotch.

Basic Recipe

1 ice cube
½ lime or ¼ lemon

1½ ounces liquor
Chilled club soda

Put the ice cube in an 8-ounce highball glass, squeeze in the juice of the lime or lemon, then drop in the shell. Add the liquor, fill with club soda and stir. Serves 1.

Hugo Rickey: Add 2 dashes grenadine and a slice of pineapple.

Puerto Rico Rickey: Add 2 dashes raspberry syrup.

Savoy Hotel Rickey: Add 4 dashes grenadine.

SANGAREES

A sangaree is made with liquor, wine or ale and a little sugar. It is always topped with grated nutmeg and served in a tumbler, large or small depending on the ingredients used. Sangarees based on brandy, gin, rum, sherry or whiskey are prepared as follows:

Basic Recipe

½ teaspoon superfine sugar   2 or 3 ice cubes
1½ ounces liquor or wine   Nutmeg

Put sugar in a small tumbler with just enough water to dissolve. Add the liquor or wine and ice, stir well and top with a little grated nutmeg. Serves 1.

The drink may be varied by adding club soda to fill a large tumbler and floating 3 tablespoons of port on top, followed by the usual dusting of nutmeg.

A few sangarees are made according to special recipes, as follows.

ALE, PORTER OR STOUT SANGAREE

½ teaspoon superfine sugar   Nutmeg
Chilled ale, porter or stout

Put the sugar in a 12-ounce tumbler and add just enough water to dissolve it. Fill with well-chilled ale, porter or stout. No ice is used. Dust the top of the drink with a little nutmeg. Serves 1.

PORT SANGAREE NO. 1

3 ounces port
1½ ounces water
½ teaspoon superfine sugar

3 to 4 ice cubes
Nutmeg

Combine all ingredients in a mixing glass and stir well. Strain into a small tumbler. Grate a little nutmeg on top. Serves 1.

PORT SANGAREE NO. 2

½ teaspoon superfine sugar
2 ounces port
2 ice cubes

Club soda
1 tablespoon brandy
Nutmeg

Put sugar into an 8-ounce tumbler and add enough water to dissolve. Add the port and ice cubes and fill with club soda. Float the brandy on top, and dust with grated nutmeg. Serves 1.

SLINGS

Slings are much like rickeys. Purists insist that plain water be used and not club soda, although many recipes call for soda. Slings should be served in 8-ounce highball or Old-fashioned glasses. They can be made with brandy, gin, vodka or whiskey.

Basic Recipe

2 ice cubes
2 tablespoons lemon juice
1 teaspoon superfine sugar

2–3 ounces liquor
Water

Combine the ice, sugar, lemon juice and liquor in a highball glass. Fill with cold water and stir. Serves 1.

Singapore Sling, the most famous of them all, is said to have originated in Raffles Hotel in Singapore. Follow the basic recipe, using gin, but add ½ ounce cherry brandy. Decorate the drink with a slice of orange and a sprig of mint, if you wish.

SMASHES

Smashes are small juleps and are served in small tumblers or Old-fashioned glasses. They are all made in the same way, using brandy, gin, rum or any whiskey.

Basic Recipe

1 teaspoon superfine sugar	1½–3 ounces liquor
2 sprigs fresh mint	Club soda
½ cup crushed ice	Fresh mint for garnish

Put sugar, mint and a little water in a small tumbler or Old-fashioned glass and muddle to crush the mint and dissolve the sugar. Add ice and pour in the liquor. Finish with a little club soda, if you like, and garnish with a sprig of mint. Serves 1.

SWIZZLES

Swizzles are a family of drinks that are all made the same way—with brandy, gin, rum or whiskey. They get their name from the swizzle stick, a twig with three to five small forked branches at its end that comes from the West Indies. It is put into the drink and twirled rapidly between the hands. (Silver swizzle sticks are copies of the natural twig.)

Basic Recipe

Crushed ice	2 ounces club soda
3 tablespoons lime juice	2 dashes Angostura bitters
1 tablespoon superfine sugar	2 ounces liquor

Almost fill a 12-ounce collins glass with crushed ice. Add lime juice, sugar and soda and stir throughly with a swizzle stick. Add the bitters and liquor and swizzle again. Serves 1.

Green Swizzle is made by adding 1 tablespoon of green crème de menthe to a Gin Swizzle.

TODDIES

Toddies may be served hot or cold. Either way, applejack, calvados, gin, rum or any whiskey may be used for them. Cold toddies are all made the same way; simply follow the recipe below. Hot toddies vary according to the liquor used, so individual recipes are given. Hot toddies are best served in mugs with handles because these are easier to hold than tumblers or Old-fashioned glasses.

BASIC COLD TODDY

1 teaspoon superfine sugar   2 or 3 ounces liquor
1 or 2 ice cubes

Put the sugar into a small tumbler or Old-fashioned glass and add just enough water to dissolve. Stir, leaving the spoon in the glass. Add ice and liquor; stir again. Serves 1.

HOT APPLE TODDY

1 medium-sized apple   8 to 12 ounces calvados or
4 teaspoons superfine sugar   applejack
                                Nutmeg

Core the apple and set in a baking pan with ⅛″ of water covering the pan. Roast in a 350° oven for 30 minutes or until tender. When cool enough to handle, cut in quarters and place each piece in an 8-ounce mug. Add a teaspoon of sugar and 2 or 3 ounces calvados or applejack to each mug, fill up with boiling water and stir. Grate a little nutmeg on top. Serves 4.

HOT BRICK TODDY

1 teaspoon sweet butter
1 teaspoon superfine sugar
⅛ teaspoon cinnamon

1 tablespoon hot water
2 ounces whiskey

Combine butter, sugar, cinnamon and hot water in a mug or Old-fashioned glass and stir to dissolve the sugar. Add the whiskey and fill with boiling water. Stir. Serves 1.

HOT GIN TODDY

2 cubes sugar
2 tablespoons lemon juice

2 or 3 ounces gin
Lemon peel or slice

Put sugar and lemon juice in a mug and stir to dissolve the sugar. Add the gin, fill with boiling water, stir, and decorate with lemon peel or slice of lemon. Serves 1.

The lemon juice is sometimes omitted and the toddy served with a little nutmeg grated on top.

HOT WHISKEY TODDY

1 cube sugar
2 ounces bourbon, rye, Scotch, Canadian or blended whiskey

Slice lemon
Nutmeg

Put sugar in a mug or small tumbler and add enough water to dissolve. Add the whiskey, fill up with boiling water and stir. Decorate with slice of lemon and grate a little nutmeg on top. Serves 1.

Hot Rum Toddy: Use rum instead of whiskey.

Hot Brandy Toddy: Use brandy instead of whiskey, and lemon peel in place of lemon slice. Omit the nutmeg.

BOTTLED DRINKS

All these drinks have one thing in common: they are mixtures that require time—varying from three days to six weeks—in a corked bottle to mellow and reach their prime. Some are served over ice in tall glasses; others make unusual and delightful liqueurs. One advantage of these bottled potables is that they are prepared ahead and therefore require no last-minute effort on the host's part. Another plus factor is their individuality. If you are looking for a drink that is somewhat unusual and not offered in every house, experiment with the folowing recipes and find one or more that truly pleases you.

Shrubs are pre-mixed bottled drinks made with spirits, citrus fruit juice and generous amounts of sugar. The origin of the name is obscure, but it may come from the Arabic *shurb,* meaning drink. Shrubs are usually poured from a large pitcher into highball glasses filled with crushed ice or ice cubes.

BRANDY SHRUB

Peel of 1 lemon
1¼ cups lemon juice
1 quart brandy

1 quart sherry
2 pounds lump sugar

Put the lemon peel in a large bowl, add the lemon juice and brandy, cover and let stand for 3 days. Add the sherry and sugar and stir until the sugar is dissolved. Strain and bottle.

HIPPOCRAS

2 lemons, quartered
2 sticks cinnamon
1 teaspoon mace
½ teaspoon freshly ground
white pepper

2 cups sugar
2 bottles Vouvray or
semi-sweet Alsatian wine

Put lemons in a large bowl, add spices, sugar and wine, stir to dissolve the sugar, cover and let stand for 12 hours. Strain the mixture through cheesecloth and bottle. Keep refrigerated until ready to use. To serve, put 3 or 4 ice cubes in a highball glass, add 4 ounces of spiced wine, and fill up the glass with club soda or Perrier water to taste. Makes about 16 servings.

PIÑA BORRACHA

3 cups fresh ripe pineapple, 1 bottle tequila
coarsely chopped

Place the pineapple and tequila in a large jar, cover securely and refrigerate for 24 hours or longer. Strain through dampened cheesecloth and rebottle. Serve as a liqueur.

POR MI AMANTE

4 cups ripe strawberries, 1 bottle tequila
halved

Place the strawberries and tequila in a large jar, cover securely and refrigerate for 3 weeks to a month. Strain through dampened cheesecloth and rebottle. Discard strawberries. Keep flavored tequila refrigerated and serve very cold as a liqueur.

RASPBERRY-SHADED VODKA

1 quart red raspberries or 1 quart vodka
sour cherries

Steep the raspberries or sour cherries in vodka for 1 week. Strain and pour flavored vodka into a bottle or decanter.

To serve, put 2 or 3 ice cubes in an Old-fashioned glass, add 2 ounces of the flavored vodka, or more to taste. For a long drink, put 2 or 3 ice cubes in an 8-ounce highball glass, add 2 ounces of the flavored vodka and fill up with club soda. Serves 1.

ROMPOPE

1 quart milk
1 cup sugar
1 vanilla bean

12 egg yolks
1 pint light rum

Combine milk, sugar and vanilla bean in a saucepan and simmer very gently for 15 minutes, stirring from time to time. Beat egg yolks in a bowl until thick and lemon-colored. Cool the milk mixture and remove the vanilla bean. Beat the egg yolks into the flavored milk and cook slowly until the mixture coats a spoon. Cool and add the rum. Bottle, cork and keep for several days before drinking. Serve in liqueur glasses as an aperitif or as a liqueur.

RUM SHRUB

3 pints orange juice
1 pound lump sugar

4 quarts dark rum

Combine the ingredients in a large crock, cover and allow to stand for 6 weeks. Strain and bottle.

SHRUB

4 Seville or bitter oranges
4 ounces granulated sugar
1 cup water

1 quart dark rum, preferably from Martinique or Guadaloupe

Peel the rinds from the oranges as thinly as possible. Boil the sugar and water until sugar is dissolved. Pour out a little rum from the bottle to make room for the sugar syrup and orange peel, recork the bottle and let stand for 2 weeks. Strain and rebottle. Serve this Shrub as a liqueur.

Fine Finales to Good Dinners

After-dinner drinking divides itself naturally into two separate and distinct periods: right after dinner and long after dinner.

Right-After-Dinner Drinking

Demitasses and right-after-dinner drinks make first-rate partners and have one important element in common: both add a subtle quality of grace and elegance to your entertaining, and should therefore be presented with style and panache. Both are more suited to sipping in the living room, on the terrace or in some other convivial place rather than at the dining table. And both require certain correct accessories.

Strong black coffee is nearly always served at the end of a meal and, because it has one of the most adaptable flavors in the world, it tastes wonderful with spirits, spices or sweets. You will find that the various coffee-based drinks such as Café Brulot or Irish Coffee are invariably popular. These concoctions are particularly delicious because the heat of the coffee brings out all the bouquet of the added spirit. One very easy solution, if you have a lot of guests, is to fill demitasses only two-thirds full with strong black coffee, have a choice of brandy and two or more liqueurs, and add a dollop of each guest's favorite to his cup. Liqueur glasses should be on hand, however, for those who prefer a separate drink. (To truly enjoy the bouquet of brandy and be able to warm it slightly with the heat of one's hand, it should be served in brandy glasses, but they are not strictly necessary.)

The brisk bitterness of strong espresso coffee is an ideal foil for small delicacies such as after-dinner mints, petits fours or really good chocolates, any of which can be served in the living room along with the demitasses, in lieu of dessert. The liqueurs that taste best with coffee are those with the less cloying flavors—such as Galliano, Benedictine, Drambuie, Strega and Anisette—but you can also temper the sweeter ones, especially the heavier coffee and chocolate liqueurs, by mixing them half-and-half with brandy. Actually, brandy of one kind or another (see page 50) is the most popular libation right after dinner, with a variety of better-known liqueurs contending for second position. (The less familiar ones are rarely in demand, but a list of both, along with their individual characteristics, is given on pages 60–61.)

Also delightful is a sizable group of mixed after-dinner drinks that are based on brandy or liqueurs rather than coffee. Most people are in somewhat of a rut as far as this classification of potables goes and—when given a choice —will invariably ask for whatever they are used to drinking. In order to widen their horizons, simply present the drink you have chosen as though it were another course. Then, if some member of the party doesn't like your masterpiece, he can always name his choice. Chances are there will be no substitutions. These mixed after-dinner drinks range from simple to highly complicated and some of them take time to prepare. In general, they are on the sweet side, but many are delicious conversation pieces, and a few are truly spectacular.

Just as the graceful way of serving demitasses is to set a tray with little after-dinner cups and saucers (the finer the china, the better), small spoons and a coffee set, so the plan-ahead hostess arranges another tray with liqueur or brandy glasses or both, and the various liqueurs she plans to offer her guests. These may be left in their own bottles, some of which are very decorative, or poured into decanters. Clear glass is more effective than a color, because many liqueurs have their own subtle or vivid colorings. The tray used to carry the paraphernalia should be bare and therefore decorative; napkins are not used. Mixed after-dinner drinks such as grasshoppers and stingers are usually served in cocktail glasses, and mists in Old-fashioned glasses. Probably for this reason, these mixtures are often referred to as "after-dinner cocktails," which is unfortunate and misleading, because bona fide cocktails are served only *before* a meal. Due to their sweetness, liqueurs and liqueur-based drinks are seldom popular at any other time than after dinner. There are exceptions, however. The Alexander, for example, can be a pleasant pick-me-up before brunch, because of its soothing, creamy content. Irish coffee is another flexible post-prandial tipple that can be equally welcome on a cold winter afternoon. Custom establishes standard procedures, but personal preference can always switch them around.

Dessert-coffee-and-liqueur parties are easy to give, demand a minimum of work and can be especially successful if you plan some sort of simple entertainment that will hold your guests' interest. This might be a particularly interesting TV program, a game such as charades or one of the more challenging word games, or a couple of hours of music with or without dancing. All you have to do by way of preparation is to make or buy a rather special dessert, brew some good, strong coffee and serve brandy, straight liqueurs or mixed liqueur-based drinks. The enjoyment of any of these is greatly enhanced if the mood is leisurely; they are not the best choice before an evening of bridge or poker. Simple highballs or beer during the game with, perhaps, sandwiches and coffee at the end of it, are the usual informal accompaniments to card playing.

Because dessert-coffee-and-liqueur parties are based on the assumption that the guests will eat the substantial part of their dinner before arriving, this form of entertainment is casual and best geared to easygoing people who live near one another. Dining at home and then driving several miles for dessert is not everyone's idea of a good time, but, given the right group of neighbors, you can have a delightful, merry party with overtones of style. These last depend largely upon the sophistication of the dessert you choose, and the way you serve it, the coffee and drinks.

Long-After-Dinner Drinking

When the feast of reason and flow of wit around the coffee table have finally slackened, the time is ripe for those long-after-dinner drinks. Some of the guests will want to coast along with their liqueurs, brandy or liqueur mixtures; others will be ready for a change. If they are serious drinkers, it is likely that highballs (or shorter versions of them) will be the order of the evening, which is easy on the host. A growing number of people these days call for beer at such a time, which is also simplicity itself. It is a nice gesture to have an assortment of beers to offer—Danish, German and Mexican among others—and Pilsner glasses to drink from. For those who have had cognac after dinner, try brandy highballs or mists—*fine à l'eau,* as the French have it. Iced champagne is good at this hour also; serve extra dry rather than brut, and don't be afraid to drop an ice cube into the glass. For those who want something very light and refreshing, keep a chilled bottle of Rhine, Moselle or Alsatian wine on hand, and make spritzers with equal parts wine and club soda.

Four Popular Types of After-Dinner Drinks

Floats are pretty to look at, smooth to sip, and may be made with any kind of liqueur. Fill a liqueur glass to within ¼ inch of the top with the liqueur of your choice, then carefully pour on cream so that it floats on top. While especially recommended for coffee or chocolate-flavored liqueurs, floats are eminently satisfactory with any liqueur you like. The traditional Brandy Float, however, is made somewhat differently: the brandy is floated on top instead of cream.

Frappés may be made with any liqueur (or liquor, for that matter), the most usual, perhaps, being crème de menthe. There are three ways of making them. All versions are good, all are drunk very cold and all should be served with short straws (regular straws cut in half), although if you happen to be out of them, no great harm is done.

1. Most usual method: Heap a cocktail glass with shaved ice and pour the liqueur slowly over it until the glass is full.

2. Put shaved ice and the liqueur in a blender, blend quickly, and pour unstrained into a cocktail glass. Half a cup of ice to a jigger of liqueur is a good proportion.

3. Half-fill a cocktail shaker with shaved ice, add a jigger of liqueur, shake quickly and strenuously, then strain into the glass. The result will be somewhat more granular than the blender method.

Mists are almost identical to frappés made by the shaved ice method, except that an Old-fashioned glass is used and a twist of lemon peel added as a final touch. While customarily made with Scotch or bourbon, mists are excellent with brandy or any liqueur. Those concocted with whiskey fit better into the long-after-dinner category, unless your liquor is of very special quality.

Pousse-cafés are in a class by themselves. They are also sometimes called, descriptively, rainbow cordials, and consist of layers of variously colored ingredients, most of which are liqueurs. To make them requires imagination, a steady hand and a slight knowledge of the specific gravities of the liqueurs and syrups involved. Practice makes perfect in the art of concocting pousse-cafés, so start with simple three-deckers and eventually you may work up to a real spectacular! One caution: When your friends learn of your accomplishments, you'll be deluged with requests. If you don't want to go to all the bother of assembling the various ingredients and making pousse-cafés, don't serve the first one.

COFFEE DRINKS

These coffee-based drinks may be made with almost any liquor or liqueur. Some are hot; others, best suited to summer enjoyment, are cold. Although brandy is most often called for in the following recipes, Jamaica rum and Irish whiskey are good choices, as are chartreuse, Kahlúa, crème de cacao, strega and Benedictine.

CAFE AUX COGNACS

Lemon
Superfine sugar

4 ounces strong hot coffee
1 ounce brandy

Rub the rim of a heavy 6-ounce goblet with lemon and then dip it in sugar. Fill the glass three-quarters full with hot coffee and float the brandy on top. Light the brandy and serve. Serves 1.

CAFE BRULOT

6 lumps sugar
9 ounces (6 jiggers) brandy
1 twist lemon peel
2 twists orange peel

2 sticks cinnamon, broken
12 whole cloves
1½ cups strong hot coffee

Place all ingredients except the coffee in the blazer of a chafing dish and heat gently, stirring. When well warmed, light the brandy and let it burn for about 1 minute. Slowly pour in the coffee, then ladle into demitasses. Serves 6.

CAFE CHARENTAIS

1 demitasse hot strong
   coffee
Sugar to taste

1 ounce brandy
1 tablespoon whipped cream

Sweeten the coffee to taste, add the brandy and top with whipped cream. Serves 1. Have coffee beans to nibble, if you like.

Café Jamaique: Substitute Jamaica rum for brandy.

Café Floride: Substitute orange peel soaked in orange liqueur for brandy.

CAFE DIABLE

This is basically the same as Café Brûlot but requires a longer blazing time. It is made with dark rum, as a rule, but brandy may also be used.

2 cinnamon sticks	Zest of 2 oranges
2 tablespoons superfine sugar	24 cloves
½ cup dark rum	6 cups strong, hot coffee

Put cinnamon sticks, sugar and rum in a chafing dish over a burner. Flame the rum. Impale the zest of the oranges, stuck together with the cloves, on a fork. Hold fork above chafing dish and pour more rum over the peel. (Use a bottle with a jigger spout, for safety.) When the peel flames, drop it into the dish, add the coffee, blend and serve. Serves 6.

CAFE ROYAL

1 demitasse strong hot coffee	1 lump sugar
	1½ ounces brandy

Hold a teaspoon over the coffee cup and place the sugar and brandy in the spoon. Light the brandy; when the flames begin to die down, pour it into the coffee. If you wish, the sugar may be omitted. Serves 1.

This drink is also known as **Cafe Brûle.**

IRISH COFFEE

1 teaspoon sugar	5 ounces strong hot coffee
1½ ounces Irish whiskey	1 tablespoon whipped cream

Rinse out a wineglass with very hot water. Put the sugar, whiskey and coffee in it. Top with whipped cream or, if preferred, float a tablespoon of unwhipped heavy cream on top. Serves 1.

Irish Mist may be used instead of Irish whiskey.

CAFE GLACE AUX LIQUEURS

½ cup sugar
1 quart strong hot coffee
1 cup brandy

4 tablespoons whipped cream
Ice cubes

Stir the sugar into the coffee until dissolved. Cool. Add the brandy and pour into tall glasses filled with ice cubes. Top with whipped cream. Serves 4.

Variations:
1. Flavor the whipped cream with sugar and cinnamon.
2. Use dark rum instead of brandy; add a twist of lemon peel. Flavor the whipped cream with vanilla.
3. Use half hot chocolate and half hot coffee.
4. Omit the sugar and use Grand Marnier instead of brandy. Top with whipped cream mixed with chopped crystallized ginger.
5. Use Irish whiskey or bourbon instead of brandy.

CAFE GRANITE

This version of the Italian water ice called *granité* serves as both after-dinner drink and dessert.

1 cup sugar
2 cups water

1 cup extra-strong espresso coffee
4 ounces coffee liqueur

Dissolve the sugar in the water over low heat. Add the coffee, cool; freeze, without stirring, in an ice-cube tray until granular. Serve in stemmed glasses and pour 1 ounce coffee liqueur into each. For a richer version, top with coffee ice cream or whipped cream. Serves 4.

CAFE LIEGEOISE

4 ounces strong coffee,
  chilled

4 ounces vanilla ice cream
1 ounce brandy

Put all ingredients in an electric blender and whirl until smooth. Serve in a large stemmed goblet. Serves 1.

COFFEE MERGER

1 jigger brandy
1 jigger Cointreau

1 jigger strong chilled black
  coffee
Ice cubes

Combine all ingredients in a cocktail shaker and shake well. Strain into a cocktail glass. Serves 1.

FLOATS

A float derives its name from the fact that cream or some other ingredient is floated on top of the drink. For how to do this, see pages 37–38.

BRANDY FLOAT

This drink is made differently from other floats in that brandy is floated on top instead of cream.

1 or 2 ice cubes
Chilled club soda

2½ ounces brandy, or less

Put the ice cubes in an Old-fashioned glass and fill two-thirds full with club soda. Float the brandy carefully on top so that it does not mix. Serves 1.

Rum or whiskey may be substituted for the brandy, and the drink's name changed accordingly.

KING ALPHONSE

2 ounces crème de cacao   ½ ounce heavy cream

Pour the crème de cacao into a large liqueur glass or little wineglass and then carefully float the cream on top. Serves 1.

This drink is also known as an **Alfonso, Angel's Tip** or **Angel's Dream.** The same recipe may be followed, however, using almost any liqueur as a base. The following are examples:

Princess: Made with apricot brandy.

Xochimilco: Made with Kahlúa.

Witching Eve: Made exactly like a King Alphonse, except that a dash of Angostura bitters follows the crème de cacao.

FRAPPES

These drinks are usually made with crème de menthe, although any liquor or liqueur is suitable. Use the basic recipe for all but the two drinks that follow it (which are somewhat different).

Basic Recipe

Crushed ice   2 ounces liquor or liqueur

Heap a cocktail glass with the ice and pour the liquor or liqueur over it until the glass is full. Serve with short straws (regular straws cut in half). Serves 1.

For two other methods of making frappés, see below.

PERNOD FRAPPE

1½ ounces Pernod   2 dashes Angostura bitters
½ ounce anisette   ½ cup shaved ice

Combine all ingredients in a cocktail shaker, shake well and pour into a cocktail glass. Serves 1.

RUM FRAPPE

1 scoop orange or lemon
sherbet

2 ounces light rum

Put the sherbet in a saucer champagne glass, pour the rum over it and stir. Serves 1.

LIQUEUR AND BRANDY DRINKS

Every bartender with any imagination, it would seem, has invented one or more drinks by combining liqueurs with other liqueurs, spirits, fruit juices or whatever was at hand. Most of these have had very short careers, but the best have survived through the years. Here are some which have stood the test of time. They are made with liqueurs or brandy or both, and some include a liquor such as gin, rum or Scotch as an ingredient.

Also see "Liqueur-Based Cocktails," pages 191–92.

AFTER DINNER

1½ ounces apricot brandy
1½ ounces curaçao
3 tablespoons lime juice

3 or 4 ice cubes
Twist of lime peel

Combine all ingredients except the lime peel in a cocktail shaker and shake vigorously. Strain into a cocktail glass, and drop in the lime peel.

After Supper: Use 2 dashes of lemon juice instead of lime juice, and omit peel.

AFTER-DINNER SPECIAL

1½ ounces Swedish Punch
¾ ounce cherry brandy

1½ tablespoons lime juice
3 or 4 ice cubes

Combine all ingredients in a cocktail shaker and shake vigorously. Strain into a cocktail glass. Serves 1.

B & B

This is simply a mixture of brandy and Benedictine. The dryness of the brandy cuts the sweetness of the liqueur. You can buy the drink bottled or make it yourself.

1–1½ ounces Benedictine   1–1½ ounces brandy

Mix together and serve in a liqueur glass, or over shaved ice as a frappé in a cocktail glass. Serves 1.

BETWEEN THE SHEETS

1 ounce brandy   ½ ounce lemon juice
1 ounce Cointreau   (optional)
1 ounce light rum   3 or 4 ice cubes

Place all ingredients in a cocktail shaker and shake vigorously. Strain into a cocktail glass. Serves 1.

BRANDY BLAZER NO. 2

1 lump sugar   1 twist lemon peel
1 twist orange peel   2–3 ounces brandy

Rinse an Old-fashioned glass with hot water to warm it. Add the sugar, orange peel, lemon peel and brandy, and mash with a spoon or muddler. Light brandy and blaze for a few seconds. Serves 1.

DIANA

Crushed ice   ½ ounce brandy
2 ounces white crème de
   menthe

Pack a 4-ounce stemmed wineglass with crushed ice and pour in the crème de menthe. Carefully float the brandy on top. Serves 1.

ETHEL DUFFY

¾ ounce apricot brandy
¾ ounce white crème de menthe

¾ ounce curaçao
3 or 4 ice cubes

Combine all ingredients in a cocktail shaker and shake vigorously. Strain into a cocktail glass. Serves 1.

GRASSHOPPER

The pale pastel green of the drink in a champagne glass makes this festive indeed.

1 ounce green crème de menthe
1 ounce white crème de cacao

1 ounce light cream
½ cup crushed ice

Pour all ingredients into a cocktail shaker, shake vigorously and strain into a saucer champagne glass. (Or whirl ingredients in an electric blender and serve in a cocktail glass.) Serves 1.

Mexican Grasshopper: Use Kahlúa instead of crème de cacao. If you wish, substitute heavy for light cream.

GREEN DRAGON NO. 1

1½ ounces dry gin
1 ounce green crème de menthe
½ ounce kümmel

½ ounce lemon juice
4 dashes peach bitters
3 or 4 ice cubes

Combine all ingredients in a cocktail shaker and shake well. Strain into a cocktail glass. Serves 1.

GREEN DRAGON NO. 2

6 ice cubes   1–1½ ounces brandy
1–1½ ounces green
    chartreuse

Put ice cubes in a mixing glass, add the chartreuse and brandy and stir briskly. Strain into a cocktail glass. Serves 1.

Praying Mantis: Add 1 ounce heavy cream. Shake drink in a cocktail shaker instead of stirring it.

Golden Gopher: Substitute white crème de cacao for the chartreuse.

GREEN DRAGON NO. 3

1½–2 ounces vodka   3 or 4 ice cubes
¾–1 ounce green crème de
    menthe

Combine all ingredients in a mixing glass and stir thoroughly. Strain into a chilled cocktail glass. Serves 1.

White Spider: Substitute white crème de menthe for green.

KAHLUA TOREADOR

1 ounce Kahlúa   1 egg white
2 ounces brandy   3 to 4 ice cubes

Combine all ingredients in a shaker and shake vigorously, or blend in an electric blender. Strain into a chilled cocktail glass. Serves 1.

LOLLIPOP

¾ ounce Cointreau   Dash maraschino
¾ ounce green chartreuse   3 or 4 ice cubes
¾ ounce kirsch

Combine all ingredients in a cocktail shaker and shake vigorously. Strain into a cocktail glass. Serves 1.

ROMAN SNOWBALL

Crushed Ice   3 coffee beans
2 ounces Sambuca

Pack an 8-ounce wineglass half full of crushed ice. Pour the
Sambuca over the ice and top with the coffee beans. The
beans are chewed like candy after they have absorbed the
flavor of the liqueur. Serves 1.

RUSTY NAIL

1–1½ ounces Drambuie   2 or 3 ice cubes
1–1½ ounces Scotch
    whiskey

Combine all ingredients in an Old-fashioned glass and stir to
mix. Serves 1.

SLEEPYHEAD

2–3 ounces brandy   2 or 3 ice cubes
Twist orange peel   Ginger ale
3 or 4 leaves fresh mint,
    bruised

Pour the brandy into an Old-fashioned glass, add the orange
peel, mint leaves and ice, and fill with ginger ale. Serves 1.

STINGER

1–1½ ounces brandy   ½ cup crushed ice
1–1½ ounces white crème
    de menthe

Combine all ingredients in a cocktail shaker and shake vigorously. Strain into a cocktail glass. Serves 1.

Rum Stinger: Substitute Jamaica rum for brandy.

Gin Stinger: Substitute gin for brandy, and reduce crème de menthe to ½ ounce. This drink is sometimes called **White Way No. 2.**

Although a Stinger is essentially an after-dinner drink, some people like to serve it before dinner as a cocktail. When making a Stinger for this purpose, reduce the sweetness by using only 1 part crème de menthe to 2 parts brandy or rum. Do not change proportions of a Gin Stinger unless you wish to cut down on the crème de menthe.

WHITE RUSSIAN

¾–1 ounce crème de cacao   1 tablespoon heavy cream
1½–2 ounces vodka   3 or 4 ice cubes

Place all ingredients in a cocktail shaker and shake vigorously. Strain into a chilled cocktail glass. Serves 1.

This is also known as a **Russian Bear.**

Black Russian: Substitute Kahlúa for the crème de cacao and omit the cream.

MISTS

These drinks are similar to frappés, but a little bigger. Mists made with Scotch or bourbon are usually best suited to long-after-dinner drinking and can also be enjoyed at other times of day. If the liquor, however, is of very special quality, it is apt to be most appreciated right after dinner. Mists concocted with brandy or any liqueur should be served immediately after demitasses.

Basic Recipe

½ cup crushed ice	**or**
2–3 ounces Scotch, bourbon or brandy	1–1½ ounces liqueur
	Twist of lemon peel

Pack the ice in an Old-fashioned glass, pour in the spirits, twist the peel over the drink to release the oil, then drop it in. Serves 1.

POUSSE-CAFES

Success in making these multi-layered after-dinner drinks depends upon keeping each layer separate and distinct from the others. The heaviest ingredient is poured first, the lightest last. When using any of the following recipes, it is essential to pour the items, *in the order listed,* into a small, straight-sided glass.

There are two accepted techniques, both of which require patience and a steady hand. Try them and see which you prefer. You can begin by setting the glass on a flat surface and pouring the first ingredient. Then tip the glass slightly and trickle the second ingredient very gently down the side so that it will flow over the one below it without blending at any point. Do the same with the third, fourth and so on. Another method is to keep the glass upright throughout, and pour each layer slowly and gently over an inverted spoon placed immediately above the glass.

As a general rule, the *higher* the proof, the *lighter* the liqueur. But it is not that simple; sugar content also has an effect. Thus, 84-proof cognac (which is dry) will float on 110-proof green chartreuse (which is very sweet), while 96-proof Kirschwasser (which combines dryness with high proof) will top them both.

Unfortunately, it is impossible to give absolutely fool-proof recipes, because liqueurs vary in density from brand to brand. However, each bottle is marked with the proof, and it is fairly easy to decide degrees of sweetness by tasting. A sound, general rule is to follow the orders given in the recipes, and experiment on your own before you try to show off in front of guests. There is no doubt that a properly made pousse-café is a colorful, dramatic achievement.

ANGEL'S DELIGHT

¼ ounce grenadine
¼ ounce Triple Sec

¼ ounce Crème Yvette
¼ ounce heavy cream

Pour in the order listed so that each ingredient floats on top of the one before it. Serves 1.

ANGEL'S KISS

¼ ounce crème de cacao
¼ ounce Crème Yvette

¼ ounce heavy cream

Pour in the order listed so that each ingredient floats on top of the one before it. Serves 1.

FIREWORKS

¼ ounce grenadine syrup
¼ ounce crème de cassis
¼ ounce apricot brandy
¼ ounce Cointreau

¼ ounce green chartreuse
¼ ounce cognac or other brandy
¼ ounce Kirschwasser

Pour all ingredients, in the order listed, into a narrow, straight-sided 2-ounce liqueur glass. Serves 1.

LAYER CAKE

½ ounce crème de cacao   ½ ounce heavy cream
½ ounce apricot brandy   Maraschino cherry

Pour in the order listed so that each ingredient floats on top of the one before it. Carefully place the cherry on top. Chill before serving. Serves 1.

Angel's Wing: Use brandy in place of apricot brandy, and omit the cherry.

PORT AND STARBOARD

This drink is fun to serve to boat-minded friends, or after dinner on a boat. It is easy to make.

1½ ounces grenadine   ½ ounce green crème de menthe

Pour in the order listed. Serves 1.

RAINBOW

¼ ounce green crème de   ¼ ounce Cherry Heering
menthe   ¼ ounce brandy
¼ ounce yellow chartreuse

Pour in the order listed so that each ingredient floats on top of the one before it. Serves 1.

SAVOY HOTEL

¼ ounce crème de cacao   ¼ ounce brandy
¼ ounce Benedictine

Pour in the order listed so that each ingredient floats on top of the one before it. Serves 1.

STARS AND STRIPES

¼ ounce crème de cassis   ¼ ounce maraschino
¼ ounce green chartreuse

Pour in the order listed so that each ingredient floats on top of the one before it. Serves 1.

This drink is sometimes made with grenadine, heavy cream and Crème Yvette, in that order.

Union Jack: Substitute grenadine for the crème de cassis. The colors of the ingredients bear no more relevance to the drink's name than do the colors of the Stars and Stripes!

ZOOMS

All zooms are made according to the following recipe. The liquor may be brandy, gin, rum or whiskey.

Basic Recipe

1 teaspoon honey   2–3 ounces liquor
1 teaspoon heavy cream   3 or 4 ice cubes

Dissolve honey in a little boiling water and pour into a cocktail shaker with the other ingredients. Shake vigorously and strain into a cocktail glass. Serves 1.

Party Punches and Eggnogs

One of the classic accompaniments to abundant and special-occasion hospitality is a brimming punch bowl, complete with ladle and circled by an array of punch cups. There was a time, particularly in England, when punch was so popular that it was served at almost every good-sized gathering. Dozens of recipes were invented and some very beautiful bowls were created. Many of these were silver; others were made of china, glass or copper. Cut-glass punch bowls were much admired by the Victorians. But punch became less and less popular as cocktails became more so. Family punch bowls collected dust on top shelves; they were used only at weddings and big, special holiday galas, or were converted into decorative containers for masses of greenery, or they went the way of so many space-consuming heirlooms and were disposed of. This is a pity, because punch is a great invention. It has a strong psychological effect on people, at once suggesting an openhanded welcome and an extremely sociable mood. It is also a very versatile drink. Punches run the gamut from mild and refreshing to heady and heart-warming to rich and nourishing; from very cold to comfortably hot. Indeed, there are delicious and suitable punches for such traditional occasions as weddings, coming-out parties and Christmas or New Year parties, for housewarmings, summertime gatherings on warm afternoons, receptions, dances of every size, après-ski and après-football games or hockey matches on blustery days. Whether a party is large or quite small, a drink-and-run affair or one where guests linger to talk, eat, drink and talk some more, a filled punch bowl surrounded by gleaming glasses, punch cups or mugs (for hot punch) is one of the most inviting of all sights.

There are a number of individual punches that can be made singly, in a glass, without benefit of a pitcher or punch bowl. As a rule, these are drinks that do not require a battery of ingredients. You will find the recipes for them grouped together alphabetically at the end of the following categories: champagne punches, liquor-based punches and eggnogs. Although you can't usually divide a party recipe and come up with the correct proportions for a single drink, you can almost always multiply quantities given in an individual recipe by any number you wish, which is what you should do with the Milk Punch recipe, for example. The only exceptions are some of the individual hot drinks (page 169) that require rather special attention.

It is not necessary to serve a blockbuster of a punch such as Artillery or Fish House. Many of the gentle, wine-based ones are delicious; so are some non-alcoholic punches that appeal to grown-ups upon occasion as well as to children and are far more fun to serve and drink than the standard "ades," iced tea or iced coffee. Finally, if further convincing is necessary, punch is easy on the host because any preliminary mixing and ripening can be done well in advance. Since almost everybody drinks the same thing at a punch party, there is no mad scramble for special concoctions to satisfy the exotic requests of some guests. One word of advice, however: punch, whatever its alcoholic components may be, should not be the only drink served at a party. Some of your guests may be more interested in the lore of such a potable than in the taste. Others may have a deep distrust of any mixed drink whose ingredients and effect are unknown to them. So always have simple drinks available for those who prefer them, although you need not provide anything more complicated than liquor with water or soda.

The Magic of Champagne Punch

It's fairly common knowledge that champagne punch is traditional at weddings, coming-out parties, anniversaries and elaborate dances. But champagne has the happy faculty of putting any pleasant occasion into particularly festive and elegant orbit. When using it in a punch, by no means open superb Dom Perignon, but substitute some lesser brand without being too penny-pinching. In punches, a sec or demi-sec is really preferable to a brut, as the slight sweetness helps to cut the acidity of fruit-juice components. The champagne, always well chilled, should be added just before serving the punch so that the bubbles don't dissipate before the glasses are filled. Naturally, the punch is best made in small batches, for the bubbles leave after awhile. It is easy to make more.

Memorable galas, the kind that call for a certain amount of ceremony, lots of style, pretty clothes and plenty of polish, are "naturals" for champagne punch because it, too, has style and polish. In addition, it evokes a high-flying mood, partly due to association, partly to the tang of its taste and partly to the lift in its makeup.

Dances, little and large: Whether you invite ten couples, roll up the rug for the evening and put your record-player to work overtime, or ask a big crowd and have a real live band, champagne punch is one of those drinks that has dancing feet. If you feel you can't serve it because of your budget, consider a recipe that combines champagne with still wine, fruit juice or other reasonably priced ingredients. And remember, as already mentioned, it is not only unnecessary, but actually rather wasteful, to use the very best champagne in a punch.

Summer-Day Parties

On a warm day, nothing looks and tastes more refreshing and joyful than a sparkling wine-based punch. Some of the recipes call for a punch bowl; others, usually known as cups, are made in a pitcher. White, red or rosé wine is used (plus champagne in various cases), along with additional ingredients that often include fruit or fruit juices or both, a measure of some liquor or liqueur and soda water. One of the prime points about such a punch is that it should *look* as summery as it tastes. Set the punch bowl on a prettily arranged table; a round one is ideal, perhaps covered with a pastel or flowered cloth. Consider circling the base of the bowl with feathery greenery and non-wilting flowers. If the table is outdoors, be sure to put it in the shade—under a tree, porch roof or awning. Have plenty of punch cups (or low glasses that are wide at the top for easy filling with a ladle), as guests tend to leave "empties" around and pick up fresh ones when they return for a refill. If you use one or more pitchers instead of a punch bowl, they should be gracefully shaped, made of clear glass and easy to pour from. Serve light nibbles or food that complements the drink.

May Day: The custom of celebrating May Day, or any other fine spring day, with a Maibowle is a pleasant one that bears reviving. The first day of May has been a spring festival since Roman times, and one that was eagerly adopted in the countries the Romans conquered. The festivities lasted from midnight to midnight and, besides May dances and Maypoles, they included bouts of eating and drinking. May wine is still made in Germany in the spring of the year from young Moselle in which the herb waldmeister (woodruff) is steeped to impart a special flavor. The original Maibowles included large quantities of that herb sprinkled with sugar and steeped in a mixture of white wine and brandy. After standing overnight, the woodruff was removed and more white wine added. Woodruff is hard to find today, so fresh fruit such as strawberries is apt to be substituted. Another version, a Bowle, calls for approximately the same ingredients but in different proportions.

An afternoon May Day party, when the garden is full of spring flowers and the trees are laden with blossoms, is enchanting to think about, so why not give one? You might ask children as well as their parents, and have a separate, wineless punch for them (page 396). If you feel truly ambitious, you could plan the party as a buffet supper, or erect a Maypole and organize a dance around it for the boys and girls. Or you could take the simpler way and concentrate on serving a delightful Maibowle accompanied by platters of sandwiches made with thinly sliced bread, plenty of cookies or little cakes for the children and straight drinks for those who never deviate from their chosen brew.

Winter Glad Tidings

In the high, far-off times, when there were such things as witches and demons, one way to get rid of unwanted warlocks was to hold a colossal wassail party. Everyone, Druids and hoi polloi alike, had a marvelous time, and the demons were successfully routed—possibly drowned—in the most agreeable way.

You may not realize, as the Christmas wassail slides down your eager throat, that you are carrying on an ancient and honorable pagan tradition. All those dances that lasted until cockcrow, libations, mysteries of barley sheaves and new wine, animal sacrifices and religious ecstasy, were far more convivial than a cocktail party and more interesting. But the general purpose of such midwinter saturnalia, both prehistoric and present-day, is the same—to rid oneself and one's friends of the cold-weather blues. The holiday season is a long one, extending from before Thanksgiving Day until after New Year, and the winter is even longer. Drinks that glow or nourish or both put you into the right humor to cope joyfully with the time of year.

Merry Christmas, Happy New Year: Just as the most thoroughly modern room is enriched by the introduction of a superb antique, so the most up-to-date party is mellowed by a touch of tradition—and Christmas is surely the one season when beloved old customs are not only appropriate but welcome. It is the ideal time to offer friends some of the old, favorite holiday bowls and punches as a change from the ubiquitous cocktail or highball.

The tradition of hot punches at the Christmas season is a carry-over from the days when carolers and revelers roamed the street, stopping here and there for a gay mug of Brandy Bishop, Hot Buttered Rum or a hot toddy. As they went along, the singing no doubt improved and the cheer grew cheerier. What a delightful way to occupy oneself on Christmas! But come Puritan times, the fun and joy were taken from the celebrations, as related in this sad quote of that period:

> All plums the prophet's son deny,
> And spice broths are too hot;
> Treason's in a December pie
> And death within the pot.

Ebullient Christmas customs, however, were too beloved to die, and were revived with gusto in the last quarter of the nineteenth century. There are choral groups in today's suburban or small communities who gather outside their neighbors' houses to sing carols every Christmas and to be rewarded with suitable refreshment. Whether your role be that of singer or host, it can be fun and very satisfying.

If you hold open house at some point during the holidays, nothing is easier to serve than one of the classic hot spiced punches and there is no better time to offer it than on a frosty afternoon, to guests coming in out of the cold. A steaming silver or copper bowl makes a decorative point of interest for a party table. You might use the recipe for Wassail Bowl, an early Anglo-Saxon drink of spiced ale originally served in a large communal cup. Over the centuries various ingredients have been added or subtracted, and each innovator devised his favorite way of making this punch. Sometimes wine replaced ale; occasionally gin was added. Often eggs were introduced. Usually, wassail is served piping hot, but some recipes advise cooling before serving. Always, however, it was, and remains, a spicy concoction.

Other less-known hot punches might be put forth in the name of holiday tradition, with a slight nod to the ancients. Although they are very good, and quality ingredients make them more so, it is not necessary to use your best wines and liquors in brews such as Aunt Betsy's Favorite, Southern Cross, Glögg (Swedish), Ogge (Danish), Orange Warmer and Cider Bishop. An eighteenth-century gentleman, Colonel Francis Negus, who had definite opinions concerning strong drink, devised a light, flavorful potion, named Negus in his honor. Scottish border folk make a spicy ale-and-whiskey drink called Het Pint for their traditional New Year's quaffing. A typically American drink for the season is Hot Buttered Applejack based on our own apple brandy. It is hearty and—take warning—slightly deceptive; the rich fruit flavor disguises the wallop. All these are served hot.

Punches that were also much favored for winter holidays in times past—and are today—often include eggs, milk or cream, or even all three. The syllabubs and possets of the sixteenth and seventeenth centuries are examples. These drinks provided nourishment as well as the lift of liquor; after a long trek through December's blasting wind and snow, a healthy swig of egg, milk and alcohol was just what a person needed. Auld Man's Milk is an ancient Scottish beverage that must have been the forerunner of our eggnog. The eggnog, popular as an "at home" drink on Christmas Day since colonial times, is traditionally made with bourbon, but there are many variations. A big bowl of eggnog is often also the center of merrymaking on New Year's Day. Eggnog should be kept in the refrigerator until served—and don't put any ice in it unless you are making an individual drink. Simply pour the mixture into the bowl at the last minute and dust the top with grated nutmeg. Another familiar holiday drink—hot and very American—is the Tom and Jerry, also made with eggs and milk, plus brandy, rum, sugar and a dusting of nutmeg.

All-winter delights: It would be a great pity if hot punches and soothing egg-and/or-milk-based ones were served only at large parties during the holiday season. For one thing, winter is interminable in many parts of the country, and if you have a good-sized party at any time during bleak weather, you can put your punch bowl to good service. For another, the many punches that call for only a few ingredients, as already explained, can be made quite easily in individual glasses or in very limited quantities if you are entertaining only a few people. Milk Punch, for example, is a soothing, restorative drink; customarily it is supposed to be frappéed, shaken with cracked ice (although it may be served warm) and poured into individual glasses. You can serve it in the late morning to guests who need a gentle, easygoing reviver, before lunch, during the afternoon, or at bedtime as a sleep inducer. It is more than one man's opinion that Milk Punch even suffices for a complete breakfast on those days when one feels the world has collapsed!

After-sports parties: Nobody has to be an active athlete to enjoy these. Perhaps you and your friends have been to a football game or a ski-jumping contest. Or a group of you may have been more energetic and spent an afternoon sledding, skating or skiing. Drinks that glow put everyone into a glowing humor after such winter exposure. One of the best of these is Rum Fustian. Mulled Wine, made in quantity, is a drink for a metal punch bowl or outsize, heavy earthenware crock and an open fireplace. If you have a log on the fire, use a clean and ash-free poker to keep the wine heated. Let the poker get red-hot and stick it into the mull from time to time or just before serving, to preserve its temperature. The sizzle and steam are spectacular, and this method adds a certain old-time taste to the brew. It is not recommended, however, unless the punch bowl is right by the fireplace and cozy informality is the order of the hour.

Skiers know this mulled wine drink as Glushein, which presumably started in the Austrian Alps but has now spread to delight après-skiers in most winter resorts. Any of the hot, spicy punches are perfect for such occasions and will be doubly enjoyed after a big dose of frosty air.

Strong Punch Dos and Don'ts

Heady brews are not everybody's cup of punch and punch should be served with definite awareness that such is the case.

Nobody feels grateful to a host who lures him into drinking unwisely by disguising the power of a punch through clever blending. Indeed, a word dropped casually here and there, "This is pretty strong," is a wise precaution. Strong punches are probably best suited to a group of men who are celebrating some event (but definitely *not* the wedding of one of them the next day), or to a sophisticated mixed group who are well aware of the deceptive power of the potable that goes down so easily. Such drinks should be limited to parties held late in the afternoon or evening, and should be accompanied by some fairly substantial food—sliced cold meat sandwiches made with dark bread, for example, gusty cheese, hot Swedish meatballs—and plenty of them.

Practical Tips for Punch Makers

Punches would seem the obvious answer to mass refreshment, but they do have their drawbacks, notably the haphazard way in which fresh batches are mixed after the first has gone (a custom that has all but outlawed punch drinking in many civilized communities), and overicing. Even the most bracingly alcoholic punch, and certainly the more subtle ones, will become pretty listless in the course of an evening unless you avoid these two pitfalls. Here is how you should proceed.

1. First, choose a punch recipe that suits the type of party, season, hour and the mood you wish to evoke. Make a complete analysis of its contents some days before the party, and assemble *all* the ingredients. To ensure a fine flavor, buy spirits and wine of good, although not top, quality.

2. Make up a batch of the essential liquors and flavorings that will not deteriorate if allowed to stand, sans ice, for a time.

3. Try out some of this batch with the perishable or dilutive ingredients to see if they blend properly.

4. If everything goes well, mix several large pitchers of the basic spine of the punch before the party, and other

pitchers containing the additives. Keep them all in cool or cold spots ready for last-minute blending at party time.

5. See that your fruit juices are freshly squeezed. In some cases, bottled fruit syrups are satisfactory substitutes, but watch out for oversweetness. When frozen concentrated juices are used, check the recipe and find out whether they should be diluted first.

6. Chill your punch bowl. If it is too big to put in your refrigerator, pack the bowl with crushed ice and let it stand long enough to get thoroughly cold all the way through. Then empty the bowl and put your punch ingredients in it immediately.

7. Chill *all* ingredients before putting them in the punch bowl.

8. Do not fill the punch bowl with lots of cut-up fruits. Your guests want a refreshing drink, not a fruit salad.

9. When tea is an ingredient of a punch, make it extra-strong by using additional tea leaves rather than by long steeping, which results in a bitter, tannic taste.

10. Strips of cucumber peel or slices of unpeeled cucumber add a nice flavor to certain punches and somehow help to blend the tastes of the other ingredients. They should be left in the mix for about fifteen minutes only, however; if they stay in too long they impart a bitter flavor.

11. As sugar is hard to dissolve in cold fruit juices and even more so in liquid containing alcohol, keep sugar syrup (see page 18) on hand.

12. For punches, a large block of ice is better than ice cubes because there is less dilution and it is easier to work around a block with a ladle. One of the surest ways to guard against the weakening of your punch caused by melting ice is to freeze the non-alcoholic liquids and use them as your ice block. (Don't try this with wine or spirits, or you will end up with nothing but a liquid mess.) If the punch has a tea base, freeze the tea in large square or round wax cardboard containers, add lemon or orange slices and more liquid—and freeze again. If fruit juices are

part of the punch, you can freeze them in blocks and use as cooling and flavoring agents.

13. Champagne or other sparkling wine, and any carbonated liquid dilutant such as soda water, should be added to the punch at the end.

14. Any punch benefits by being made in a series of relatively small quantities. It tastes fresher and dilutes less. However, this requires a diligent eye on the part of the host, because he has to refill the bowl more frequently and should blend his ingredients with the same care and in the right order each time.

15. Hot punches should be warm enough to bring out the flavor, but not so hot that guests are fearful of burning their lips or mouths and feel they must sip cautiously.

16. Cold punches may be served in a bowl of any material. Hot punches may crack a glass or china bowl; metal is the proper choice, and sturdy mugs are often preferred to cups or glasses, particularly at informal parties. To avoid cracking a glass or glass punch cup, put a silver spoon in it before filling it with a hot drink. (A demitasse spoon should be used in small punch cups.)

17. A gallon of punch fills about 32 punch cups, and each guest will drink 2 to 3 cups of punch. So you can count on a gallon to serve about twelve people. It is important to figure in advance how much you will need, and so avoid the discouraging sight of an empty punch bowl.

COLD PUNCHES

Champagne Punches for Parties

BELLINI

1 quart puree of fresh
 peaches
Sugar to taste

1 tablespoon lemon juice
3 quarts chilled champagne

Sweeten the peaches to taste, stir in the lemon juice and put into a punch bowl. Add the champagne and mix well. Serve in 8-ounce highball glasses. Makes about 12 servings.

BOMBAY PUNCH

3 cups lemon juice	¼ pint maraschino
1 cup superfine sugar, or to taste	¼ pint curaçao
1 large block ice	4 quarts champagne
1 quart brandy	2 quarts club soda
1 quart medium-dry sherry	Fruits in season

Stir lemon juice and sugar together until the sugar is dissolved. Taste for sweetness and pour into a large punch bowl. Add the block of ice and all remaining ingredients in the order listed, except the fruits. Stir gently to mix. Decorate with fruit. Serve in 4-ounce punch glasses. Makes about 70 servings.

BOWLE

1 pound sliced fresh peaches or strawberries	1 pint medium-dry white wine, well chilled
Superfine sugar to taste	3 quarts iced champagne

Sweeten fruit to taste, put in a bowl, add the white wine and stir gently. Refrigerate for about 2 hours. At serving time, put the mixture in a punch bowl, add the iced champagne, and stir gently. Serve in 4-ounce punch glasses, each with a little of the fruit. Makes about 26 servings.

CHAMPAGNE-ORANGE PUNCH

2 quarts orange sherbet	1 cup Grand Marnier, chilled
3 quarts champagne, well chilled	1 cup brandy (optional)
	Orange slices

Have ready a well-chilled punch bowl. Combine all ingredients except the orange slices. Garnish with these, and serve in 4-ounce punch glasses. Makes about 40 servings.

This punch may be varied by using three or four 6-ounce cans of frozen concentrated orange juice instead of sherbet and by adding an extra quart of champagne. Lemon or raspberry water ice or home-made strawberry or cassis sherbet may be substituted for the orange sherbet. Lemon slices and strawberries may be used as alternate garnishes.

CHAMPAGNE PUNCH NO. 1

3 cups lemon juice
1 cup superfine sugar
1 large block ice
½ pint maraschino
1 pint curaçao

1 pint brandy
2 quarts chilled champagne
1 quart chilled club soda
Fruits in season

Combine the lemon juice and sugar and stir until the sugar is dissolved. Place the ice in a punch bowl, add the sweetened lemon juice together with the maraschino, curaçao and brandy. Pour in the champagne and club soda and stir gently. Decorate with fruits in season and serve in 4-ounce punch glasses. Makes about 40 servings.

CHAMPAGNE PUNCH NO. 2

1 cup orange juice
½ cup lemon juice
½ cup superfine sugar
½ cup light rum

½ cup dark rum
1 cup pineapple juice
1 large block of ice
2 bottles chilled champagne

Combine all ingredients, except the champagne, in a large punch bowl. Stir gently. Add the block of ice and pour in the champagne. Decorate with fruit if desired and serve in 4-ounce punch glasses. Makes about 20 servings.

CHAMPAGNE PUNCH NO. 3

1 quart strong, cold black
tea
1 large block ice
1 bottle dark rum
1 bottle bourbon
1 bottle brandy

2 cups Grand Marnier or
Cointreau
2 cups orange juice
Superfine sugar, to taste
2 bottles chilled champagne

Pour the tea over ice in a punch bowl and add the rum,
bourbon, brandy, Grand Marnier, orange juice and sugar.
Stir well. When ready to serve, add the champagne and stir
gently. Serve in 4-ounce punch glasses. Makes about 50 servings.

CHAMPAGNE PUNCH NO. 4

4 teaspoons sugar
1 teaspoon orange bitters
½ cup lemon juice
½ cup orange juice

6 ounces brandy
Block of ice
2 bottles chilled champagne

Put the sugar in the bottom of a punch bowl and add the
bitters. Pour in the fruit juices and brandy and stir until the
sugar is dissolved. Add a block of ice and, just before serving,
pour in the champagne and stir gently. Serve in 4-ounce
punch glasses. Makes about 16 servings.

DRAGOON PUNCH

This is said to be the cavalryman's answer to Artillery Punch.

3 pints porter
3 pints ale
½ pint brandy
½ pint sherry

½ cup sugar syrup
3 large lemons, thinly sliced
Block of ice
2 bottles chilled champagne

Pour porter, ale, brandy, sherry and sugar syrup into a punch
bowl. Add lemon slices and a block of ice. Add the champagne. Serve in 4-ounce punch glasses. Makes about 40 servings.

HONOLULU PUNCH

2 medium-sized ripe
pineapples
1 cup superfine sugar
1 cup lemon juice

1 pint brandy
1 pint dark rum
Block of ice
4 bottles chilled champagne

Peel and coarsely grate the pineapples. Sprinkle with sugar and let stand for an hour or so. Add lemon juice, brandy and rum, stir well, cover and refrigerate overnight. When ready to serve, pour mixture into a punch bowl with a large block of ice and add the champagne. Stir gently and serve in 4-ounce punch glasses. Makes about 45 servings.

LAFAYETTE PUNCH

6 oranges
1 cup superfine sugar
1 bottle chilled Moselle wine

Block of ice
4 bottles chilled champagne

Peel oranges, carefully removing all the white pith. Slice thinly and place in a shallow bowl. Sprinkle with sugar, pour the Moselle wine over them, and refrigerate for an hour or more. When ready to serve, slide the orange and wine mixture into a punch bowl, add a block of ice and pour in the champagne. Serve in 4-ounce punch glasses. Makes about 34 servings.

UNCLE HARRY'S PUNCH

1 large block of ice
2 bottles chilled Rhine wine
½ cup orange juice
½ cup lemon juice
¾ cup curaçao

¾ cup golden rum
2 quarts chilled club soda
2 bottles chilled champagne
Mint leaves
Orange and lemon slices

Put block of ice in a punch bowl and pour in all the ingredients in the order listed except the garnish. Stir gently to mix, float mint leaves, lemon and orange slices on top. Serve in 4-ounce punch glasses. Makes about 45 servings.

VODKA-CHAMPAGNE PUNCH

1 bottle iced vodka	Lemon slices
2 bottles chilled champagne	Strips cucumber peel

Thoroughly chill a punch bowl. Pour in the vodka and champagne; garnish with lemon slices and strips of cucumber peel. Serve in 4-ounce punch glasses. Makes about 18 servings.

Champagne Punches for Individuals

BALI HAI

Crushed ice	2 ounces Tom Collins mix
1 ounce light rum	3 ounces lime juice
1 ounce okolehao	2 ounces champagne

Fill a large tumbler three-quarters full with crushed ice. Pour in the rum, okolehao, Tom Collins mix and lime juice and stir. Top with champagne. Serves 1.

CHAMPAGNE PUNCH

4 ice cubes
2 tablespoons lemon juice
1 ounce framboise

1 slice orange
8 ounces chilled champagne

Put ice cubes into a 14-ounce tumbler and add the lemon juice, framboise and orange slice. Pour in the champagne. Stir gently and serve with straws. Serves 1.

SUMMER PUNCH

2 or 3 ice cubes
3 tablespoons crème de cassis

Dash kirsch
10 ounces chilled champagne

Put ice cubes in a 12-ounce glass, add cassis and kirsch and fill up with champagne. Stir gently. Serves 1.

Liquor-Based Punches for Parties

APPLEJACK PUNCH

2 quarts applejack
6 ounces grenadine
2 cups orange juice

Block of ice
2 quarts chilled ginger ale
Fruit to garnish

Combine all ingredients except ginger ale and fruit garnish in a punch bowl with a block of ice. Pour in the ginger ale and stir lightly. Decorate with fruit. Serve in 4-ounce punch glasses. Makes about 35 servings.

ARTILLERY PUNCH

1 quart rye whiskey
1 pint dark rum
½ pint gin
½ pint brandy
3 ounces Benedictine
1 bottle dry red wine

2 cups orange juice
1 cup lemon juice
1 quart strong black tea
1 large block Ice
Sugar syrup (optional)
Twist lemon peel

Combine all ingredients, except sugar syrup and lemon peel, in a large punch bowl with a block of ice. Stir gently and add a little sugar syrup. Decorate with lemon peel twists. Serve in 4-ounce punch glasses. Makes about 36 servings.

For a more flavorful punch, make the block of ice from the tea. This will reduce the servings to about 28.

ATHOLE BROSE

This traditional Scottish brew or "brose" is named for the mountainous region of Athole.

3 cups oatmeal
1 cup water

4 tablespoons honey
1 bottle Scotch whiskey

Place oatmeal in a bowl, stir in the water, and let steep for an hour. Strain oatmeal, pressing out all the liquid. There should be about ½ cup of creamy-colored oatmeal water. Blend this with the honey and stir in the whiskey. Shake well and serve at room temperature in 4-ounce punch glasses. Makes about 8 servings.

AULD MAN'S MILK

6 large eggs, separated
½ pound superfine sugar
1 quart half-and-half
  (½ milk, ½ cream)

1 pint Scotch whiskey
Nutmeg

Beat egg yolks until thick and lemon-colored. Add sugar and half-and-half and stir until sugar dissolves. Slowly stir in the Scotch. Beat egg whites until light and frothy, and fold into the whiskey mixture. Grate a little nutmeg over the punch and serve in 4-ounce punch glasses. Makes about 16 servings.

AZTEC PUNCH

1 gallon tequila
3 cups lemon juice
1 cup superfine sugar
4 46-ounce cans grapefruit
   juice
2 quarts strong, cold black
   tea
1½ teaspoons ground
   cinnamon
Block of ice

Combine all ingredients and allow to stand for an hour or so to blend. Pour over block of ice in a large punch bowl. Serve in 4-ounce punch glasses. Makes a little over 3 gallons or about 120 servings.

BIMBO PUNCH

6 large lemons, thinly sliced
1½ quarts brandy
1 pound lump sugar
1 large block of ice
Orange and lemon slices

Steep lemon slices in brandy for 8 hours or overnight. Strain the brandy. Dissolve the lump sugar in boiling water, cool, and add to the brandy. Chill. Put block of ice in a punch bowl and pour the liquor over it. Decorate with orange and lemon slices. Serve in 4-ounce punch glasses. Makes 16 servings.

BRANDIED MOKA

1 quart strong hot coffee
1 quart rich hot chocolate
1¼ pints brandy
30 coffee-ice cubes
Whipped cream
Shaved chocolate, or
   cinnamon

Combine hot coffee and chocolate. Allow to cool and then stir in the brandy. Put 3 coffee-ice cubes in ten 12-ounce collins glasses and add the brandy mixture. Top with whipped cream and a little shaved chocolate, or a dusting of cinnamon. Serves 10.

If preferred, the coffee-ice may be made in a block and placed in a punch bowl and the brandy mixture added, with cream to taste instead of whipped-cream topping.

CARDINAL PUNCH

3 cups lemon juice
1 cup superfine sugar
1 large block ice
1 pint brandy
1 pint rum
2 quarts claret, or other dry red wine
1 cup sweet vermouth
1 bottle chilled champagne, or other sparkling white wine
1 quart club soda
1 orange, thinly sliced
3 slices fresh pineapple

Mix lemon juice and sugar together and stir until the sugar is dissolved. Put block of ice in a large punch bowl, add the lemon juice, brandy, rum, claret and vermouth, and stir to mix. Just before serving, pour in the champagne and club soda and decorate with orange and pineapple slices. Serve in 4-ounce punch glasses. Makes about 50 servings.

COLONIAL TEA PUNCH

12 lemons
1 quart strong tea
2 cups sugar
1 quart dark rum
1½ ounces brandy
4 cups crushed ice

Peel the lemons as thinly as possible and put peels in a punch bowl. Add juice from the lemons, the tea and sugar, and allow to stand for about 1 hour. Add rum, brandy and crushed ice. Stir and serve in 4-ounce punch cups or wine-glasses. Makes about 20 servings.

FISH HOUSE PUNCH NO. 1

3 cups lemon juice
1 cup superfine sugar
Block of ice
1½ quarts brandy
1 pint peach brandy

1 pint rum
1 quart club soda
1 quart strong cold black tea
 (optional)
Fruits in season

Place the lemon juice and sugar in a punch bowl and stir until sugar is dissolved. Add a large block of ice, brandy, peach brandy, rum, club soda, tea (if you wish) and stir well. Decorate with fruits in season. Serve in 4-ounce punch glasses. Makes about 40 servings if tea is included, 32 without tea.

FISH HOUSE PUNCH NO. 2

3 six-ounce cans frozen
 concentrated lemonade
2 bottles dark rum
2 bottles golden rum
2 bottles brandy

1 cup peach brandy
 (optional)
1 block tea ice made from
 1 quart medium-strong tea
3 quarts water

Combine lemonade concentrate, rums, brandy and peach brandy. Allow to steep for about 2 hours at room temperature. When ready to serve, add tea ice and water and stir. Serve in 4-ounce punch glasses. Makes about 65 servings.

FISH HOUSE PUNCH NO. 3

1 cup water
1½ cups superfine sugar
3 cups lemon juice
3 pints dry white wine
1 bottle dark rum

1 bottle golden rum
1 bottle brandy
4 ounces peach brandy
Block of ice

Pour the water into a punch bowl, add sugar and lemon juice and stir until sugar is dissolved. Pour in wine, both rums, brandy and peach brandy. Let the mixture stand at room temperature for 2 to 3 hours, stirring occasionally. Just before serving, add a block of ice. Serve in 4-ounce punch glasses. Makes about 42 servings.

PARLOR PUNCH

12 lemons
2 pounds sugar
2 tablespoons English
Breakfast or Darjeeling tea

1 cup dark rum
1 cup raspberry syrup
Club soda (optional)

Grate the rinds of 3 lemons into the sugar. Add 1 quart of water and bring to a boil over high heat. Boil for 15 minutes, strain and, when cool, add the juice of the 12 lemons. Pour 1 pint of boiling water over the tea and steep for ½ hour. Strain into the sweetened lemon mixture. Refrigerate overnight. When ready to serve, add rum and raspberry syrup and blend well. Put 2 or 3 ice cubes in 10-ounce tumblers and fill with punch, or punch and a dash of soda. Makes about 20 servings.

PHILIP BROWN'S PUNCH

4 bottles dry white wine
1 bottle brandy
1 bottle golden rum
3 ounces (half a 6-ounce
can) frozen lemonade

Block of ice
2 quarts club soda

Combine wine, brandy, rum and lemonade concentrate in a punch bowl and allow to stand for about an hour. When ready to serve, add a block of ice and the club soda, a bottle at a time. Stir lightly and serve in 4-ounce punch glasses. Makes about 50 servings.

PINEAPPLE-OKOLEHAO PUNCH
(From Trader Vic's)

Block of ice
2 bottles chilled okolehao
1½ quarts chilled pineapple
juice

1 cup chilled lemon juice
1 pint chilled club soda
Strawberries for garnish

Put block of ice in a punch bowl and add all ingredients except strawberries. Stir lightly, then garnish with berries. Serve in 4-ounce punch glasses. Makes about 30 servings.

RUM PUNCH

1 bottle medium-dark rum
2 vanilla beans
Large block of tea ice

1 cup fresh lime juice
4 cups cold strong black tea

Put vanilla beans in bottle of rum, allow to steep for 2 to 3 hours, then strain. Set block of tea ice in a punch bowl and add rum, lime juice and tea. Stir. Serve in 4-ounce punch glasses. Makes about 16 servings.

TEA PUNCH

1½ quarts freshly brewed
strong hot tea
2 6-ounce cans frozen
concentrated lemonade
1 cup frozen concentrated
orange juice

1 bottle vodka
1 large block ice
Lemon and orange slices
Strawberries in season

Combine tea with frozen juices and allow to cool. Add vodka and stir to mix well. Put ice in a punch bowl and pour in the vodka mixture. Decorate with orange and lemon slices, and strawberries in season. Serve in 4-ounce punch glasses. Makes about 20 servings.

VODKA-ORANGE PUNCH

3 bottles iced vodka
3 6-ounce cans undiluted
frozen concentrated
orange juice

1 cup Cointreau
Dash lemon juice
Orange slices (optional)

Combine ingredients in a large jug, stir well and set in a bowl of ice. Serve in 4-ounce punch glasses, garnished with a slice of orange. Makes about 25 servings.

WHISKEY PUNCH

1½ cups lemon juice
4 cups orange juice
2 tablespoons superfine
  sugar
Block of ice
3 ounces curaçao

1½ bottles bourbon, rye or
  blended whiskey
2 quarts chilled club soda,
  or 1 quart iced tea and
  1 quart club soda
Fruits to garnish

Combine orange and lemon juice with sugar and stir until sugar is dissolved. Pour over a block of ice in a punch bowl and add all the remaining ingredients. Stir gently. Serve in 4-ounce punch glasses. Makes about 35 servings.

Liquor-Based Punches for Individuals

KAMEHAMEHA RUM PUNCH

½ cup crushed ice
1 ounce light rum
2 ounces pineapple juice
1 tablespoon lemon juice
1 teaspoon grenadine
1 teaspoon blackberry
  brandy

1 teaspoon superfine sugar
3 to 4 ice cubes
1 ounce dark rum
Stick pineapple
Maraschino cherry

Combine crushed ice, light rum, pineapple juice, lemon juice, grenadine, blackberry brandy and sugar in a mixing glass and stir well. Put ice cubes in a highball glass and pour the mixture over them. Float dark rum on top. Decorate with pineapple stick and cherry. Serves 1.

MAI KAI NO

1½ cups crushed ice
  (approx.)
1 ounce light rum
1 ounce 151-proof Demerara
  -rum
½ ounce dark rum
1½ tablespoons lime juice

Dash Angostura bitters
½ ounce passion-fruit juice
½ ounce honey
Chilled club soda
Pineapple stick
Fresh mint sprigs

Fill a 14-ounce double Old-fashioned glass to the three-quarters mark with crushed ice. Add the three rums, lime juice, bitters, passion-fruit juice and honey; stir to mix well. Add a splash of soda and a little more ice if necessary. Stir again. Garnish with pineapple and mint. Serves 1.

MYRTLE BANK PUNCH

2 ice cubes
1½ ounces 151-proof
  Demerara rum
1½ tablespoons lime juice

1 teaspoon grenadine
1 teaspoon superfine sugar
Crushed ice
1 tablespoon maraschino

Combine ice cubes, rum, lime juice, grenadine and sugar in a cocktail shaker and shake vigorously. Put crushed ice in a 10-ounce goblet, strain rum mixture over the ice, and float maraschino on top. Serves 1.

PISCO PUNCH

1 ice cube
1 teaspoon lime juice
1 teaspoon pineapple juice

1 cube pineapple
3 ounces pisco brandy

Place ice cube in an 8-ounce wineglass or goblet and add the other ingredients. Fill glass with iced water and stir to mix. Serves 1.

PLANTER'S PUNCH NO. 1

3 tablespoons lime juice
2 teaspoons superfine sugar
Finely crushed ice
2–3 ounces rum
2 dashes Angostura bitters

2 ounces club soda
Slice each, orange and
    lemon
Pineapple stick
Maraschino cherry

Mix lime juice and sugar together and stir until the sugar is dissolved. Fill a collins glass with crushed ice to the three-quarters mark and stir until glass is frosted. Add lime juice, rum, bitters and club soda and stir to mix. Decorate with the orange and lemon slices, pineapple stick and cherry. Serves 1.

PLANTER'S PUNCH NO. 2

Crushed ice
1 tablespoon lime juice
2 tablespoons lemon juice
¼ cup orange juice
1 teaspoon pineapple juice
1½–2 ounces light rum
¾–1 ounce dark rum

Slice each, orange and
    lemon
Pineapple stick
Maraschino cherry
Mint sprig dipped in
    confectioners' sugar

Pack a 14-ounce collins glass two-thirds full with crushed ice. Add the fruit juices and light rum and stir until glass is frosted. Add the dark rum. Garnish the drink with orange and lemon slices, pineapple stick, cherry and mint sprig. Serves 1.

PLANTER'S PUNCH NO. 3

1 ounce lime juice
2 tablespoons superfine
    sugar
3 ounces dark rum

4 ounces crushed ice
Dash Angostura bitters
Nutmeg

Pour lime juice into a cocktail shaker and add sugar. Stir until sugar is dissolved. Add rum, ice and bitters and shake vigorously. Pour mixture, unstrained, into a 9-ounce goblet. Grate a little nutmeg on top of drink. Serves 1.

This is the traditional Planter's Punch that follows the old rhyme:

> One of sour (lime juice),
> Two of sweet (sugar);
> Three of strong (rum),
> Four of weak (ice or water).

RUM PUNCH

2 ounces orange juice
2 ounces pineapple juice
2 ounces papaya nectar
1 ounce lime juice

2 ounces medium-dark rum
Sprig mint, or fruit garnish
2 or 3 ice cubes

Mix fruit juices together and chill thoroughly. When ready to serve, put ice cubes in a 14-ounce collins glass, add rum and chilled juices, stir to mix and garnish with mint or appropriate fruit. Serves 1.

SOUTHERN PUNCH

Crushed ice
1½ ounces bourbon
½ ounce brandy
1 ounce lemon juice

½ ounce sugar syrup
Club soda
1 tablespoon rum

Fill a 12-ounce collins or highball glass about three-quarters full with crushed ice. Combine the bourbon, brandy, lemon juice and sugar syrup in a cocktail shaker and shake vigorously. Pour into the glass, which will frost. Fill almost to the top with soda and float the rum on top. Serves 1.

Wine Punches

CASSIS PUNCH

2 cups whole, hulled
    strawberries

½ cup crème de cassis
3 bottles dry white wine

Place strawberries in a bowl, pour the cassis over them and let them steep for an hour or so. Strain. Put a block of ice in a punch bowl and pour in the cassis and wine. Stir. Float the strawberries on top. Serve in 4-ounce punch glasses with a strawberry in each. Makes about 20 servings.

Champagne may be used instead of white wine for a more festive punch.

CLARET PUNCH

3 cups lemon juice
1 cup superfine sugar
1 large block ice
½ pint curaçao
1 pint brandy

3 quarts claret
    (red Bordeaux wine)
1 quart chilled club soda
Fruits in season

Combine lemon juice and sugar and stir until sugar is dissolved. Put ice in a punch bowl and pour the sweetened lemon juice over it. Add the curaçao, brandy, wine and club soda, and stir. Decorate with fruit. Serve in 4-ounce punch glasses. Makes about 46 servings.

DUBONNET PUNCH

6 limes
1 bottle Dubonnet
1 pint gin

1 quart chilled club soda
Crushed ice
Mint leaves

Squeeze limes and reserve shells. Pour the lime juice, Dubonnet and gin into a large glass pitcher; add lime shells and soda. To serve, pack 10-ounce collins or highball glasses with crushed ice to the three-quarters mark, fill up with punch and decorate with mint leaves. Makes 15–20 servings.

KAYSER SOUR

1 bottle chilled Rhine wine
3 cups lemon juice

6 tablespoons superfine
  sugar
Ice cubes

Thoroughly chill the wine. Combine lemon juice and sugar and stir until juice is dissolved. Add wine and stir to blend. Put 12 to 16 ice cubes in a pitcher, pour the wine mixture over them, and serve in 4-ounce punch glasses. Or put 1 or 2 ice cubes in wineglasses and fill with 4 ounces of the mixture. Makes about 12 servings.

MADEIRA PUNCH

12 16 ice cubes
1 bottle medium dry
  Madeira
½ cup brandy
Superfine sugar, to taste

Lemon and orange slices
Fresh peach slices
Halved fresh strawberries
1 quart chilled club soda

Put ice cubes in a large pitcher, pour the Madeira and brandy over them and sweeten to taste. Garnish with fruit and pour in the club soda. Serve in 4-ounce punch glasses. Makes 16 servings.

MAIBOWLE

1 quart ripe strawberries
6–8 tablespoons superfine
  sugar

3 bottles chilled Moselle
  wine
1 bottle chilled champagne
Large block of ice

Wash and hull strawberries, sprinkle with sugar, pour 1 bottle Moselle over them and refrigerate for several hours. At serving time, put a large block of ice in a punch bowl, add strawberry mixture, remaining 2 bottles of Moselle and the champagne. Stir gently. Serve in 4-ounce punch glasses, with a strawberry in each. Makes about 25 servings.

RHINE WINE PUNCH

1 block ice
1 cup sugar syrup
2 cups lemon juice
1 pint dry sherry
½ pint brandy
½ pint strong cold black tea

3 quarts chilled dry Rhine wine
8–10 thin strips cucumber peel
1 quart chilled club soda

Put a block of ice in a punch bowl and pour in all the liquid ingredients except the club soda. Stir, add cucumber peel and let punch steep for 15 minutes. Remove peel. Add club soda, stir and serve in 4-ounce punch glasses. Makes about 45 servings.

ROSE LEMONADE

2 bottles California rosé wine
2 6-ounce cans frozen concentrated lemonade

1 quart club soda
12 to 16 ice cubes

Thoroughly chill wine and club soda. Pour wine into a large pitcher, add lemonade concentrate and stir to blend. Add club soda and ice cubes, and stir gently. Serve in 4-ounce punch or wineglasses. Makes about 20 servings.

SANGRIA CALIFORNIA STYLE

2 gallons California Zinfandel
1 cup brandy
½ cup Cointreau or Strega
2 quarts orange juice
2 cups lemon juice
12 to 16 ice cubes

2 quarts chilled club soda
3 oranges, thinly sliced
3 lemons, thinly sliced
1 cup superfine sugar

Thoroughly chill all ingredients. Pour the wine, brandy and

Cointreau (or Strega) into a large punch bowl. Stir orange and lemon juice with the sugar until sugar has dissolved. Then add to bowl and stir to blend. Add ice cubes and soda, and garnish with fruit slices. Serve in 4-ounce punch or wineglasses. Makes about 100 servings.

SANGRIA
(Cesar Ortiz's Version)

2 cups orange juice
1 cup lemon juice
Superfine sugar to taste

1 bottle Spanish red wine, preferably from the south
Ice cubes

Combine fruit juices with sugar and stir until sugar is dissolved. Pour into a glass pitcher. Add the wine and stir to mix. Refrigerate until ready to serve. Put 2 or 3 ice cubes in each 8-ounce goblet and fill with Sangría. Makes about 10 servings.

SANGRIA NO. 1

1 orange, sliced
1 lemon, sliced
1 apple, cored and cut into 8 wedges
1 bottle dry red wine, preferably Spanish

2 ounces brandy, preferably Spanish
1 pint chilled club soda
Ice cubes
¼ cup superfine sugar

Combine cut-up fruits and sugar in a large glass pitcher, pour in wine and brandy and stir to mix well. Refrigerate until thoroughly chilled. At serving time add club soda and ice cubes, stir and serve in 8-ounce goblets. Makes about 6 servings.

ANGRIA NO. 2

1 quart dry red wine
1 quart chilled club soda
Orange, lemon and lime slices

Peel of 1 orange, cut in a spiral
Sugar syrup to taste
12 to 16 ice cubes

Blend all ingredients except the ice cubes. Put ice cubes in a large glass pitcher and pour the wine mixture and garnishes over them. Serve in 4-ounce punch glasses or small wineglasses. Makes 16 servings.

SANGRIA NO. 3

½ cup freshly made sugar
  syrup
1 thinly sliced orange
1 thinly sliced lime

1 bottle chilled red wine,
  preferably Spanish
12 to 16 ice cubes

Make sugar syrup (page 18) and pour, while still hot, over orange and lemon slices in a bowl. Let them marinate for at least 4 hours. Put ice cubes in a large pitcher, add the syrup with fruit, and the wine. Stir well and serve in 4-ounce wine or punch glasses with a slice of both fruits in each serving. Makes about 8 servings.

SUMMER PUNCH

1 block ice
3 bottles dry white wine
1½ cups crème de cassis

12 orange slices, halved
1 pint strawberries

Put block of ice in a punch bowl. Pour in wine and cassis, and stir. Float orange slices and strawberries on top. Serve in 4-ounce punch glasses. Makes about 20 servings.

WINE REFRESHER

1 bottle rosé wine
3 cups unsweetened
  grapefruit juice

Ice cubes (optional)

Chill wine and grapefruit juice thoroughly, then pour into a pitcher and stir to blend. Put 1 or 2 ice cubes into 8-ounce wineglasses and pour 4 ounces of the wine punch over them. Or serve punch without ice, in 4-ounce wineglasses. Makes 12 servings.

Dry red wine and orange juice are used to make this drink in France.

Wine Cups

Cups are really wine drinks or punches in which various liqueurs are combined with wines, as a general rule. Sparkling wine or soda makes many cups effervescent. Presented in glass pitchers and chilled, these drinks are served in small wineglasses.

When made in very large quantities, cups are sometimes served from a punch bowl instead of a pitcher. Bigger glasses may also be used if preferred.

CHABLIS CUP NO. 1

12–16 ice cubes
2 slices lemon
3 slices pineapple

1½ ounces Benedictine
1 bottle Chablis

Put ice cubes into a large pitcher and add all the remaining ingredients. Stir gently and serve in wineglasses. Makes about 6 servings.

A peeled ripe peach may be substituted for the pineapple slices. Any white Burgundy wine may be used instead of Chablis.

CHABLIS CUP NO. 2

½ cup kirsch
½ cup Grand Marnier
2½ cups sliced fresh fruits
    such as peaches or
    strawberries, including
    1 orange and 1 lemon

12–16 ice cubes
1 bottle Chablis or other dry
    white wine
2 or 3 sprigs fresh mint

Combine the kirsch, Grand Marnier and fruits in a bowl and refrigerate for several hours. Put the ice cubes in a large pitcher. Pour the fruit and liqueur mixture over them, add the wine and stir to blend. Garnish with the mint sprigs. Serve in 4-ounce wineglasses. Makes about 10–12 servings.

CHAMPAGNE CUP NO. 1

Large chunk or 12–16 cubes
    of ice
4 slices fresh pineapple
4 ounces fresh strawberries
4 long slivers cucumber peel

2 ounces brandy
2 ounces curaçao
1 pint club soda
1 bottle chilled champagne

Place a chunk of ice in a large wide-mouthed pitcher. Add pineapple, strawberries, cucumber peel, brandy, curaçao and club soda and stir gently. Add champagne, stir again gently and serve in 5-ounce wineglasses. Serves about 8.

CHAMPAGNE CUP NO. 2

1 pint medium-dry sherry
Juice and peel of 1 lemon
8 thin slices unpeeled
    cucumber

Large block of ice
4 bottles chilled champagne

Combine sherry, lemon juice and peel, and cucumber slices in a bowl. Refrigerate for 3 to 4 hours, removing the cucumber slices at the end of 20 minutes. Take from the refrigerator, put in a punch bowl, add the ice and pour in the champagne. Stir lightly. Serve in 4-ounce punch glasses. Makes about 30 servings.

CIDER CUP NO. 1

1 quart sweet cider	Apple slices
4 ounces sweet sherry	1 pint chilled club soda
4 ounces brandy	

Pour the cider, sherry and brandy into a large pitcher. Add chunks of ice or 12–16 ice cubes and the apple slices. Add club soda and stir gently. Serve in 4-ounce punch glasses or wineglasses. Makes about 14 servings.

Children's Cup: Omit the sherry and brandy and use fizzy lemonade instead of club soda.

CIDER CUP NO. 2

12–16 ice cubes	1½ ounces curaçao
Lemon or orange peel	1½ ounces brandy
1 quart sweet cider	12 ounces chilled club soda
1½ ounces maraschino	

Put the ice cubes in a large glass pitcher, decorate with the peel and add all the other ingredients, with the soda last. Serve in wineglasses. Makes about 12 servings.

CLARET CUP NO. 1

Block of ice	½ cup curaçao
1 cup lemon juice	¼ cup maraschino
1 cup sugar syrup	2 bottles claret (red
2 cups orange juice	Bordeaux wine)
½ cup pineapple juice	2 quarts chilled club soda

Place a block of ice in a punch bowl and add all the ingredients except the club soda. Stir. Allow the mixture to blend and chill. Just before serving, add the club soda. Serve in 5-ounce wineglasses. Makes about 25 servings.

Burgundy Cup: Substitute Burgundy for claret and Benedictine for maraschino.

CLARET CUP NO. 2

12–16 ice cubes
4 teaspoons superfine sugar
6 ounces chilled club soda
½ ounce Triple Sec
½ ounce curaçao
2 ounces brandy

1 pint claret (red Bordeaux wine)
Fruits in season
Cucumber peel
Mint sprigs

Half-fill a large glass pitcher with ice cubes and add the sugar, soda, Triple Sec, curaçao, brandy and claret. Stir to mix well. Decorate with fruit, cucumber peel and mint sprigs. Serve in 6-ounce wineglasses. Makes about 4 servings.

EMPIRE PEACH CUP

2 large, ripe peaches
2 bottles chilled Moselle
2 tablespoons superfine sugar

1 bottle sparkling Moselle, chilled
Crushed ice

Peel the peaches and drop into a large glass pitcher or bowl. Add one of the bottles of Moselle and the sugar, stir and refrigerate for half an hour. Add the second bottle of Moselle and the sparkling Moselle and serve immediately. Serve in wineglasses. Makes about 18 servings. Set the bowl or pitcher in a bed of crushed ice to keep cold.

KALTE ENTE

Rind 1 lemon
3 ounces curaçao
1 bottle chilled Moselle

1 bottle sparkling Moselle, chilled
Crushed ice

Put the lemon rind in a large pitcher and add the remaining ingredients. Serve in wineglasses. Makes about 12 servings. Set the pitcher in a bed of crushed ice to keep cold.

MOSELLE CUP

12–16 ice cubes
3 large ripe peaches
12 maraschino cherries
1½ ounces Benedictine

1 bottle chilled Moselle
1 bottle sparkling Moselle, chilled

Put the ice cubes in a large pitcher and add the peaches, peeled, pitted and quartered, the cherries, Benedictine and Moselle. When ready to serve pour in the sparkling Moselle. Serve in wineglasses. Makes about 12 servings.

RHINE WINE CUP

12–16 ice cubes
1 bottle Rhine wine
Fruits in season
½ ounce Triple Sec

½ ounce curaçao
6 ounces club soda
Cucumber peel
Mint sprigs

Put the ice cubes in a large pitcher and add the Rhine wine, fruits, Triple Sec, curaçao and club soda. Decorate with the cucumber peel and mint sprigs. Serve in wineglasses. Makes about 8 servings.

SAUTERNE CUP

1½ ounces brandy
1½ ounces curaçao
1½ ounces maraschino
2 bottles chilled Sauterne

8 ounces chilled club soda
Crushed ice
Lemon and orange slices

Combine all ingredients except the fruit slices in a large pitcher or punch bowl, stir gently and set in a bed of crushed ice. Garnish with the lemon and orange slices. Serve in wineglasses. Makes about 15 servings.

HOT PUNCHES

For Parties

AUNT BETSY'S FAVORITE

1 bottle dry red wine
2 cups tawny or ruby port
1 cup brandy
8 cubes sugar

Peel of 2 oranges
6 cloves
1 stick cinnamon

Combine all ingredients in a heavy saucepan and heat slowly without allowing the mixture to reach simmering point. Pour into 4-ounce punch glasses. Makes about 12 servings.

BRANDY BISHOP

1 large orange
20 cloves (approx.)
2 tablespoons sugar (brown
   if you prefer)

1 quart port
6 ounces brandy

Stud the orange with cloves and roast in a 350° oven for 30 minutes. Remove, cut into quarters, and place in a heavy saucepan with the sugar and port. Heat for 20 minutes without letting wine come to a boil. Pour an ounce of brandy into 6 warmed 6-ounce mugs and fill with the hot wine. Serves 6.

Archbishop: Use a red Bordeaux instead of port.
Pope: Use red Burgundy instead of port.
Cider Bishop: Use hard cider instead of port and 2 teaspoons honey in place of sugar. This drink may be made with brandy or applejack.

COLUMBIA SKIN

1 lemon
9 ounces Scotch whiskey

2 cups boiling water

Remove the peel from the lemon, slicing it as thinly as possible so that practically none of the white is included. Slice the lemon thinly. Put the Scotch in a warmed glass pitcher, add the lemon peel and boiling water. Stir gently. Serve in Old-fashioned glasses garnished with a slice of lemon. Serves 4.

GLOGG

1 bottle tawny port	1 stick cinnamon
1 bottle Madeira	½ pound lump sugar
1 bottle medium dry sherry	½ cup brandy
½ bottle dry red wine	1 cup raisins
15 cloves	1 cup blanched almonds
15 cardamom seeds	

Combine all ingredients except the sugar, brandy, raisins and nuts in a heavy saucepan and heat slowly. When the wine mixture is hot, place a rack on top of the saucepan so that it covers half of it. Arrange the sugar cubes on the rack, warm the brandy, pour it over the sugar and set it alight. Ladle the wine mixture over the flaming sugar until sugar is dissolved. Serve in 8-ounce mugs, garnished with the almonds and raisins. Makes about 10 servings.

There are a number of variations of this traditional Scandinavian Yuletide drink. Dry red wine, muscatel and sweet vermouth, with aquavit in place of the brandy, may be used. In another version, 2 bottles of dry red wine, preferably Bordeaux, are used with the quantity of aquavit increased to a whole bottle, which is poured over the flaming sugar.

HET PINT

2 quarts ale
1 whole nutmeg, grated
Superfine sugar to taste

2 whole eggs and 1 yolk
1 cup Scotch whiskey

Pour the ale into a heavy saucepan with the grated nutmeg, bring just to a boil and sweeten with sugar to taste. Remove from the heat. Beat the eggs with the extra yolk and slowly whisk into the hot ale, taking care not to let the mixture curdle. Add the Scotch and warm through. Pour the liquid from a height into a heated tankard and continue pouring it back and forth until it foams. Serve at once in warmed 8-ounce mugs. Makes about 8 servings.

Ale Flip: Reduce nutmeg to ½ teaspoon.

HOT BUTTERED APPLEJACK

1 quart sweet cider
4 teaspoons superfine sugar
Nutmeg
4 twists lemon peel

4 cinnamon sticks
4 ounces applejack
4 pats sweet butter

Heat cider to just under the boiling point. In each of four 10-ounce mugs put a teaspoon of sugar, a grating of nutmeg, a twist of lemon peel, a cinnamon stick and an ounce of apple-jack. Fill up with cider and top with a pat of butter. Stir with cinnamon stick. Serves 4.

OGGE

4 egg yolks
2 ounces sugar syrup

1 quart beer
Nutmeg

Beat the egg yolks until light and lemon-colored, then stir in the sugar syrup. Heat the beer to just under the boiling point and slowly add to the sweetened egg yolks, beating constantly. Serve in warmed 8-ounce mugs and grate a little nutmeg on top of each. Serves 4.

ORANGE WARMER

6 cups boiling water
6 teaspoons tea
6 cups orange juice
½ cup superfine sugar

1 cup Grand Marnier or
  Cointreau
Orange slices, halved
Whole cloves

Pour the boiling water over the tea and steep for 3 minutes. Strain into a punch bowl. Meanwhile, heat the orange juice with the sugar, stirring until the sugar is dissolved. Add to the punch bowl, together with the Grand Marnier or Cointreau. Garnish with orange slices studded with whole cloves. If preferred, this punch may be served from a chafing dish over medium heat. Serve in 8-ounce mugs. Makes about 12 servings.

RUM FUSTIAN

The "rum" in this drink's name does not refer to the liquor, rum. In the past in England, "rum" simply meant any strong and pleasant drink. "Rum fustian" actually means "knave's brew."

6 egg yolks
1 quart beer or ale
1 pint gin
1 pint medium dry sherry

1 stick cinnamon
Dash nutmeg
Twist lemon peel

Beat the egg yolks until lemony and frothy. Beat in the beer; beat in the gin. Put the sherry in a saucepan with the cinnamon, nutmeg and lemon peel and heat just to the boiling point. Remove the cinnamon. Beat the hot wine into the egg mixture, and serve at once, while it is still warm, in heated 8-ounce mugs. Makes about 8 drinks.

SOUTHERN CROSS

1 bottle tawny port
2 tablespoons superfine
  sugar
½ teaspoon mixed spice

½ cup grapefruit juice
Juice and rind of 1 lemon
¼ cup raisins
1 cup water

Pour wine into a heavy saucepan and add all ingredients except the raisins and water. Heat gently. Meanwhile, put the raisins into a small saucepan with the water and slowly bring to a boil. Add to the hot wine mixture and pour into a metal punch bowl. Serve in 4-ounce punch glasses. Makes about 8 servings.

WASSAIL

10 small apples	3 allspice berries
10 teaspoons brown sugar	1″ stick cinnamon
2 bottles dry sherry or dry Madeira	2 cups superfine sugar
½ teaspoon grated nutmeg	½ cup water
1 teaspoon ground ginger	6 eggs, separated
3 cloves	1 cup brandy

Core the apples and fill each with a teaspoon of brown sugar. Place in a baking pan and cover the bottom with ⅛″ water. Bake in a 350° oven for 30 minutes, or until tender. Combine the sherry or Madeira, nutmeg, ginger, cloves, allspice berries, cinnamon, sugar and water in a large, heavy saucepan and heat without letting the mixture boil. Leave on very low heat. Beat the egg yolks until light and lemon-colored. Beat the whites until stiff and fold them into the yolks. Strain the wine mixture and add gradually to the eggs, stirring constantly. Add the brandy. Pour into a metal punch bowl, float the apples on top and serve in 8-ounce mugs. Makes about 10 servings.

WASSAIL BOWL—HOT SPICED BEER

12 small apples	½ teaspoon nutmeg
12 teaspoons brown sugar	1½ cups orange juice
1 cup superfine sugar	1½ cups cranberry juice
1 teaspoon cinnamon	2 quarts beer or ale
½ teaspoon ginger	

Core the apples and fill each with a teaspoon of brown sugar. Place in a baking pan and cover the bottom with ⅛″ water. Bake in a 350° oven for 30 minutes, or until tender. Combine the sugar and spices in a 4-quart saucepan. Add the juices and beer and heat the mixture for 15 minutes without letting it come to a boil. Pour the mixture into a metal punch bowl and float the baked apples on top. Serve in 8-ounce mugs. Makes 12 servings.

EGGNOGS

For Parties

BALTIMORE EGGNOG

12 eggs, separated	½ pint peach brandy
2 cups superfine sugar	3 pints milk
1 pint brandy	1 pint heavy cream
½ pint light rum	Nutmeg

Beat the egg yolks and sugar together until thick. Slowly stir in the brandy, rum, peach brandy, milk and cream. Refrigerate until thoroughly chilled and pour into a punch bowl. Beat the egg whites until stiff and fold gently into the eggnog. Grate a little nutmeg on top and serve in 4-ounce punch glasses. Makes about 30 servings.

BOURBON EGGNOG

12 eggs, separated	1 quart milk
1½ cups superfine sugar	1 quart bourbon
Cracked ice	Nutmeg
1 quart heavy cream	

Beat the egg yolks with the sugar until thick. Set the container in a large bowl filled with cracked ice. In a separate bowl, beat the cream until stiff, add the milk, and slowly stir in the bourbon. Combine both mixtures in a punch bowl. Beat the egg whites until stiff and fold gently into the eggnog. Grate nutmeg on top and serve in 4-ounce punch glasses. Makes about 30 servings.

Brandy Eggnog: Substitute brandy for bourbon.

INSTANT EGGNOG

2 quarts French vanilla ice cream	½ cup dark rum
1 bottle bourbon	Nutmeg

Put the ice cream in a punch bowl and stir in the bourbon and rum until thoroughly blended. Grate nutmeg on top. Serve in 4-ounce punch glasses. Makes about 25 servings.

PENDENNIS EGGNOG

1 bottle bourbon	2 quarts heavy cream
1 pound superfine sugar	Nutmeg
12 eggs, separated	

Pour the bourbon into a bowl and stir in the sugar. Set aside for 2 hours. Beat the egg yolks until light and slowly beat in the bourbon. Set aside for another 2 hours. When ready to serve, beat the cream until stiff; beat the egg whites until they stand in peaks. Pour the bourbon mixture ino a punch bowl and fold in the cream, then the egg whites. Grate a little nutmeg on top. Serve in 4-ounce punch glasses. Makes about 30 servings.

For Individuals

BASIC EGGNOG

2–3 ounces brandy or light
    rum
1 whole egg
1 tablespoon superfine sugar

1 cup milk
½ cup crushed ice
Nutmeg

Combine all ingredients except the nutmeg in a cocktail shaker and shake vigorously. Strain into a tall glass. Grate a little nutmeg on top. Serves 1.

Breakfast Eggnog: Use 2 ounces brandy. Add ½ ounce curaçao, and omit sugar.

BALTIMORE EGGNOG

1 egg
1 cup milk
1 teaspoon superfine sugar
1 ounce dark rum

1 ounce brandy
1 ounce Madeira
3 or 4 ice cubes
Nutmeg

Break the egg into a cocktail shaker and add the rest of the ingredients except the nutmeg. Shake vigorously and strain into a 12-ounce highball glass. Grate a little nutmeg on top. Serves 1.

GENERAL HARRISON'S EGGNOG NO. 1

1 whole egg
1 teaspoon superfine sugar
½ cup crushed ice

8 ounces claret
Nutmeg

Combine the egg, sugar and crushed ice in a cocktail shaker and shake vigorously. Strain into a 12-ounce Tom Collins glass, fill with claret and stir gently. Grate a little nutmeg on top. Serves 1.

For a non-alcoholic version of this drink, see page 400.

Non-Alcoholic Drinks That Join the Fun

The enormous quantities of bottled and canned sodas, colas, ginger ale and other non-alcoholic drinks sold in this country are proof positive that we're a thirsty people with a pronounced taste for potables containing no alcohol whatever. The same individuals who relish cocktails, highballs and a gamut of other mixed drinks are equally enthusiastic about non-alcoholic brews. Which they prefer depends upon mood and circumstance. After a couple of sets of tennis, for example, a tall glass of lemonade may appeal most, whereas after eighteen holes of golf a Tom Collins or Scotch and soda may get the vote. One guest may want a glass of spiced tomato juice before lunch; another may want a Bloody Mary. A host can never be sure when a friend is going to ask for a non-alcoholic drink, unless that friend never drinks anything else or is on the wagon temporarily for one reason or another. And, while it is a wise precaution to have a supply of such staples as Coca-Cola and ginger ale on hand, it is good entertaining strategy to whip up more personal and unusual concoctions upon occasion.

If you are expecting guests for cocktails, or a meal preceded by cocktails, be prepared to offer a non-alcoholic substitute to those who want it. Anyone can pour chilled tomato juice from a can or bottle into a glass, but this won't win compliments. Why not serve, instead, one or more of the sixteen drinks based on tomato or V-8 juice that are included in this section? Or simply dress up ginger ale as directed for a Pussyfoot, or club soda for a Club Cocktail. Or experiment with clam juice. Since all these "cocktails" are more generous in size than those made with liquor, they are served in Old-fashioned glasses, goblets or small tumblers. Any one of them will make a guest feel that he is being just as pampered as the cocktail drinkers. It's the personal touch that wins—plus a fresh taste experience.

If a house guest finally appears on Sunday morning looking rocky and feeling squeamish, due to having enjoyed Saturday night's party too enthusiastically, you can often make him feel considerably better by giving him a pick-me-up. He will probably have decided opinions about the type that will do him the most good. Some people are convinced that "a hair of the dog" is the most help. Others shudder at the mere thought. If he belongs to the non-alcoholic-cure school, consider serving him a Prairie Oyster No. 2 or one of its variations. If he wants something stronger, consult the section on pick-me-ups (page 304).

For those occasions when a long drink is indicated, there are many kinds to please many palates. Some are based on yogurt, some on fruit juice, others on milk, and on and on. For a friend with a sweet tooth, one of the drinks that calls for a scoop of ice cream is a good choice. At a holiday party, a non-alcoholic eggnog has very suitable seasonal appeal. On a cold afternoon or evening, try counteracting the temperature with a Spiced Cider Cup, a Hot Grapefruit Toddy, or—if calories can be ignored— Superb Hot Chocolate with or without a dash or two of Grand Marnier.

A non-alcoholic punch can strike just the right note of cheer at some gatherings. Sherbet Punch, made with orange sherbet and ginger ale, is bound to appeal to the young; a tea-based punch served in a pitcher is generally popular on a summer day; a punch made with fruit juice and an effervescent mixer, then garnished with fruit slices and mint sprigs, looks inviting enough for the most festive party.

One important point about non-alcoholic drinks is that they should not only *taste* good but *look* attractive. If you have handsome goblets, don't hesitate to use them instead of everyday Old-fashioned glasses or tumblers. When you can plan ahead, chill tall drinks with ice cubes that you have frozen around bits of garnish such as mint leaves, lemon or orange peel, or that you have colored pink with Angostura bitters. Even as simple a drink as a Horse's Neck becomes something of a triumph when a long, unbroken spiral of lemon peel curls down through the ice cubes and ginger ale.

There is a non-alcoholic drink that can turn any hour into an occasion. All you need do is consult the following recipes.

NON-ALCOHOLIC COCKTAILS AND MEDIUM-SIZED DRINKS

BARLEY WATER

2 ounces pearl barley	Peel of ½ lemon
3 teaspoons sugar	1 pint boiling water

Put barley in a small saucepan and cover with cold water. Bring to a boil and boil for about 3 minutes. Strain barley and put in a jug with sugar, lemon peel and boiling water. Cover and let stand until cold. Strain. Serve plain, or add lemon juice and sugar to taste, or dilute half and half with milk, or serve over ice.

Barley water traditionally is a refreshing drink for invalids, and is given to children. It deserves wider use. It is usually served in small tumblers. Makes 2 to 4 servings according to use.

BLENDER TOMATO JUICE (WITH VARIATIONS)

All recipes except No. 16 are based on 1 cup tomato juice, and all make one serving. V-8 juice may be used instead of tomato juice in all instances.

1. *With celery:* Combine juice, ½ cup chopped celery, and salt to taste, in an electric blender and blend at high speed until smooth. Pour over ice cubes in an Old-fashioned glass or a goblet.

2. *With cucumber and onion:* Combine juice, 4 thin slices cucumber and 1 thin slice onion. Blend on high speed until smooth. Serve in a sour glass without ice, or on the rocks in an Old-fashioned glass or a goblet.

3. *With carrots:* Combine juice, ½ cup thinly sliced raw carrots, ¼ teaspoon salt and a dash of Tabasco. Blend on high speed until smooth. Pour over ice cubes in an Old-fashioned glass or a goblet.

4. *With green pepper:* Combine juice, ½ cup thinly sliced green pepper, ¼ teaspoon salt and a dash of Tabasco. Blend on high speed until smooth. Serve in a chilled glass, or over ice.

5. *With (hot) chili pepper:* Combine juice, a peeled canned green chili and a dash of lemon juice. Blend on high speed until smooth. Serve in an Old-fashioned glass or a goblet with ice.

6. *With parsley and onion:* Combine juice, 6 sprigs parsley, 3 or 4 slices onion, a dash of Tabasco and a pinch of salt. Blend on high speed until smooth. Serve chilled or with ice in an Old-fashioned glass.

7. *With herbs and onion:* Combine juice, 2 leaves fresh basil (or ½ teaspoon dried), slice of onion, a sprig of parsley, dash of Tabasco, salt and freshly ground pepper to taste. Blend on high speed until smooth. Serve in a chilled glass.

8. *Tomato Juice Provençale:* Combine juice, 1 clove garlic, 4 or 5 leaves fresh basil (or 1 teaspoon dried), ¼ teaspoon salt and a dash of lemon juice. Blend for 1 minute. Serve over ice cubes in a chilled glass.

9. *Tomato Juice Mexicaine:* Combine juice, ½ peeled canned chili, 3 thin slices avocado, a pinch of oregano and ¼ teaspoon salt. Blend for 1 minute. Serve over ice cubes in a chilled glass.

10. *Tomato Juice British:* Combine juice, 3 or 4 sprigs watercress and 1 sprig parsley (both without stems), dash of Worcestershire sauce and ¼ teaspoon salt. Blend for 1 minute. Serve over ice cubes in a chilled glass.

11. *Tomato Juice Italienne:* Combine juice, 4 or 5 leaves fresh basil (or ½ teaspoon dried), one ¼″ slice red Italian onion, ½ teaspoon freshly ground pepper and a dash of salt. Blend for 1 minute. Serve over ice cubes in a chilled glass.

12. *Tomato Juice Piquant:* Combine juice, 3 tablespoons lime juice, dash of Tabasco, freshly ground pepper to taste

and ¼ teaspoon salt. Blend for 1 minute. Serve over ice cubes in a chilled glass.

13. *Tomato Juice Cajun:* Combine juice, 1 strip green pepper, dash of Tabasco, ¼ clove garlic, dash of lime juice and ¼ teaspoon salt. Blend for 1 minute. Serve over ice cubes in a chilled glass.

14. *Tomato Juice Californian:* Combine juice, ½ cup shredded raw carrot, 2 sprigs parsley without stems, 1 tablespoon lemon juice, dash of Worcestershire sauce and ¼ teaspoon salt. Blend for 1 minute. Pour over ice cubes in a chilled glass. Serve with a topping of sour cream and a sprinkling of paprika.

15. *Tomato Juice New England:* Combine juice, ½ cup clam juice, 1½ tablespoons lime juice, dash of Tabasco and ¼ teaspoon salt. Blend for 1 minute. Serve over ice cubes in a chilled glass.

16. *Tomato and yogurt:* Combine ½ cup tomato juice, ½ cup yogurt, ½ small sliced onion and 2 or 3 sprigs watercress without stems (or 2 or 3 cucumber slices). Blend on high speed for 1 minute. Serve in a tumbler over ice.

CLAM JUICE COCKTAIL

1 teaspoon tomato catsup	5 ounces clam juice
⅛ teaspoon celery salt	1 to 2 ice cubes
2 dashes Tabasco sauce	

Combine all the ingredients in a cocktail shaker and shake vigorously. Strain into a tumbler or goblet. Serves 1.

Clam Juice Tomato Cocktail: Omit the tomato catsup and use half clam, half tomato juice.

CLUB COCKTAIL

1 cube sugar	2 or 3 ice cubes
2 dashes Angostura bitters	Chilled club soda
Peel from 1 lemon, cut in a spiral	

Put the sugar in an Old-fashioned glass or goblet and add the bitters, peel and ice cubes. Fill with soda and stir lightly. Serves 1.

MANGOADE

2 cups ripe mango coarsely
  chopped, or canned mango
  drained and chopped
¼ cup sugar, or to taste
2 cups orange juice

¼ cup lime or lemon juice
2 cups cold water
1 teaspoon grated orange
  rind

Combine all ingredients except orange rind in a blender and blend on high speed for about 30 seconds. Strain and pour into a pitcher. Sprinkle with orange rind and serve in 8-ounce tumblers or goblets with 2 or 3 ice cubes in each. Makes about 8 servings.

ORANGE JUICE HAWAIIAN

⅔ cup chilled orange juice
1 slice pineapple
Dash lemon juice

2 or 3 ice cubes
Sprig mint

Put all ingredients except ice cubes in an electric blender and blend for 30 seconds on high speed. Serve in a chilled tumbler or goblet over ice cubes. Garnish with mint. Serves 1.

PRAIRIE OYSTER NO. 2

1 egg yolk
1 teaspoon Worcestershire
  sauce

2 dashes vinegar
Dash Tabasco
Pinch salt and pepper

Slip the unbroken egg yolk into a 4–6-ounce wineglass, sour glass or champagne saucer glass. Add the rest of the ingredients. Serves 1.

When drinking, the egg yolk should be swallowed whole.

Prairie Oyster No. 3: Use an entire egg instead of the yolk alone, and add 1 teaspoon tomato catsup.

Prairie Hen: Use an entire egg.

PUSSYFOOT

4 ounces ginger ale   Thin slice orange
½ teaspoon grenadine   2 or 3 ice cubes
Twist lemon peel

Combine all ingredients in an Old-fashioned glass or small
tumbler. Stir gently. Serves 1.
This is also called a **Shirley Temple.**

NON-ALCOHOLIC LONG DRINKS

ANGOSTURA HIGHBALL

2 or 3 ice cubes   Ginger ale
1 teaspoon Angostura bitters

Put the ice cubes in a highball glass, add the bitters and fill
with ginger ale. Serves 1.

AYRAN

1 pint plain yogurt   2 tablespoons crushed, dried
1 pint cold water   mint (optional)
Salt to taste

Pour yogurt into a bowl and beat until smooth, add water
and continue beating until thoroughly blended, or combine in
an electric blender and blend until smooth. Season to taste
with salt and dried mint. Chill thoroughly and serve in tall
glasses, with ice. Makes 4 servings.

This drink, which is popular throughout the Middle East, is
also known as **Abdug** or **Laban.** A similar drink, **Lassi,** is
popular in India: it is often sweetened with sugar and may
also be seasoned with a little ground cardamom. If seasoned
with ginger, onion and hot green chili peppers, it is called
Sambaran.

BLACK AND TAN

1 or 2 ice cubes   Milk
Cola

Put ice cubes in a 10-ounce highball glass and fill two-thirds with cola. Fill up with milk and stir gently. Serves 1.

BLACK COW

8 ounces sarsaparilla   1 or 2 scoops vanilla
                                  ice cream

Pour sarsaparilla in a 14-ounce collins glass, add ice cream and stir. Serves 1.

FLORIDA CRUSH NO. 1

1 6-ounce can frozen   Crushed ice
  concentrated orange,   Water
  grapefruit or tangerine   Lime slices
  juice   Fresh mint sprigs

Put 3 tablespoons concentrated citrus juice in each of 4 tall glasses. Add crushed ice and ½ cup water to each glass. Stir to mix thoroughly and garnish with a slice of lime and a sprig of mint. Serves 4.

FLORIDA CRUSH NO. 2

1 6-ounce can frozen   Crushed ice
  concentrated orange or   Watermelon balls
  grapefruit juice   Mint sprigs
4 tablespoons superfine
  sugar

Put 2 tablespoons of frozen citrus juice in each of 4 tall glasses and add 1 tablespoon of sugar. Add crushed ice and another tablespoon of concentrated juice and blend thoroughly. Garnish with watermelon balls and fresh mint sprigs. Serves 4.

GRAPEFRUIT FROSTEDS

2 18-ounce cans grapefruit juice

Fresh mint sprigs
Lime slices

Pour contents of 1 can of grapefruit juice into a freezer tray with the ice-cube compartments in place. Freeze until firm. Fill 4 tall glasses with the frozen grapefruit juice and add the juice from the second can. Garnish with fresh mint sprigs and lime slices. Serves 4.

Grapefruit Jubilee: Add ½ cup cassis syrup to the second can of grapefruit juice.

HORSE'S NECK

1 lemon
3 or 4 ice cubes

Ginger ale

Peel the lemon in an unbroken spiral and put the peel in a highball glass with one end hooked over the rim. Add the ice cubes, fill up with ginger ale and drop in a slice of lemon. Serves 1.

For Horse's Neck with liquor see page 297.

ICED MINT TEA

1 bunch fresh mint, or
⅔ ounce dried mint
2 cups boiling water
1 quart cold water
Sugar to taste

Ice cubes
6 strips lemon peel
6 mint sprigs, dusted with powdered sugar

Pour the boiling water over the mint and steep for half an hour in a double boiler over hot water. Strain, and combine the liquid with the cold water and sugar to taste. Pour into tall glasses filled with ice cubes; garnish with lemon peel and fresh mint dusted with powdered sugar. Serves 6.

LEMONADE

2 tablespoons lemon juice
1½ tablespoons lime juice
2 tablespoons superfine
sugar

6–8 ice cubes
2 cups cold water

Pour lemon and lime juice into a pitcher, add sugar and stir until dissolved. Add ice cubes and water and stir. Serve in tumblers. Serves 2.

PARISETTE

2 or 3 ice cubes
1 tablespoon grenadine

1 cup cold milk

Put ice cubes in a 10-ounce highball glass; add grenadine and milk. Stir gently. Serves 1.

Ginger ale, ginger beer, chilled club soda or lemonade may be used instead of milk, but the drink cannot then properly be called a Parisette.

PERFECT LEMONADE

4 tablespoons lemon juice
1 teaspoon superfine sugar
1 cup chilled club soda, or
plain water

3 or 4 ice cubes

Combine lemon juice and sugar and stir until sugar is dissolved. Add soda or water and stir. Put ice cubes in a tall glass and pour lemonade over them. Serves 1.

To vary the drink, substitute 1½ ounces cassis syrup, raspberry syrup or cherry syrup for the sugar. Or use half grape juice and half soda instead of all soda. Or use chilled apple juice in place of club soda.

Limeade: Substitute lime juice for lemon juice.

ROSY SQUASH

2 or 3 ice cubes
2 tablespoons lemon juice

1 tablespoon grenadine
Chilled club soda

Put ice cubes in a 12-ounce highball glass and add the lemon juice and grenadine. Fill with soda and stir. Serves 1.

RUSSIAN ICED TEA

2 tablespoons English
Breakfast or Darjeeling tea
3 cups sugar
1 cup fresh mint leaves
1 cup lemon juice

Crushed ice
Lemon slices
Mint sprigs
Powdered sugar

Pour a quart of boiling water over the tea and steep for 3 hours. Make a syrup of the sugar and 1 cup of cold water by boiling for 10 minutes. Add the mint leaves and infuse for 2 hours or until the tea is ready. Strain tea and syrup and combine with the lemon juice. Serve in 12- or 14-ounce glasses filled with crushed ice. Garnish with lemon slices and mint sprigs and dust the top with powdered sugar. Without the garnish, this brew will keep for several days in the refrigerator. Makes 12–14 servings.

SARATOGA

2 tablespoons lemon juice
½ teaspoon superfine sugar
2 dashes Angostura bitters

2 or 3 ice cubes
Ginger ale

Put lemon juice, sugar and bitters in a tall glass with the ice cubes, stir to mix and fill with ginger ale. Serves 1.
Chilled club soda may be used instead of ginger ale.

SUMMER DELIGHT

2 or 3 ice cubes
3 tablespoons lime juice
¾ ounce raspberry syrup

Chilled club soda
Fruits for garnish (optional)

Put ice cubes in a 10-ounce highball glass and add lime juice and syrup. Fill with soda and stir. Garnish with fruit. Serves 1.

SUMMER GIRL SODA

1 teaspoon grenadine
2 teaspoons whipped cream
1 ounce chilled club soda
1 scoop vanilla ice cream

1 scoop each raspberry and
   orange sherbet
Chilled club soda

Put grenadine in a 12-ounce glass with whipped cream, stir, add 1 ounce club soda and stir again. Add the vanilla ice cream and two sherbets, fill with club soda and sip through a straw. Serves 1.

YOGURT-FRUIT DRINK

3 tablespoons frozen,
   concentrated orange juice

½ pint plain yogurt

Combine ingredients in an electric blender and blend on high speed. Serve in a tall glass over ice cubes. Serves 1.

Half a cup of pineapple juice may be used instead of orange juice.

NON-ALCOHOLIC PUNCHES

AGUA DE JAMAICA

This popular Mexican soft drink is made from the sepals of a tropical flower known variously as flor de Jamaica, rosella, roselle and sorrel. It can be bought in Puerto Rican and Latin American markets as rosella.

4 ounces rosella sepals
2 quarts boiling water

Superfine sugar to taste

Put rosella sepals into a large jug and pour boiling water over them. Let stand until cool. Strain, sweeten to taste and serve in tumblers with 2 or 3 ice cubes per serving. Makes about 10 servings.

ANGEL PUNCH

1 cup sugar syrup
1 pint lemon juice
1 quart strong green tea

2 quarts white grape juice
1 block ice
2 quarts chilled club soda

Combine all ingredients except soda, and refrigerate for an hour or two. Pour over ice in a punch bowl and add the soda. Serve in 4-ounce punch glasses. Makes about 45 servings.

If this drink is made with ordinary black tea it is known as **Temperance Punch.**

BASIC TEA PUNCH

2 cups strong freshly brewed tea
6 cups any fruit juice
2 cups chilled ginger ale or club soda

Sugar syrup to taste
Block of ice

Combine all ingredients and sweeten to taste. Put ice in a punch bowl and pour the mixture over it. Serve in 4-ounce punch glasses. Makes about 20 servings.

CARRY NATION PUNCH

1 cup sugar syrup
3 cups lemon juice
1 quart orange juice
1 cup pineapple juice

1 block ice
2 quarts chilled ginger ale
Slices of orange and lemon

Mix sugar syrup and juices together and pour over ice in a punch bowl. Add ginger ale and garnish with the fruit slices. Serve in 4-ounce punch glasses. Makes about 35 servings.

FLORIDA PUNCH

2 cups superfine sugar
3 cups water
2 46-ounce cans blended
   orange and grapefruit juice

1½ cups lime juice
1½ quarts ginger ale
16 ice cubes

Combine sugar and water in a saucepan and cook over low heat, stirring constantly until the sugar is dissolved. Cool. Combine the sugar syrup with the fruit juices and pour over ice cubes in a punch bowl. Add the ginger ale and serve at once in 8-ounce goblets. Makes about 24 servings.

ORANGE MILK

Peel from 2 oranges
1 pint milk

2 tablespoons superfine
   sugar

To make this non-alcoholic milk punch, put the orange peel in a deep bowl, heat milk to boiling point and pour over the peel. Allow to steep for about 15 minutes, then stir in sugar until dissolved. Remove peel. Chill drink thoroughly; serve in tumblers. Serves 2.

PEANUT PUNCH

2 tablespoons cornstarch
½ cup water
2 cups milk

6 tablespoons peanut butter
Sugar to taste

Mix cornstarch and water in a small saucepan, add milk, peanut butter and sugar to taste. Cook over moderate heat, stirring with a whisk until thoroughly smooth and thick. Cool and refrigerate before serving. Serve in tumblers or goblets with or without ice. Serves 2.

This may be converted into an alcoholic drink with the addition of 2 ounces dark rum per serving. Stir in when ready to serve.

PENSACOLA PUNCH

2 cups superfine sugar
6 cups water
1 46-ounce can grapefruit
  juice
3½ cups lime juice

Crushed ice
1 pound grapefruit sections
Lime slices, maraschino
  cherries, mint sprigs

Combine sugar and water in a saucepan and cook over low heat, stirring constantly until the sugar is dissolved. Cool. Chill fruit juices and pour over crushed ice in a punch bowl. Add the sugar syrup and grapefruit sections. Garnish with lime slices, maraschino cherries and mint sprigs. Serve in 8-ounce goblets. Makes about 18 servings.

SHERBET PUNCH

1 large piece ice
1 pint orange sherbet

1 quart ginger ale
Mint leaves

Put ice in a punch bowl and add sherbet and ginger ale, stirring to break up sherbet. Garnish with mint leaves. Serve in 4-ounce punch cups. Makes about 12 servings.

SPICED LEMONADE

1 cup sugar syrup
12 whole cloves
1 stick cinnamon

1½ cups lemon juice
1 quart water
Crushed ice

Put sugar syrup, cloves and cinnamon in a small saucepan and simmer together for 5 minutes. Add lemon juice and let stand for one hour. Strain and combine with the water in a pitcher. Stir and pour into tumblers over crushed ice. Makes about 12 servings.

TAMARIND PUNCH

This drink is popular in both Mexico and India; indeed, with slight variations it is popular wherever tamarinds are readily available.

½ pound ripe tamarinds,
shelled

3 quarts cold water
Superfine sugar to taste

Put tamarinds in a large pitcher, add water and allow to soak for about 4 hours or until the pulp has thoroughly softened. Strain through a fine sieve, and sweeten to taste. Serve in 8-ounce tumblers with 2 to 3 ice cubes. Makes about 16 servings.

TEA PUNCH

1 large block ice
3 cups strong black tea
1 quart orange juice
1 cup lime juice

2 cups raspberry syrup
1 cup crushed pineapple
2 quarts chilled club soda

Pour all ingredients over ice in a punch bowl, adding soda just before serving. Serve in 4-ounce punch glasses. Makes about 40 servings.

MISCELLANEOUS NON-ALCOHOLIC DRINKS

EGGNOG

1 whole egg	¼ teaspoon vanilla
1 tablespoon superfine sugar	1 cup milk
Pinch salt	Nutmeg

Beat the egg with the sugar and salt and pour into a 10-ounce highball glass. Add vanilla and milk and stir to mix. Grate a little nutmeg on top.

GENERAL HARRISON'S EGGNOG NO. 2

1 whole egg	8 ounces sweet cider
1 teaspoon superfine sugar	Nutmeg
½ cup crushed ice	

Combine egg, sugar and crushed ice in a cocktail shaker and shake vigorously. Strain into a 12-ounce collins glass, fill with cider and stir gently. Grate a little nutmeg on top. Serves 1.

HOT GRAPEFRUIT TODDY

2 tablespoons superfine sugar	1 teaspoon whole cloves
2" stick cinnamon	6 cups grapefruit juice

Combine sugar and spices in a saucepan, stir in the grapefruit juice and heat slowly. Pour into 6-ounce mugs. Makes 8 servings.

ORANGE EGGNOG

3 tablespoons frozen orange concentrate, thawed	¾ cup milk, chilled
	1 egg

Place all ingredients in an electric blender and blend on high speed. Pour into a chilled tumbler or goblet. Serves 1.

RASPBERRY VINEGAR

This drink is a non-alcoholic shrub. Like the alcoholic versions (page 317), it is made ahead of time and bottled.

12 pounds fresh, ripe raspberries	3 quarts cider or malt vinegar Sugar

Wash and clean a third of the berries and pour a third of the vinegar over them. Let stand for 3 days. Drain off and reserve the juice and strain the berries through cheesecloth or a jelly bag. Set all the liquid aside. Repeat with a fresh batch of berries and add the liquid to that set aside earlier. Repeat with remaining berries.

Measure the juice and for each quart add 1 pound of sugar. Boil gently for 5 minutes and bottle. To serve, pour over ice in tall glasses and add a more or less equal portion of chilled club soda to fill. Add sugar to taste.

This drink, sometimes known as **Raspberry Shrub**, was a standard party drink for children earlier in the century.

SPICED CIDER CUP

1 quart sweet cider	½ teaspoon whole cloves
¼ cup sugar	¼ teaspoon whole allspice
2″ cinnamon stick	

Combine the ingredients in a saucepan and heat to the boiling point. Remove from the heat and allow the spices to steep for 3 or 4 hours. Strain, chill and serve with ice cubes in tumblers or goblets. If liked, the drink may be reheated and served in 8-ounce mugs. Makes 4 servings.

SUPERB HOT CHOCOLATE

6 ounces semi-sweet
chocolate bits
1 pint heavy cream

Pinch cinnamon
Whipped cream flavored with
vanilla

Melt chocolate bits in a double boiler over hot water and stir in the cream. Heat just to boiling point, stirring constantly. Add the cinnamon and serve in 8-ounce chocolate cups topped with flavored whipped cream. Makes about 4 servings.

For mint-flavored chocolate, place a mint patty in the bottom of each cup before pouring in the hot chocolate.

For a less rich drink, use half milk and half cream, or plain whole milk in place of the heavy cream.

To vary the drink and make it slightly alcoholic, use 1 or 2 dashes Grand Marnier instead of cinnamon.

Drinks for the Calorie-Conscious

Although it is highly caloric, alcohol contains very little food value. But since it does not require digestion it is one of the most highly assimilable of foods. Unlike most other foods, alcohol passes through the walls of the stomach and small intestine directly into the bloodstream, and immediately goes to work producing energy. Once the alcohol has entered the bloodstream, it remains there until it has all been oxidized. The normal rate for the elimination of alcohol from the system is about ⅓ ounce per hour. This rate remains constant, whether you exercise, lie in bed or sit in a sauna. Of course it is only the absolute alcohol that is absorbed directly into the bloodstream. The other components of the spirit pass through the digestive system, which is why you have to take their calories into account, as well as alcohol's, when you are drinking.

It is difficult, if not totally impossible, to give the caloric content of mixed drinks as accurately as might be desired. A change in brand name, in proportions, in size of drink can affect the calorie count. One hundred percent alcohol (200 proof) would deliver about 200 calories per ounce. Thus, 100-proof spirits have 100 calories per ounce; 86-proof, 86 calories, etc., *plus* extra calories if they also contain sugar or a measurable amount of some other caloric ingredient. The number of calories is unchanged, of course, no matter how much ice, water or soda mixers you use to dilute the spirits. Water and club soda do not contain any calories, and there are "low-calorie" mixers on the market that yield only 1 or 2 calories per 12-ounce bottle. Regular (non-diet) ginger ale and other soft drinks add about 10 calories per ounce, and sugar adds about 20 calories for each teaspoon used.

Calorie-Counter Chart

Here are the approximate calories per ounce of some of the more popular drinks and mixers:

ALCOHOLIC DRINKS	CALORIES PER OUNCE
Beer (American)	14
Beer (imported)	16
Benedictine	110
Bourbon	*
Brandy	75
Chartreuse (green)	100
Chartreuse (yellow)	125
Crème de menthe	104
Gin	*
Martini (very dry), most other dry cocktails	60
Port	45–50
Rum	*
Scotch	*
Sherry, dry	40
Table wines, dry	20

ALCOHOLIC DRINKS	CALORIES PER OUNCE
Tom Collins	35
Vermouth, dry	25
Vermouth, sweet	44
Vodka	*
Grenadine	25
Grape juice	10
Grapefruit juice	7
Quinine water	11
Tomato juice	3

Low-Proof Spirits and Wines

Most popular spirits, such as whiskey, gin, vodka and rum, range from 80 to 86 proof, or 40 to 43 percent alcohol. When these are diluted with ice, club soda, water or other mixers, your drink will be about 20 to 25 percent alcohol, which is roughly the same strength as fortified wines such as sherry, port and Madeira. Table wines contain somewhat less alcohol, usually from 11 to 12½ percent. Wine, the result of fermentation rather than distillation, has more nutritional value than distilled spirits, since many of the vitamins and minerals in the grapes are retained through the fermenting and aging processes. When Louis Pasteur made his often-quoted statement: "Wine is the most healthful and hygienic of beverages," vitamins were as yet unknown, but his investigations had convinced him that wine was indeed a great boon to mankind.

---

* Same as proof. For example, an ounce of 80-proof contains 80 calories.

Some Low-Calorie Drinks

For those times when you're striving to keep on the diet rails but you would be an oddity without a glass in your hand, here is a choice of non-alcoholic drinks that sip smoothly without swallowing up too many calories.

Bouillon on the rocks: Pour beef bouillon over ice and season with lots of lemon juice and a dash of Worcestershire.

Clam broth: Season it with lemon juice, celery salt and a dash of Tabasco. Serve on ice.

Clam and tomato juice: Combine them half-and-half. Season with salt or soy sauce and freshly ground black pepper, celery salt, lemon juice and Tabasco.

Perrier water: (James Beard calls it the champagne of dieters.) Add a lemon slice, or pep it up with a dash of syrup of grenadine or cassis, and ice.

Lemon juice and soda: Serve it on the rocks and add a dash of Angostura bitters for tanginess (or use ice cubes colored with the bitters).

Tea: Try it spiced and iced in hot weather. When the temperature drops, try hot sassafras tea for a change.

A cocktail isn't taboo if you choose from these low-calorie drinks that won't cut into your daily allowance too heavily. Light combinations of white wine and soda are good; so are spirits if the shot is *very* modest.

Spritzer: For this Rhine wine highball, add 2 ounces of dry white wine (approximately 40 calories) to 2 ounces of charged water and a twist of lemon, on ice.

Brandy: Pour 1 ounce (about 75 calories) over ice and douse with soda.

A Scotch, bourbon, vodka or gin drink: Make any one of these with only ½ ounce of spirits (100-proof alcohol has 100 calories an ounce; 86-proof spirits, 86 calories, etc.). Add soda and ice.

Pear in wine: Peel a pear and soak it in white wine. Drink the wine as an aperitif; eat the pear for dessert.

A simulated Lillet: Combine 2 ounces of dry white wine, a dash of lemon or orange juice, grated peel and a squirt of seltzer.

A Campari soda: Splash a little Campari over ice cubes, add a twist of lemon and soda for a cocktail with a blush and a tang.

Dry vermouth: Pour just 2 ounces (approximately 50 calories) over plenty of ice. Add a twist of lemon.

Tomato vermouth: Mix 4 ounces of tomato juice (25 calories) with 2 ounces of dry vermouth (50 calories). Pour over ice and add a twist of lemon.

Flavored white wine: Splash a dry white wine such as a Graves (2 ounces—approximately 40 calories) on the rocks with a dash of cherry essence or the juice of canned or frozen cherries.

Spiced cider: To make a low-calorie winter drink (1 cup: 100 calories), heat 1 quart of natural, unsweetened cider in a heavy saucepan with 1 cinnamon stick or ¼ teaspoon cinnamon, 4 or 5 cloves, ¼ teaspoon nutmeg, a pinch of mace and 4 or 5 thin slices of lemon. Simmer for half an hour. (For non-dieting guests, add a jigger of dark rum per glass.)

IV

Wines for New and
Old Wine Lovers

A Case of Wine—The Farsighted Gift

Anyone can go into a wineshop, order a case of dependable wine and send it to a friend on some special occasion. But there are more original and interesting ways to express your good wishes with wine.

A wine of the month: We have had a cheese and a fruit of the month; why not a wine? What more exciting and thoughtful gift for the wine enthusiast, connoisseur or novice than the promise of wine on six, eight or twelve different occasions during the months to come! If the wines are related to seasonal food, so much the better. Here are five different plans built around presents of one or two cases of wine.

1. Make up a case of twenty-four different wines that you have tasted and enjoyed. Arrange to have your wine dealer deliver the bottles in several installments during the year or, if this is not possible, send the entire case at once. Enclose a card with each bottle, describing its contents and giving your opinion of it. In this selection, it would be imaginative to include a good sherry or Montilla, perhaps

409

a Madeira, and that delicately flavored aperitif wine,
Lillet, which may be unfamiliar to many people.

As an alternative, you might send a case of all American wines, representing the range from sherry to champagne.

2. Give a case of wine to be sent, three bottles at a
time, in four installments during the year. At Christmas:
three bottles for holiday drinking—perhaps a first-rate
sherry, a port and a Madeira—or a good dry champagne.
In April: two bottles of a fine white wine, and one of a
lesser but interesting white. In July: three German Rhine
and Moselle wines, so pleasant for summer drinking. The
final wines in this series, sent in the late fall: great reds—
maybe one Burgundy and two Bordeaux. Thus you will
have covered the year in seasonal fashion and offered as
widely varied a selection as anyone could wish.

3. An interesting but more opulent plan involves two
cases of wine, chosen to complement eight special dinners
and geared to different times of year. Naturally, the dish
or food you have in mind should be suggested in the note
accompanying each installment. Here are some ideas to
consider:

December: Three bottles of champagne brut for New
Year's morning, to be used as an aperitif or to accompany
the first meal of the year.

March: A bottle of good Riesling or a Muscadet for
oysters, and two bottles of California Cabernet Sauvignon
for a filet of roast beef.

April: Three white wines, two dry ones for shad and
shad roe or similar fish and a bottle of fine Sauternes for
dessert.

May: A bottle of Montrachet for the salmon season
and two bottles of a Médoc to go with lamb, which is at
its peak at this time.

June: A bottle of Pinot Chardonnay for a first course
of crab meat, a Pinot Noir for a steak grilled outdoors
and a fine Cabernet Sauvignon for cheese.

July: A trio of hot-weather wines—a Pouilly-Fuissé or
Pouilly-Fumé to be drunk with lunch, a domestic rosé,

and good Beaujolais to serve at an outdoor meal or, cooled, with a cold supper.

August: Three fine Moselle wines for a breakfast or lunch party or for a refresher on a hot afternoon.

October or November: Three great red wines—two of Bordeaux to be drunk with pheasant, duck or wild turkey; a Burgundy to accompany venison.

4. Two cases might also be divided into monthly offerings—two bottles a month. For suggestions, consult the food and wine charts, pages 426-57. Choose a dish or food appropriate for each month and select one of the wines recommended as a suitable partner.

5. A final and definitely luxurious gift: six or twelve magnums to be delivered all at once or on a monthly basis. Attach a note to each bottle. It is a novelty and a grand gesture to serve a magnum of wine with dinner, so this present is bound to please.

A joyous wedding present: There is no happier and more practical way to give a marriage a good send-off than to provide the cornerstone for a future wine cellar— a case or two of carefully chosen wines coupled with a sound, informative book on the subject. If you wish to heap bounty upon bounty, you might include one or more of the appurtenances of wine storing and serving—a sturdy wine rack, a workmanlike corkscrew, a handsome decanter, classic clear crystal wineglasses.

Here might be the contents of one case of wine, sent as a wedding present:

1. A great red Bordeaux.
2. A fine Burgundy.
3. Two country wines such as a Muscadet, a Beaujolais, a Pouilly-Fumé or a Sancerre.
4. A great Rhône, either an excellent Côte Rôtie or a Hermitage.
5. A German wine such as a fine Niersteiner or a Bernkasteler.
6. A typical wine from the Rheingau—a Schloss Vollrads or a Schloss Johannisberger.

7. An Italian wine—a light Valpolicella or a rougher, heavier Barolo.
8. A wine from Spain or Portugal—a Rioja or a vinho verde.
9. A fine California Cabernet Sauvignon and a Pinot Chardonnay.
10. A first-rate champagne.

A case of mixed California and New York State wines would be an equally exciting gift and one that would enable a young couple to develop their wine palates on the fine U.S. varietals. Include a fine Cabernet Sauvignon, an excellent Pinot Noir, a Zinfandel, a Johannisberg Riesling, a Pinot Chardonnay, a rosé, a dry champagne, one of the native American varietals such as an Elvira or Catawba, a wine from the High Tor vineyards, a flowery Gewürztraminer and a sweet dessert wine.

How to Give a Wine-Tasting Party

Whether you and your friends aspire to become wine connoisseurs or not, you can all have a very good time at a wine-tasting party—if you like wine. Simply gear the party to your guests' expertise or lack of it, and you can't miss. This kind of entertaining has a lot to recommend it: an appealing "difference" that sets it apart from the ubiquitous cocktail and buffet party routines; a flexibility that gives you plenty of opportunity to create your own pace and pattern; a common denominator—i.e., judging wines —that promotes easy conversation and new friendships.

The first and most important single point to remember about any wine tasting is that the wines themselves should all belong to a specific group. Just as you cannot compare apples and oranges, so it is impossible to compare, for example, a red Burgundy to a white Moselle. Aside from the fun of it, a wine tasting is for the purposes of comparison and judgment—to judge the product of one château against another, or the white wines of the Rhine and Moselle against those of Alsace. You might stick to the wines of one country or one area that produces a great many: all-Bordeaux or all-Burgundies, reds from Italy, or a group of whites or reds from different vintners in California or New York State. Or you could plan along broader lines, and settle for all reds, all dry whites, or several rosé wines, and forget geography. For an unusually festive party, plan a tasting around several champagnes (all brut).

A sherry-tasting party can be very pleasant, particularly if you serve tapas along with the sherries, as the Spanish do. These miniature hors d'oeuvre, arranged on large platters or individual plates, consist of such goodies as lobster claws, little cubes of steak and onions, pieces of cucumber, olives and crumbled cheese or shrimp, small red-hot chillies and so on. Another group of wines that warrants a tasting is the vermouths. Select three or four dry vermouths and the same number of sweet ones—from France, Italy and the United States. Since the two types must be judged separately, arrange them on the table accordingly.

There are two basic varieties of wine tastings, and it's up to you to decide which will intrigue your guests more. One method is to expose all the wine labels so that everybody can read and study them while tasting, and talk over their opinions with one another as they progress from bottle to bottle. If you decide upon this pattern, choose wines that, in your opinion, will really interest your friends, or ask each couple to bring a bottle of a wine they particularly like which belongs to the group you've settled on—Rhine, rosé or whatever. Such general participation can be very satisfactory if a number of people get together frequently for wine tastings and are seriously interested in the subject. They not only can share each other's enthusiasms and learn from them but they also share the costs. The role of host rotates; he is responsible for table arrangements and any food, but for only one bottle of wine.

The second method makes more of a game of wine tasting, its aim being to see who can most accurately list the wines in the order of their established, recognized reputation. The bottles are wrapped in metal foil so that all labels are covered, and numbers are used for identification. Thus, each person must base his judgment on tasting alone, and list his decision by number. As host, you must use care when choosing the wines. You might pick three to five that range from poor to pleasant, one that is quite good, one that's even better and one that is superb. Your selection of the last three should be backed up by expert opinion and may require careful research. This type of wine tasting has all the zest of competition, and is most apt to intrigue guests who like, but have little knowledge of, wines. You might even give the winner a prize of —you guessed it—a bottle of wine! Again, costs may be shared, but only in terms of dollars. The host must be responsible for selecting wines that range from everyday to very special, or the tasting party loses its point.

Most people can sample as many as eight wines without overindulging; you can have fewer, but you should not attempt to have more. There is a limit to the number that any nonprofessional can try successfully at one session. As the average serving is 1½ to 2 ounces from each bottle, eight bottles will be sufficient for up to sixteen people, allowing for about half a bottle a person. (These figures do not apply to sherries and vermouths, which should be sipped more sparingly.)

To set up your party, space out the bottles on a large table covered with an attractive cloth. If you are providing only one glass per person, group the glasses at the head of the table. The best type are large-bowled, all-purpose wineglasses that allow the taster to swirl the wine around and get the full fragrance of its bouquet. Somewhat smaller glasses are fine for sherry, and long, slim flutes that hold the bubbles are the most pleasant for champagne, although all-purpose wineglasses do very well. Place several bowls of water on the table so that guests can rinse their glasses after each tasting. Put a small pile of linen or paper towels beside every bowl. If the taste-rinse-dry idea doesn't appeal to you, you may ask your guests to lend you their wineglasses for the evening, or you can rent them. You will need a glass per guest for each bottle of wine—or forty-eight glasses for eight people to taste six wines each. This means a sizable cleanup after the party.

Provide something to clear the palate between wines; pieces of French bread, breadsticks or plain unsalted crackers are best. Cheese doesn't help the flavor of most white wines, but cubes of a mild variety such as Gruyère or Muenster make excellent foils for reds.

Have a small pad and sharp pencil ready for each guest so that he can list his decisions and make any notes about names, vintages, etc., that he wants to remember.

Be sure that your wines are at the proper temperature when you set them out—room temperature for reds, chilled (not icy) for whites and rosés, slightly chilled for sherries and vermouths. Champagnes should stand in buckets of ice. When you uncork the bottles—and this should be done with red wines about an hour before the tasting—place the corks beside them. True connoisseurs like to sniff the cork to get an idea of the condition and bouquet of the wine. Amateurs will have fun doing this, whether or not it influences their judgment.

A more elaborate and less authentic type of wine tasting is a lunch or dinner party with wines and a menu that complement each other to perfection. Entertaining this way, you have a latitude that extends from the classic dinner with its progression of great dishes and great wines to a festive but simple buffet of French country wines and ragoûts. Try a champagne and charcuterie buffet, for example, or southern European wines and seafood, or Swiss wines and fondues. The combinations are endless; but they must be compatible because judgments will be affected by the success of the partnerships between the wines and the food as well as by the quality of the wines themselves.

There are three things to note about a wine: color, bouquet and taste. Pour no more than 2 ounces into your glass (measure by eye) and hold it up to the light. Is the color clear and brilliant, or dull? Then roll the wine around in the glass, put your nose to it and sniff deeply.

Does the wine have a light and delicate bouquet, a rich fragrance, a fruity one or none at all? If it is made from one of the great varieties, can you detect the characteristic fragrance of the grape? Now take a sip and roll it around your mouth and over your tongue. If you can, suck air through your lips and let it swirl through the wine, a professional trick that points up the flavor. Finally swallow slowly, carefully noting the body, the smoothness of the wine and the aftertaste, if any. Did the wine have a light, rippling feeling in your mouth or was it round and full-bodied? Was it smooth or harsh or thin and watery? If it had an aftertaste, was it pleasing or not? Don't be influenced by the opinions of the other tasters, no matter how expert. The best wine for you is the one you like best. But if there are certain wines in a group that are truly outstanding and have a much better reputation than the others, you can learn a great deal about quality by concentrating on tasting. Remember that it is always permissible and often necessary to return to a wine and taste it again if you're undecided. If you plan to make careful comparisons that require more than one sampling of the various bottles, limit the amount of each so that the total adds up to no more than 2 ounces per bottle.

Wines to Complement Every Meal

In food and wine, what goes with what? There are many people today who tend to dismiss the entire question of choosing appropriate wines by saying that the one you like is the best one to serve with whatever you happen to be eating. This point of view may be somewhat high-handed but it is not as arbitrary as that of the woman who always served white wine because red wine, if spilled, would stain her tablecloth! Neither takes into account the fact that some time-honored partnerships deserve consideration—notably the one about white wine with most fish and red wine with hearty red meats or game—simply because they make good culinary sense. There are exceptions, of course. It is perfectly legitimate to serve a light red, slightly chilled, perhaps a young Beaujolais, with a rich, oily fish cooked in red wine—salmon, for instance. Certain delicate game birds such as quail taste better with the less dominant white wines. And, if you happen to like white wines, you can also serve them with the lighter, whiter meats: veal, pork, ham and, in the poultry group, chicken, roast or poached turkey, and even goose—a flowery Moselle or the acidity of a Meursault can help cut its rich fattiness. Duck, on the other hand, seems to need the rich assertiveness of a red wine. When a poultry dish is cooked with wine, the obvious procedure is to serve a similar wine with it, and the same holds true of meat dishes. Remember that richer foods take more robust wines to do them justice and that in every country there are regional foods and regional wines that go hand in hand.

Once you have learned the basic rules and more especially the simple concepts that back them up, you can depart upon occasion from the rules and be more adventuresome. After all, good dining should be a personal adventure and not an exercise in rigid discipline. Any wine should be chosen not only to go with the food but also to enhance the mood, the time and the place. And don't be afraid to please your own taste buds. The one drastic mistake to avoid is flagrant mismating—a heavy red wine with a delicate, light dish or a very dry wine with a sweet dessert.

Generally speaking, wines do not belong with the hors d'oeuvre course unless you are having something like oysters or other seafood or perhaps a pâté or quiche, with which you could serve an Alsatian or German wine. Nor are table wines often served with soup today, although you might have a glass of dry Madeira or amontillado with consommé, turtle or game soup, or seafood bisque. Wines belong with fish, meat, poultry, game, and cheese when the latter is served as a course on its own after the entrée. Wine is seldom served anymore with the dessert course. Most people prefer to invest in the dry table wines, which are more effective and necessary. However, if you choose to be elegant and traditional, it is also important to be correct. Wines that complement various fresh fruits are discussed further on, as are wines to serve with sweet desserts or after dinner.

If you have a maxim, let it be, "The better the dish, the better the wine." Food that is a work of art deserves a wine of consequence; food that is simple, home cooking just rates something pleasant to drink.

If you are serving more than one wine with a meal, the progression is the same as at a wine tasting—white before red, dry before sweet, young before old, light- before full-bodied, modest before great. Most people, however, settle for one wine, chosen to complement the main dish. With the average three-course dinner—entrée or soup, main course and dessert—one wine is sufficient. Only make sure that you have enough of it. If you select a dry wine, you can also serve it before the meal as an aperitif, but this is not a good idea if your guests are indifferent to wine and prefer the ubiquitous cocktails instead.

Brut champagne and rosé wines are in slightly separate categories as companions to food from the range of reds and whites. Some connoisseurs subscribe to the theory that champagne can be served with any course throughout a meal, as well as before it. Others believe that champagne belongs on its own or with something as grand as fresh caviar or a marvelous foie gras. Either way, you can't go wrong. Rosés have their place on a menu—with certain lamb and veal dishes, occasionally with pork or ham, although they are really at their best with cold or simple summer food.

Foods Unfriendly to Wines

It is important to realize that some foods do not go well with wines. They are either so overpowering in flavor that they kill the taste of the wine, or they alter it and make the taste unpleasant. Following is a list of such foods, and suggestions for coping with the problem:

Asparagus makes wine taste sweet, so follow the sensible French custom and serve it as a separate course, either as a first course or after the meat.

Artichoke makes wine taste metallic and should also be served as a separate course after the meat, or as a first course, cold or hot.

Salad dressing made with vinegar is not favorable to wine. If you are having a large salad as a main course for a summer luncheon or buffet, serve it with a sour cream or mayonnaise type of dressing and offer a light, gay white wine such as an Alsatian or California Riesling, or a summery rosé. The safest and wisest thing to do, however, is to substitute lemon juice or dry white wine for the vinegar in your salad dressing.

Hot Mexican dishes and curries are highly spiced and have too much heat for wines. Serve beer with them.

Sweet-sour dishes, such as sweet-sour spareribs, drown the taste of wine. Again, serve beer with these.

Oriental dishes, for the most part, do not go well with wines, although champagne is very acceptable. With them serve beer or oriental rice wine.

A few fruits, such as oranges and pineapples, refuse to blend with any wine, but are delightfully companioned by various brandies.

Cranberries, so often partnered with holiday turkey, are another enemy of most wines. Champagne is a good choice, for it can withstand the tart sweetness of cranberry sauce. Otherwise, try a good old-fashioned hard cider.

For Chilly-Day Meals

Winter wine drinking has one great advantage over wine drinking in summer: it never turns into a losing battle against thirst. There are moments on sweltering hot days when we don't really care what the wine is so long as it is cold and there is plenty of it. In contrast, winter's more deliberate meals and evenings spent by the fireside provide the opportunity to drink wine for wine's sake rather than for its ability to refresh.

In cold weather, we eat not only heavier, heartier food, but more of it. As hot meat is the first food to regain favor when the temperature drops, the full-bodied red wines are in demand. Next to meat come cream and egg yolks for thickening and enriching of sauces that require the headier, more scented wines. And the rich fruit pies bring forth the luscious, sweet golden wines, chilled and carried sweating to the table.

Wine and soup: Perhaps the wintriest of all dishes, and the one most often associated with comforting, warming and reviving, is a steaming soup bowl. The question of whether to serve wine with soup worries many gourmets; they don't like the idea of drinking two liquids in alternate sips. There is a lot to be said for this point of view, and the way around it is to drink the wine not *with* the soup, but *in* it. If there are any traditional wines to drink with soup, they are sherry and Madeira. A glass of either is certainly good with a bowl of almost any soup, thick or clear. Having a higher alcoholic strength and a more powerful flavor than ordinary table wines, they act almost as an added seasoning (and, indeed, are often used for this purpose). Amontillado among sherries, and Verdelho or Rainwater among Madeiras, have enough pungency and body to hold up against a really savory broth or cream soup.

In London clubs, where the drinking of soup is reckoned a serious matter, a little cruet bottle, the kind that usually contains vinegar, is put on the table with the soup. It contains a mixture of sherries—leftovers from the bottom of many bottles. The custom is to shake a few drops into a bowl of soup as a seasoning—and highly effective it is, too. The even more serious soup lovers who can be seen in any French workmen's café like to make what they call a chabrot. Starting with a large bowl of soup—from the rich stockpot and heavy with vegetables—they eat half, then pour a big glass of ordinary red wine into the rest, producing a pink-tinged mixture that is sharp and appetizing.

Red wine and meat: In winter, roast meat comes into its own. Historically, this was the season when the livestock could no longer be fed. All animals, save a few for breeding, were slaughtered for the Christmas feast, and for a few weeks there was a glut of beef, pork and lamb.

A tradition, originally French, connects beef with Burgundy and lamb with Bordeaux. This may only stem from the fact that the Charolais (the hill pastures above Burgundy) is France's most famous cattle country, and the salt marshes below Bordeaux are renowned for their lamb. As a principle for choosing wine, it certainly works. The difference between beef and lamb gives a rough idea of the differences between the wines that go with them. If you were to say that Burgundy, like beef, is more savory, rich in flavor, something to chew, you would not be far wrong. Bordeaux, like lamb, has a lighter texture and a more delicate—although just as appetizing—savor.

Winter-weight white wines: Some wine connoisseurs have a full-fledged enthusiasm for white wine in winter. They refuse to confine it to fish as many people do, and drink it with veal, pork and frequently chicken, just as they would in summer. One often-forgotten wine country that makes an excellent cold-weather white wine is Hungary. The Hungarian word of praise for a wine is "fiery." By this they do not mean rough and immature, as hooch is fiery, but warming, generous, full of flavor. Hungarian wines are like the southernmost of the great Rhine wines of Germany, only more so. They tend to be sweet and to taste of the grape and the earth. They have a unique Hungarian taste which suggests the very essence of autumn —something gold and lingering. They are wines of tremendous character and, like the pepper-hot goulash that is the heart of Hungarian cooking, they are eminently keepers-out of the cold. If you want a special and different white for winter drinking and can find it in your local store, Hungarian fits the role perfectly.

This is not to say that other white wines are not appropriate to winter dinners. Rich chicken and sweetbread dishes call for the suavity of the great white Burgundies. The brilliant, brittle quality of young Muscatel or Gros Plant is perfect with oysters, clams, mussels and other *fruits de mer,* while the scented dryness of a fine Pouilly-Fumé or Sancerre tastes especially good with crab or lobster. The softness of a good Traminer or Gewurtztraminer from Alsace or California is a delicious accompaniment to pork or veal and to choucroute.

Wines for fireside sipping: The wintriest of all wines, port, was an invention of the age before central heating, when the cold was felt almost as much indoors as out. Snug before the fire with a glass of port, a dog and a decanter, the contented drinker could forget the needles of icy draft whistling through the house. By these standards, however deep the snow, loud the wind or bitter the frost, our winters are feeble, emasculated seasons, and it is easy to see why port is no longer on every sideboard. It is in memory of times past, rather than in any great need for inner warmth, that port tastes so extraordinarily comforting and appropriate when the evenings turn cold.

The port to keep on hand, the ideal wine to offer if guests come round on a stormy night, is named after its color—tawny. Time has faded its original deep ruby to a brick-red and has smoothed its taste into the richest, roundest, most luscious sweetness in the whole world of wine. (For more about port, see pages 65–66.)

For Summer-Day Meals

When the season is sultry and stifling and cold foods are at their most inviting, a bottle of wine should have, above all, the power to refresh. Not every wine possesses this, by any means—reds decidedly less than whites. It is a matter of the trace of acidity that a white wine, like a ripe apple, keeps in its flavor. The best rosés have the same quality, but in a red wine this characteristic would produce a thin and feeble taste. Hence the preference for white and rosé wines in hot weather. Even dishes that would be natural partners for red wines if served hot— red meat, duck and game, for example—go well with a lighter wine when served cold.

Salads, no matter what their basic ingredients, give rosé wine real distinction, provided you recognize that vinegar is the deadly enemy of wine; one drop in a bottle will turn all of it sour. Make your French dressing 8 parts oil to 1 of vinegar and add a little sugar; the salad will taste all the fresher and the wine will be unaffected. If the wine is very special, cut out the vinegar altogether and substitute a little lemon juice or dry white wine.

Paradoxically, it is the people of northern countries who are the great eaters of cold food. No hot country makes a specialty of a cold table as the Scandinavians do with their smorgasbord. Apart from Spain's sharp iced soup, gazpacho, few of the parched southern countries have evolved light, cooling summer dishes. One reason is that they are chronically short of greenery, the heart of a salad. Another difficulty arises with many southern wines. A picturesque fallacy has it that nothing is better than local wines with local foods, but no one in his right mind would drink a dark, overpowering local red on a sweltering Sicilian evening if he could get a bottle of northern Moselle, cool and green as the moss by a waterfall.

Green wines: *Vinho verde* is Portugal's pleasantest, coolest, most attractive wine. It becomes a habit, in hot weather, to drink a bottle of it as casually as an American would drink a can of beer. *Vinho verde* may be white, red or pink. The red is the least successful, as it tends to be cloudy. The pink (not officially classed as *vinho verde* although made in the same manner) has become tremendously popular. The brands destined for export are sweetened because their natural sharpness is too marked for people unused to the taste. Their white cousins, on the other hand, are shipped in something nearer to their natural state, only slightly sweetened. All are heat-wave wines, to be drunk as an aperitif before, as well as with, a cold meal in very hot weather. One bottle, under these circumstances, goes nowhere at all. For a dinner party, you almost have to allow a bottle per person.

No other European country so far south produces a wine as suitable to its climate as Portugal. In Spain, red wine is mixed with citrus fruit and ice to make the drink called sangría. In summer, particularly in Andalusia, sangría is drunk with any food at all, simply for its thirst-quenching properties. Being only very moderately alcoholic, it is a good party drink. If you prefer a red wine with meat, many connoisseurs suggest that in hot weather the best choice is a light red, such as an Italian Valpolicella, French Beaujolais, or California Mountain Red. They also advise that the wines are more refreshing when slightly chilled.

Rosés: The world's best rosé wines come from France, Italy and California. California rosés resemble the French in that they are true rosés, where Italian *rosati* tend to be more like bright, light cherry reds.

The finest rosés are made from the Grenache grape which in France produces Tavel, the only rosé never omitted in a list of the world's great wines. It is usually rather strong, positive and forceful in character, not easily drowned by the flavor of food, however assertive. The most widespread alternative to Tavel from Provence in the south of France is Anjou Rosé from the valley of the Loire. Between them, these rosés can take care of most cold meals. The first is best for boldly flavored dishes involving garlic or onions, the second for more delicate lunch-type foods—cold chicken and ham, veal, fish, and simple salads of lettuce and tomatoes or cottage cheese with a lemon and oil dressing.

The Grenache is also the grape that produces some of northern California's outstanding rosé wine. The other popular California rosé grape is the Gamay, which gives a slightly softer, light wine with less character. Grenache and Gamay, like Tavel and Anjou, carve up the field of cold food between them.

The Italian *rosati* remain the least explored. Remarkably little fuss is made about them, yet Chiaretto del Garda is one of the softest, most appealing and brightest colored of all pink wines. Color, after all, is an important part of the appearance of a meal, and a carafe of brilliant cherry-red wine adds as much to the table as a bowl of summer flowers. Some of the Swiss rosés, although less vivid in color, also are light and fresh in flavor.

Rosés are often treated too offhandedly and left in the refrigerator as though they were orange juice or lager. If the bottle immediately forms a heavy dew when taken out, the wine is too cold, will have no taste except a vague sharpness, and no aroma at all. Leave it only until it acquires a refreshing coolness. Ice-cold, all wines taste alike.

Northern white wines: There is a strong similarity between the white wines of northernmost France (leaving aside Champagne) and Germany, a quality between sweet and sharp. With their distinct flowery and grapy scent, you can't really characterize the flavor—fresh fruit is the best analogy. And nothing tastes better with fresh fruit such as peaches, apples or grapes—or with cold dishes— than some of these wines.

Although the finest great growths of German white wines are the most wonderful of their kind in the world, it's the lower-priced, more common Rhines and Moselles that make the most summery and reviving accompaniment to cold meals. These lesser wines are not to be compared with the distinguished ones in scent and depth of flavor, but they have the edge on them for casual, thirsty drinking.

By the same token, it is not the best of the French Loire wines that make perfect matches for cold foods, but the simple, inexpensive Muscadet (especially for fish and shellfish), Anjou Blanc, Saumur, and Pouilly-Fumé. The equivalent wines from Alsace or Switzerland fall into the same category. They are good value for the money. With cold meals in hot weather, two bottles of one of these moderately priced wines make more sense than one of something twice as expensive.

WINE AND MEAT

Although the pairing of wine and meat, like all good marriages, is ultimately a matter of individual choice and preference, there are some well-established guidelines that can contribute greatly to the happiness of the liaison. The rule of thumb about serving a red wine with a red meat, for example, is generally a sound one when you are having a roast. Yet the dicta about what goes with what are more relaxed these days. While you would usually choose a light red to accompany a veal roast, some people drink, with perfect assurance, a white with this delicate meat. And although a perfectly roasted filet should certainly be accorded the compliment of a fine Burgundy, Bordeaux, or premium American red, it would be folly to lavish the same wine on a hamburger or a beef stew, where a modest European red wine or an American Mountain Red would be more appropriate and compatible. Common sense is an excellent guide to follow when picking a wine for a dish. The following chart lists the established marriages of wine and meat, and also indicates where other choices are just as good.

BEEF	ACCOMPANYING WINE
Porterhouse, sirloin, and similar hearty steaks, plainly cooked, London broil, hamburgers	RED: Châteauneuf-du-Pape; Pommard; Médoc; Spanish Rioja; California Cabernet Sauvignon. For summer outdoor eating, lightly cooled Beaujolais
Steak au poivre, steak Diane, steak au Roquefort	RED: Hermitage; young Juliénas or Fleurie; California Pinot Noir, Zinfandel
Filet mignon, tournedos, chateaubriand, whole roast filet, beef	RED: Médoc or St. Emilion of a good year; Vosne-Romanée or Corton of a good year; Côte Rôtie of a good

Wellington, beef scallops, beef Stroganoff	year; California premium Cabernet Sauvignon
Roast prime ribs, roast sirloin	RED: Graves such as an Haut-Brion; Pomerol; Burgundy such as Gevrey-Charbertin, Clos de Tart
Braised beef, pot roasts, beef stews, beef Bourguignon	RED: An inexpensive wine that may also be used in the cooking, such as a domestic red; a French Macon Rouge, Beaujolais or regional Burgundy; Chianti
Pot-au-feu	RED: Beaujolais or Cabernet Sauvignon; Dão from Portugal WHITE: Hermitage or white Burgundy

VEAL	ACCOMPANYING WINE
Roast saddle of veal, veal rump, noix or langue de veau	RED: Light Burgundy such as Volnay or Chassagne-Montrachet; Médoc; California Pinot Noir; Valpolicella
Braised veal, veal Marengo, paupiettes de veau, alouettes sans têtes, braised veal chops, stuffed shoulder or breast of veal, Sicilian veal, paprika schnitzel	RED: Beaujolais such as Moulin-à-Vent ROSÉ: Tavel; Grenache Rosé WHITE: Pouilly-Fuissé or California Pinot Chardonnay
Ossi bucchi	WHITE: Soave; Johannisberger Riesling
Vitello tonnato	WHITE: Verdicchio; Orvieto; Muscadet; Pouilly-Fumé
Blanquette de veau	WHITE: Pouilly-Fuissé; Soave; Moselle
Scaloppine· cooked with white wine	WHITE: Frascati; Pinot Chardonnay; Chante-Alouette

| Plainly sautéed or cooked with sherry or Marsala | RED: Valpolicella; Beaujolais
ROSÉ: Tavel |

LAMB, MUTTON	ACCOMPANYING WINE
Roast gigot, boned and rolled shoulder of lamb	RED: Light Médoc or red Graves; St. Emilion; Chambertin; Beaune Village; Bonnes Mares ROSÉ: Tavel
Roast saddle, rack, crown roast of lamb	RED: Médoc or Pomerol of a good year; La Tâche or Echézeaux; Hermitage of a good year; Fleurie
Roast leg of mutton	RED: Hermitage; Côtes du Rhône; California Barbera
English mutton chops	None. Beer or ale goes best
Lamb chops	RED: Châteauneuf-du-Pape; Moulin-à-Vent
Shish kebab, shashlik, barbecued lamb	RED: A cooled Beaujolais such as Morgon ROSÉ: Tavel; Grenache Rosé
Braised lamb, lamb stews, navarin	RED: Beaujolais; California Pinot Noir; Rioja; Châteauneuf-du-Pape
Moussaka	ROSÉ: Tavel; Gamay; Grenache Rosé RED: Beaujolais such as Juliénas

PORK, HAM	ACCOMPANYING WINE
Pork roasts, pork pot roasts, braised pork, broiled or sautéed pork tenderloin, chops, spareribs, choucroute garnie, ham	WHITE: Champagne; occasionally a fruity white like an Alsatian, a white Graves or Moselle RED: California Zinfandel ROSÉ: Grenache Rosé Many pork dishes are admirably suited to beer, both light and dark

SPECIALTY MEATS, PIES, PÂTÉS, COLD MEATS	ACCOMPANYING WINE
Tripe: Niçoise, à la mode de Caen; Genovese tripe dishes made with tomato, such as Tripe Creole	WHITE: Muscadet: Sancerre; Alsatian or Johannisberger Riesling; New York State Vin Blanc Sec RED: Barbera; Zinfandel; Châteauneuf-du-Pape
Sweetbreads, brains	WHITE: Pouilly-Fuissé; Pouilly-Fumé; Sancerre; Haut Brion Blanc; California Pinot Blanc or Chenin Blanc; champagne
Liver	RED: Beaujolais such as Fleurie; California Pinot Noir
Tongue	RED: Beaujolais ROSÉ: A Burgundian Rosé
Kidneys	RED: Light Médoc; Fleurie; Corton; California Pinot Noir
Stuffed beef heart; braised oxtail	Inexpensive American red wines or beer
Grilled pigs' feet	WHITE: Riesling ROSÉ: Tavel
Sausages: Hot, en brioche, or with potato salad	WHITE: Pouilly-Fuissé; white Hermitage; Riesling
As an hors d'oeuvre	WHITE: Riesling; Pouilly-Fumé
Cold, as a snack	ROSÉ: Tavel, or beer
Meat pies and hot pâtés, served as a main course	WHITE: Sancerre; Pouilly-Fumé: Moselle; champagne
Cold cuts	WHITE: Muscadet RED: Beaujolais

Beef in aspic, meat salads   RED: Médoc, California Cabernet
                                Sauvignon
                             WHITE: Muscadet
                             ROSÉ: Tavel

CHOOSING A WINE FOR A CASSEROLE

Carafe is the wine word that matches the food word casserole; in both cases, the name of the container has christened its contents. A carafe wine is a good plain blended table wine; a casserole is a sustaining, all-in-one dish. It is no coincidence that the two go together.

Carafe wines are wines without a vintage year, without the name of a particular vineyard or even, necessarily, of a specific region. They are consistent from bottle to bottle; having been blended, they do not reflect the vagaries of weather. In England and France, carafe wines are those drawn from the barrel and sold in bulk. In this country, the corresponding wines—either imported or domestic— are usually sold in gallon and half-gallon jugs. A carafe wine should have—and this is where you distinguish good from indifferent ones—recognizable style and character. It is possible to produce plain, uncharacteristic wine by endless filtering and sterilizing, but unless wine has something of its own to say it is uninviting and you would not want a second glass.

The secret of serving a carafe wine is to make it run like a river. On the table, a bottle with a five- or six-glass capacity soon comes to an end. A carafe, which suggests that there is a barrel of wine for replenishment somewhere in the background, has no such limitations. It never seems to be either full or empty. The same implication of plenty should come across in the glasses. In France, a carafe wine is served more often than not in tumblers. Sturdy stemmed water goblets are a good choice for your own parties.

As for temperature, the rule here is to relax. In Italy,

white carafe wine is often barely below room temperature. In Spain, red wine is always iced in summer. Neither —you may say—is perfectly served; but are they any the worse for that? The main factors are to have the right wine and the easy feeling of an ample flow. Both attributes, in natural wine-drinking countries, are always present.

When shopping for a carafe wine, you can find any number of cut-price offers, gallon jugs and quantity deals. One of them might be a real bargain, but it is only a great buy if you like the taste of the contents. Some wine from gallon jugs might easily put you and your guests off wine for weeks. Nevertheless, conditions in certain parts of the world do make the wines of those countries naturally inexpensive.

Red Wines

Vin ordinaire, the carafe wine of the daily wine-drinking workingman of France and the other Mediterranean countries, is red. Simple people, who have no notions or conventions of gastronomy and never experiment beyond the monotonous food they grew up with, drink red wine unquestioningly. There are local exceptions, of course, in areas where only white grapes grow, but it is no surprise to see a Spaniard washing down a fried fish with strong red wine. Unquestionably, red carafe wine is more agreeable than white with some dishes, not so good with others. It is best for casseroles with a rich base of meat stock, with beans, mushrooms, strong seasonings, and for creamy or spicy chicken casseroles.

While white wine is often called for in a recipe, it is not necessarily the best partner for the dish at table.

The ideal red carafe wine is dark, strong-flavored and dry, with a good hint of the savor of grapes in it, although not the sugar that usually goes with that taste. This may sound like rather a tall order. As it is notoriously difficult to put your finger on any taste—wine eludes every kind of verbal analysis—naming names is the only way. The following red wines, then, have the qualities to look for.

Dão (pronounced, more or less, Dong), from the valley of the river Dão, almost in the center of Portugal, has the very properties most suitable in a carafe wine. There are two qualities: the better is called Reserva and is usually about ten years old. Ordinary Dão must be three or four years old to be drinkable, but you don't have to worry, because it is never bottled until it is. The brand name Grão Vasco is reliable.

Rioja (pronounced Reeoha with a hard *h*): The Rioja area in the center of northern Spain, hardly two hours' drive from the French border, has virtually a monopoly of high-quality Spanish table wine. Red Rioja can be superb in extreme old age, but very seldom has the chance to demonstrate how superb. At four years old, when normally sold, it is good. Some Riojas are labeled "claret," others "Burgundy," although they are nothing like either French wine, but have a perfectly good character of their own. "Claret" Riojas are often rosé wines; the ones to look for are the real reds, such as the Castel Pomal or Bodegas Bilbainas.

Barolo: This Italian wine is grown in a limited area in the hilly, inviting hunting country southeast of Turin, not a hundred miles from the French border. It is a dark-colored, profoundly scented and flavored wine. Game is its natural companion; one of the best-known *cantinas* (wineries) was once a royal hunting lodge. But any meaty, savory casserole with onions and spices in its makeup will gain enormously from the partnership.

Côtes du Rhône: French *vin ordinaire* can be amazingly ordinary, but the wines of the Rhone Valley as it enters Provence seem to keep their standards up and their prices down. Châteauneuf-du-Pape is the great name among them, and the archetype of carafe wine for a casserole meal.

U.S.: For carafe consumption, fine domestic wine starts with a price disadvantage due to labor costs. The California Pinot Noir, although not bargain-priced, would be ideal with a lamb casserole. Some of the more reasonable domestic reds in gallon and half-gallon jugs make very satisfactory carafe wines; in this case, do some tasting and choose the vineyard carefully.

White Wines

The qualities to look for in a white carafe wine—with seafood casseroles and sweet-sour German pork ones in mind —are firmness, dryness and substance. We say a casserole is substantial; we should be able to say that about its white wine partner, too. Often such wines have a strong golden color. Their scent is not particularly marked, but they are rich drinking even when they are as dry as a bone. In Spain, with luck, you are served such a wine with the bread as part of the table setting. It announces immediately its cousinship—although distant—with sherry. It reminds you of that intensely appetizing undercurrent of nuttiness in a dust-dry fino from Jerez. But such a wine isn't exported, although the sherry is, of course.

Spanish sherry, chilled and very dry, served at the table in a carafe, is excellent with some of the seafood casseroles, rather than drunk as an aperitif. Because sherry is strong, you need only half as much of it as you would of a normal table wine. But with prawns and shrimp, casseroled or cold, it is matchless. It also goes well with some Chinese food.

Dão and Rioja: Both these areas on the Iberian peninsula produce white wines as well as red. The whites may not be quite so good, but in terms of value for money, and served as the carafe white for a family meal or large party, they are almost impossible to beat. Viña Paceta of Bodegas Bilbainas is the Rioja to remember; Grão Vasco is the Dão.

Côtes du Rhône: In France it is the Rhone Valley again that grows such wines as White Hermitage and white Châteauneuf-du-Pape. Both are wines with fine strong tastes, mellow to the mouth and nose, golden to look at. A winter shrimp casserole does not call for the same wine as a dish of fresh shrimp at a summer lunch. In summer, you would look for a delicate, hardly alcoholic, slightly prickly wine—a Moselle perhaps. But the seasonings in a casserole—the herbs, spices, salt, pepper and garlic—all call for something stronger.

Traminer: Anyone who likes a white wine to be dry but as wonderfully scented, luscious, spicy and interesting as wine can be will fill his carafe with the Traminer of Alsace or a California Gewurtztraminer. Casseroles with a sweet or sweet-and-sour element—with fruit, nuts, sauerkraut and pork, or ginger—are possible candidates for a red wine, but may also be paired off superbly with this type. It is an equally successful carafe wine, chilled, with pork.

Rosé Wines

If for some reason you could have only one wine, always, in your carafe—a wine for all seasons, dishes and guests— it would be a rosé. This is the great compromise wine, safe and never wrong, even if it is rarely exactly right. Crackling rosés have their moments and sweet ones their devotees, but for the general-purpose carafe, a still, dry rosé is safest. It should come to the table chilled but not icy. One of the simplest ways to choose a rosé is by the bottle: if it is perfectly plain and simple, with no decoration, gold wire, silver paper or Vistavision labels, you know the money has been spent on the important part—the wine. France, Italy, Portugal, Spain and the U.S. all make admirable rosés.

A Choice

As a host, you can sidestep the responsibility of deciding whether a red or white wine will suit the food and guests best by offering both. Stand a carafe of red at one end of the table, one of white at the other. If the party is big enough, there is no reason why a carafe of pink (rosé) should not be placed in the middle. Guests might well start by trying two and settling for one after the first course.

WINE AND POULTRY

No controversy rages more relentlessly in the realm of food and drink than the one over the proper wine to serve with poultry. Feuds can blossom while good friends debate the merits of a white or red with turkey. Not too long ago, when Americans were less knowledgeable about wine than they are today, the issue seldom came up. The standard accompaniment for turkey was sparkling Burgundy, and the quantity sold on national holidays was staggering. Fortunately, this fashion has passed into history, but its memory lingers on in the form of rosé—an equally unfelicitous companion for a hot, crisp-skinned bird.

Although the choice between a white and red wine is largely a matter of individual preference, a turkey that is fragrant with truffles slipped beneath the skin and carefully roasted with bastings of sweet butter seems to suggest a red wine such as a fine Burgundy. On the other hand, poached chicken served with a *sauce à la crème* may easily turn one's thoughts to a majestic Meursault or Montrachet, while duck and certain goose dishes appear clearly destined for a good Burgundy or Rhône red, or possibly champagne.

Cold poultry is quite another thing. A nicely roasted and cooled chicken, a chicken in aspic or cold duck with mayonnaise is best with chilled white wine or rosé. Or slightly chilled red wine such as Beaujolais can be delicious with cold duck, cold turkey, or succulent grilled or spitted chicken from the barbecue. Here are some suggestions for selecting wines to serve with hot and cold poultry.

POULTRY	ACCOMPANYING WINE
Capon	
Truffled and roasted	Château-bottled Bordeaux; La Tâche; California Pinot Noir
Chicken	
Barbecued	Rosé; California Zinfandel; Beaujolais; Meursault
Fried	Rosé; California Pinot Chardonnay; Muscadet; Beaujolais
Roasted	Fleurie; Meursault; light Bordeaux; California Cabernet Sauvignon
Roasted, served with cream sauce	Graves; Pouilly-Fumé; Pinot Blanc; champagne
Sautéed with white wine	For cooking and drinking: Muscadet; Pouilly-Fuissé; softer Riesling (Alsatian or California); California Sauvignon Blanc
Sautéed with red wine, spicy and highly herbed	Fleurie; Châteauneuf-du-Pape; California Cabernet Sauvignon or Zinfandel
Sautéed with sherry or port and a dark sauce	Fleurie; California Pinot Noir
Chicken casseroles	
With white wine	For cooking and drinking: Alsatian Riesling; California Johannisberg Riesling; Muscadet
With red wine	California Pinot Noir or Cabernet Sauvignon; Morgon; Juliénas
Coq au vin	Ideally, a Chambertin for both cooking and drinking; California Pinot Noir; Hermitage Rouge

POULTRY	ACCOMPANYING WINE
Chicken curry	Rosé, although beer is the best accompaniment for curries
Paella	Spanish white from Rioja or from around Valencia; Muscadet; Pinot Blanc
Poule au pot	Meursault; Montrachet; California Pinot Chardonnay
Chicken livers In a pâté	White wine; champagne
Sautéed, with Madeira	Beaujolais; light Bordeaux; California Cabernet Sauvignon
Duck Roasted with fruits or a fruit glaze	Burgundy Bourgueil; Châteauneuf-du-Pape; Chante-Alouette; Moselle; Rhine
Duck casseroles With beans	Hermitage Rouge; St. Estèphe; Pomerol; California Barbera
Rock Cornish game hens	Juliénas; Côte Rôtie; Pinot Noir; white Clos des Mouches; Moselle; Grey Riesling
Squab Roasted	Médoc; Nuits-St. Georges; Chassagne-Montrachet Rouge
Deviled	Pomerol; Vosne-Romanée; Juliénas
Goose Roasted	Hermitage; Médoc; Fleurie; Meursault; Vouvray; flowery Moselle

POULTRY	ACCOMPANYING WINE
Turkey Roasted	Light Médoc or Graves; Beaune Villages; Fixin; champagne; California Sauvignon Blanc
Poached, en demi-deuil	Meursault; Montrachet; California Pinot Chardonnay; Moselle
Braised, with white wine	For cooking and drinking: Chassagne-Montrachet; Pouilly-Fumé; Sancerre
With red wine	Crozes-Hermitage; Fleurie; California Pinot Noir
Scalloped turkey **or chicken**	Rosé; Vouvray; California Sauvignon Blanc
Turkey or chicken **tetrazzini**	Pinot Chardonnay; Alsatian or California Johannisberger Riesling; Vouvray

Ever since the days of the racy Edwardians with their
"cold bird and a bottle of bubbly," game and wine have
had a connotation of sybaritic pleasure, gastronomically
speaking. What could be more deliciously, almost sinfully
self-indulgent than a midnight snack of cold quail and
chilled champagne or a lunch of doves with a superb white
Burgundy?

Although it is often said that game meats and game
birds should always be served with the greatest red wines
of Bordeaux and Burgundy, this is not necessarily true or
even desirable. There are many times when a game dish
tastes better with a rich German Rhine or Moselle, a
hearty Rhône red, a delicate white Burgundy, a gay white
from the Loire Valley, a domestic red, champagne—or
even a rosé.

Scotch grouse, beautifully roasted, does demand a great
claret to do it justice, but light-meated birds such as quail

take to white wines. A young saddle of succulent venison should have the honor of one of the important reds but game fish, like most fish, are complemented by white wines, although the rich-meated salmon is also good teamed with a light red, a rosé or simply beer.

When serving a wine with game, consider the way you are preparing the game. Pheasant with sauerkraut, for example, is enhanced by a flowery Alsatian wine, while a spicy dish like venison chili or hearty venisonburgers is better paired with cold beer than wine. If you have any doubts, select two or three wines as possibilities, try them out several days in advance, and choose the one most suited to your dinner.

Finally, never serve wine if you wish to accompany game with fruit jellies such as currant jelly or, at most, serve something unpretentious. Great wines are ruined when teamed with such sweet concoctions and many gourmets agree that fine game needs no such cloying additions, anyway.

The following guide will help you to choose the right wine for your game dinner.

WINE AND GAME

GAME	ACCOMPANYING WINE
Wild duck	FINE RED BURGUNDY: Vosne-Romanée, Romanée-Conti, Clos de Vougeot, Bonnes Mares
	FINE RED BORDEAUX: Médoc such as Châteaux Mouton-Rothschild, Latour, Montrose, Margaux, Lascombes; St. Emilion such as Châteaux Cheval-Blanc, Ausone; Pomerol such as Château Petrus, or Graves such as Château Haut-Brion
	FINE RHÔNE RED: A well-aged Hermitage
	LIGHT RED: Juliénas, Fleurie, fine California Pinot Noir

GAME	ACCOMPANYING WINE
Wild goose	**LIGHT RED:** Lighter Bordeaux, Beaujolais, Chinon, Côte Rôtie, Bourgeuil **ALSATIAN:** Sylvaner or Traminer **FINE RHINE OR MOSELLE**
Quail	**FINE WHITE BURGUNDY:** Montrachet; Meursault **FINE RHINE OR MOSELLE** **LIGHT RED:** Beaujolais; Chinon; lighter Médoc
Pheasant	**FINE RED BORDEAUX:** Médoc such as Chateaux Lafite, Beychevelle, Léoville-Las Cases; St. Emilion such as Châteaux la Gaffelière-Naudes or Ripeau; Graves such as La Mission-Haut-Brion **FINE WHITE BURGUNDY:** Montrachet or Meursault **ALSATIAN:** Sylvaner or Traminer **FINE RHINE OR MOSELLE:** Rüdesheimer; Bernkasteler-Doktor-Auslese; Piesporter **LIGHT RED:** Beaujolais; Chinon; Côte Rôtie
Partridge	**FINE RED BURGUNDY:** Le Richebourg; Pommard; Chambertin **FINE RED BORDEAUX:** St. Emilion such as Château Ausone **FINE RHÔNE RED:** Aged Hermitage **LIGHT RED:** Beaujolais
Grouse	**FINEST RED BORDEAUX:** Châteaux Haut-Brion, Mouton-Rothschild, Montrose
Woodcock	**FINE RED BURGUNDY:** Corton; Clos de Bèze; Gevrey-Chambertin; Fixin; Nuits-St. Georges **RED BORDEAUX:** St. Emilion such as Château Pavie **RED:** California Cabernet Sauvignon

GAME	ACCOMPANYING WINE
Snipe	FINE RED BORDEAUX: Médoc such as Châteaux Lascombes, Beychevelle, Margaux LIGHTER RED BURGUNDY: Pommard; Chassagne-Montrachet; Beaujolais
Wild turkey	FINE RED BURGUNDY: Beaune; Châteauneuf-du-Pape FINE RHÔNE RED: Richebourg Red Rhône; Côte Rôtie
Dove	RED: Médoc or California Cabernet Sauvignon FINE WHITE BURGUNDY: Meursault; Montrachet; Corton Charlemagne WHITE LOIRE: Sancerre
Smoked game birds	CHAMPAGNE FINE ROSÉ: Tavel or California Grenache
Venison	BIG RED BURGUNDY: Vosne-Romanée; Clos de Vougeot; Musigny; Echézeaux; Grands-Echézeaux BIG RED BORDEAUX: Châteaux Haut-Brion; Cheval-Blanc; Petrus
Hare	RED RHÔNE: Côte Rôtie; Châteauneuf-du-Pape CHAMPAGNE
Cold game and game birds	CHAMPAGNE ALSATIAN: Sylvaner or Traminer; California Gewurtztraminer LIGHT WHITE LOIRE: Pouilly-Fumé
Trout	WHITE BURGUNDY: Meursault; Chablis LIGHT WHITE LOIRE: Muscadet; Sancerre SWISS NEUCHÂTEL DOMESTIC RIESLING

GAME	ACCOMPANYING WINE
Salmon	LIGHT RED: Beaujolais; California Zinfandel WHITE BURGUNDY: Chassagne-Montrachet WHITE BORDEAUX: Haut-Brion Blanc ROSÉ: California Gamay

These are a perfect duo when wisely matched. Most wine guides specify white wine with fish and, indeed, brisk white wines suit fish almost universally. But the "almost" is important because you cannot be certain that *all* white wines go well with *all* fish. A brittle, dry wine may be in order with oysters, clams and other shellfish, but richly spiced fish calls for richer, more full-bodied and flowery white wines such as the great white Burgundies. The English and Germans prefer good "hock"—the fine wines of the Rhine and Moselle—with their fish course. And in Venice or along the Italian coast, the wealth of *frutti di mare* is best enjoyed with the small, soft Italian white wines.

There are occasions when a red wine is used in the preparation of fish dishes, and here a light red is the ideal accompaniment. Certain fish are heavy and oily enough in themselves to warrant a red wine, and shad, in some forms, takes a light, full-flavored red.

Fortified wines are also used in and with fish dishes. All good fish soups invite the company of fine sherry or Madeira, especially at a formal dinner. Naturally you would not serve a cream or dry cocktail sherry, but one that is mellow and slightly nutty with a dry overtone.

Sometimes a fish dish calls for beer rather than wine. A salmon or shad recipe prepared with beer, shrimp or lobster cooked in beer, and certain fried fish dishes such as whitebait and oysters should be eaten with beer. In fact, many people invariably choose to drink beer, ale or stout with their oysters, clams and other seafoods.

There is one wine that can be served with all fish dishes infallibly, it seems—champagne.

Some smoked and cured fish present a problem when it comes to choosing a complementary wine because they

are so strong in character that it would be a waste to serve
a beautiful flowery or fruity white wine with them. Again,
champagne does the trick. Aside from that, stick to such
brisk small wines as Muscadet, Pouilly-Fumé or California
Mountain White when serving herring, salmon belly or salt
fish.

The following chart lists a goodly number of fish dishes
along with the most companionable wines. Except where
noted, all should be chilled.

WINE AND FISH

FIRST COURSE	ACCOMPANYING WINE
Anchovy	
Toast	Pouilly-Fumé
With eggs	Sancerre
Clams	Pouilly-Fuissé; Muscadet; champagne, well chilled
Steamed with butter	California Sauvignon Blanc
Coquille St. Jacques	Bâtard-Montrachet
Crabmeat	Meursault
With mayonnaise or other sauces	Champagne, well chilled
Deviled crab	California Johannisberg Riesling
Crabmeat salad	Pouilly-Fumé, Vouvray
Eels	
Broiled	Muscadet
Smoked	Pouilly-Fumé

FIRST COURSE	ACCOMPANYING WINE
Hot fish hors d'oeuvre	Champagne, well chilled
Lobster	
Cold	California Pinot Chardonnay
Cold, with mayonnaise, rémoulade or herb sauce	Champagne; Muscadet
Mussels	Muscadet
Marinière	California Sauvignon Blanc
Ravigote	Pouilly-Fumé
Oysters	
With any sauce	Champagne; Chablis
With sausage	Muscadet
Scallops	Champagne, well chilled
Raw	Muscadet
Provençale	Chassagne-Montrachet
Pan roast	Pouilly-Fuissé
Seafood salad	California Chenin Blanc
Shrimp	California Mountain White (dry)
With mayonnaise	Meursault
With cocktail sauce, rémoulade or Russian dressing	Champagne, well chilled

FIRST COURSE	ACCOMPANYING WINE
Smoked fish	Rhine
Smoked whitefish	Pouilly-Fumé
Soups (fish chowders, seafood bisques, turtle soup)	Sherry, lightly chilled

MAIN DISH	ACCOMPANYING WINE
Abalone steak	Domestic Chablis
Bass Sea bass, broiled	California Pinot Chardonnay
Striped bass, cold	Pouilly-Fumé
Striped bass flambé au fenouil	Meursault, young
Bouillabaisse	Cassis Chassagne-Montrachet
Clams Casino	Muscadet
Fried	Pouilly-Fumé
Fritters	California Mountain White or Pinot Blanc
Spanish, with rice	Beaujolais, very young; may be chilled
Coquille St.-Jacques	Le Montrachet, young
Crab Barbecued	Beaujolais, very young; may be slightly chilled (or beer)

MAIN DISH	ACCOMPANYING WINE
Deviled	Muscadet
Soft-shell crabs amandine	California Sauvignon Blanc
Eel Estouffade of eel	Chassagne-Montrachet
Matelote of eel	Rhine
Smoked eel	Dry sherry, chilled
Finnan haddie Delmonico	Pouilly-Fumé
Poached	Riesling
Halibut Broiled	Chablis
Cold	Pouilly-Fumé
Poached	California Pinot Chardonnay
Herring in mustard sauce	Beaujolais, very young; may be slightly chilled
Lobster A l'Américaine	Meursault; Beaujolais
Chausson	Le Montrachet, young
Fra Diavolo	Beaujolais, very young; may be slightly chilled; Verdicchio
Grilled	California Sauvignon Blanc
Newburg	Meursault, young
Mussels marinière	Chablis

MAIN DISH	ACCOMPANYING WINE
Oysters Casino, fried, omelette or pan roast	Muscadet
Pike, poached	Moselle
Red snapper, poached	Chassagne-Montrachet
Salmon Baked, braised or in red wine	Beaujolais, very young; may be chilled
Cold	Chassagne-Montrachet; Pouilly-Fumé; Moselle
Cold, with chambertin jelly	Beaujolais, very young; may be slightly chilled
Mousse	Le Montrachet, young
Poached	Rhine, California Johannisberg Riesling
Smoked	Dry sherry, chilled
Sand dabs meunière	Domestic Chablis; Pouilly-Fumé
Sardines, grilled	Muscadet
Scrod, broiled	Domestic Chablis
Shad and shad roe	Pouilly-Fumé; Moselle
Shrimp Creole	Beaujolais, very young; may be slightly chilled

MAIN DISH	ACCOMPANYING WINE
Fried	Muscadet; California Sauvignon Blanc
Sole	
Filets, cold	Pouilly-Fumé; Chassagne-Montrachet
In red wine	Beaujolais, very young; may be chilled
Grilled	Chablis
Mousse of sole	Le Montrachet
Rex sole	Chablis
Sole amandine	California Pinot Chardonnay
Sole bonne femme	Meursault, young
Sole dieppoise	Muscadet
Sole marguery	Meursault, young
Sole mousseline	Puligny-Montrachet, young
Sole meunière	Domestic Chablis; Pouilly-Fumé
Sole normande	California Sauvignon Blanc
Spaghetti with red clam sauce	Beaujolais such as Juliénas; may be chilled
Swordfish Barbecued or broiled	Beaujolais such as Moulin-à-Vent; may be chilled
Trout	
Trout farcie	Meursault, young
Trout meunière	Pouilly-Fumé; Chablis
Truite au bleu	Chablis; Moselle

MAIN DISH	ACCOMPANYING WINE
Truite au lac, braisée	California Chenin Blanc

Tuna
Braised, with wine
    and herbs
	Beaujolais, very young; may be slightly
	    chilled

Fresh, broiled	Beaujolais, very young; may be slightly chilled; California Pinot Chardonnay
Whitebait	Chassagne-Montrachet

Purists will tell you that cheese should always be accompanied by red wine. In general, this is a good rule to follow when planning lunch or dinner menus, particularly if you are serving one of the great cheeses such as Brie or Camembert. But in this country we frequently entertain quite informally and don't stand in awe of rules. Certain cheeses team well with dry white wine, champagne, dry sherry or ale. A fine Bel Paese or cream brick cheese served with rolls, sweet butter and fruit makes a refreshing conclusion for a weekend brunch, with the champagne, Alsatian or dry white wine that accompanied the meal. A smooth Port Salut or Pont l'Evêque with unsalted crackers and sweet butter, fruit and chilled dry sherry or champagne is a delightful midday snack, light yet satisfying. Some cheeses (aged sharp Cheddar, Emmenthal, aged Edam, Port Salut, Muenster, Liederkranz, Tilsit) are known as "beer cheeses." They go well with beers and ales and a simple spread of cold meats and salad or with pumpernickel and rye breads for a late snack.

Certain classic cheese dishes call for wine or ale as an accompaniment and, interestingly enough, the wine is often white. You might accompany a Swiss cheese fondue or a quiche Lorraine with a dry white wine (Neuchâtel), an Alsatian, a dry Moselle, or an American Riesling. A Welsh rabbit is best teamed with fine English ale. A cheese soufflé made with sharp Cheddar is complemented by ale, too, or a chilled Beaujolais, Valpolicella or American Zinfandel. When a soufflé is made with Parmesan, Valpolicella again, or Barolo, aged Chianti or American red table wine is a good choice. And of course any of these are excellent companions for pasta with Italian cheese.

Among food lovers everywhere, an important cheese such as Brie or Roquefort often appears as a separate course following the meat course at dinner. It is served with French bread, sweet butter and sometimes a simple green salad with oil and lemon juice dressing (vinegar is unkind to wine). With the cheese goes the finest red wine of the meal, an excellent Bordeaux or light Burgundy. Cheese served with fruit, dry biscuits and good red wine may also replace the dessert course at lunch or dinner.

The English enjoy a cheese such as a ripe Stilton after dessert, with port. If you copy this idea, be sure the wine has the distinction of maturity; young port is much too blatant and sugary.

If you serve red wine and cheese as a dessert course at a meal or as a course on its own, you should consider the specific qualities of the cheese when you choose the wine. The chart that follows lists the better-known natural cheeses and the red wines that complement them.

WINE AND CHEESE

CHEESE	ACCOMPANYING WINE
CHEDDAR: A flaky hard or semi-hard cheese. Top-quality, natural aged Cheddar has a sharp tang and is pale yellow in color	Lightly chilled Juliénas; Fleurie; Valpolicella; California Cabernet Sauvignon; Zinfandel
DOUBLE GLOUCESTER: Similar to Cheddar, this English cheese	Good Bordeaux; light Burgundy (Volnay, Pommard, red

CHEESE	ACCOMPANYING WINE
is richer, smoother and more pungent	Montrachet); Châteauneuf-du-Pape
PORT SALUT: A creamy, rich cheese with a definite cheesy flavor	See Cheddar, above
OKA: Similar to Port Salut with a very pungent taste	See Cheddar, above
EDAM: A firm, smooth cheese that can be mild or a little sharp, depending on age. The older, the better	See Cheddar, above
EMMENTHAL: The popular "Swiss" cheese with large holes; when well aged, firm and slightly sharp; if too young, rubbery in texture	Lightly chilled Beaujolais (Morgon, Moulin-à-Vent); regional Bordeaux; Châteauneuf du Pape; California Cabernet Sauvignon
GRUYÈRE: One of the great cheeses, creamier and richer than Emmenthal; used in Swiss fondue and in many fine cheese dishes	Fine Bordeaux; light Burgundy (Volnay, Pommard); fine Rhône red (Côte Rôtie, Hermitage)
PROVOLONE: A dry, firm, slightly crumbly cheese with a rather sharp taste and a definite cheese aroma	Italian Barolo; Bardolino; aged Chianti; Rhône red; California Cabernet Sauvignon
MONTEREY JACK: A good everyday cheese from California, light and creamy with a delicate flavor	Light Italian red (Valpolicella, aged Chianti)
CAERPHILLY: A mild, creamy cheese from Wales, similar to Jack cheese	Regional Bordeaux; light Italian red; California Barbera; lightly chilled Beaujolais

CHEESE	ACCOMPANYING WINE
BLUE CHEESE: If properly aged, cream-colored with blue-green veins, smooth and rich in texture with a sharp, slightly salty taste	Lightly chilled Beaujolais or Valpolicella; California Zinfandel
GORGONZOLA: A creamy, rich blue cheese that originated in Italy; smoother than other blue cheese and riper in flavor	Italian Bardolino; good Bordeaux; light Burgundy (Volnay, Pommard); fine Rhône red
STILTON: The English version of blue cheese; creamy, rich and pungent	Fine Bordeaux; light Burgundy; Hermitage
ROQUEFORT: The most famous of the blue cheeses and one of the greats; French Roquefort is made from sheep's milk and, unlike other blues, remains chalky white after aging; rich and heady	See Stilton, above
BRIE: A French cheese considered by many food lovers to be the greatest of all; if thoroughly ripened, rich and creamy with a strong odor	The finest Bordeaux or elegant light Burgundy
CAMEMBERT: A widely imitated cheese; the true product from Normandy, France, is similar to Brie; runny and soft with a rich flavor	See Brie, above
PONT L'ÉVÊQUE: A ripe, creamy French cheese with a rich flavor	Fine Bordeaux; light Burgundy; Châteauneuf-du-Pape

CHEESE	ACCOMPANYING WINE
CREMA DANICA: A creamy, soft cheese from Denmark with a rich, not too sharp flavor	Light Burgundy; California Pinot Noir; lightly chilled Beaujolais
BEL PAESE: A rather firm but creamy cheese with a delicate flavor	Lightly chilled Beaujolais or Valpolicella; California Barbera
TALEGGIO: A creamy Italian cheese, similar in texture to Bel Paese, but with a more definite flavor	Lightly chilled Beaujolais or Valpolicella; Hermitage; California Mountain Red
CREAM BRICK: An aged cream cheese made in the United States; rich in texture, smooth and creamy with a light, sharp tang	Light Italian or California Pinot Noir or Zinfandel

WINE AND DESSERT

Unless you are one of those people who likes to indulge in true gourmet perfection upon occasion, you will have little interest in dessert wines except as flavorings for various dishes. Few people serve these sweet wines anymore although, as already mentioned, nothing finishes off a dinner with more élan than a well-chosen dessert wine. It adds a highly civilized and elegant touch that is part of a distinguished tradition. Down through the years, the great dessert wines have been the inspiration for some of the world's most amusing, penetrating, inspirational talk. Hosts and guests always were—and still are—at their best and most relaxed with the candlelight playing on glasses and decanters at the end of dinner.

The range of dessert wines is wide, varying from a brisk, festive sweet champagne that goes with a very special sweet soufflé or bombe to a rich, tawny port so appropriate with a contemplative browse among the nuts. Dessert wines fall into two main groups: the fortified and the unfortified.

Fortified wines—port, Madeira and sherry—are almost twice as rich in alcohol as natural table wines. All, with the exception of white port, the dry sherries and the medium-dry Madeiras, are sweet, which makes them ideal end-of-dinner drinks, usually served after, rather than with, the dessert. A good ruby, tawny or—rare treat indeed—vintage port, a Bual, Malmsey or Rainwater Madeira, an old, fine cream sherry, are excellent candidates, look most inviting in clear decanters and taste better still when accompanied by walnuts and almonds. They should be served in colorless glasses, either cut or plain, not quite so large as regular wineglasses but definitely not small. A brimming thimbleful is a nightmare; it gives you no opportunity to enjoy the scent of the wine and offers every chance for pouring the drink down your neck. Err, always, on the side of too-big wineglasses, and fill them one-third full.

For a more detailed explanation of the wide range of types among the "big three" fortified wines, including their characteristics, see pages 63–68.

Unfortified dessert wines, in contrast to the red and brown tones of fortified wines, are pale golden and go well with ice cream, fresh fruit (except citrus) or other desserts at the end of the meal. Oddly enough, although you can happily sip glass after glass of port or Madeira, nobody seems to drink more than two or three glasses of a fine Sauternes, lingering over them for hours. A fine Sauternes is intensely sweet—the more so the better. The best Sauternes is Château d'Yquem, but there are other good château Sauternes that are much less expensive and well worth looking for.

The dessert wines of the Rhine are Beerenauslese and Trockenbeerenauslese, in that order of sweetness. Hungary produces Tokay, a dessert wine so individual that it has always had a royal reputation; the aroma and taste of Tokay are celestial butterscotch. Again, with Tokay, sweetness is all—the sweeter the more desirable (and more expensive).

The dessert wines of the world do not end with the few just mentioned. There is, for example, sweet champagne, which may be described on the bottle with un-Gallic understatement as *demi-sec* (half-dry), but is sometimes more correctly labeled *doux* or sweet. A fairly powerful dose of sugar is added to the wine at the last moment, which makes it a very different matter from the dry type. The latter is too light to accompany a sweet dessert; the effect is often unpleasantly acid.

Every wine-producing and -drinking community has its sweet wines for the leisurely end of dinner. Another one is muscatel. The muscat grape, with its strong fruity smell, is cultivated all over southern Europe, and perhaps most successfully in Portugal, to produce a heavy brown wine that makes admirable everyday after-dinner sipping.

WINE AND FRUIT

Wine is the fermented juice of a fruit, so it seems quite natural that wine and fruit should be happy together. Epicures have long delighted in the combination, whether it be a ripe pear and a glass of red wine or a fine bowl of raspberries laved with port. As is the case with most generalities, however, there are exceptions to this felicitous partnership. Some wines—Chablis, for example—are too dry and flinty to accompany fruit, and some fruits— notably those of the citrus family—do not team well with wines although they are quite happy with brandies. (Brandies, being the distillation of wines, go well with almost all fruits.) The following table will help you to choose wines to serve with various fresh fruits and wine for flavoring suitable fruits.

FRESH FRUIT ACCOMPANYING WINE

Strawberries   TO DRINK: Beaujolais, lightly cooled; light
Bordeaux, red; sweet white wine from the Rhine
and Moselle regions, cooled; a rich German
dessert wine such as Forster Jesuitengarten
Trockenbeerenauslese
TO FLAVOR: Port; cream sherry; Madeira; Marsala;
champagne sec or extra dry; sweet white Rhine
or Moselle wine; red Bordeaux or Beaujolais

Raspberries   TO DRINK: Saumur; Anjou; light Moselle
TO FLAVOR: Port; Marsala; crème de cassis

Fresh figs   Red wine from the Loire region, such as a Chinon
or a Bourgueuil; very young Beaujolais or
Juliénas, lightly cooled; Valpolicella; fine Anjou;
port; cream sherry

Figs and   The light reds suggested above, gently cooled
   prosciutto

Melons   TO DRINK: A soft white such as Pouilly-Fumé or a
Meursault; a soft champagne
TO FLAVOR: Port; cream sherry; Madeira;
Sauternes

Melon and   Meursault; a good fruity rosé; Beaujolais, lightly
   prosciutto   cooled; Valpolicella

To fill a   Cut out a small plug and fill melon with soft white
   watermelon   wine, champagne or cognac; replace plug and
chill melon in ice for several hours

Apricots   Fine Sauternes; good Barsac; sweet German wine
such as Beerenauslese; Monbazillac from
Gascony (a luscious sweet wine)

Peaches   TO DRINK: Champagne sec; good red wine
TO FLAVOR: Champagne sec; dash of cognac and
champagne; kirsch; framboise

FRESH FRUIT ACCOMPANYING WINE

Pears	Good claret; St. Emilion or Pomerol (with Bartletts); Anjou; Sauternes; cognac
Pears and fine cheese	Excellent Burgundy or Bordeaux
Apples	Montrachet; Gewurtztraminer; German white, Auslese; sparkling cider

WINE FOR HOLIDAY FEASTS

The holiday season with its richer, more lavish food obviously calls for richer, more lavish wines than usual to do it justice. But what are they, and how do you recognize them? The sensible approach is to try out ahead of time a few likely candidates in the fine-wine category that will complement the food you are planning to serve. Spend a half-hour with the manager of your local liquor store, going over the possibilities, and take home two or three half bottles to sample and compare. Once you decide, order your wine—and have it delivered—early. Then you will be sure of getting what you want, rather than what happens to be left in stock on Christmas Eve.

First of all, you will need a principal wine for the main meal of the holiday—a wine that will go with the turkey, the ham, the goose or whatever you are having. Taking into account the sauces and accompanying dishes, the hors d'oeuvres and dessert, a traditional holiday dinner adds up to a heavy, rich meal. At such a time you need a fine, forcefully flavored wine. Whether it is white or red is up to you. While beef and lamb are pretty well committed to red wine, most of the game, poultry and other traditional main dishes that are served at Christmas are a toss-up. For turkey, ham and goose, there are adherents on both sides of the fence. As turkey has both red (dark) and white (light) meat, those who like the breast may prefer white wine with it, while those who go for a drumstick are more likely to want red. You are going to need more than one bottle anyway, so an easy and pleasant solution is to set out both and let each guest choose his favorite.

When it comes to selecting a white wine, it should probably be a Rhine, a Burgundy or a Moselle. Among the heavier, more forceful white wines with a touch of gentleness that makes them festive drinking, pride of place is taken by the best of the Rhine wines. The ordinary ones don't have this quality. The dry, rich flavor of a white Burgundy with its vaguely fruity perfume is a perfect complement for a holiday bird.

At the other end of your table, looking even more tempting than the cool, tall bottle of Rhine wine, you might place a carafe of red—one of France's or California's most richly savory, scented, high-colored wines. If it is French, it will be from the Rhône Valley, Burgundy or the hill country east of Bordeaux. If it is Californian, most likely it will be a Cabernet Sauvignon.

Fine Burgundies inevitably cost more than the Rhône reds and it is important to find one that justifies its price. Look for those that carry on their labels the name of the vineyard after the name of the village—for example, Chambolle-Musigny Les Amoureuses (Chambolle-Musigny, the village; Les Amoureuses, "Women in Love," the vineyard). Such wines are almost always better than plain village-named wines where no vineyard is mentioned because you are assured that the wine is from the vineyard named and is not a blend.

Serving two wines concurrently at a holiday meal has another advantage—you can offer both in the classic progression of white before red.

A first course of smoked salmon, oysters, clams or caviar is best enjoyed with a chilled white wine. Give each guest two wineglasses, and he can start the meal with the white wine, then decide later if he wants to go on to the red for the main course or stay with the white.

The only other wine you may then want for your Christmas dinner (and indeed it is really an elegant extra rather than a necessity) is a sweet wine for dessert. The choice is endless—from the obvious golden Sauternes of France to the often neglected Madeira. You might follow a somewhat unusual but pleasant procedure—and serve that wonderful old American favorite, sweet Madeira, with—rather than after—the dessert course, particularly if you have a creamy dessert. Malmsey and Boal are the types to pick; the others tend to be a bit dry with a sweet dish.

To calculate how much wine to buy for the holiday season, see pages 12–13.

Always overestimate, rather than underestimate, your wine-buying needs. It makes sense to keep any surplus on hand for future celebrations; wine only improves with a few months' storage on its side in a dark cupboard.

At buffet meals, however well organized and delicious, it is better to be generous with a modest wine and, as choice is one of the charms of informal meals, have not one wine but two or three. A row of carafes of different colors, gleaming among the buffet food, is a very cheering, welcoming sight. White, rosé, red—to offer the spectrum is to make sure that everyone gets exactly what he or she wants.

Finally, champagne comes naturally to mind when we think of celebrations. Nothing compares with it for getting a party off the ground, although some people tire of it after a while, especially with food, and feel frustrated if they think it is to be the only drink of the entire evening. If you are planning to have champagne at a buffet meal, it is a good idea to offer an alternative, such as a red wine. At a formal meal, you might serve a very dry champagne as the aperitif and with the first course, a still red or white wine with the main course, and then (if you like) a bottle of sweet champagne with the dessert.

WHAT TO DRINK WITH EXOTIC FOREIGN FOODS

The word "exotic," as used here, simply means the less familiar foods that are served in Chinese, Japanese, Scandinavian, Indian, Greek and Middle Eastern restaurants in this country, or that you may serve at home to guests. When you travel, you can follow the local customs and experiment with the local drinks described in various guidebooks or recommended by restaurants. But here in America it is helpful to know what drinks are best suited to the dishes you order or cook and to sample them, at any rate.

Chinese Food

Ask the average American what the Chinese drink with their meals and he will say, "Tea, of course." The idea is about as accurate as the European notion that Americans usually drink Coca-Cola with dinner. Tea with meals is conventional in today's Chinese-American restaurants, but in the China of bygone days it was a between-meals beverage, consumed in large quantities in the midmorning and midafternoon, especially when visitors dropped by. However, if the Chinese don't drink tea with dinner, what do they drink?

An old Chinese proverb says, "Without wine in the bottle it is hard to have guests." The wine of the proverb is not available in this country, but was somewhere between a medium sherry and a Chablis. Many old China hands enjoy a very dry Manzanilla (a sherrylike wine), slightly chilled, as an accompaniment to Chinese dishes. Or you might try a dry Moselle with just a few drops of crème de cassis in it.

If you are a confirmed cocktail drinker, consider having a Gimlet made with fresh lime and a little sugar, or a

Martini, before a Chinese meal. A gin and tonic is another possibility on a warm evening.

An excellent choice for the cocktail hour is champagne or dry white wine that can be served right through the meal. But if you are eating or serving sweet-sour dishes, be careful about your selection of a beverage. Very dry white wines tend to taste sour when sipped with sweetish foods. Beer or ale is more satisfactory. In fact, a fine beer goes well with a variety of tastes in Chinese cuisine. If yours is an adventuresome palate, you might drink a good Burgundy or a lightly chilled Beaujolais with one of the duck-based Chinese dishes.

Japanese Food

Whiskey and soda is perhaps the most satisfactory drink to order or serve before a Japanese meal. As the Japanese are now making their own whiskey, it is becoming increasingly popular with them, too.

With the meal, nothing can equal sake served warm in little sake cups. If this seems too alien for your Western palate, you might compromise by having the sake chilled. It may also be drunk on the rocks before a meal. Beer is another good accompaniment to Japanese dishes, especially those based on beef, and Japanese beer is excellent.

The after-dinner drink is a matter of choice—possibly brandy or one of the less sweet liqueurs.

Scandinavian Food

Probably the wisest plan is to copy the Scandinavians and start the meal with chilled aquavit in small glasses. Partner it or follow it with selections from the smorgasbord. During the rest of the meal, you will find that beer is a highly suitable beverage. As you may know, the Scandinavians brew many fine beers, some of which are available in this country.

Aquavit is sometimes served mixed with coffee after dinner, and Cherry Heering, a Danish cherry liqueur, is a good after-dinner choice.

Mexican Food

Any of the tequila-based drinks make a first-rate beginning to a Mexican meal. Possibly the Margarita is the most popular.

Beer, particularly imported Mexican beer, is a perfect partner for the more robust Mexican dishes such as mole poblano. Lighter dishes can be accompanied by wines, dry red or dry white, following the usual procedures for when to serve which. Domestic rosé wines are a particularly felicitous choice with Mexican food.

Kahlúa, the Mexican coffee liqueur, is an excellent drink after dinner.

Indian Food

Although many Indians do not drink alcoholic beverages because of religious prohibitions, there is a logical precedent for drinking wine with Indian food. When the Moguls came down from Persia through the Khyber Pass into India in the early sixteenth century, they brought wine with them, and for awhile it was drunk at their courts and flowed like fountains in their summer pleasure gardens in Kashmir. Wine drinking in India died a natural death for a simple reason: fine wines are wasted on Indian dishes. Champagne, however, lives up to its reputation of tasting good with anything. Drink brut with most dishes, but sec with those that contain raisins or other sweetening. With curries, you can also drink a rosé wine, although beer and ale are very popular with both Indians and Westerners.

Instead of alcohol, the majority of Indians take water, lemonade or buttermilk with their food—all three suit it well. Fresh lemon- or limeade can be flavored with a colorful pinch of saffron and a few crushed cardamom seeds. Buttermilk will help to quench the flames in the throat of anyone who has swallowed a hot pepper unexpectedly!

On a very hot summer afternoon, many Indians find refreshment in an icy drink called *lassi,* based on yogurt. Sherbet, an Indian word, was originally a drink rather than a frozen concoction. Indians drink all fruit juices, either pure or blended with soda. Milk with spice of flavoring is also popular, as is the "milk" from a fresh green coconut.

Even if you are so devoted to espresso that you think you never want anything else, try your after-dinner demitasse with cream and a few spiced cashew nuts. You can also put whole or powdered cardamom or cinnamon in with the coffee when you are brewing it at home, a trick that gives it a subtle and exotic Indian flavor.

Greek and Middle Eastern Foods

Many Middle Eastern countries are opposed to the drinking of alcohol on religious grounds. However, this need not affect your own conscience, and an excellent beginning to a typical Middle Eastern meal would be one of the anis drinks such as ouzo or arak, served on the rocks with water.

If you develop a taste for Greek retsina or other Greek wines, you can drink it with the meal. Or switch to a more familiar dry white or red wine, following the standard and most accepted procedure about which goes best with what dishes. But if the dish is very highly spiced, icy cold beer or ale is a far better choice.

Greek Metaxas brandy is a good after-dinner drink, or you may prefer a more familiar French brandy.

V

Toasts You Can Use with Assurance

Although the early Greeks and Romans practiced a ritual of drinking to their gods and their dead, the toast as we know it is supposed to have originated in France during the reign of Francis I. By that time—the early sixteenth century—life for the rich had become both leisurely and luxurious. They ate elaborate meals, in the course of which they listened to music, recounted stories and quaffed wine from tall goblets. It became the gallant custom to drink to the health of various ladies in their midst. A bit of toasted bread was placed in the bottom of a goblet, which was then filled with wine. After a man had proposed the health, the goblet was passed from hand to hand around the table, and each person sipped from it. The last one to receive it was the woman herself; the bit of wine-saturated toast was hers, along with the compliments of the assembled company. Thus a courteous and courtly custom came to be known as a "toast." At any rate, so goes one explanation.

Many toasts today are very short. "Here's how!" "Luck!" "Happy days!" and others like them are familiar to everyone. They are most informal and not really suitable to anything resembling an occasion. In France, "Santé!" is the popular toasting word, in Italy "Salute!" in Scandinavia "Skoal!" in Germany "Prosit!" in Spanish-speaking countries "Salud!" and so on around the world. When these seem too banal and impersonal, a short line such as "I'd like to propose a toast to our host and hostess," or ". . . to the bride" or "Here's wishing ———— much happiness and a long life" is always acceptable and certainly preferable to a long-drawn-out rigmarole that slows down the party pace. But if you wish to have a few gracefully worded, apt toasts tucked up your sleeve, you can find several in this collection that will appeal to you and make sense on specific occasions. Not all of them start off in the standard way with "Here's to . . ." or "To . . ." or "Let's drink to . . ." Some are short verses or sayings that you can emphasize by simply raising your glass to the person or group you are toasting. Or you can always start off by saying, "I'd like to propose a toast." If sitting at the dining table, it is customary to rise. Another custom that may be followed or not is for everyone to touch glasses after the toast has been proposed but before drinking it. Sometimes people all applaud after drinking the toast. When toasts are drunk in a public restaurant, however, the entire procedure should be quiet and inconspicuous.

Upon occasion, people are moved to toast the effects of drinking or the contents of their glass. Here are a few examples.

> O water, pure, free of pollution,
> I vainly wish that I dared trust it,
> But I've an iron constitution
> And much I fear that water'd rust it.

> Here's to champagne, the drink divine,
> That makes us forget our troubles;
> It's made of a dollar's worth of wine
> And eight dollars' worth of bubbles.

[The figure "eight" can be changed to whatever you want.]

If wine tells truth, and so have said the wise,
It makes me laugh to think how brandy lies.
—OLIVER WENDELL HOLMES

Claret is the liquor for boys; port for men; but he who aspires
to be a hero must drink brandy.
["Brandy" may be changed to suit the situation.]
—SAMUEL JOHNSON

Here's to good old whiskey,
So amber and so clear.
'Tis not so sweet as woman's lips
But a damned sight more sincere.

Fill up the goblet and reach me some;
Drinking makes wise, but dry fasting makes glum.

Here is a riddle most abstruse;
Canst read the answer right?
Why is it that my tongue grows loose
Only when I grow tight?

I wish that my room had a floor;
I don't care so much for a door,
But this walking around
Without touching the ground
Is getting to be quite a bore.

At the goblet's brink
Let us pause and think
How they do it in Japan:
First the man takes a drink,
Then the drink takes a drink,
Then the drink takes the man.

Here's to the heart that fills as the bottle empties.

Here's champagne to our real friends
And real pain to our sham friends.

The man that isn't jolly after drinking
Is just a driveling idiot, to my thinking.
—attributed to Euripides,
but no doubt a very free translation

The Frenchman loves his native wine;
The German loves his beer;
The Englishman loves his 'alf-and-'alf
Because it brings good cheer;
The Irishman loves his "whiskey straight"
Because it gives him dizziness;
The American has no choice at all
So he drinks the whole damned business.

Upon occasion, a guest may want to toast his host, or vice versa. This is a particularly pleasant gesture at a meal, if wine is served, and here are some of the forms it can take.

Let's drink to our friend and host. May his generous heart, like his good wine, only grow mellower with the years.

To the sun that warmed the vineyard,
To the juice that turned to wine,
To the host that cracked the bottle
And made it yours and mine.

Here's a toast to the host who carved the roast;
And a toast to the hostess—may she never "roast" us.

To our host, an excellent man;
For is not man fairly judged by the company he keeps?

Here's a toast to the hostess, a toast to the host;
May we meet again ere we give up the ghost.

A glass in the hand's worth two on the shelf—
Tipple it down and refresh yourself!

Here's a toast to all who are here,
No matter where you are from;
May the best day you have seen
Be worse than your worst to come.

I drink to the general joy of the whole table.
—WILLIAM SHAKESPEARE

Good bread, good meat—
Good God, let's eat!

Salt this food with humor, pepper it with wit, and sprinkle over it the charm of good fellowship. Never poison it with the care of life.

BREAD—to feed our friendship,
SALT—to keep it true,
WATER—that's for welcome,
WINE—to drink with you.

The following toasts to friendship include many that may be drunk to one's host or guests as well as on other occasions.

Friendship's the wine of life.
Let's drink of it and to it.

Here's to mine and here's to thine!
Now's the time to clink it!
Here's a flagon of old wine
And here we are to drink it.

Happy are we met, happy have we been,
Happy may we part and happy meet again.

Old wood to burn,
Old books to read,
Old wine to drink,
Old friends to trust.
    —FRANCIS BACON

Don't ask me to give you a toast from my head,
For straightway its warmth will depart;
But here's to our friendship—I pledge you instead,
'Tis a toast that was made in my heart.

The world is gay and colorful
And life itself is new;
I am very grateful for
The friend I found in you.

May the roof over your head never fall in,
And those beneath it never fall out.

Old friends are scarce,
New friends are few;
Here's hoping I've found
One of each in you.

Pretend we've known you all along,
That you're an old-time friend.
Perhaps before the evening is o'er,
The make-believe will end.

(This toast to a new acquaintance is quite different from the next one, which is a heartfelt one to a very old and intimate friend.)

I have eaten your bread and salt,
I have drunk your water and wine;
The deaths ye died I have watched beside
And the lives ye lived were mine.
—RUDYARD KIPLING

Among the next toasts to men or women, both collectively and individually, some are complimentary, some ironic.

Here's to woman! Would that we could fall into her arms without falling into her hands.
—AMBROSE BIERCE

A drink, my lass, in a deep clear glass
Just properly tempered by ice,
And here's to the lips mine last have kissed;
And if they were thine, here's twice.

May these ladies distrust man in general,
But not us in particular!

God made the world—and rested;
God made man—and rested;
Then God made woman.
Since then, neither God nor man has rested.

May you always be happy
And live at your ease,
Get a kind husband
And do as you please.

Here's to beefsteak when you're hungry,
Whiskey when you're dry,
All the girls you ever want
And heaven when you die.

To the men I've loved,
To the men I've kissed;
My heartfelt apologies
To the men I've missed.

Here's to bachelors, created by God for the consolation of widows and the hope of maidens.

[Note: This toast might be given by a man to his ushers at his bachelor dinner before his wedding.]

Here's to man—something a beautiful woman fascinates, a clever woman interests and a sympathetic woman gets.

The following toasts are intimate ones concerned with courtship and love.

I have known many,
Liked a few,
Loved one—
Here's to you.

Here's to you and here's to me,
Here's to what we used to be;
Here's to what we might have been,
And here's to what we'll be again.

I drink to your health when I'm with you,
I drink to your health when I'm alone,
I drink to your health so often
I'm beginning to worry about my own!

To our two selves, dear!

If I were I, and you were you, would you?
There are times I would and times I wouldn't,
Times that I could and times I couldn't;
But the times I could and would and I feel game
Are the times I'm with you, dear.
Do you feel the same?

The toasts below can come in very handily and neatly, provided you are one of a group of three or four, respectively.

I'm as dear to you as he,
He's as dear to me as thee,
You're as dear to him as me;
Here's to "Three's good company."

["He" and "him" can be changed to "she" and "her" without spoiling the rhyme.]

Here's to the four of us;
Thank God there's no more of us!

God bless me and my son John,
Me and my wife, him and his wife;
Us four and no more.

[Again, the words can be altered to suit the situation, as "my friend Joe," "me and my girl," "him and his girl," etc.]

If you two like we two like we two like you two,
Then "Here's to us four."
But if you two don't like we two
Like we two like you two, then
"Here's to us two and no more!"

Following are many toasts that may be used whenever they seem suitable.

Let us toast the fools; but for them the rest of us could not succeed.

—MARK TWAIN

May all your troubles be little ones;
May all your troubles be small;
May all your troubles be light as bubbles;
May you have no troubles at all.

Here's a health to all those that we love,
Here's a health to all those that love us,
Here's a health to all those that love them that love those
That love them, that love those that love us.

Here's to hell!
May the stay there
Be as much fun as the way there!

Here's to us that are here, to you that are there, and the rest
of us everywhere.
—RUDYARD KIPLING

Here's that we may all go up the hill of Prosperity and never
meet a friend—coming down.

Not the laurel—but the race;
Not the quarry—but the chase;
Not the dice—but the play;
May I, Lord, enjoy alway.

There is so much good in the worst of us,
And so much bad in the best of us,
That it hardly becomes any of us
To talk about the rest of us.

I like ———. He's every other inch a gentleman.
—NOEL COWARD

Mingle with the friendly bowl
The feast of reason and the flow of soul.
—ALEXANDER POPE

Drink to the girls and drink to their mothers,
Drink to their fathers and to their brothers;
Toss their dear healths as long as you're able,
And dream of their charms while under the table.

Here's to you, as good as you are,
And here's to me, as bad as I am;
But as good as you are, and as bad as I am,
I am as good as you are, as bad as I am.
—AN OLD SCOTCH TOAST

Here's to today—the tomorrow you worried about yesterday.

Eat, drink and be merry, for tomorrow ye diet.

Good company, good wine, good welcome—make good people.
—WILLIAM SHAKESPEARE

May the most you wish for be the least you get.

There may be a toast I'd like to say,
If I could only think it;
So fill your glass to anything,
And, thank the Lord, I'll drink it.

Following are three toasts that can be used quite gracefully at weddings. Any of them can be made to the bride alone or to her and her groom.

I wish you all the joy that you can wish.
—SHAKESPEARE

Quiet days, fair issue and long life.
—SHAKESPEARE

A health to you
And wealth to you
And the best that life can give to you.
May fortune still be kind to you
And Happiness be true to you
And Life be long and good to you—
Is the toast of all your friends to you.

Index